New Directions
in Organizational Psychology
and Behavioral Medicine

Psychological and Behavioural Aspects of Risk Series

Series Editors: Professor Cary L. Cooper and Professor Ronald J. Burke

Risk management is an ongoing concern for modern organizations in terms of their finance, their people, their assets, their projects and their reputation. The majority of the processes and systems adopted are very financially oriented or fundamentally mechanistic; often better suited to codifying and recording risk, rather than understanding and working with it. Risk is fundamentally a human construct; how we perceive and manage it is dictated by our attitude, behaviour and the environment or culture within which we work. Organizations that seek to mitigate, manage, transfer or exploit risk need to understand the psychological factors that dictate the response and behaviours of their employees, their high-flyers, their customers and their stakeholders.

This series, edited by two of the most influential writers and researchers on organizational behaviour and human psychology explores the psychological and behavioural aspects of risk; the factors that:

- define our attitudes and response to risk,
- are important in understanding and managing 'risk managers', and
- dictate risky behaviour in individuals at all levels.

Titles Currently in the Series Include:

Risky Business
Psychological, Physical and Financial Costs of High Risk Behavior in Organizations
Edited by Ronald J. Burke and Cary L. Cooper

Safety Culture
Assessing and Changing the Behaviour of Organizations
John Bernard Taylor

Crime and Corruption in Organizations
Why It Occurs and What To Do About It
Edited by Ronald J. Burke, Edward C. Tomlinson and Cary L. Cooper

New Directions in Organizational Psychology and Behavioral Medicine

Edited by

ALEXANDER-STAMATIOS ANTONIOU
University of Athens

CARY COOPER
Lancaster University

LONDON AND NEW YORK

First published 2011 by Gower Publishing

Published 2016 by Routledge
2 Park Square, Milton Park, Abingdon, Oxon OX14 4RN
711 Third Avenue, New York, NY 10017, USA

Routledge is an imprint of the Taylor & Francis Group, an informa business

Copyright © Alexander-Stamatios Antoniou and Cary Cooper 2011

Alexander-Stamatios Antoniou and Cary Cooper have asserted their moral right under the Copyright, Designs and Patents Act, 1988, to be identified as the editors of this work.

All rights reserved. No part of this book may be reprinted or reproduced or utilised in any form or by any electronic, mechanical, or other means, now known or hereafter invented, including photocopying and recording, or in any information storage or retrieval system, without permission in writing from the publishers.

Notice:
Product or corporate names may be trademarks or registered trademarks, and are used only for identification and explanation without intent to infringe.

Gower Applied Business Research
Our programme provides leaders, practitioners, scholars and researchers with thought provoking, cutting edge books that combine conceptual insights, interdisciplinary rigour and practical relevance in key areas of business and management.

British Library Cataloguing in Publication Data
New directions in organizational psychology and behavioral
  medicine. -- (Psychological and behavioural aspects of
  risk)
  1. Psychology, Industrial. 2. Quality of work life. 3. Job
  stress. 4. Employees--Mental health.
  I. Series II. Antoniou, Alexander-Stamatios G. III. Cooper,
  Cary L.
  158.7-dc22

Library of Congress Cataloging-in-Publication Data
New directions in organizational psychology and behavioral medicine / [edited by] Alexander-Stamatios Antoniou and Cary Cooper.
    p. cm. -- (Psychological and behavioural aspects of risk)
  Includes index.
  ISBN 978-1-4094-1082-9 (hbk. : alk. paper) -- ISBN 978-1-4094-1083-6 (ebook) 1. Psychology, Industrial. 2. Organizational behavior--Psychological aspects. 3. Industrial hygiene. I. Antoniou, Alexander-Stamatios G. II. Cooper, Cary L.
  HF5548.8.N473 2010
  158.7--dc22

2010034181

ISBN 13: 978-1-4094-1082-9 (hbk)

Contents

List of Figures   ix
List of Tables   xi
List of Contributors   xiii
Foreword   xvii

Introduction: New Directions in Organizational Psychology
and Behavioral Medicine   1
Alexander-Stamatios Antoniou and Cary Cooper

PART I   NEW CHALLENGES FOR OCCUPATIONAL HEALTH PSYCHOLOGY

1   A Short History of Occupational Health Psychology:
A Biographical Approach   7
Amy Christie and Julian Barling

2   Well-Being at Work, a New Way of Doing Things?
A Journey through Yesterday, Today and Tomorrow   25
Philip C. Gibbs and Simon B. Burnett

3   The Changing World of Work and Occupational Health   43
Maria Armaou and Alexander-Stamatios Antoniou

4   Stress Medicine: From Bench to Bedside   63
Dirk H. Hellhammer and Juliane Hellhammer

PART II   WORK AND DISPOSITIONAL OCCUPATION SOURCES OF HEALTH

5	Work Hours, Work Intensity and Work Addiction: Risks and Rewards	79
	Ronald J. Burke and Lisa Fiksenbaum	
6	Gender Differences in Burnout: A Literature Review	107
	Ayala Malach-Pines and Sigalit Ronen	
7	American Adolescents in the Workplace: Exploration of Health-Related Psychosocial Issues	123
	Donald E. Greydanus, Helen D. Pratt and Dilip R. Patel	
8	Emotional Intelligence as a Personality Trait	139
	Konstantinos V. Petrides	
9	Self-Efficacy as a Central Psychological Capacity within the Construct of Positive Organizational Behavior: Its Impact on Work	147
	Magdalini Koutsoumari and Alexander-Stamatios Antoniou	
10	Professional Efficacy and Social Support in Nurses During the SARS Crisis in Canada and China	169
	Esther R. Greenglass, Zdravko Marjanovic, Lisa Fiksenbaum, Sue Coffey, Kan Shi, and Xue Feng Chen	

PART III   HEALTH, MANAGEMENT AND ORGANIZATIONAL EFFECTIVENESS

11	An Integrative Framework of Supervisor Responses to Workgroup Conflict	191
	Kirsten Way, Nerina L. Jimmieson, and Prashant Bordia	
12	Determinants of Work Satisfaction, and Physical and Psychological Health in German Managers	221
	Elizabeth Austin, Bruce Kirkcaldy and Terence Martin	
13	Employee Health and Presenteeism: The Challenge for Human Resources Management	239
	Robert A. Roe and Bas van Diepen	

| 14 | Non-Standard Work Schedules and Retention Management
Robert R. Sinclair and Kristin E. Charles | 259 |

PART IV   JOB INSECURITY, UNEMPLOYMENT AND MENTAL HEALTH

15	Health Effects of Unemployment and Job Insecurity *Gisela Mohr and Kathleen Otto*	289
16	Job Insecurity: Implications for Occupational Health and Safety *Tahira M. Probst*	313
17	Mental Health and Unemployment: The Coping Perspective *Alexander-Stamatios Antoniou and Marina Dalla*	329

PART V   SPECIFIC ISSUES OF OCCUPATIONAL HEALTH PSYCHOLOGY

18	Brain versus Nature: How the Internet Affects Physical Activity *Panagiotis Perros and Alexander-Stamatios Antoniou*	355
19	Health Professionals and Community Stigma toward People who Engage in Substance Abuse *Alexander-Stamatios Antoniou and Marina Dalla*	367
20	Immigration, Acculturation and Responses to Perceived Employment Discrimination: A Study of Albanian and Bulgarian Immigrants in Greece *Alexander-Stamatios Antoniou and Marina Dalla*	385

Index   397

List of Figures

Figure 4.1	Neuropattern Test Set	69
Figure 4.2	The Neuropattern circle	70
Figure 10.1	Theoretical model of the relationship among organizational support, perceived feedback, preventive coping, and professional efficacy	173
Figure 10.2	Model relating organizational support, perceived feedback, preventive coping, and professional efficacy in Canadian nurses	180
Figure 10.3	Model relating organizational support, perceived feedback, preventive coping, and professional efficacy in Chinese nurses	181
Figure 11.1	An integrative framework of supervisor responses to workgroup conflict	195
Figure 12.1	Path model, predicting work satisfaction (PMI) from personality (Type A, locus of control), coping style, occupational stress and demographic variables (age and hours of work)	232
Figure 12.2	Path model, predicting mental health (PMI's psychological well-being) from personality (Type A, locus of control), coping style, occupational stress and demographic variables (age and hours of work)	232
Figure 12.3	Path model, predicting physical health (PMI) from personality (Type A, locus of control), coping style, occupational stress and demographic variables (age and hours of work)	233
Figure 14.1	A model of work schedule effects on retention outcomes	263
Figure 19.1	Means of discrimination towards substance users as a function of education	375
Figure 20.1	Interaction of separation by ethnicity in predicting active reaction toward discrimination	393

List of Tables

Table 7.1	Types of mood disorders	129
Table 7.2	Psychological therapies for depression	129
Table 7.3	Medications used to treat adult nicotine addiction	131
Table 7.4	Consequences of adolescent alcohol consumption	132
Table 7.5	Medications used to treat adult alcoholics	133
Table 8.1	Trait EI versus ability EI	141
Table 8.2	The sampling domain of trait EI	143
Table 9.1	Intercorrelations among study variables	162
Table 9.2	Intercorrelations among occupational self-efficacy and work engagement dimensions	162
Table 9.3	Summary of stepwise regression analyses for variables predicting work engagement and occupational self-efficacy	163
Table 10.1	Canadian and Chinese nurses' area and role during the SARS crisis	175
Table 10.2	Means, standard deviations, and intercorrelation matrix of variables	178
Table 10.3	Goodness of fit indices for models	179
Table 12.1	Correlations between demographic, job-related, outcome and personality variables	227
Table 12.2	Gender differences for job-related, outcome and personality variables	228
Table 12.3	Linear multiple regression analyses. Subscales of coping as determinants of outcome measures (work satisfaction, psychological and physical health)	229
Table 12.4	Fit statistics for the structural equation models	231
Table 13.1	Common health conditions in presenteeism	245
Table 17.1	Means and standard deviation of low and high scores of GHQ-28 and STAI according to Ward analysis	338
Table 17.2	Participants with low and high scores of GHQ-28 and STAI according to Crosstab analysis	338

Table 17.3	Means of personality and anger expression variables as a function of age and gender	339
Table 17.4	Means of personal value variables as a function of age and gender	340
Table 17.5	Means of personal interest and work variables as a function of age and gender	341
Table 17.6	Hierarchical regression for the prediction of well being (general health and state trait anxiety) from gender, age, personality and work variables	344
Table 19.1	Means of discrimination as a function of gender	375
Table 19.2	Means of just world beliefs as a function of interaction of gender and education	376
Table 19.3	Hierarchical regression for the prediction of stigmatization from just world beliefs	377
Table 20.1	Acculturation, perceived injustice and responses to perceived injustice as a function of ethnicity and gender	391
Table 20.2	Hierarchical regression for the prediction of behavior reaction to discrimination from perceived injustice and acculturation	392

List of Contributors

Alexander-Stamatios Antoniou, National and Kapodistrian University of Athens, Greece

Maria Armaou, University of Warwick, UK

Elizabeth Austin, Department of Psychology, University of Edinburgh, Scotland, UK

Julian Barling, Queen's School of Business, Kingston, Ontario, Canada

Prashant Bordia, School of Management, University of South Australia, Australia

Ronald J. Burke, York University, Toronto, Canada

Simon B. Burnett, Lancaster University Management School, UK

Kristin E. Charles, Assessment Scientist Kronos, Inc., USA

Xue Feng Chen, Chinese Academy of Sciences, Beijing, China

Amy Christie, Queen's School of Business, Kingston, Ontario, Canada

Sue Coffey, York University, Toronto, Canada

Cary Cooper, Lancaster University Management School, UK

Marina Dalla, University of Athens, Greece

Lisa Fiksenbaum, York University, Toronto, Canada

Philip C. Gibbs, Lancaster University School of Health and Medicine, UK

Esther R. Greenglass, York University, Toronto, Canada

Donald E. Greydanus, Michigan State University College of Human Medicine, USA

Dirk H. Hellhammer, University of Trier, Germany

Juliane Hellhammer, University of Trier, Germany

Nerina L. Jimmieson, School of Psychology, The University of Queensland, Australia

Bruce Kirkcaldy, International Centre for the Study of Occupational and Mental Health, Düsseldorf, Germany

Magdalini Koutsoumari, Panteion University of Social and Political Sciences, Athens, Greece

Ayala Malach-Pines, Ben-Gurion University, Israel

Zdravko Marjanovic, York University, Toronto, Canada

Terence Martin, International Centre for the Study of Occupational and Mental Health, Düsseldorf, Germany

Gisela Mohr, University of Leipzig, Institute of Psychology II, Work and Organizational Psychology, Germany

Kathleen Otto, University of Leipzig, Institute of Psychology II, Work and Organizational Psychology, Germany

Dilip R. Patel, Michigan State University College of Human Medicine, USA

Panagiotis Perros, University of Athens, Greece

Konstantinos V. Petrides, Institute of Education, University of London, UK

Helen D. Pratt, Michigan State University College of Human Medicine, USA

LIST OF CONTRIBUTORS

Tahira M. Probst, Washington State University Vancouver, USA

Robert A. Roe, Maastricht University, the Netherlands

Sigalit Ronen, McGill University, Montreal, Canada

Kan Shi, Chinese Academy of Sciences, Beijing, China

Robert R. Sinclair, Portland State University, Department of Psychology, USA

Bas van Diepen, Maastricht University, the Netherlands

Kirsten Way, School of Psychology, The University of Queensland, Australia

Foreword

This volume makes a timely contribution to organizational psychology and behavioural medicine. Its five parts comprehensively cover topics that point the reader towards not just new developments in the field of occupational health psychology but the challenges the discipline faces. The volume is important not just because it captures a number of issues that are changing or about to change the nature of occupational health psychology but because it comes at a time when organizations, researchers and practitioners are witnessing social, economic and political turbulence that are themselves a source of work stress and strain.

All those concerned about the field will find this volume useful because in this time of turbulence the various contributors are expanding our understanding and identifying different perspectives that challenge traditional approaches and call for a more balanced approach to occupational health psychology. To illustrate this balanced approach the editors have gone beyond simply exploring traditional, but still important aspects of occupational health and stress to emphasizing aspects of positive psychology and positive organizational behaviour that explore how individuals can flourish, maximize their potential and experience meaningful work; nicely capturing resource depletion as well as resource accumulation.

The volume also challenges the reader to go beyond current conceptual boundaries to better understand concepts like presenteeism and the costs of stress, the significance of mental health issues at work, the need for partnerships that extend beyond the organization when developing interventions, the benefits of providing good work, the importance of the social environment in shaping work behaviours that will be valued, the practical value of carrying out stress audits and the importance of human resource policies that ensure that future working relationships are based on trust, authenticity and partnership.

It is clear that as researchers we are being asked to think as much about the positive aspects of work as we have about work's negative aspects, as managers we are being asked to think as much about value driven organizations as we have about organizational control and as practitioners as much about the processes, nature and evaluation of interventions as we have about their management. This volume provides an opportunity to be challenged by the work of the contributors. Change is necessary and innovation is called for if we are to fulfil our moral obligation to those whose working lives we study. The rest is up to us.

Philip Dewe
Professor of Organizational Behaviour
Department of Organizational Psychology
Birkbeck, University of London
Vice Master at Birkbeck, University of London

Introduction:
New Directions in Organizational Psychology and Behavioral Medicine

Alexander-Stamatios Antoniou and Cary Cooper

The purpose of this volume is to review the short history of occupational health psychology (OHP) and to include empirical research showing the dynamic relationship between work, health and satisfaction. OHP is an applied field of psychology that aims to improve the quality of work life, and to protect and promote the safety, health and well-being of workers (NIOSH, 2009). It is the study of psychological, social and organizational aspects of the dynamic relationship between work and health. The European perspective suggests that the areas of psychology that might be applied in addressing occupational health include health psychology, work and organizational psychology, and social and environmental psychology. Meanwhile, North American researchers integrate psychological procedures, practices and methodologies with a diverse number of specialties, principally health and occupational health psychology, preventive, occupational and behavioral medicine, political science, sociology and business.

OHP studies have focused on psychosocial work environments, stress theory and stress intervention, managerial behavior and intervention to promote health at work. In today's changing world, research on organizational psychology and behavioral medicine is a dynamic area. Personal and job environmental factors related to employee health and job satisfaction, performance management, unemployment and job insecurity, technical innovation and increased cultural diversity are all topics more related to the contemporary nature of work than traditional issues such as leadership, work values and so on. Furthermore, the term "health" used in OHP has a positive connotation that includes a state of complete physical, mental and social well-being.

This new volume aims to provide insight into: (a) new challenges for occupational and health psychology, (b) work and dispositional occupational sources of health, (c) health, management and organizational effectiveness, (d) job insecurity, unemployment and mental health and (e) specific issues of occupational psychology.

Part I: New Challenges for Occupational Health Psychology

This section provides an introduction to the short history of OHP. Although concerns for worker health have a long tradition, OHP developed as a psychological discipline as recently as 1990s. It is both a scientific discipline and an applied field that operates at the intersection of science and society. The focus of Part I is on positive aspects of health and well-being.

Part II: Work and Dispositional Occupational Sources of Health

The focus of this part is related to different levels of explanation of work health, including the job environment and dispositional factors, job factors (e.g. work overload and work intensity) and personality resources (e.g. emotional intelligence, self-efficacy). Special attention is given to the psychological problems of vulnerable groups in the workplace (e.g. adolescents, women).

Part III: Health, Management and Organizational Effectiveness

The management of people at work is an integral subject of the research of OHP. The positive model of management is comprised of two integrated systems: productivity and effectiveness, and work satisfaction.

Part IV: Job Insecurity, Unemployment and Mental Health

Unemployment and job insecurity results in the significant deterioration of mental health. This part addresses the effects on health of unemployment and job insecurity. The relation of personality traits, anger experience and personal systems of values and work interests to the well-being of the unemployed is also examined.

Part V: Specific Issue of Occupational Health Psychology

The final part of this volume identifies three major areas of OHP. The first chapter deals with people's Internet behavior, the psychological impact of Internet use and the potential for certain people to engage in Internet abuse. The second chapter focuses on aspects of working with drug abusers, such as social discrimination and the behavior of health professionals towards drug abusers. The third chapter addresses problems faced by immigrants in relation to work and employment.

* * *

At this point we would like to express our sincere thanks to all those who contributed to this volume. It has been an honor for us to welcome such an international team of experts, academics and professionals from so many universities and research centers worldwide. Their enthusiasm and commitment has provided original and in-depth insights on current issues of working life. Finally, we also thank the Gower staff for their invaluable contributions throughout the various stages of this project.

References

National Institute for Occupational Safety and Health (2009). *Occupational Health Psychology*. Available at: http://www.cdc.gov/niosh/topics/stress/ohp/ohp.html [Accessed: 22 March 2010].

PART I
New Challenges for Occupational Health Psychology

1

A Short History of Occupational Health Psychology: A Biographical Approach

Amy Christie and Julian Barling

The past century has seen many fascinating changes in the way in which people are viewed within the work context. There has been a shift from a perspective in which workers were valued primarily for their ability to be productive, with anything interfering with the potential for productivity seen as a hindrance to be controlled (Taylor, 1911), to a focus on employee well-being. The large body of research now focusing on the topic of employee well-being demonstrates the magnitude of this shift. This interest transcends the world of research, with organizations showing concern about the health of the workforce as well. Seminal in this transformation of the view of work, workers and their well-being has been the work of international researchers over the past century. This chapter presents and evaluates their substantial contribution. How substantial has this contribution been? A traditional academic perspective would examine, for example, citations to various articles or authors, or note that this field now has a formal name (occupational health psychology), its own acronym (OHP), and two flagship journals. We offer a different perspective, exploring the history of OHP by considering some of the most seminal contributions to the field. There are certainly not many social scientists who have had a rock band named in their honor, or a knighthood bestowed on them for their work. In this chapter, however, we will meet two social scientists, among others, involved in OHP research who can make such claims!

Marie Jahoda: Unemployment and Mental Health

There are surely very few people for whom it could be said that their lifetime's work helped shape an entire field; that they served as a role model to the field; that their publishing career spanned eight decades—and eventually had a rock band named after them![1] But this is certainly true of Marie Jahoda, and it is in appreciation of her life and her influence that we begin this chapter. In witnessing a life so rich, the challenge is not what to include, but rather what can we afford to omit?

Marie Jahoda was born in Vienna on January 26, 1907. Her first publication appeared in 1926. Her early influence, however, derived principally from the results of research into the mental health effects of unemployment within the Marienthal community (Jahoda, 1933; Jahoda, Lazarsfeld, and Zeisel, 1933). That this book would continue to influence research on unemployment is all the more remarkable given that most copies of the first published edition were burned by the Nazis because of the three authors' Jewish origins. Jahoda's focus on research into the nature and consequences of unemployment for mental health continued for the rest of the century, with her retirement in 1972 simply being the occasion for an extraordinary burst of research and writing.

This trajectory culminated in a book Jahoda published in 1982, which described the psychological nature and experience of unemployment (and employment). Jahoda (1982; 1989) posited that work is a fundamental human activity that is critical for mental health, noting that people would often prefer "bad" jobs to unemployment. From her understanding of unemployment, she identified two major functions of employment. The manifest function of employment was the provision of sufficient financial resources, and could be contrasted with latent or psychological functions, which included the provision of a time structure, social contacts, and personal identity. The absence of any of the latent consequences would be detrimental to mental health, and her theory is sometimes referred to as the "deprivation theory of unemployment."

A chapter on the life and influence of Jahoda would be remiss if it were limited to a focus on her research on unemployment and mental health; her interests and her impact were much broader. Aside from the numerous professional awards and honorary degrees bestowed on her, a professional

---

[1] The rock band NOJAHODA chose this name because, they noted, they exhibited none of the seven attributes of mental health identified by Jahoda. Their first recording was entitled "Jahoda's witness."

chair named in her honor in Germany, and the fact that she held a junior cabinet position in the United Kingdom, Jahoda was also a lifelong social activist. She was jailed in Austria in 1936–37 for her leadership role in the Austrian socialist youth movement, and exiled immediately thereafter to England in 1937 where she spent the war-time years. After emigrating to the United States at the end of World War II, she worked actively against the excesses of McCarthyism, became a board member of the American Civil Liberties Union, and was the first female president of the Society for the Psychological Study of Social Issues. Her social activism was inseparable from her professional career (e.g., Jahoda, 1956; 1959), culminating in her interests in action research (e.g., Jahoda, Deutsch, and Cook, 1951).

Marie Jahoda characteristically remained engaged in thinking and writing throughout her life. Demonstrating the breadth of her interests and influence, one of her last works (published five years before her death in 2001) was a translation into English of the sonnets of Louise Labe, the sixteenth-century French proto-feminist poet (Jahoda, 1997).

Arthur Kornhauser: Work and Mental Health

The term "occupational health psychology" was first penned in 1990 by Jonathan Raymond (Raymond, Wood, and Patrick, 1990), however, interest in the health and well-being of workers emerged much earlier. Some have argued (e.g., Zickar, 2003) that industrial psychologist Arthur Kornhauser's commitment to identifying organizational factors thought to improve the well-being of workers was instrumental to the development of the field. Beginning in the 1920s, Kornhauser was devoted to the study of worker well-being, and pioneered efforts to understand the effects of work on mental health at a time when prevailing interest concentrated on how pre-existing mental illnesses affected organizational efficiency. Instead, Kornhauser was interested in the range of mental health, both positive and negative, including all those psychological and behavioral attributes indicating life satisfaction, adjustment, and effectiveness. He believed that developing scientific, practical methods of morale or opinion surveying and psychological testing could be beneficial to improving the lives of workers and society overall (see Zickar, 2003). Contrary to the Tayloristic principles of the early twentieth century, Kornhauser's lifetime work fuelled the surge of research interest that, in the decades following his retirement, would explore the impact of organizational factors on employee mental health (Sauter and Hurrell, 1999). Likewise, during this era, Kornhauser's counterparts in Europe were also revealing the erroneous assumptions of scientific management, specifically indicating its deleterious effects for the health and adjustment of employees doing specialized work (e.g., Trist and Bamforth, 1951).

Kornhauser's final contribution to the field was probably his most influential: an in-depth study of Detroit autoworkers' work and well-being in the 1950s (Kornhauser, 1965). This incredible undertaking, consisting of over 400, four-hour interviews, was published in 1965 as the now classic book, *Mental Health of the Industrial Worker*. In his quest to explore the psychological condition of factory workers in the mass-production industry, Kornhauser offered a number of conclusions that only much later became part of mainstream thinking and conventional programs of research. For example, in his comparison of autoworkers at various organizational levels, Kornhauser found that mental health was stratified by occupational category, such that men in lower employment grades experienced worse mental health than those in higher grades—a phenomenon later investigated at length, and supported empirically, by Marmot and his colleagues (discussed in more detail later). For Kornhauser, the key to understanding this stratification was job satisfaction, which, like mental health, varies across organizations, making salient organizational and managerial influences on the mental health of workers. Accordingly, he identified a number of job characteristics thought to detract from positive mental health, including the lack of opportunity for self growth and esteem, financial stress, task repetitiveness, aspects of supervision and other human interaction, career immobility, job insecurity, and adverse physical conditions. Finally, well before the work-family conflict literature gained such prominence, Kornhauser was investigating the interface between work, family, and leisure in his interviews, concluding that job dissatisfaction could spill over into non-work domains, a notion which is now held to be axiomatic.

The seminal findings of the Detroit autoworker's study are infused into the research of today and form part of the foundation of occupational health psychology itself.

Robert Kahn

Another critical early influence in the development of OHP was Robert L. Kahn from the University of Michigan's Institute for Social Research, the home of so many early contributions to the discipline of social psychology. In 1949, Rensis

Likert, whose influence has permeated the field in its own right, founded and became the first director of the Institute for Social Research (ISR) at the University of Michigan, where Kahn served as the director of its survey research department from 1970 to 1976. The ISR remains one of the most long-standing American research institutions in the social sciences, continuing its influential interdisciplinary social research today. Kahn first became an expert in survey methodologies, and was perhaps initially most widely known for his book, *The Social Psychology of Organizations*, co-authored with Daniel Katz (Katz and Kahn, 1966). As the title suggests, he and Katz applied the principles of social psychology to large corporations, and a second edition of the book appeared in 1978. However, while Katz continued his work in social psychology, Kahn was already interested in how organizations influenced employee health. His second groundbreaking contribution to OHP started with his now-classic research on the relationship between role stressors and health (Kahn, Wolfe, Quinn, Snoek, and Rosenthal, 1964), an issue that continues to attract empirical attention today (Beehr and Glaser, 2005).

Kahn et al. (1964) showed that role conflict, role ambiguity, and role overload (both quantitative and qualitative) were important stressors for men in their national sample of the US labor force. Outcomes such as lower job satisfaction, job-related tension, withdrawal, and lower self-confidence were associated with role stress. Kahn et al. (1964) also showed that organizational factors influence role expectations and pressures that ultimately determine workers' experiences of inter-role conflict and ambiguity, and that interpersonal relations and personality factors moderate this relationship. Subsequent research over the next 40 years validated and extended their findings; and Kahn's 1980 book, appropriately entitled *Work and Health*, further extended the way in which this link is viewed.

Kahn has continued to publish well into his retirement years, with a particular focus on aging, including a broadly successful book about aging well co-authored with physician John Rowe (Rowe and Kahn, 1998).

Jeffrey Greenhaus and Nicholas Beutell: Work and Family Conflict

Kahn and colleagues predominantly focused on role conflict within the domain of work, however, their pioneering research inspired Greenhaus and Beutell's (1985) seminal article exploring inter-role conflict between work and non-work pressures. While certainly not the first to consider the work and family interface (authors such as Robert Hoppock studied this issue as early as 1935), Greenhaus and Beutell (1985) offered a theoretical framework for understanding the work-family conflict concept that legitimized its study in the management field. The main focus of this literature has been to understand how work and family functioning mutually influence one another. Changes in the composition of the workforce, with more women working outside the home, more single-parent families, and a greater number of dual-earning households, have amplified the importance of this endeavor over the past few decades. Today, the focus on work-family conflict is widespread, being studied in at least 37 different countries (Bellavia and Frone, 2003).

Based on role theory (Kahn et al., 1964), Greenhaus and Beutell (1985) define work-family conflict as occurring when an individual's work roles and family roles are in some way incompatible, and specifically identify time-based, strain-based, and behavior-based conflict as the most prevalent forms of such incompatibility. In this way, time constraints, strain, and in-role behavior in the work domain can make meeting role demands in the family domain difficult or impossible, and vice versa, a concept first modeled and empirically tested by Frone, Russell, and Cooper (1992; 1997). Many theories of work-family conflict have been offered today that promise to make valuable contributions to our understanding of the way in which people experience the intersection of work and family, and their joint influence on employee well-being. However, Greenhaus and Beutell (1985)'s conceptual article remains the most widely cited in the work-family conflict literature (197 citations as of 2001) even after controlling for the number of years since its publication.[2]

Sir Michael Marmot: The Whitehall Studies

Arguably the most rigorous and influential investigation of social and occupational status and health came from the now famous Whitehall studies conducted by Sir Michael Marmot and colleagues over the last 30 years—a program of research that earned Marmot a knighthood in the United Kingdom. The first Whitehall study, Whitehall I, beginning in 1967, was a longitudinal study of cardiovascular and other diseases in 18,000 male civil servants in London. The results were striking. Mortality rates were highest among men in low employment grades and lowest among those in higher grades, a finding made even more intriguing considering that civil servants certainly do not fall

---

[2] http://wfnetwork.bc.edu/loppr/top100.pdf [accessed December 9, 2010].

at the extremes of society's social status hierarchy (Marmot, Shipley, and Rose, 1984). The relationship was in fact monotonic, such that at each level of the status hierarchy, those with lower social standing were more vulnerable to morbidity and mortality than their higher status colleagues (Marmot, 2004). Although the findings from Whitehall I countered the hypothesis that the demanding and "stress-filled" atmosphere experienced by executives left them most at risk for coronary heart disease, it could not uncover what *caused* the social gradient in health. Moreover, after controlling for risk factors such as age, smoking, plasma cholesterol, systolic blood pressure, body mass index, physical activity, height, and family history, two-thirds of the gradient remained, thus giving birth to a second major study, Whitehall II.

Whitehall II began with over 10,000 men and women in the civil service in 1985 and continues through its seventh phase today with its purpose being to understand what underlies the health gradient. In this effort, Marmot and colleagues have illuminated the role of the psychosocial work environment in creating social health inequalities, and in doing so, point out the salience of work itself and its organization (Marmot and Shipley, 1996). These ideas transcend the domain of epidemiology, having been accepted by psychologists, sociologists, and organizational researchers. Over the course of Whitehall II, diverse factors have been identified as contributing to the social gradient, including job demands, control, social support, effort-reward imbalance, job insecurity, organizational change, work-home balance, and retirement, all of which can be observed in the over 250 published works based on the study that had already been published by 2005.[3] Such research has directed health policy makers away from looking solely to individual behaviors and lifestyle factors in their efforts to prevent chronic diseases in society. In fact, the impact of the Whitehall studies has extended beyond that of the research community, and has directed British health policy changes over the last decade, creating a primary focus on reducing societal health inequalities in the country.

Christina Maslach and Susan Jackson: Job Burnout

With the intensity of research occurring in the second half of the twentieth century that focused on understanding the link between the organization and the well-being of workers, came an interest in the most extreme manifestations of psychologically demanding work. In the 1970s, researchers began to study the phenomenon of job burnout intensively, even though practitioners had already

---

3 http://www.ucl.ac.uk/whitehallII [accessed December 9, 2010].

recognized the ill effects of emotionally defeating work, particularly in the service sector. Early work conducted by psychiatrist Herbert Freudenberger and social psychologist Christina Maslach was mainly qualitative and aimed to define the nature of burnout, and verify its existence (Freudenberger, 1975; Maslach, 1976). However, it is really Maslach and Jackson's (1981) introduction of the Maslach Burnout Inventory (MBI), a psychometrically sound measure of burnout, that sees the beginning of the extensive quantitative literature on burnout now available. Remarkably, although slightly updated from 1981, the MBI is still the most commonly used measure of burnout today (Maslach, Schaufeli, and Leiter, 2001) and has been cited over 300 times at the time of this writing.

In their original conceptualization of burnout (designed for service workers), Maslach and Jackson (1981) introduced a multidimensional measure of experienced burnout based on earlier qualitative evidence, specifically identifying emotional exhaustion, depersonalization, and diminished personal accomplishment as its integral components. Emotional exhaustion reflects the depletion of once-present emotional resources, which then leaves individuals unable to reenergize each day for work. The second component, depersonalization, occurs when workers feel detached and cynical about their work, often denying the humanity of their clients. Finally, a diminished sense of personal accomplishment or competence characterizes the third dimension.

Originally, burnout was considered to be specific to the services and education industries. More recently, however, the burnout literature has focused on a much wider variety of occupations and roles. Likewise, in the past two decades, the process, consequences, and situational and individual causes of job burnout have been investigated extensively using the MBI by prominent researchers such as Michael Leiter, Wilmar Shaufeli, and Christina Maslach.

Robert Karasek and Töres Theorell: The Demand-Control-Support Model

Any history of occupational health psychology surely must speak to Robert Karasek and Töres Theorell's theory of work design and health, probably the most influential and widely-researched theory in occupational health psychology. Karasek and Theorell's work was inspired by the long tradition of research and practice in the Nordic countries that countered Tayloristic formulas for job design, and explained the link between health, well-being, and work. At the University of Stockholm, Karasek worked under the influence of psychologist Bertil Gardell, himself a pioneer of OHP who had a well-established research program on alienation, mental health, autonomy, and participation at work (e.g., Gardell, 1971; 1977). Gardell's work was continued after his death by his colleague, Marianne Frankenhaeuser, who studied the relationship between psychosocial factors and health in great depth (e.g., Frankenhaeuser and Johansson, 1986). Similarly, at the Karolinska Institute in Sweden, Theorell worked with Lennart Levi, head of the Institute's Stress Research Laboratory and founder of the National Institute for Psychosocial Factors and Health (established in 1981), with Theorell later assuming the directorship. Quite rightly, both Levi and Gardell are credited with having inspired and shaped Swedish and European legislation that has strived to improve working life by enhancing the psychosocial work environment (Kompier, 2002).

Karasek's original publication in 1979 outlined the demand-control (or decision latitude) model, arguing that job control gives employees the latitude to manage or cope with the demands of their jobs, thus buffering negative health effects. Those jobs that are both highly demanding and low in controllability would result in the most psychological strain (the "strain" hypothesis; Karasek, 1979). A later publication expanded this model to account for physical health, specifically cardiovascular disease, in a longitudinal population study of Swedish men (Karasek, Baker, Marxer, Ahlbom, and Theorell, 1981). *Healthy Work* (1990), a book authored by Karasek and Theorell (1990), extended the theory further to account for the positive health consequences of social support—a major focus of behavioral science research in the 1980s, enhancing the theory's legitimacy and popularity for a widespread audience. In fact, the demand-control-(support) literature has attracted so much empirical attention that it has enabled a number of comprehensive reviews with sample sizes of 36 studies after 15 years (Schnall and Landsbergis, 1994) and 63 studies after 20 years (van der Doef and Maes, 1999). Furthermore, while limiting their search to only "high quality" studies, de Lange et al. (2003) included 45 longitudinal studies in their review of the demand-control-(support) literature at the turn of the century.

While debate continues about the validity of the statistical interaction between demands and latitude, such debate can only be constructive for the field of occupational health psychology. In this respect, it is not the validation of the DCS model that has been most critical to occupational health psychology, but instead the way in which Karasek and Theorell's job strain model has stimulated other researchers to consider the range of psychosocial work factors critical to employee health, and led to the development of other theories such as Johannes Siegrist's effort-reward imbalance model (Siegrist, 1996).

Peter Warr, Toby Wall, and the Institute of Work Psychology

Research conducted at the University of Sheffield's Institute of Work Psychology (IWP)[4] has consistently yielded a considerable influence on the field of occupational health psychology. Started in 1968 (Warr, 1999), the IWP has played host to national and international postgraduate students, as well as sabbaticants, many of whom have either moved or returned to countries all over the world (e.g., John Cordery, Mark Griffin, Sharon Parker, and Kerrie Unsworth to Australia; Natalie Allen, Gary Johns, and Nick Turner to Canada; Olga Epitropaki to Greece; Mike Burke and Steven Rogelberg to the United States), thereby extending its pervasive influence.

One of the stalwarts of the IWP is Peter Warr, who has spent several decades within this Institute, many of them as the Director. Perhaps not surprisingly given that the IWP is situated in Sheffield, Warr's earlier research focused on the nature and effects of unemployment. Warr and his colleagues at the Institute focused on the effects of unemployment on diverse groups (e.g., young people experiencing unemployment; Jackson, Stafford, Banks, and Warr, 1983) and a wide range of outcomes. Moreover, Warr and his colleagues also focused on the nature of unemployment, noting presciently in 1984 how unemployment constitutes more than simply the loss of employment and the consequent provision of money. Instead, Warr (1984) pointed out how unemployment requires individuals to assume new and difficult roles, deal with uncertainty and unpredictability, cope with feelings of loss of control, and identity issues.

Subsequently, Peter Warr (1987) published his seminal theory of how employment and unemployment both influence mental health. While acknowledging that any attempt to summarize a seminal work in a few sentences is inevitably incomplete, it is worth noting that Warr went further than contemporary approaches to understanding how intrinsic work characteristics affected well-being (e.g., the job characteristics model; Hackman and Oldham, 1976; 1980) by explicitly incorporating extrinsic components in his theory. In addition, Warr's (1987) model also shows that work characteristics (named "vitamin factors" in his model) need not only exert linear effects on well-being.

---

4 In earlier years, this was known as "The Social and Applied Psychology Unit" (Warr, 1999).

Peter Warr was succeeded as Director of the IWP by Toby Wall, who was already situated at the Institute. Wall has made significant advances to our understanding of the effects of task-related autonomy both indirectly through his supervision of doctoral studies of people who themselves have gone on to publish influential research in OHP (e.g., Sharon Parker), and directly through his own research. Wall's now-classic quasi-experimental study establishes the long-term benefits of even small amounts of task-related autonomy on mental health and productivity (Wall, Corbett, Martin, Clegg and Jackson, 1990).

Dov Zohar: Occupational Safety

Occupational safety now attracts considerable attention within OHP. However, this was not always the case; most of the research in this area has been conducted in the past 25 years. Early safety research concentrated on identifying the characteristics of "accident-prone" employees (for example, Wong and Hobbs, 1949) so that organizations could manage accident rates through their selection processes (or more realistically, the process of excluding certain employees). Today there is a vast literature assuming that human error explains only a small portion of workplace accidents, and suggests that unsafe behavior, often motivated by the need for efficiency, is instead the primary culprit (Zohar, 1980).

Historically, the focus on safety was legitimized in 1980 with Dov Zohar's introduction of the notion of safety climate, a specific type of organizational climate. Zohar (1980) argues that safety climate is a shared perception of an organization's policies, procedures, and practices about safety. In a sample of Israeli organizations, Zohar (1980) showed that employee perceptions of management's attitudes towards safety are most important in predicting safety climate level. Climate, however, is not determined by the totality of safety procedures or practices (for example, the number of policies, emphasis on safe working, protective gear, training), but by their relative importance against other managerial responsibilities (particularly in the trade-off between efficiency on one hand, and safety on the other) (Zohar, 2000).

The occupational safety literature has advanced to become a significant contributor to the field, its focus clearly consistent with the central tenets of OHP. Barling and Hutchinson (2000) argue that while most commonly organizations use a control-based orientation towards safety by attempting to ensure compliance to existing safety regulations through reward and punishment, a commitment-based orientation, which builds employees' trust in management and commitment to the organization, is more effective. Recent research has reflected this reasoning, exploring commitment-based antecedents to safe behavior, such as performance-based pay, training, teamwork (Kaminski, 2001), autonomy (Barling, Kelloway, and Iverson, 2003; Parker, Axtell, and Turner, 2001), job insecurity (Probst, 2002), leadership (Hofmann, Morgeson, and Gerras, 2003), and high performance work systems (Zacharatos, Barling, and Iverson, 2005), thus demonstrating how the issue of occupational safety is now considered to be integral to organizational functioning.

The Organizations

Scholars of organizations have known for millennia that organizations have the ability to influence the behavior of individuals. Thus, it will come as no surprise that individuals' research on occupational health psychology has been significantly influenced by the activities of several different organizations.

Perhaps the first organization that should be acknowledged is the US National Institute for Occupational Health Psychology (NIOSH) developed in 1970.[5] Beginning in the 1980s, NIOSH identified occupational stress as one of the primary factors that potentially compromised the well-being of employees, and ever since, has focused considerable efforts on providing research-driven solutions for organizational interventions. Its activities in this regard have been numerous. In 1990, three prominent researchers employed by NIOSH published their influential paper laying out an agenda for research and interventions on work stress (Sauter, Murphy, and Hurrell, 1990). NIOSH has also been instrumental together with the American Psychological Association (APA)[6] in organizing eight research-based conferences since 1990, with the ninth conference scheduled to be held in Orlando, 2011. These conferences have had a significant impact on bringing together OHP researchers from across the world. NIOSH also joined with the APA to sponsor graduate-level courses in OHP. Of course, organizations cannot exert the influence that NIOSH has had, people do! In this respect, the influence of Sauter, Murphy, and Hurrell through all these efforts on the field of occupational health psychology cannot go unnoticed.

As well as joining together with NIOSH in these endeavors, the APA has been instrumental as the publisher of *Journal of Occupational Health Psychology*

---

5 http://www.cdc.gov/niosh/homepage.html [accessed December 9, 2010].
6 http://www.apa.org/ [accessed December 9, 2010].

(*JOHP*).[7] In keeping with organizational wisdom that every cause needs a champion, Gwendolyn Keita has played a leading role within the APA in all of these endeavors

In 1999, the European Academy of Occupational Health Psychology (EA-OHP)[8] was formed, and was structured specifically around three goals, namely research, education, and practice. With Tom Cox taking a primary leadership role, the EA-OHP has organized several conferences, and currently holds one biannually that is attended by several hundred people from across the world. These conferences tend to focus more intensively on education and practice than those organized by the APA and NIOSH, which predominantly focuses on research.

The contributions of other organizations have not been trivial, whether for-profit publishing companies that have been very welcoming of the idea of work and well-being (e.g., Taylor and Francis, Wiley, Sage), international organizations that have funded a considerable amount of research (e.g., the International Labour Organization), or university-based institutes that have developed researchers through graduate training (e.g., the Institute of Work Psychology at the University of Sheffield). Nonetheless, space dictates that we limit our observations and major comments to those organizations that have exerted the greatest direct influence of occupational health psychology.

The Editors

Many of the people introduced above have substantially influenced the quality and direction of the field of occupational health psychology directly through their research. However, others have influenced the field of OHP through the development and nurturing of academic journals that provide an outlet for academic research, and a forum for discussion. The critical role of the editors, themselves usually well-established as researchers in the specific area, should therefore not be discounted. Existence of such journals then serves as evidence for the maturity of the field.

Several years before the appearance of the first journal devoted specifically to occupational health psychology, Cary L. Cooper started the *Journal of Occupational Behavior* (which later became the *Journal of Organizational Behavior*).[9]

---

7   http://www.apa.org/journals/ocp/ [accessed December 9, 2010].
8   http://www.ea-ohp.org/ [accessed December 9, 2010].
9   http://www3.interscience.wiley.com/cgi-bin/jhome/4691 [accessed December 9, 2010].

The masthead of the journal, first published in 1980, specifically invited articles that focused on issues such as work stress and work and family, and this journal initially published many seminal articles in the field. As one early example, Christina Maslach and Susan Jackson published their seminal work on the measurement of burnout in the second volume of the (then) *Journal of Occupational Behavior*. The role of Cary Cooper goes further than the editorship of this journal: he has also consistently provided opportunities for researchers around the world to share their thoughts on topics for which they have specific expertise in chapters in his edited books.

Several years later, in 1986, Tom Cox at the University of Nottingham began to edit *Work and Stress*.[10] Unlike the *Journal of Organizational Behavior*, as its title indicates, *Work and Stress* was always focused specifically on employees' well-being and the factors that influence that well-being. As such, *Work and Stress* holds the distinction of being the first specific journal in the area. To this day, Tom Cox continues as editor, and a hallmark of this journal is the fact that its readership probably includes more practitioners than is true of many other academic journals, perhaps extending the benefits of the knowledge derived from empirical research to more organizations and more people. Like Cary Cooper, Tom Cox has also been instrumental in editing numerous books.

The contributions of Cooper and Cox has been appropriately recognized beyond the confines of academic research, with Cary Cooper being awarded the Commander of the Order of the British Empire (CBE) in 2001 and Tom Cox the CBE in 2000, both very significant achievements.

Some ten years following the appearance of *Work and Stress*, the *JOHP* was first published by the American Psychological Association. James (Jim) Quick served as the first editor of *JOHP* from 1996 through 1999. He was followed by Julian Barling, who recently completed his term as editor, having served between 2000 and 2005. Perhaps a mark of the maturity of this specific journal is that it is now on its third editor, with Lois Tetrick having assumed the role of editor as of 2006. The very fact that the journal can afford to rotate its editorships, and that the second editor (Barling) was from outside of the United States despite the fact that the journal was published by the American Psychological Association, is further evidence of the breadth of occupational health psychology research.

---

10 http://www.tandf.co.uk/journals/titles/02678373.asp [accessed December 9, 2010].

In conclusion, occupational health psychology has come a long way since the days of scientific management in the early part of the twentieth century, helping to shape a new recognition of the importance of the health and well-being of workers. The individuals, organizations, and journals discussed in this chapter were instrumental in this respect. Of course, we take for granted that the field of OHP today is a function of the efforts of many researchers, in many countries, unfortunately, however, space prohibits us from mentioning these significant contributions in this chapter. As we continue in the twenty-first century, our understanding of the link between work and health will no doubt be solidified and extended, with the likelihood that we will see the knowledge gained applied to help employees and the organizations that employ them.

References

Barling, J. and Hutchinson, I. (2000). Commitment vs. control-based safety practices, safety reputation, and perceived safety climate. *Revue Canadienne des Sciences de l'Administration*, 17(1), 76–84.

Barling, J., Kelloway, E.K., and Iverson, R.D. (2003). High quality work, employee morale and occupational injuries. *Journal of Applied Psychology*, 88, 276–83.

Beehr, T.A. and Glaser, S. (2005). Organizational role stress. In J. Barling, E.K. Kelloway, and M.R. Frone (eds), *Handbook of Work Stress* (pp. 7–33). Thousand Oaks, CA: Sage.

Bellavia, G.M. and Frone, M.R. (2003). Work-family conflict. In J. Barling, E.K Kelloway, and M.R. Frone (eds), *Handbook of Work Stress* (pp. 113–48). Thousand Oaks, CA: Sage.

de Lange, A., Taris, T., Kompier, M., Houtman, I., and Bongers, P. (2003). "The *very* best of the millennium": longitudinal research and the demand-control-(support) model. *Journal of Occupational Health Psychology*, 8(4), 282–305.

Frankenhaeuser, M. and Johansson, G. (1986). Stress at work: psychobiological and psychosocial aspects. *International Review of Applied Psychology*, 35, 287–99.

Freudenberger, H.J. (1975). The staff burnout syndrome in alternative institutions. *Psychotherapy: Theory, Research, and Practice*, 12(1), 72–83.

Frone, M.R., Russell, M., and Cooper, M.L. (1992). Antecedents and outcomes of work-family conflict: testing a model of the work-family interface. *Journal of Applied Psychology*, 77, 65–78.

Frone, M.R., Russell, M., and Cooper, M.L. (1997). Relation of work-family conflict to health outcomes: a four-year longitudinal study of employed parents. *Journal of Occupational and Organizational Psychology*, 70, 325–35.

Gardell, B. (1971). Technology, alienation and mental health in the modern industrial environment. In L. Levi (ed.), *Society, Stress and Disease*, vol. 1. Oxford: Oxford University Press.

Gardell, B. (1977). Autonomy and participation at work. *Human Relations*, 30, 515–33.

Greenhaus, J.H. and Beutell, N.J. (1985). Sources of conflict between work and family roles. *Academy of Management Review*, 10(1), 75–88.

Hackman, J.R. and Oldham, G.R. (1976). Motivation through the design of work: test of a theory. *Organizational Behavior and Human Performance*, 16, 250–79.

Hackman, J.R. and Oldham, G.R. (1980). *Work Redesign*. Reading, MA: Addison-Wesley.

Hofmann, D.A., Morgeson, F.P., and Gerras, S.J. (2003). Climate as a moderator of the relationship between leader-member exchange and content specific citizenship: safety climate as an exemplar. *Journal of Applied Psychology*, 88(1), 170–78.

Hoppock, R. (1935). *Job Satisfaction*. New York, NY: Harper and Row.

Jackson, P.R., Stafford, E.M., Banks, M.H., and Warr, P.B. (1983). Unemployment and psychological distress in young people: the moderating role of employment commitment. *Journal of Applied Psychology*, 68, 525–35.

Jahoda, M. (1933). The influence of unemployment on children and young people in Austria. In The Save the Children International Union (ed.), *Children, Young People and Unemployment* (pp. 115–37) (vol. 2, part 2). Geneva: Eigenverlag.

Jahoda, M. (1956). Psychological issues in civil liberties. *American Psychologist*, 11(5), 234–40.

Jahoda, M. (1959). Conformity and independence. *Human Relations*, 12(2), 99–120.

Jahoda, M. (1982). *Employment and Unemployment: A Social Psychological Analysis*. Cambridge: Cambridge University Press.

Jahoda, M. (1989). Economic recession and mental health: some conceptual issues. *Journal of Social Issues*, 44(4), 13–24.

Jahoda, M. (1997). *Louise Labe. Vierundzwanzig Sonette in drei Sprachen*. Munster: Johann Lang.

Jahoda, M., Deutsch, M., and Cook, S.W. (1951). *Research Methods in Social Relations with Especial Reference to Prejudice*. New York: The Dryden Press.

Jahoda, M., Lazarsfeld, P.F., and Zeisel, H. (1933). *Marienthal: The Sociography of an Unemployed Community* (English translation 1972). London: Tavistock.

Kahn, R.L., Wolfe, D.M., Quinn, R.P., Snoek, J.D., and Rosenthal, R.A. (1964). *Organizational Stress: Studies in Role Conflict and Ambiguity*. New York, NY: Wiley.

Kaminski, M. (2001). Unintended consequences: organizational practices and their impact on workplace safety and productivity. *Journal of Occupational Health Psychology*, 6(2), 127–38.

Karasek, R.A. (1979). *Job Demands, Decision Latitude, and Mental Strain: Implications for Job Design*. Ithaca, NY: Cornell University Press.

Karasek, R.A., Baker, D., Marxer, F., Ahlbom, A., and Theorell, T. (1981). Job decision latitude, job demands, and cardiovascular disease: a prospective study of Swedish men. *American Journal of Public* Health, 71, 694–705.

Karasek, R.A. and Thorell, T. (1990). *Healthy Work: Stress, Health, and the Reconstruction of Working Life*. New York, NY: Basic Books.

Katz, D. and Kahn, R. (1966). *Social Psychology of Organizations*. New York, NY: Wiley.

Kompier, M. (2002). The psychosocial work environment and health: what do we know and where should we go? *Scandinavian Journal of Work, Environment and Health*, 28(1), 1–4.

Kornhauser, A. (1965). *Mental Health of the Industrial Worker*. New York, NY: Wiley.

Marmot, M.G. (2004). *The Status Syndrome: How Social Standing Affects Our Health and Longevity*. New York, NY: Times Books.

Marmot, M.G. and Shipley, M.J. (1996). Do socioeconomic differences in mortality persist after retirement? 25 year follow up of civil servants from the first Whitehall study. *British Medical Journal*, 313, 1177–80.

Marmot, M.G., Shipley, M.J., and Rose, G. (1984). Inequalities in death: specific explanations of a general pattern? *The Lancet*, 323, 1003–6.

Maslach, C. (1976). Burned-out. *Human Behavior*, 5(9), 16–22.

Maslach, C. and Jackson, S.E. (1981). The measurement of experienced burnout. *Journal of Occupational Behavior*, 2, 99–113.

Maslach, C., Schaufeli, W.B., and Leiter, M.P. (2001). Job Burnout. *Annual Review of Psychology*, 52, 397–422.

Parker, S.K., Axtell, C.M., and Turner, N. (2001). Designing a safer workplace: importance of job autonomy, communication quality, and supportive supervisors. *Journal of Occupational Health Psychology*, 6(3), 211–28.

Probst, T.M. (2002). Layoffs and tradeoffs: production, quality, and safety demands under the threat of job loss. *Journal of Occupational Health Psychology*, 7(3), 211–20.

Raymond, J.S., Wood, D., and Patrick, W.K. (1990). Psychology doctoral training in work and health. *American Psychologist*, 45, 1159–61.

Rowe, J.W. and Kahn, R.L. (1998). *Successful Aging*. New York, NY: Pantheon Books.

Sauter, S.L. and Hurrell, J.J. (1999). Occupational Health Psychology: Origins, Content, and Direction. *Professional Psychology: Research and Practice*, 30(2), 117–122.

Sauter, S.L., Murphy L.R., and Hurrell, J.J. (1990). Prevention of work-related psychological disorders: a national strategy proposed by the National Institute for Occupational Safety and Health (NIOSH). *American Psychologist*, 45(10), 1146–58.

Schnall, P.L. and Landsbergis, P.A. (1994). Job strain and cardiovascular disease. *Annual Review of Public Health*, 15, 381–411.

Siegrist, J. (1996). Adverse health effects of high-effort/low-reward conditions. *Journal of Occupational Health Psychology*, 1, 27–41.

Taylor, F.W. (1911). *Principles of Scientific Management*. New York, NY: Harper and Brothers.

Trist, E.L. and Bamforth, K.W. (1951). Some social and psychological consequences of the longwall method of coal-getting. *Human Relations*, 14, 3–38.

van der Doef, M.P. and Maes, S. (1999). The job demand-control-(support) model and psychological well-being: a review of 20 years of empirical research. *Work and Stress*, 13, 87–114.

Wall, T.D., Corbett, J.M., Martin, R., Clegg, C.W., and Jackson, P.R. (1990). Advanced manufacturing technology, work design and performance: a change study. *Journal of Applied Psychology*, 75, 691–7.

Warr, P.B. (1984). Job loss, unemployment and psychological well-being. In V.L. Allen and E. van der Vliert (eds), *Role Transitions* (pp. 263–85). New York: Plenum Press.

Warr, P.B. (1987). *Work, Unemployment and Mental Health*. Oxford: Oxford University Press.

Warr, P.B. (1999). *Work, Well-Being and Effectiveness: A History of the MRC/ESRC Social and Applied Psychology Unit*. Sheffield: Institute of Work Psychology.

Wong, W.A. and Hobbs, G.E. (1949). Personal factors in industrial accidents: a study of accident proneness in an industrial group. *Industrial Medicine*, 18, 291–4.

Zacharatos, A., Barling, J., and Iverson, R.D. (2005). High-performance work systems and occupational safety. *Journal of Applied Psychology*, 90(1), 77–93.

Zickar, M.J. (2003). Remembering Arthur Kornhauser: industrial psychology's advocate for worker well-being. *Journal of Applied Psychology*, 88(2), 363–9.

Zohar, D. (1980). Safety climate in industrial organizations: theoretical and applied implications. *Journal of Applied Psychology*, 65, 96–102.

Zohar, D. (2000). A group level model of safety climate: testing the effects of group climate on microaccidents in manufacturing jobs. *Journal of Applied Psychology*, 85, 587–96.

2

Well-Being at Work, a New Way of Doing Things? A Journey through Yesterday, Today and Tomorrow

Philip C. Gibbs and Simon B. Burnett

Introduction

The contemporary interest in well-being is far from novel. Decades, or as could even be argued, centuries, of thought and research have regarded this concept and its myriad constituent aspects, including happiness, subjective appreciation of the values and quality of life, fulfilment and satisfaction, many of which can be unearthed with the minimum of effort. Consideration can be tracked even as far back as ancient Socratic philosophy, and most if not all religious and spiritual movements express considerable concern and insight into how people should pursue happier and more meaningful lives. In a more contemporary context, humanistic psychologists such as Abraham Maslow (regarded as the 'father' of the discipline [Maslow, 1998:3]) and Carl Rogers shared similar holistic visions of pursuing, understanding and influencing the productive capacities of mankind through concentrating on the development of uniquely human issues and experiences such as health, hope, love, creativity, self-actualisation and meaning (Gable and Haidt, 2005:104). Further, other organisational-humanists, such as Elton Mayo, have attempted to treat the endemic Marxian structural and systemic problems of work, seen to be caused by Tayloristic systems of organisation that were repetitive, dehumanising and alienating for workers (see O'Connor, 1999):

> *[Researchers] had empirically discovered that one may organize, and apparently scientifically, a carefully contrived enquiry into a human industrial problem and yet fail completely to elucidate the problem in any particular. (Mayo, 1946:53)*

As a result much has been written on *human* needs and desires within the workplace over reifying the processes of *production* (Bohart and Greening, 2001; Gillespie, 1991:267).

Despite such widespread interest however, the term 'well-being' is neither uniformly defined, nor a topic seemingly easily amenable to empirical, evidence-based scientific analysis. Nevertheless, especially in recent years, it has progressively become an increasingly pervasive and popular concern for many organisations, governments and academics alike, many of whom believe that discovering, measuring and harnessing the effects and essence of human *wellness*, what makes people happy, healthy and productive, may be as important as the more historically traditional psychological focus on assessing and curing mental *illness*: reducing sickness, absence and eliminating individual suffering. One new, prominent and influential school of thought, positive psychology, spearheaded by Martin Seligman, 1998 President of the American Psychological Association (APA), has assumed as its very *raison d'être* the modern cause of promoting the study of well-being through rigorous quantitative research; and can arguably be considered as vanguard and representative of such positive, well-being-oriented organisational and academic movements.

Numerous, varying definitions of well-being are hence available: Warr (2007) explains that it is essential to think of concepts like happiness and well-being as *multidimensional* constructs. They embody various facets and spectrums which can range from feelings of anxiety to comfort, satisfied to unsatisfied, bad to good, or depression to enthusiasm. Further, Waddell and Burton (2006:4) contend it is 'the subjective state of being healthy, happy, contended, comfortable, and satisfied with one's quality of life', whilst Huppert, Baylis and Keverne (2005) describe it as a positive and sustainable condition that can enable individuals, organisations and even nations to thrive, arguing that it is more than just pleasant and pleasurable emotions. More recently, Drach-Zahavy (2008:199) declared 'well-being refers to people's multidimensional evaluations of their lives, including cognitive judgments of life satisfaction as well as affective evaluations of moods and emotions'.

As these definitions highlight, there is no clear consensus, but rather a predominant 'multi-dimensional' complexity and popularity surrounding the subject. Bohart and Greening (2001) thus reason: were theorists such as Maslow and Rogers just simply ahead of their time? This chapter is, in part, a response to such a question, in light of the recent, burgeoning prominence of interest evident in a variety of disciplines, such as occupational health and organisational psychology. It considers the progression of interest in well-being through some of its past, present and (possible) future trajectories and manifestations, attempting to highlight the complexities, both inherent to the individual *and* the wider, societal environment, that are sometimes overlooked. As a result, this chapter draws upon literature from a variety of scholarly approaches and practical organisational examples, demonstrating the increasing permeation of well-being throughout many elements and arenas of contemporary life.

Yesterday: The Foundations of the Present

A HISTORY OF NEGATIVE EMPHASIS AND PREVENTATIVE INTERVENTIONS

Since its modern formal inception, psychology has commonly been regarded as a science and profession predominantly concerned with healing. Resulting from significant enhances in funding from multi-national socialistic governments post the Second World War, a majority of practitioners have commonly focused their efforts and resources on curing or fixing damaged mental health and human functioning. Research into the understanding of psychological disorders and the negative effects of environmental stressors (Huppert et al., 2005; Seligman and Csikszentmihalyi, 2000) was widely deemed to be able to ease societal ills. The general empirical focus of the discipline is hence described as having become generally negatively-orientated:

> *After 50 years and 30 billion dollars of research, psychologists and psychiatrists can boast that we are now able to make troubled people less miserable, and that is surely a significant scientific achievement.* (Seligman, Parks and Steen, 2004:1379)

To date there have been rapid developments within this field, with a great emphasis on exploring the psychological and behavioural effects of work-related illness and stress. This has provided organisations with a greater awareness of the negative consequences and subsequent impacts that such pathological conditions can have on both employee and business functioning. These are well documented in a number of international reviews as being linked to financial and human costs at individual (e.g. anxiety, burnout and depression) and organisational (e.g. accidents and workplace violence) levels. For instance, the harmful personal and organisational impacts of employees' lack of influence in decision making, little control over the physical work environment, work overload, poor social support, role ambiguity and unclear management are discussed by Michie and Williams (2003), Dollard et al. (2007) and Richardson and Rothstein (2008). Similarly, empirical findings have highlighted that having constant supervision or being closely monitored by managers can likewise exacerbate individuals' stress levels (Faragher, Cooper and Cartwright 2004).

Figures show that in the United States alone around 54 percent of reported sickness absence results from work-related stress and associated health problems (Kompier and Cooper, 1999). Stambor (2006) highlighted how the American Institute of Stress calculated that organisations lose circa $300 billion a year due to workplace stress, staff turnover, absenteeism and healthcare costs. Similarly, in the UK, the Health and Safety Executive (HSE) report that on average 30.2 working days are lost in each case of stress-related health issues. They calculated that from 2006 to 2007 a total of 13.8 million working days were lost due to work-related stress, anxiety and depression (HSE, 2007). In accordance with such an environment and Seligman et al.'s comments above, Smail infers that:

> *The notion that there is something 'wrong' with the person in distress which has to be put 'right' is absolutely central to the medical and psychological disciplines which have grown up over the past 150 years.*
> *(Smail, 1993:19)*

In the post-war era, many employers have hence, understandably, embraced the axiomatic belief that reducing work-related stress and targeting its sources within the workplace will ultimately improve their bottom-line financial performance alongside employee well-being. This has led to a huge organisational demand for the designing and implementing of preventative interventions such as stress risk assessments and management programmes (Biron, Cooper and Bond, 2008; Wright, Cropanzano and Bonett, 2007; Grawitch, Gottschalk and Munz, 2006; Adkins, 1999).

OCCUPATIONAL HEALTH SERVICES

As consequence, there has been a rapid expansion of in-house occupational health services and centres: 'Over the past 25 years wellness programs have been adopted by organizations in an attempt to develop high functioning employees ... it has been estimated that 90% of companies provide at least one subset of a wellness program for their employees' (Parks and Steelman, 2008:58). For further corroboration see also Murphy and Sauter (2003), Caulfield and Chang et al. (2004) and Quick and Quick et al. (1997). Such services are commonly designed to optimise not just individual health and well-being through applying behavioural science principles but also that of the organisation (Adkins, 1999). Nigram, Murphy and Swanson (2003) examined the quality of work life amongst organisations that offer stress management programmes compared to those which do not, and concluded that where such initiatives *are* provided, there did appear to be a good indication of that company being considered a better place to work because they were more employee-centred. The modern world of work has then been influenced through the input of health psychologists in terms of generating theory and research but importantly also through practice (Quick and Tetrick, 2003).

Significantly though, in accordance with the cultural-historical predilection towards negativity as highlighted by both Seligman et al. and Smail above, many of these principles and initiatives applied within workplaces are based upon research into ill-health and disease. Blustein (2008) highlighted that one reason for this is that many corporate occupational health services traditionally operate within health and safety mindsets, which are largely driven by governmental legislation based on illness prevention. Consequently, they generate interventions through targeting and addressing health-related problems acquired at the workplace (Drach-Zahavy, 2008; Quick and Quick, 2004; Quick 1999).

A common related pressure upon in-house occupational health services is the need often to justify their continued existence. It is fairly typical for large organisations to invest in such support services in the belief that they will have a positive impact upon the organisation. Traditional justification of their required economic expenditure has relied on reported rates of sickness absence, as it is considered relatively straightforward to calculate and compare the economic impact of an individual employee not being present (Miller, Whynes and Reid, 2000). However, occupational health services can do much more than implement programmes designed to reduce sickness absence and work-related stress, such as promoting the health and well-being of employees and boosting organisational morale (Grawitch, Trares and Kohler, 2007). Whilst it may be relatively easy to calculate the input costs for such services, the output costs are not as tangible. This is particularly relevant in terms of calculating the expense of psychological outcomes such as the subjective appreciation of well-being, which are often not directly, externally observable and, as stated above, are multi-faceted and multi-dimensional.

Today: The Present State of Affairs

As a remedy to the identified and lamented historical 'imbalance' towards psychological illness, Seligman used his APA presidency to launch a 'new science of human strengths' (Seligman, 1999:126:7), wherein increased *happiness and well-being* would be the deliberately desired and sought after outcomes (Seligman, 2003:127), rather than continuing the presiding emphasis on negativity. This 'new science', as indicated in the introduction, has come to be known as 'positive psychology' and is referred to as 'an umbrella term for the study of positive emotions, characteristics, processes and institutions that assist both individuals and organisations to thrive' (Seligman and Csikszentmihalyi, 2000:410). It is not merely an approach for studying topics like strengths and happiness, but is a systematised emphasis on identifying, examining and promoting optimal human functioning and flourishing. Seligman claims the idea struck whilst gardening with his five-year-old granddaughter, who told him that, as she had decided to stop being so whiny, he should, accordingly, try to 'stop being such a grouch' (Seligman, 2005:3–4). A *positive psychology* had thus been born, specifically designed to focus upon:

> ideally ... document[ing] what kind of families result in the healthiest children, what work environments support the greatest satisfaction among workers, and what policies result in the strongest civic commitment. (Seligman, 1999:126–7)

Seligman then dedicated his efforts towards articulating the foundations upon which a 'scientifically viable positive psychology might rest' (2003:127). He was not long alone in his cause, for Fredrickson and Branigan similarly argue that positive emotions have been too neglected and received little empirical attention (2005), and Csikszentmihalyi (publishing with Seligman [2000]) contributed to outlining a workable framework for a 'science' of positive psychology. Further, Arnold and Turner et al. (2007:194) stated that 'recent contributors to the field of occupational health (e.g. Hofmann and Tetrick, 2003; Snyder and Lopez, 2002) have argued that well-being goes beyond the absence of ill health to include the presence of positive states'. Roberts (2006) pointed out how there has been a rapid increase in empirical efforts to study well-being at work; in addition to the formation of the associated 'positive organizational behavior' and 'positive organizational scholarship' movements, Luthans and Youssef (2007), for instance, have highlighted how an assemblage of recent research has correlated well-being with attractive organisational outcomes: such as greater job satisfaction, positive affectivity, humour, organisational commitment, motivation, organisational justice and self determination. Equally, Grawitch, Gottschalk and Munz (2006) highlight the increasing recognition that work-life balance, health and safety, and employee growth, development and involvement are all key categories of healthy workplace practices that promote well-being; once again demonstrating its inherent complexity and it multi-dimensionality.

SHIFTS IN ASSESSING AND PROMOTING HEALTH AND WELLNESS AT WORK

The importance of work for individual psychological health has been well documented, to the point where it is now generally considered a central part in the development and sustenance of the healthy human being (Blustein, 2008; Martin, 2007). One of the most prominent indications of how important work is to mental health has been provided through research looking at individuals who have lost their jobs or are out of work; much of which highlights how many can often suffer from ensuing mental health problems such as depression and anxiety (Blustein, 2008; Lucas, Clark, Georgellis and Diener, 2004; Marrone and Golowka, 1999). As a result, work is deemed important as it fulfils certain positive qualities for individuals, such as: providing social interaction, a means of economic support and stability, status and self-development, accomplishment and also enhancing well-being (Blustein, 2006).

In recent years organisations have started to refocus their efforts from viewing ill-health as a business cost to viewing good health as a business benefit. It has become notable that organisations increasingly believe that discovering the essence and effects of well-being within the workplace and positive working climates may be as important to employee health as focusing on problems such as illnesses and work-related stress (Quick and Quick, 2004). Similarly, as Wilson and DeJoy et al. (2004) highlighted, attention has also begun to shift from preventative actions concentrated at an *individual* level where employees are empowered to promote their own health, to the *organizational*, with focus on diagnosing and repairing potential issues that affect the health of the organization (Drach-Zahavy, 2008). Blustein thus states:

> *rapid growth in the study of occupational health psychology has generated a keen interest in the way in which work functions in the broader spectrum of health and wellness. Furthermore the recent advances in positive psychology have identified the critical role that satisfying work plays in psychological well-being across various domains of human functioning. (2008:231)*

Evidence of this can be seen in a growing number of organisations who are starting to provide and implement forms of organizational *wellness* programmes (OWP), to target and help promote the health and well-being of their employees. Wolfe, Parker and Napier (1994) described OWP as services provided that attempt to rectify ill-health issues or promote good health practices within the workplace in an attempt to control absence rates and healthcare costs. One practical, contemporary example of this can be seen in the UK organisation The Royal Mail, who have recently announced an initiative to recruit in-house 'health trainers'. The role of these individuals will be to encourage and promote well-being within the workplace and provide access to relevant information and help (Brockett, 2008). Furthermore, an article published in *The Wall Street Journal* by Covel (2008) highlighted how a rising number of smaller companies within the United States are implementing incentive-based wellness programmes. One such company was Wesley Willows Corporation, a retirement community who sought external help to implement an incentive-based weight-loss programme. Employees who volunteered to take part in the programme were given financial incentives to lose weight. They also organised additional team weight-loss and wellness competitions (e.g. walking 10,000 steps a day) through awarding points and monthly prize for the teams that lost the most weight. They emphasised that all involvement was voluntary and encouraged employees to have fun. They were cautious not to encourage any unnecessary weight loss, although they did state how some employees took the competition a little too seriously.

However, whilst it is widely assumed that employees who participate in such health promotion programmes become more psychologically and physically fit as a result, certain researchers suggest that there is still relatively little empirical evidence to support this belief (Aldana, Merrill, Price, Hardy and Hager, 2005). This, though, is beginning to change; for example, Wilson et al. (2004) present research into how organisational climate, job design and job future are important predictors of employee health. Furthermore, Parks and Steelman (2008) recently performed a meta-analysis of organisational wellness programmes, the results of which indicated that participation in an organisational wellness programs *was* associated with higher reported job satisfaction and lower absenteeism. They concluded that their results did offer some empirical support for the effectiveness and continuation of such programmes within organisations.

Tomorrow: Speculation on the Impacts of Such a Turn of Events

At first glance such well-being and positive-oriented endeavours, very much indicative of the discipline and concerns of positive psychology, appear to echo themes previously expressed by various humanistic psychologists. Both focus on identifying, measuring and influencing positive and healthy traits, rather than the negative or pathological, embracing the assumption that they are inherent to the human agent. Bell and Taylor therefore suggest that the humanists of Maslow's era were 'primarily important' as 'cultural visionaries or prophetic voices' for the subsequent 'human potential movement' (2004:440); and Martin states:

> *[Positive psychology's] manifesto could have been written by humanistic psychologists such as ... Abraham Maslow, but positive psychologists aspire to be far more experimentally oriented than them. (2007:89)*

However, Seligman et al. have recently gone to significant efforts to distance themselves from humanistic psychology, contending that their discipline is one based on *quantitative* evidence and science, not 'a narcissistic and anti-scientific lack of research' (Seligman, cited in Taylor, 2001:13). Seligman hence argues that humanistic psychologists were generally associated with *qualitative* research methods and thus lacked a sufficient cumulative empirical base. Alternatively, as argued above, positive psychology is an endeavour to take the methods and practices of treating mental illness and adapt them to create a new positive approach, which is, above all, scientifically robust. It is believed this generates an evidence-based practice for *operationalising* and applying positivity, leading to the widespread securing of 'wellbeing, positive individuals, flourishing communities and a just society' (Seligman, 1999:126) which can be expanded out as a replicable programme of 'best practice'.

RETAINING THE RESTRICTIVE 'MEDICAL' MODEL

In furtherance to that stated in the first section, Huppert and Whittington (2003) explain that within Western cultures particularly it is usually accepted when categorising people's health status that the focus will be on disease, disability, illness and negative mental states. Importantly, this is reinforced culturally by primary conceptions of epidemiology neglecting positive functioning, as they continue to use a negative discourse by addressing rates of mortality and morbidity. As a result they state the 'relative neglect of positive well-being is probably related to the prevailing medical model which tends to dichotomise health and disease, regarding health as simply the absence of disease or disorder' (2003:108) – something which Seligman and his discipline has attempted to redress. However, such a perspective is indicative of considering positive and negative well-being as opposing, polar, incommensurable ends of the same continuum. This prevailing climate, and disenchantment with various remedying stress-focused initiatives, has resulted in a social condition from which the seductive ideas of Seligman et al., promoting that which is *positive* and empowering and *adding* to life (rather than merely the neutralising of negative states) and based on an actionable, scientific foundation, could emerge and be taken very seriously.

Joseph and Linley propose, though, that by focusing primarily on opposing *positive* forces, 'positive psychology as a movement largely continues to operate within the medical model and thus implicitly condones the [dichotomising] "medicalization" of human experience' (2006:333). Evidence of this can be seen in the very discourse used by the protagonists of the movement. For instance, Seligman et al. (2005) suggested that positive interventions could one day supplement traditional negative ones, implying positivity and negativity do indeed run along a single spectrum of human functioning. Further, Held highlights the residual bias inherent to one of Seligman's books, *Authentic Happiness*, in which he 'reinforces his negative views about negativity ... for example, he says, "Pessimism is maladaptive in most endeavours ... Thus, pessimists are losers on many fronts"' (Seligman, quoted in Held, 2004:20). This culminates, she argues, in a prevailing 'tyranny of the positive attitude' (Held, 2004:11). Joseph and Linley (2006) hence express that positive psychologists need to make their agenda clear and outright oppose and move away from the 'medical model', otherwise their agenda runs the danger of being assimilated by it. Equally, Seligman's criticism of the stress-focused literature becomes somewhat difficult to sustain when it appears he is acting to maintain the bi-polar division he apparently established positive psychology in order to re-balance.

Positive psychology, despite its intentions, has hence not yet solved the problems it intended to, sufficiently providing widespread, scientifically robust systems with which companies can enhance well-being; and could even be postulated as having contributed to their continuance. Despite tireless attempts to distance themselves 'not only from humanistic psychology but from the rest of psychology (and social science) as well' (Held, 2004:36), it could be asked then: 'are positive psychologists [actually] that different from [other] *negative psychologists*?'; as the attempts of those who focus on conditions such as illness and stress are doing so in the 'positive hope of living better too' (Held, 2004:39). If this is sustainable, Seligman et al. may then be rushing to exclude on *a priori* grounds both the humanistic tradition their own theories represent (Taylor, 2001:13) and the rest of a field from which they are not actually overly differentiated, suggesting, despite efforts to disguise the fact, humanistic psychologists were indeed somewhat 'ahead of their time', being conceptual predecessors of the current cultural concerns with *being well*.

The path to assessing effectively well-being within individuals and organisations is thus still rather unclear. Whilst there is considerable academic, corporate and personal interest in such an endeavour, there remains ambiguity surrounding its very definition; Seligman even states, 'I use "happiness" and "well-being" interchangeably' (2003:127). At present, many organisational measures of health and well-being are either too limited (e.g. only focusing on job satisfaction), too negative (e.g. only focusing on ill-health such as distress, strain, or sickness), fixed on the presence or absence of psychological symptoms (e.g. anxiety, depression and low self-esteem) or often too narrow (e.g. not considering cross-cultural elements) (Luthans, Avolio, Avey and Norman, 2007; Warr, 2007; 2006; Ryan et al., 2000), and remain entrenched along a problematic conceptual bi-polar scale. As a result, despite the developments of OWPs, organisations still have few clear exemplars and guidelines to follow demonstrating what constitutes established 'good practice' and manners in which to demonstrate the validity of occupational health services in implementing such programmes.

THE COMPLEXITY OF EXTERNAL PRESSURES AND INFLUENCES

As indicated throughout this chapter, well-being is a multi-dimensional concept, which can be, and is, conceived of and understood in a variety of manners. Dame Carol Black, author of the *Working for a Healthier Tomorrow* report presented to the UK government in March 2008, states: 'A myriad of factors influence health and well-being, though many are familiar only to those who experience them'

(2008:4). However, such a quagmire is itself further complicated by the array of *external* pressures that come to bear upon the concept and human interpretation and actioning of it, but are often overlooked or ignored. This final discussion shall now attend to some of the potential issues, both present and future, regarding attempts to foster organisational well-being that stem from entwined, constitutive environmental factors such as ethics, legislation, economics and politics.

The *People Management* publication reported in April 2008, that the British government is intending to 'help get employees "Fit for Work"' by providing individual case workers, early interventions and 'a reformed sick note' system. Referencing the work of Carol Black, it discloses that one of the primary motivations behind the deliberate and pro-active governmental action is the estimated £100 billion loss per annum suffered by the economy due to employee ill-health issues and stress-related absence; a figure equivalent to the annual running of the whole National Health Service (Brockett, 2008:15). Demonstrating an example of the emerging shift from a negative orientation to a positive one, 'sick notes' are to be replaced by 'fit notes', reflecting which duties an employee is still capable of performing despite any condition they may be suffering. This example not only demonstrates the unavoidably *political* aspect of well-being, but denotes the maintenance of the medical dichotomisation of health discussed earlier. Similarly, for possible sceptics it poses questions such as: are these efforts just simply a rebranding or relabeling of a negative orientation, designed to give the *impression* they are more positive? As Luthans and Avolio (in press:2) stated, there are times when the focus does appear to be different, however, after reflection and taking careful consideration have we just 'again been fooled by that "old wine in new bottles" illusion'? Well-being, impacts a variety of stakeholders, including politicians, healthcare professionals, employers, employees and trade unions (Brockett, 2008:15), representing the necessity for the creation and sustainment of an active collaboration between all such diverse groups in order to redress the production and financial losses, and improve employee wellness. Both the Chartered Institute of Personnel Development and the British Medical Association (BMA) have released statements in favour of this shift. However, clearly caution must be retained, as indicated by a spokesperson for the BMA, that doctors do not become 'a policing arm of the Department for Work and Pensions' (Brockett, 2008:15).

Covel likewise considers the embracement of this trend in a variety of North American work organisations, where 'incentive-based wellness programmes' have been initiated, designed to encourage employees to become fitter by providing lower health-care costs (2008; c.f. also Shelly, 2008). Under their medico-political system of privatised medicine, where reportedly 40 million citizens cannot even afford insurance premiums and are thus entirely without healthcare unless provided gratis by their employer, this acts to complicate the ethicality of the organisational well-being issue. Without moralising either way, questions can be raised as to whether the burden of providing healthcare for these individuals should indeed be tackled at a governmental, organisational or an individual level. Further, if an employee is dependent on their work for health insurance, is their ability to protect their interests or resist unreasonable employer requests effectively diminished or undermined? This gives rise to another ethical consideration regarding motivation, as many of these initiatives seem to be driven by desires to cut costs and medical absenteeism and increase work activity, rather than by a genuine humanitarian concern first and foremost to improve the lives of human beings. The significance of this point depends on one's own opinion, and political position, but the issue should at the very least be sufficiently addressed in the well-being literature.

Barrett proffers another similar example, in an article entitled 'Drop That Weight Or Your Fired!' (2008), reporting on efforts to combine reducing healthcare costs and boost productivity. Perhaps worryingly, she suggests that 'now companies are wondering just how far they can go', and intimates that enabling organisations to appropriate jurisdiction over employee well-being is a 'slippery slope' (2008:18). Should companies be able to demand or enforce participation? Should they be able to punish those who don't achieve the standards and results organisationally required of them? Ultimately Barrett suggests there are 'big legal and ethical issues with pushing employees to change their behaviour ... And big costs if they don't' (2008:18; c.f. Mello and Rosenthal, 2008).

Consideration of well-being in contemporary and future times therefore raises two important questions that must be clearly articulated for the future: how far do we want these developments to impinge on our personal lives?; and who should have jurisdiction over their future developments? With a variety of groups being unavoidably involved in the determination of an answer to either question, including occupational therapists, organisational sociologists, politicians, HR departments, company shareholders, managing directors, employees, doctors and economists – to name but a few – care must be taken. As of yet there is still very little research demonstrating the financial return on investment for wellness programmes and many of those which are in operation still consider it in simplistic terms of a continuum, and do not provide sufficient reference to or awareness of the external factors and multiplicity of the many groups with a vested interest. Carol Black thus suggests:

My recommendations point to an expanded role for occupational health and its place within a broader collaborative and multi-disciplinary service. Ultimately I believe such a service should be available to all, whether they are entering work, seeking to stay in work, or trying to return to work without delay in the wake of illness or injury. (Black, 2008:foreword)

It is hence a contention of the authors of this chapter that occupational and health psychologists should play a prominent role as harbingers of new theories and practices in organisational and personal well-being. This chapter has highlighted some of the complexities and difficulties psychologists have and still face surrounding well-being in terms of research and its application and practice within applied settings, but they arguably reside upon a valid and influential theoretical platform from which to enact *positive* change.

However, now even 'health economists' are becoming more interested in this field, and over the coming years psychologists will likely work more closely with them on establishing a benefit-cost ratio and demonstrating the return on investment associated with such programmes. Psychology as a discipline can be seen to be becoming more multidisciplinary, as issues such as well-being cross many boundaries. So the disciplines of health psychology, along with occupational, cognitive, clinical and counselling psychology to name but a few, are all searching for answers. All have their own methods and perspectives on how to view well-being. Furthermore, other non-psychological schools of thought are also offering increasing insight and knowledge. As stated though, we believe that psychology needs to take more ownership of this field and integrate other useful contributions from disciplines outside the psychological literature to offer a more holistic approach. There also needs to be increased communication between government and large, medium and small firms to facilitate a more widespread programme rather than discrete occurrences in the provision and promotion of an environment and climate in which individuals can achieve and enhance a sense of *wellness*, provided it does not become part of an enforced dictatorial regime.

References

Adkins, J.A. (1999). Promoting organizational health: the evolving practice of occupational health psychology. *Professional Psychology Research and Practice*, 30, pp.129–37.

Aldana, S.G., Merrill, R.M., Price, K., Hardy, A. and Hager, R. (2005). Financial impact of a comprehensive multisite workplace health promotion program. *Preventive Medicine*, 4, pp.31–137.

Arnold, K.A., Turner, N., Barling, J., Kelloway, E.K. and McKee, M.C. (2007). Transformational leadership and psychological wellbeing: the mediating role of meaningful work. *Journal of Occupational Health Psychology*, 12, pp.193–203.

Barrett, J. (2008). Drop that weight or your fired! *Newsweek*, 151(15), p.18.

Bell, E. and Taylor, S. (2004). From outward bound to inward bound: the prophetic voices and discursive practices of spiritual management development. *Human Relations*, 57(4), pp.439–66.

Biron, C., Cooper, C.L. and Bond, F.W. (2008). Mediators and moderators of organizational interventions to prevent occupational stress. In S. Cartwright and C.L. Cooper (eds), *Oxford Handbook of Organizational Well-being* (pp. 441–65). Oxford: Oxford University Press.

Black, C. (2008). Working for a healthier tomorrow [online]. Available at: http://www.workingforhealth.gov.uk/Carol-Blacks-Review/> [Accessed 21st June 2008].

Blustein, D.L. (2006). *The Psychology of Working: A New Perspective for Career Development, Counseling, and Public Policy*. Mahwah, NJ: Erlbaum.

Blustein, D.L. (2008). The role of work in psychological health and well-being: a conceptual, historical, and public policy perspective. *American Psychologist*, 63(4), pp.228–40.

Bohart, A.C. and Greening, T. (2001). Humanistic psychology and positive psychology. *American Psychologist*, 56, pp.81–2.

Brockett, J. (2008). Government to help get employees 'fit for work'. *People Management*, 14(7), p.15.

Caulfield, N., Chang, D., Dollard, M.F. and Elshaung, C. (2004). A review of occupational stress interventions in Australia. *International Journal of Stress Management*, 11, pp.149–66.

Covel, S. (2008). Small business link: companies win as workers lose pounds; incentive-based wellness programs give employers rewards – with a payoff of lower health-care costs. *The Wall Street Journal (Eastern Edition)*, 252(8), p.B6.

Dollard, M.F., LaMontagne, A.D., Caulfeild, N., Blewett, V. and Shaw, A. (2007). Job stress in the Australian and international health and community services sector: a review of the literature. *International Journal of Stress Management*, 14, pp.417–45.

Drach-Zahavy, A. (2008). Workplace health friendliness: a cross-level model for predicting workers' health. *Journal of Occupational Health Psychology*, 13(3), pp.197–213.

Faragher, E.B., Cooper, C.L. and Cartwright, S. (2004). A shortened stress evaluation tool (ASSET). *Stress and Health*, 20, pp.189–201.

Fredrickson, B.L. and Branigan, C. (2005). Positive emotions broaden the scope of attention and thought-action repertories. *Cognition and Emotion*, 19(3), pp. 313–32.

Gable, S. and Haidt, J. (2005). What (and why) is positive psychology? *Review of General Psychology*, 9(2), pp.103–10.

Gillespie, R. (1991). *Manufacturing Knowledge: A History of the Hawthorne Experiments*. Cambridge and New York, NY: Cambridge University Press.

Grawitch, M.J., Gottschalk, M. and Munz, D.C. (2006). The path to a healthy workplace: a critical review linking healthy workplace practices, employee well-being, and organisational improvements. *Consulting Psychology Journal; Practice and Research*, 58, pp.129–47.

Grawitch, M.J., Trares, S. and Kohler, J.M. (2007). Healthy workplace practices and employee outcomes. *International Journal of Stress Management*, 14, pp.275–93.

Health and Safety Executive (2007) [online]. Why tackle work-related stress. Available at: <http://www.hse.gov.uk> [Accessed 5th July 2008].

Held, B.S. (2004). The negative side of positive psychology. *Journal of Applied Humanistics*, 44, pp.9–46.

Hofmann, D.A. and Tetrick, L.E. (eds) (2003). *Health and Safety in Organizations*. San Francisco, CA: Jossey-Bass.

Huppert, F.A., Baylis, N. and Keverne, E.B. (eds) (2005). *The Science of Well-being*. Oxford: Oxford University Press.

Huppert, F.A. and Whittington, J.E. (2003). Evidence for the independence of positive and negative well-being: implications for quality of life assessment. *British Journal of Health Psychology*, 8, pp.107–22.

Joseph, S. and Linley, P.A. (2006). Positive psychology versus the medical model? *American Psychologist*, 60, pp.332–3.

Kompier, M. and Cooper, C.L. (1999). *Preventing Stress, Improving Productivity*. London: Routledge.

Lucas, R.E., Clark, A.E., Georgellis, Y. and Diener, E. (2004). Unemployment alters the set-point for life satisfaction. *Psychological Science*, 15, pp.8–13.

Luthans, F. and Avolio, B.J. (in press). The point of positive organizational behaviour. *Journal of Organisational Behavior*, pp.1–34.

Luthans, F., Avolio, B.J., Avey, J.B. and Norman, S.M. (2007). Positive psychological capital: Measurement and relationship with performance and satisfaction. *Personnel Psychology*, 60, pp.541–72.

Luthans, F. and Youssef, CM. (2007). Emerging positive organizational behavior. *Journal of Management*, 33(3), 321–49.

Marrone, J. and Golowka, E. (1999). If work makes people with mental illness sick, what do unemployment, poverty, and social isolation cause? *Psychiatric Rehabilitation Journal*, 23, pp.187–93.

Martin, M.W. (2007). Happiness and virtue in positive psychology. *Journal for the Theory of Social Behaviour*, 37(1), pp.89–103.

Maslow, A.H. (1998). *Maslow on Management*, New York: Wiley.

Mayo, E. (1946) (2nd edition). *The Human Problems of an Industrial Civilization*. Cambridge, MA: Murray.

Mello, M.M. and Rosenthal, M.B. (2008). Wellness programs and lifestyle discrimination: the legal limits. *New England Journal of Medicine*, 359(2), pp.192–9.

Michie, S. and Williams, S. (2003). Reducing work related psychological ill health and sickness absence: a systematic literature review. *Occupational and Environmental Medicine*, 60, pp.3–9.

Miller, P., Whynes, D. and Reid, A. (2000). An economic evaluation of occupational health. *Journal of Occupational Medicine*, 50, pp.159–63.

Murphy, L.R. and Sauter, S.L. (2003). The USA perspective: current issues and trends in the management of work stress. *Australian Psychologist*, 38, pp.151–7.

Nigam, J.A.S., Murphy, L.R. and Swanson, N.G. (2003). Are stress management programs indicators of good places to work? Results of a national survey. *International Journal of Stress Management*, 10, pp.345–60.

O'Connor, E. (1999). Minding the workers: the meaning of 'human' and 'human relations' in Elton Mayo. *Organization*, 6, pp.223–46.

Parks, K.M. and Steelman, A.A. (2008). Organizational wellness programs: a meta-analysis. *Journal of Occupational Health Psychology*, 13(1), pp.58–68.

Quick, J.C. (1999). Occupational health psychology: historical roots and future directions. *Health Psychology*, 18, pp.82–8.

Quick, J.C. and Quick, J.D. (2004). Healthy, happy, productive worker: a leadership challenge. *Organizational Dynamics*, 33, pp.329–37.

Quick, J.C., Quick, J.D., Nelson, D.L. and Hurrell, J.J., Jr. (1997). *Preventive Stress Management in Organizations*. Washington DC: American Psychological Association.

Quick, J.C. and Tetrick, L.E. (eds) (2003). *Handbook of Occupational Health Psychology*. Washington, DC: American Psychological Association.

Richardson, K.M. and Rothstein, H.R. (2008). Effects of occupational stress management intervention programs: a meta-analysis. *Journal of Occupational Health Psychology*, 13, pp.69–93.

Roberts, L.M. (2006). Shifting the lens on organizational life: the added value of positive scholarship. *Academy of Management Review*, 31, pp.292–305.

Ryan, A.M., Horvath, M., Ployhart, R.E., Schmitt, N. and Slade, L.A. (2000). Hypothesizing differential functioning in global employee opinion surveys. *Personnel Psychology*, 53, pp.531–62.

Seligman, M.E.P. (1999). The president's address (Annual Report). *American Psychologist*, 54, pp.126–7.

Seligman, M.E.P. (2003). Positive psychology: fundamental assumptions. *The Psychologist*, 16, pp.126–7.

Seligman, M.E.P. (2005). Positive psychology, positive prevention, and positive therapy. In C.R. Snyder and S.J. Lopez (eds) (2005), *Handbook of Positive Psychology* (pp.3–9). Oxford; Oxford University Press.

Seligman, M.E.P. and Csikszentmihalyi, M. (2000). Positive psychology: an introduction. *American Psychologist*, 55, pp.5–14.

Seligman, M.E.P., Parks, A.C. and Steen, T. (2004). A balanced psychology and a full life. *The Royal Society*, 359, pp.1379–81.

Seligman, M.E.P., Steen, T.A., Park, N. and Peterson, C. (2005). Positive psychology progress: empirical validation of interventions. *American Psychologist*, 60(5), pp.410–21.

Shelly, M. (2008). Beyond the copayment: using wellness programs and technology to address rising health care costs. *Managed Care Outlook*, 21(14), pp.1–6.

Smail, D. (1993). *The Origins of Unhappiness: A New Understanding of Personal Distress*. Glasgow: HarperCollins.

Snyder, C.R. and Lopez, S.J. (2002). *Handbook of Positive Psychology*. London: Oxford University Press.

Stambor, Z. (2006). Employees: a company's best asset. *Monitor on Psychology*, 37, pp.28–30.

Taylor, E. (2001). Positive psychology and humanistic psychology: a reply to Seligman. *Journal of Humanistic Psychology*, 41, pp.13–29.

Waddell, G. and Burton, A.K. (2006). *Is Work Good for Your Health and Well-Being?* London: The Stationery Office.

Warr, P. (2007). *Work, Happiness and Unhappiness*. London: Psychology Press.

Wilson, M.G., DeJoy, D.M., Vandenberg, R.J., Richardson, H.A. and McGrath, A.L. (2004). Work characteristics and employee health and well-being: test of a model of healthy work organization. *Journal of Occupational and Organizational Behavior*, 77, pp.565–88.

Wolfe, R., Parker, D. and Napier, N. (1994). Employee health management and organizational performance. *Journal of Applied Behavioral Science*, 30, pp.22–42.

Wright, T.A., Cropanzano, R. and Bonett, D.G. (2007). The moderating role of employee positive well being on the relationship between job satisfaction and job performance. *Journal of Occupational Health Psychology*, 12, pp.93–104.

3

The Changing World of Work and Occupational Health

Maria Armaou and Alexander-Stamatios Antoniou

The world of work has changed dramatically during the last decades as technological advancements, organisational restructuring and new forms of employment have become common place for most organisations. According to Kompier (2006) the major changes that organisations have faced involve globalisation, increased utilisation of information technology, changes in the workforce, flexibility and new organisational practices, together with their effect on job characteristics and employees' health and well-being.

In fact, the European Agency for Safety and Health in Work (2007), based on the results of an expert forecast on emerging psychosocial risks related to occupational safety and health (OSH), categorised them as either new or increasing. New risks were identified as either 1) previously unknown and caused by new processes, new technologies, new types of workplace, or social or organisational change, 2) long-standing issues newly considered as risks due to changes in social or public perceptions or 3) new scientific knowledge allowing a long-standing issue to be identified as a risk. Subsequently, risks are characterised as being on the increase if 1) the number of hazards leading to them is growing, 2) the likelihood of exposure to the hazard leading to them is increasing (exposure level and/or the number of people exposed) or 3) the effect of the hazard on workers' health is getting worse (seriousness of health effects and/or the number of people affected).

The expert survey actually revealed that emerging psychosocial OSH risks for employees were often related to technical and organisational as well as to some socioeconomic, demographic and political changes, including the phenomenon of globalisation. In particular, the top 10 emerging risks were categorised into five main topics: new forms of employment and job insecurity; OSH risks for the ageing workforce; work intensification; high emotional demands at work; and poor work–life balance.

New Technology, Computerisation and Work Intensification

The introduction of new technology in the working environment has largely meant the computerisation of today's workplace. Indeed, it has been estimated that at least 76 million people in the United States used a computer in their workplace in 2003, accounting for at least 56 percent of all employed adults aged 18 years and older (US Census Bureau, 2005). This has changed the way in which work is organised, adding to today's work intensification, which is associated with deterioration in working conditions, whether they are assessed in terms of physical or psychological discomforts, nuisance or occupational risks (Ashkenazy, 2004; European Foundation for the Improvement of Living and Working Conditions, 2006). Specifically, it is those changes in the working conditions, where there is an exposure to risk factors, that are believed to influence all types of health and safety issues (Berthet and Gauthier, 2000). For example, the European working conditions survey, 2000 (European Foundation for the Improvement of Living and Working Conditions, 2005) showed that the higher the pace constraints are, the more probable is workers' perception that their health is threatened (Burchell, 2004).

Moreover, it has been reported that work intensification often causes employees to neutralise the safety systems of machinery and equipment in order to work faster and maintain production rates, which may lead to injuries. The results of different studies indicate that work intensification can have a direct influence on the occurrence of epidemics of musculoskeletal disorders (MSDs) and stress-related diseases (Chouanière, 2006; European Foundation for the Improvement of Living and working Conditions, 2002; Kompier and Levy, 1994), though it is also indicated that the harmful character of work intensity depends on the interrelationship between aspects of the work (e.g. work rhythm pressure or tight deadlines) and aspects of the situation (personal, work or job-related).

Griffiths et al. (2007) investigated the impact of the computerised work environment on professional occupational groups and subsequent risk factors for musculoskeletal symptoms by reviewing papers published between 1980 and 2007. Overall, the computerised work environment involves a number of biomechanical and psychological work demands that depict certain psychosocial stressors, causing behavioural and physiological responses that lead to an increased risk of upper body musculoskeletal symptoms. As far as biomechanical work demands are concerned, job computerisation may include the introduction of more repetitive upper limb work, with longer periods of sedentary postures, resulting in reduced task diversity and variability of muscle activity (Waersted and Westgaard, 1997). With regards to psychosocial work demands, these may include increased information processing requirements and greater demands on attention and memory (Carayon and Smith, 2000; Smith, 1997), high precision and concentration (Birch et al., 2000), and multi-tasking demands.

Regarding the psychosocial stressors of computerised work, these involve increased workload demands, reduced discretionary control over task scheduling, increased workpace, deadline and electronic performance monitoring pressures, the need for sustained concentration with diminished social interaction, a sense of being rushed and a tendency for increased supervisory control with reduced autonomy (Griffiths et al., 2007). There is growing evidence that such psychosocial factors associated with computer work may also increase the risk of upper body musculoskeletal symptoms and disorders, particularly neck/shoulder pain (Griffiths et al., 2007).

In addition, some researchers assert that psychosocial risk factors are at least as important as the biomechanical risk factors in the aetiology of work-related musculoskeletal symptoms and disorders (Lundberg, 2002; Winkel and Westgaard, 1992) and may increase the effect of the biomechanical loading (Hanse, 2002; Melin and Lundberg, 1997). Behavioural responses related to the above work demands and psychosocial work stressors involve working long hours, fast-paced work, applying excessive forces to the keyboard or mouse and inadequate work breaks; while the physiological ones involve increased stress response and heightened muscle tension (Griffiths et al., 2007).

New Organisational Practices, New Forms of Employment Contracts and Job Insecurity

There are several taxonomies of new organisational practices, such as lean manufacturing, total quality management, call centres, telehomeworking etc., all of which have flexibility in common (Kompier, 2006). Flexibility has several types, including structural (flatter hierarchies), functional (e.g. lean manufacturing), numerical (e.g. part-time, temporary work), geographic (e.g. telework) and job-based flexibility (e.g. re-designing jobs for better control) (Sparrow and Marchington, 1998); it can also be distinguished as quantitative (e.g. overtime work, temporary work, part-time contracts etc.) and qualitative (job rotation, job enrichment etc.) flexibility (Kompier, 2006). These new organisational practices can have a positive effect on employees' health if organisational redesign efforts intend to create jobs of high intrinsic quality so that employees can experience less strain (Brockner et al., 2004; Karasek and Theorell, 1990).

Otherwise, such changes can be detrimental to employees' health and well-being. Osthus (2007) addressed these issues by examining the outcome of downsizing and internal reorganisation on the quality of jobs and work-related health problems for workers in Norway. He noticed that all of these changes generally led to poor quality jobs and higher work-related effort, while increasing demands were not followed by increasing rewards (e.g. more control over work processes). In general, both type of changes had a negative effect on employees' health but the effect was stronger in the case of internal reorganisation.

An example of geographic flexibility is telework and just like all recent changes in the workplace it can have either a positive or a negative effect on employees' health. Specifically, telehomeworking is considered to help workers cope with the mutual incompatibility of paid work and home obligations (Baruch and Nicholson, 1997) as well as enabling them to work at convenient times and plan their work activities more efficiently (France et al., 2002; Tremblay, 2002; Vittersø et al., 2003). However, Peters and van der Lippe, (2007), on examining time-based and strain-based work–home interference in a sample of Dutch employees, noticed that heavy telehomeworking practices were accompanied by higher levels of strain spilling into the home domain, and by longer working hours. Similarly, a case study by Kellihera and Anderson (2008) showed that such flexible working arrangements, even when they are chosen by the workers themselves, may aggravate and generate stress and have a negative impact on opportunities for learning and development.

The most typical example of organisational flexibility is the numerical flexibility that involves different types of non-standard forms of work such as temporary, part-time, on-call, day-hire or short-term work or self-employment (Cooper, 2002). These types of employment contracts are often described as precarious work as there is growing evidence that there are specific risks for health and safety in the workplace connected with the conditions that characterise these forms of work (Rodgers and Rodgers, 1989). For example, temporary workers are more often exposed to adverse conditions in their physical work environment, such as noise, painful and tiring positions, and repetitive movements. They also have less control over working times, often work in less skilled jobs and have less insight into their work environment, mainly resulting from a lack of training (Benach et al., 2002a; Benach et al., 2000; European Foundation for the Improvement of Living and Working Conditions, 2001a).

In addition, temporary workers have fewer opportunities for training and lifelong learning (European Foundation for the Improvement of Living and Working Conditions, 2001a). Indeed, a study by the Organisation for Economic Cooperation and Development (OECD) (2002) found that in 12 investigated European countries, temporary workers were far less likely to receive formal training. Apart from training, it is also indicated that personal protective equipment is made available less often to temporary workers than to permanent workers (McLaren et al., 2004). Thus, fewer workers are reached by OSH measures and adequately trained in the field of OSH. For example, an Italian survey carried out on a sample of 800 workers in different economic sectors showed that atypical workers tended to underestimate work-related risks. In fact, as regards psychosocial risks, 57.8 percent of atypical workers versus 41.4 percent of standard workers had a tendency to consider that they were very rarely, or never exposed to these risks (Battaglini, 2007).

Finally, due to the wide range of flexible employment contracts, it is important to examine the differences among them with regards to workers occupational health. Aronsson et al. (2002), when examining the Swedish workforce, noticed significant differences among different types of employment contracts. Specifically, they found that work conditions for project employees and people in probationary employment were most similar to those of permanent employees. Substitutes occupied an intermediate position, whereas seasonal workers and persons working on-call operated under conditions most dissimilar to permanent employees. Regarding health, only workers on-call and substitutes showed strikingly more health complaints than those in other forms of employment.

Nevertheless, the effects of different forms of precarious employment vary, and are not always negative. Self-employed workers, for example, enjoy greater control over working time and have a higher level of autonomy. However, at the same time they have very little social support. Part-time employees also show lower levels of health-related absenteeism and report less stress, particularly when they choose voluntarily to work part-time (Benach et al., 2002b; McLaren et al., 2004). A few studies report no difference at all in implications for the health of precariously employed workers in comparison to permanent workers (Bardasi and Francesconi, 2003). For example, two surveys of the European Foundation for the Improvement of Living and Working Conditions in 2001 showed no evidence that temporary or part-time employment had negative long-term effects on mental health among British men and women during the 1990s (2001a; 2001b).

Worse health outcomes were only found for certain kinds of jobs such as in lean production or self-employment when compared with other forms of employment (European Foundation for the Improvement of Living and Working Conditions 2001a; 2001b). Furthermore, in a UK study on call centres (Sprigg et al., 2003), employees with non-permanent contracts reported better well-being than permanent employees. Fixed-term or temporary workers were less anxious, less depressed and more satisfied with their job. Such differences have not been identified for part-time workers. Finally, a study among workers with different work contracts in Brazil showed no statistically significant health outcomes at all (Santana and Lomis, 2004).

It is no surprise that the recent trends for organisational restructuring and downsizing have been followed by an increase in perceived job insecurity. For example, Worall and Cooper (1998) found that over 60 percent of a national sample of 5,000 British managers had undergone such major organisational changes and the main consequences were that nearly two thirds experienced increased job insecurity, reduced morale and erosion in motivation and loyalty. Attention has been given to the issue of the health consequences of job insecurity as there is evidence that perceived job insecurity is significantly related to medically certificated, long-term (i.e. greater than three days) sickness absence (Vahtera, Kivimaki and Pentti, 1997). Researchers have often focused on its effects on mental health rather than physical health, and studies usually indicate a relationship between job insecurity and poorer mental health. In these types of studies, mental health is usually measured using the general health questionnaire (GHQ). This is a scale developed for the purpose of detecting non psychotic mental health symptoms (such as sleeping problems, anxiety and depression) in the population. In a few studies, other indicators of mental well-being have been used, for example burnout, job-induced tension and depression.

A meta-analysis by Sverke et al. (2002) showed that the higher the job insecurity, the poorer the mental health. This relationship was confirmed by longitudinal studies which unequivocally showed that job insecurity should be treated as the cause of worsening mental health and that a reverse relationship is statistically irrelevant (Ferrie et al., 2003). Perhaps not surprisingly, the aspect of job insecurity that is most connected with decreasing mental health is the fear of job loss (Hellgren et al., 1999). Furthermore, the impact of job insecurity on mental health is more frequently reported in men (De Witte, 1999; Ferrie et al., 1998; Kinnunen et al., 2000).

As far as the relationship between job insecurity and physical health is concerned, there is less evidence of that than of the relationship between job insecurity and mental health. Nevertheless, Sverke's (2002) meta-analysis also showed that the higher the job insecurity, the poorer the physical health. Indeed, high job insecurity is connected with worse self-reported health, more frequent somatic ailments (e.g. headaches and spinal aches) and the appearance of long-lasting illnesses. Some studies found that the above relationships were identified only for men, others identified them for women also. In Switzerland, a survey carried out in 2002 revealed that 37 percent of workers who feared losing their job suffered serious functional disorders such as headaches, back pains and sleeping disorders, compared with 17 percent of those who did not fear losing their job (Steinman, 2006). Some studies have used physiological health indicators and show that job insecurity might be connected with heightened systolic and diastolic blood pressure, with ischaemia and with higher BMI (Ferrie et al., 1998; Kinnunen et al., 2000).

Flexibility and Work Patterns

Technology development and rapid organisational change has also greatly altered employees' work patterns, which has been found to affect their mental and physical health. Among the most common changes in work patterns to have been investigated are overtime work, extended working hours, irregular or unpredictable working hours and long working hours. There are many studies which show that working long hours increases the risk for hypertension and cardiovascular disease (Hayashi et al., 1996; Liu et al., 2002; Nakanishi et al., 2001; Yang et al., 2006); while others have detected relationships between long hours at work and musculoskeletal injuries (Lipscomb et al., 2002; Trinkoff et al., 2006), diabetes (Kawakami et al., 1999) and chronic infections (Mohren et al., 2001). Evidence also suggests that overtime and extended work schedules can lead to depression and other psychological conditions (Glass and Fujimoto, 1994; Shields, 1999).

Overtime work refers to those hours worked beyond the contractual working hours (Riedmann et al., 2006). According to the report *Time and Work: Duration of Work* (Boisard et al., 2003), a rather large proportion of employees (around 17 percent of full-time employees and 14.2 percent of all employees) work long hours. For this reason, the concepts of long working hours and overtime work are often used interchangeably within the literature. Bourdeaud'hui and Vanderhaeghe (2006) studied to what extent overtime had an influence on work stress, well-being and work–life balance in the Flemish workforce. They concluded that overtime work increases the number of workers with work-related stress and problems in their work–life balance. This was true for all groups studied, independent of gender, age, family situation, sector, job, company dimensions and management or non-management function.

Moreover, the level of work stress was at its lowest when the worker did not work overtime and at its highest when the worker had to work overtime and was not compensated for it. Also, Dembe et al. (2005) found that work schedules involving overtime hours had the highest risk of injury (61 percent) among non-standard schedules. However, it is important to differentiate between long working hours and overtime work with regards to part-time and full-time employees, as for the latter overtime work is related to their work motivation (Beckers et al., 2007).

Long work hours, on the other hand, can be defined as hours that exceed the standard full-time work-week that implies by definition a certain number of overtime hours. Most studies agree that working long hours is an important occupational stressor that increases the risk of mental health problems. For example, a NIOSH report provided an integrative review of 52 research reports recently published in the United States that examined the associations between long working hours and health outcomes. There was a pattern of poorer performance on psychophysiological tests, especially when the employees worked long shifts and when shifts of more than 12 hours were combined with more-than-40-hour work-weeks. Some of these studies mentioned that the ninth to twelfth hours of work were associated with feelings of decreased alertness and increased fatigue, lower cognitive function, reduced vigilance on task measures or increased injuries (Caruso et al., 2004).

The report *Time and Work: Duration of Work* (Boisard et al., 2003) showed that employees clearly perceive increased working time as being linked to health and safety risks. In particular, employees tended to blame their work as being a risk to their health and as the reason for their health problems if they were forced to work long hours. This link was also noted with regards to specific health problems such as headaches, fatigue, anxiety and insomnia. In the same way, employees who had atypical working time schedules also blamed this for a number of health problems. Night work, working days of more than 10 hours and the changing of schedules within a month were seen as particularly detrimental to their health. Almost 70 percent of the employees who worked at least one night per month were of the opinion that their work affected their health. The effects most frequently reported were insomnia, stress, fatigue and irritability.

In addition, working long hours can also affect employees' domestic relationships, as employees working long hours report high levels of stress and work–family conflict. For example, Grosch et al. (2006) found that employees working more than 48 hours per week were significantly more likely to have disruptions in family life compared to those working 35–40 hours per week. Similarly, Spurgeon (2003), on examining British male, white-collar workers, found that 50 percent of them reported that their family life suffered due to their long working hours, while 20 percent thought that their partner had been negatively affected.

However, the relationship between long working hours and stress or psychological health seems to be mediated by individual factors such as the amount of control the workers feel that they have, and the way in which they regard their job (White and Beswick, 2003). Bourdeaud'hui and Vanderhaeghe (2006) found that overtime work can increase work stress when it concurs with the risk factors of high workload and low autonomy. In particular, they indicated that workers with low autonomy, high workload and overtime work without compensation report the highest prevalence of work-related stress.

However, Spurgeon et al. (1997) noticed that there is a particular shortage of studies that focus solely on the relationship between long working hours and health problems related to stress, such as gastrointestinal disorders, musculoskeletal disorders and depression of the immune system. Another problem arises from the lack of well-controlled and comparative studies. Consequently, there is no clear evidence-based recommendation for the design of flexible working hours (Janssen and Nachreiner, 2004). However, it appears that it is important for workers' well-being that they are involved in the decisions about how their work time is organised.

Extended working hours refers to work when the hours of the standard shift are extended. This implies a high number of hours worked either during a day or a shift, or a high number of days worked per week. Extended working hours generally refer to a working week of more than 48 hours or to 10- to 12-hour shifts instead of 8-hour shifts (Harrington, 2001). According to the Fourth European Working Conditions survey, 14 percent of all European employees work longer than 48 hours per week, while Americans work longer hours and more weeks per year than workers in other industrialised nations (Caruso et al., 2004). Research in nursing work shows that extended working hours are associated with increased MSD (Engels et al., 1996; Lipscomb et al., 2002). For example, Engkvist et al. (2000) found that Swedish nurses working full-time were at increased risk of back injury. Recently, Trinkoff et al. (2006) using a longitudinal, three wave survey of 2,617 registered nurses in the United States found that the work schedule independently increased nurses' risk of developing an MSD.

There is also some evidence that irregular working hours may have an effect on work-related accidents. This is thought to originate from the increased fatigue resulting from long working hours, influencing workers' behaviour and attention during work. Specifically, unconventional shift work, including night shifts, evening shifts and rotating shifts can disrupt circadian rhythms and sleep patterns, resulting in stress, fatigue and impaired performance among affected workers (Akerstedt et al., 2002; Costa, 2003; Harrington, 2001; Hughes and Stone, 2004; Knutsson, 2003). As a matter of fact, industrial accidents and injuries are more likely to occur on night and evening shifts than on day shifts (Brogmus and Maynard, 2006; Dembe et al., 2006; Folkard et al., 2005; Spurgeon, 2003). Furthermore, it has been shown that unconventional shift work can increase the risk of suffering sleep disturbances (Akerstedt, 2003; DeMoss et al., 2004; Lee, 1992), digestive problems (Caruso et al., 2004), particular types of cancer (Davis et al., 2001; Hansen, 2001; Schernhammer et al., 2003) and reproductive problems (Axelsson and Rylander, 1989).

In addition, Hanecke et al. (1998) studied more than a million German injury reports and found that there is a higher risk of injuries after the eighth and ninth hour at work for all shifts. Researchers have also documented increased risks of accidents and injuries among unconventional shift workers in a variety of industries including health care, public safety, manufacturing, construction and transportation (Horwitz and McCall, 2004). Likewise, recent evidence suggests that construction workers are particularly susceptible to job injuries on the evening shift, compared to day or night shifts (Dembe et al., 2008).

Finally, it has been suggested that non-standard work schedules weaken injured workers' rehabilitation (Anema et al., 2004; Kearney, 2001; Krause et al., 1997). For example, Dembe et al. (2007) investigated the relative effects of different types of work schedules on the likelihood of injured workers resuming their work successfully following an injury. Overall, they found that job re-entry following an occupational injury was more difficult for workers returning to non-standard schedules, especially schedules involving overtime and long working hours. They also identified differences among different types of non-standard schedules. For example, among workers on extended work-hour schedules the greatest likelihood of them quitting their job after an injury or working less than full time following an injury were seen in those with jobs involving long hours per day and long hours per week. Employees working overtime schedules experienced the greatest risks of being temporarily assigned to another job, being unable to perform normal duties and facing any kind of job disruption following injury. Employees with long commuting schedules by far had the greatest danger of being fired or changing occupations following an injury, compared to injured workers in other kinds of extended hour schedules.

References

Akerstedt, T.E. (2003). Shift work and disturbed sleep/wakefulness. *Occupational Medicine*, 53, 89–94.

Akerstedt, T., Knutsson, A., Westerholm, P., Theorell, T., Alfredsson, I. and Kecklund, G. (2002). Sleep disturbances, work stress and work hours: a cross-sectional study. *Journal of Psychosomatic Research*, 53, 741–8.

Anema, J.R., Cuelenaere, B., van der Beek, A.J., Knol, D.L., de Vet, H.C. and van Mechelen, W. (2004). The effectiveness of ergonomic interventions on return-to-work after low back pain; a prospective two year cohort study in six countries on low back pain patients sicklisted for 3–4-months. *Occupational and Environmental Medicine*, 61, 289–94.

Aronsson, G., Gustafsson, K. and Dallner, M. (2002). Work environment and health in different types of temporary jobs. *European Journal of Work and Organizational Psychology*, 11(2), 151–75.

Ashkenazy, P. (2004). *Les désordres du travail, enquête sur le nouveau productivisme.* Paris: Seuil.

Axelsson, G. and Rylander, R. (1989). Outcome of pregnancy in relation to irregular and inconvenient work schedules. *British Journal of Industrial Medicine*, 46, 306–12.

Bardasi, E. and Francesconi, M. (2003). The impact of atypical employment on individual well-being: evidence from a panel of British workers. *Working Papers of the Institute for Social and Economic Research*, Paper 2003-2, University of Essex, Colchester.

Baruch, Y. and Nicholson, N. (1997). Home, sweet work: requirements for effective home working. *Journal of General Management*, 23, 15–30.

Battaglini, E. (2007). *Percezione dei rischi nell'Impresa post-fordista.* Rome: IRES Istituto di Ricerche Economiche e Sociali.

Beckers, D.G.J., van der Linden, D., Smulders, P.G.W., Kompier, M.A.J., Taris, T.W. and van Yperen, N.W. (2007). Distinguishing between overtime work and long workhours among full time and part-time workers. *Scandinavian Journal of Work, Environment and Health*, 33(1), 37–44.

Benach, J., Amable, M., Muntaner, C. and Benavides, F.G. (2002a). Working conditions. The consequences of flexible work for health: are we looking at the right place? *Journal of Epidemiology and Community Health*, 56, 405–6.

Benach, J., Benavides, F.G., Platt, S., Diez-Roux, A. and Muntaner, C. (2000). The health damaging potential of new types of flexible employment: a challenge for public health researchers. *American Journal of Public Health*, 90(8), 1316–17.

Benach, J., Gimeno, D. and Benavides, F.G./European Foundation for the Improvement of Living and Working Conditions (2002b). *Types of Employment and Health in the European Union.* Luxembourg: Office for Official Publications of the European Communities. Available at: http://eurofound.europa.eu/publications/htmlfiles/ef0221.htm [Accessed: 12 October 2009].

Berthet, M. and Gauthier, A.-M. (2000). *L'exposition aux risques professionnels. Intégrer organisation du travail et prévention.* Lyon: ANACT.

Birch, L., Juul-Kristensen, B., Jensen, C., Finsen, L. and Christensen, H. (2000). Acute response to precision, time pressure and mental demand during simulated computer work. *Scandinavian Journal of Work, Environment and Health*, 26(4), 299–305.

Boisard, P., Cartron, D.C., Gollac, M. and Valeyre, A./European Foundation for the Improvement of Living and Working Conditions (2003). *Time and Work: Duration of Work.* Luxembourg: Office for Official Publications of the European Communities. Available at: http://www.eurofound.eu.int/publications/htmlfiles/ef0211.htm [Accessed: 12 October 2009].

Bourdeaud'hui, R. and Vanderhaeghe, S. (2006). *Werkbaar werk en overwerk: Technische nota*. Brussels: Sociaal Economische Raad Vlaanderen, STV Innovatie and Arbeid.

Brockner, J., Spreitzer, G., Mishra, A., Hochwarter, W., Pepper, L. and Weinberg, J. (2004). Perceived control as an antidote to the negative effects of layoffs on survivors' organizational commitment and job performance. *Administrative Science Quarterly*, 49(1), 76–100.

Brogmus, G. and Maynard, W. (2006). Safer shift work through more effective scheduling. *Occupational Health and Safety*, 75(12), 16.

Burchell, B. (2004). Gender and the intensification of work: evidence from the European working conditions surveys. *Eastern Economic Journal*, 30(4), 627–42.

Carayon, P. and Smith, M.J. (2000). Work organization and ergonomics. *Applied Ergonomics*, 31(6), 649–62.

Caruso, C., Hitchcock, E., Dick, R., Russo, J.M. and Schmit, J.M. (2004). Overtime and extended work shifts: recent findings on illnesses, injuries, and health behaviors (US Centers for Disease Control, National Institute for Occupational Safety and Health, Cincinnati), *Publication*, 2004–143. Available at: http://www.cdc.gov/niosh/docs/2004-143/pdfs/2004-143.pdf [Accessed: 12 October 2009].

Chouanière, D. (2006). Stress et risques psychosociaux: concepts et prevention. *Documents pour le Médecin du Travail*, 106, 169–86.

Cooper, C.L. (2002). The changing psychological contract at work. *Occupational and Environmental Medicine*, 59(6), 355.

Costa, G. (2003). Shift work and occupational medicine: an overview. *Occupational Medicine*, 53, 83–8.

Davis, S., Mirick, D.K. and Stevens, R.G. (2001). Night shift work, light at night, and risk of breast cancer. *Journal of the National Cancer Institute*, 93, 1557–62.

Dembe A.E., Delbos, R.G., Erickson, J.B. and Banks, S.M. (2007). Associations between employees' work schedules and the vocational consequences of workplace injuries. *Journal of Occupational Rehabilitation*, 17, 641–51.

Dembe, A.E., Erickson, J.B. and Delbos, R.G. (2008). *Industry and Occupation Variations in the Injury Risks Related to Shift Work and Extended Work Hours*. Working Paper, Ohio State University Center for Health Outcomes, Policy and Evaluation Studies.

Dembe, A.E., Erickson, J.B., Delbos, R.G. and Banks, S.M. (2005). The impact of overtime and long hours on occupational injuries and illnesses: new evidence from the United States. *Occupational and Environmental Medicine*, 62, 588–97.

Dembe, A.E., Erickson, J.B., Delbos, R.G and Banks, S.M. (2006). Nonstandard shift work and the risk of job-related injuries: a national study from the United States. *Scandinavian Journal of Work, Environment and Health*, 32(3), 232–40.

DeMoss, C., McGrail, M., Haus, E., Crain, A.L. and Asche, S.E. (2004). Health and performance factors in health care shift workers. *Journal of Occupational and Environmental Medicine*, 46, 1278–81.

De Witte, H. (1999). Job insecurity and psychological well-being: review of the literature and exploration of some unresolved issues. *European Journal of Work and Organizational Psychology*, 8, 155–77.

Engels, J., van der Gulden, J., Senden, T., van't Hof, B. (1996). Work related risk factors for musculoskeletal complaints in the nursing profession: results of a questionnaire survey. *Occupational Environmental Medicine*, 53, 636–41.

Engkvist, I.L., Hjelm, E.W., Hagberg, M., Menckel, E. and Ekenvall, L. (2000). Risk indicators for reported over-exertion back injuries among female nursing personnel. *Epidemiology*, 11(5), 519–22.

European Agency for Safety and Health in Work (2007). Expert forecast on emerging psychosocial risks related to occupational safety and health. Available at: http://osha.europa.eu/en/publications/reports/7807118 [Accessed: 12 October 2009].

European Foundation for the Improvement of Living and Working Conditions (2001a). *The Impact of New Forms of Work Organisation on Working Conditions and Health*, Background paper to the European Union Presidency Conference 'For a Better Quality of Work'. Luxembourg: Office for Official Publications of the European Communities. Available at: http://www.eurofound.eu.int/publications/htmlfiles/ef0164.htm [Accessed: 12 October 2009].

European Foundation for the Improvement of Living and Working Conditions (2001b). *Working Conditions in Atypical Work: Resumée*. Luxembourg: Office for Official Publications of the European Communities. Available at: http://eurofound.europa.eu/publications/htmlfiles/ef0159.htm [Accessed: 12 October 2009].

European Foundation for the Improvement of Living and Working Conditions (2002). *Quality of Work and Employment in Europe: Issues and Challenges*. Luxembourg: Office for Official Publications of the European Communities. Available at: http://www.eurofound.eu.int/pubdocs/2002/12/en/1/ef0212en.pdf [Accessed: 12 October 2009].

European Foundation for the Improvement of Living and Working Conditions (2005). *Third European Survey on Working conditions 2000*. Available at: http://www.eurofound.europa.eu/pubdocs/2001/21/en/1/ef0121en.pdf (Accessed: 12 October 2009).

European Foundation for the Improvement of Living and Working Conditions (2006). *A Review of Working Conditions in France*. Luxembourg: Office for Official Publications of the European Communities. Available at: http://eurofound.europa.eu/ewco/surveys/FR0603SR01/FR0603SR01.pdf [Accessed: 12 October 2009].

Ferrie, J.E., Shipley, M.J., Marmot, M.G., Stansfeld, S. and Smith, G.D. (1998). The health effects of major organizational change and job insecurity. *Social Science and Medicine*, 46, 243–54.

Ferrie, J.E., Shipley, M.J., Stansfeld, S., Smith, G.D. and Marmot, M.G. (2003). Future uncertainty and socioeconomic inequalities in health: the Whitehall II study. *Social Science and Medicine*, 57, 637–46.

Folkard, S., Lombardi, D.A. and Tucker, P.T. (2005). Shiftwork: safety, sleepiness and sleep. *Industrial Health*, 43(1), 20–23.

France, E., Akselsen, S., Jones, M. and Tracy, K. (2002). Telework and quality of life: some social impacts and practical implications. *Journal of the British Telecommunications Engineers*, 3(1), 57–66.

Glass, J. and Fujimoto, T. (1994). Housework, paid work, and depression among husbands and wives. *Journal of Health Society and Behavior*, 135, 179–91.

Griffiths, K.L., Mackey, M.G. and Adamson, B.J. (2007). The impact of computerized work environment on professional occupational groups and behavioural and physiological risk factors for musculoskeletal symptoms: a literature review. *Journal of Occupational Rehabilitation*, 17, 743–65.

Grosch, J.W., Caruso, C.C., Rosa, R.R. and Sauter, S.L. (2006). Long hours of work in the US: associations with demographic and organizational characteristics, psychosocial working conditions, and health. *American Journal of Industrial Medicine*, 49, 943–52.

Hanecke, K., Tiedemann, S., Nachreiner, F. and Grzech-Šukalo, H. (1998). Accident risk as a function of hour at work and time of day as determined from accident data and exposure models for the German working population. *Scandinavian Journal of Work, Environment and Health*, 24(3), 43–8.

Hanse, J.J. (2002). The impact of VDU use and psychosocial factors at work on musculoskeletal shoulder symptoms among white-collar workers. *Work Stress*, 16(2), 121–6.

Hansen, J. (2001). Increased breast cancer risk among women who work predominantly at night. *Epidemiology*, 12(1), 74–7.

Harrington, J.M. (2001). Health effects of shift work and extended hours of work. *Occupational and Environmental Medicine*, 58, 68–72.

Hayashi, T., Kobayashi, Y., Yamaoka, K. and Yano, E. (1996). Effect of overtime work on 24-hour ambulatory blood pressure. *Journal of Occupational Medicine*, 38, 1007–11.

Hellgren, J., Sverke, M. and Isaksson, K. (1999). A two-dimensional approach to job insecurity: consequences for employee attitudes and well-being. *European Journal of Work and Organizational Psychology*, 8, 179–95.

Horwitz, I.B. and McCall, B. (2004). The impact of shift work on the risk and severity of injuries for hospital employees: an analysis using Oregon workers' compensation data. *Occupational Medicine*, 54, 556–63.

Hughes, R. and Stone, P. (2004). The perils of shift work. *American Journal of Nursing*, 104, 60–63.

Janssen, D. and Nachreiner, F. (2004). Health and psychosocial effects of flexible working hours. *Revista de Saúde Pública*, 38(Suppl.), 11–18. Available at: http://www.scielo.br/scielo.php [Accessed: 12 October 2009].

Karasek, R. and Theorell, T. (1990). *Healthy Work: Stress, Productivity, and the Reconstruction of Working Life*. New York: Basic Books.

Kawakami, N., Araki, S., Takatsuka, N., Shimizu, H. and Ishibashi, H. (1999). Overtime, psychosocial working conditions, and occurrence of non-insulin dependent diabetes mellitus in Japanese men. *Journal of Epidemiology and Community Health*, 53, 359–63.

Kearney, J. (2001). A closer look at work resumption. In Bloch, F.S. and Prins, R. (eds), *Who Returns to Work and Why: A Six-Country Report of Work Incapacity and Reintegration* (pp. 193–215). Somerset, NJ: Transaction Publishers.

Kellihera, C. and Anderson, D. (2008). For better or for worse? An analysis of how flexible working practices influence employees' perceptions of job quality. *The International Journal of Human Resource Management*, 19(3), 419–31.

Kinnunen, U., Natti, J. and Happonen, M. (2000). Organizational antecedents and outcomes of job insecurity: a longitudinal study in three organizations in Finland. *Journal of Organizational Behavior*, 21, 443–59.

Knutsson, A. (2003). Health disorders of shift workers. *Occupational Medicine*, 53, 103–8.

Kompier, M.A.J. (2006). New systems of work organization and workers' health. *Scandinavian Journal of Work, Environment and Health*, 32(6), 421–30.

Kompier M. and Levy, L./European Foundation for the Improvement of Living and Working Conditions (1994). *Stress at Work: Causes, Effects and Prevention: A Guide for Small and Medium Sized Enterprises*. Luxembourg: Office for Official Publications of the European Communities.

Krause, N., Lynch, J.W., Kaplan, G.A., Cohen, R.D., Goldberg, D.E. and Salonen, J.T. (1997). Predictors of disability retirement. *Scandinavian Journal of Work Environment and Health*, 23(6), 403–13.

Lee, K.A. (1992). Self reported sleep disturbances in employed women. *Sleep*, 15, 493–8.

Lipscomb, J., Trinkoff, A.M., Geiger-Brown, J. and Brady, B. (2002). Work-schedule characteristics and reported musculoskeletal disorders of registered nurses. *Scandinavian Journal of Work, Environment and Health*, 28(6), 394–401.

Liu, Y., Tanaka, H. and The Fukuoka Heart Study Group (2002). Overtime work, insufficient sleep, and risk of non-fatal acute myocardial infarction in Japanese men. *Occupational and Environmental Medicine*, 59, 447–51.

Lundberg, U. (2002). Psychophysiology of work: stress, gender, endocrine response, and work-related upper extremity disorders. *American Journal of Industrial Medicine*, 41, 383–92.

McLaren, E., Firkin, P., Spoonley, P., Dupuis, A., de Bruin, A. and Inkson, K. (2004). *At the Margins: Contingency, Precariousness and Non-Standard Work*. Research Report Series, 2004/1, Labour Markets Dynamics Research Programme, Massey University, Auckland. Available at: http://lmd.massey.ac.nz/publications/At%20the%20Margins.pdf [Accessed: 12 October 2009].

Melin, B. and Lundberg, U. (1997). A biopsychosocial approach to work-stress and musculoskeletal disorders. *Journal of Psychophysiology*, 11, 238–47.

Mohren, D.C., Swaen, G.M., Kant, I.J., Borm, P.J. and Galama, J.M. (2001). Associations between infections and fatigue in a Dutch working population: results of the Maastricht cohort study on fatigue at work. *European Journal of Epidemiology*, 17(12), 1081–7.

Nakanishi, N., Yoshida, H., Nagano, K., Kawashimo, H., Nakamura, K. and Tatara, K. (2001). Long working hours and risk for hypertension in Japanese male white-collar workers. *Journal of Epidemiology and Community Health*, 55, 316–22.

Organisation for Economic Cooperation and Development (2002). Taking the measure of temporary employment. *OECD Employment Outlook*. Paris: OECD. Available at: http://www.oecd.org/dataoecd/36/8/17652675.pdf [Accessed: 12 October 2009].

Osthus, S. (2007). For better or worse? Workplace changes and the health and well-being of Norwegian workers. *Work, Employment and Society*, 21(4), 731–50.

Peters, P. and van der Lippe, T. (2007). Home-based telework: a gendered strategy to cope with demanding work and family responsibilities. *International Journal of HRM*, 18, 430–47.

Riedmann, A., Bielenski, H., Szczurowska, T. and Wagner, A./European Foundation for the Improvement of Living and Working Conditions (2006). *Working Time and Work–Life Balance in European Companies: Establishment Survey on Working Time 2004–05*. Luxembourg: Office for Official Publications of the European Communities. Available at: http://www.eurofound.eu.int/publications/htmlfiles/ef0627.htm [Accessed: 12 October 2009].

Rodgers, G. and Rodgers, J. (1989). *Precarious Jobs in Labour Market Regulation: The Growth of Atypical Employment in Western Europe*. Brussels: International Institute for Labour Studies, Free University of Brussels.

Santana, V.S. and Lomis, D. (2004). Informal jobs and non-fatal occupational injuries. *Annals of Occupational Hygiene*, 48(2), 147–57.

Schernhammer, E.S., Laden, F., Speizer, F.E., Willett, W.C., Hunter, D.L., Kawachi, I., Fuchs, C.S. and Colditz, G.A. (2003). Night-shift work and risk of colorectal cancer in the nurses' health study. *Journal of the National Cancer Institute*, 95, 825–8.

Shields, M. (1999). Long working hours and health. *Health Reports*, 11, 33–48.

Smith, M. (1997). Psychosocial aspects of working with video display terminals (VDTs) and employee physical and mental health. *Ergonomics*, 40(10), 1002–15.

Sparrow, P.R. and Marchington, M. (1998). *Human Resource Management: The New Agenda.* London: Financial Times Pitman Publications.

Sprigg, C.A., Smith, P.R and Jackson, P.R (2003). *Psychosocial Risk Factors in Call Centres: An Evaluation of Work Design and Well-Being*, Research Report 169. London: Health and Safety Executive. Available at: http://www.hse.gov.uk/research/rrpdf/rr169.pdf [Accessed: 12 October 2009].

Spurgeon, A. (2003). *Working Time: Its Impact on Safety and Health.* Geneva: International Labour Organisation. Available at: http://www.ilo.org/public/english/protection/condtrav/publ/wtwo-as-03.htm [Accessed: 12 October 2009].

Spurgeon, A., Harrington, J.M. and Cooper, C.L. (1997). Health and safety problems associated with long working hours: a review of the current position. *Occupational and Environmental Medicine*, 54, 367–75.

Steinman, R.M. (2006). Santé psychique: stress. Bases scientifiques pour une stratégie nationale en matière de prévention du stress et de promotion de la santé psychique en Suisse (condensed). Promotion Santé Suisse, Berne and Lausanne. Available at: http://www.gesundheitsfoerderung.ch/f/leistungen/psychische_gesundheit/psychische_gesundheit_stress/default.asp [Accessed: 12 October 2009].

Sverke, M., Hellgren, J. and Naswall, K. (2002). No security: a meta-analysis and review of job insecurity and its consequences. *Journal of Occupational Health Psychology*, 7, 242–64.

Tremblay, D.G. (2002). Balancing work and family with telework? Organizational issues and challenges for women and managers. *Women in Management Review*, 17, 157–70.

Trinkoff, A.M., Le, R., Geiger-Brown, J., Lipscomb, J. and Lang, G. (2006). Longitudinal relationship of work hours, mandatory overtime, and on-call to musculoskeletal problems in nurses. *American Journal of Industrial Medicine*, 49, 964–71.

US Census Bureau (2005). Computer and Internet use in the United States: 2003. Available at: http://www.census.gov/prod/2005pubs/p23-208.pdf2005 [Accessed: 12 October 2009].

Vahtera, J., Kivimaki, M. and Pentti, J. (1997). Effect of organisational downsizing on health of employees. *Lancet*, 350, 1124–8.

Vittersø, J., Akselsen, S., Evjemo, B., Julsrud, T.E., Yttri, B. and Bergvik, S. (2003). Impacts of home-based telework on quality of life for employees and their partners: quantitative and qualitative results from a European survey. *Journal of Happiness Studies*, 4, 201–33.

Waersted, M. and Westgaard, R.H. (1997). An experimental study of shoulder muscle activity and posture in a paper version versus a VDU version of a monotonous work task. *International Journal of Industrial Ergonomics*, 19, 175–85.

White, J. and Beswick, J. (2003). Working long hours. Health and Safety Laboratory, Sheffield. Available at: http://www.hse.gov.uk/research/hsl_pdf/2003/hsl03-02.pdf [Accessed: 12 October 2009].

Winkel, J. and Westgaard, R. (1992). Occupational and individual risk factors for shoulder-neck complaints: Part II – the scientific basis (literature review) for the guide. *International Journal of Industrial Ergonomics*, 10, 85–104.

Worrall, L. and Cooper, C.L. (1998). *Quality of Working Life Survey of Managers' Changing Experiences*. London: Institute of Management.

Yang, H., Schnall, P., Jauregui, L.M., Su, T.-C. and Baker, D. (2006). Work hours and self-reported hypertension among working people in California. *Hypertension*, 48, 744–50.

4

Stress Medicine: From Bench to Bedside

Dirk H. Hellhammer and Juliane Hellhammer

Stress-related disorders show a continuous increase in industrialized countries and considerably impair physical and mental health. Accidents, absenteeism, employee turnover, diminished productivity, direct medical, legal and insurance costs, workers' compensation awards, etc. all sum up to a tremendous financial burden in consequence of stress (Andlin-Sobocki et al., 2005; Lademann et al., 2006). According to the World Health Organization (WHO, 2003), stress-related conditions count for up to half of all disability. Although countless research papers have been published on stress-related disorders, most of this knowledge has not been translated to treatment strategies for such conditions. This chapter will first address some premises for efficient treatment strategies, which may help to improve medical care in these patients, and then offer such a clinical approach, which has recently been developed in Trier. The interested reader will find more and detailed information in a book we recently published on this issue (Hellhammer and Hellhammer, 2008).

Premises for Neurobehavioral Medicine

Neurobehavioral medicine faces several challenges, which are in part unique and in part generally admitted. The following five challenges have to be met, once efficient diagnostic and therapeutic strategies have been established.

MISSING CO-VARIANCE OF THE PSYCHOLOGICAL AND PHYSIOLOGICAL STRESS RESPONSE

Stress may result in both a psychological and physiological stress response. While perceived psychological stress can be assessed by interviews and questionnaires, peripheral physiological measures routinely assess autonomic parameters (e.g. blood pressure, heart rate, epinephrine, norepinephrine, etc.), and endocrine (e.g. ACTH, cortisol) or immune responses (e.g. proinflammatory cytokines, etc.). Interestingly, the psychological and the physiological stress response show either no, weak or inconsistent correlations. It seems that the brain processes a stressor on different levels, and not all of the processes are conscious, thus limiting perception of physiological responses. Although the missing covariance of the psychological and biological stress response has been known for many decades, it is often neglected in clinical research and practice. Practically, a patient can only report perceived psychological stress, but not provide reliable information about his physiological stress response. Thus, the doctor may wrongly interpret the impact of stress in a given patient, and finally assign an inappropriate treatment. Consequently, the missing covariance of the psychological and the peripheral physiological stress response is the first specific and serious challenge for neurobehavioral medicine.

COMPLEXITY AND HETEROGENEITY OF AETIOLOGICAL MECHANISMS

The aetiology and pathogenesis of stress-related disorders always reflect a complex interplay of diverse biological, social and psychological determinants. Even patients sharing similar disorders or diseases are likely to have different constellations of such determinants: 1) genetic dispositions are different among individuals, affecting the ability to adapt to stress, 2) epigenetic determinants programme gene expression, particularly in pre- and postnatal life, 3) socioeconomic conditions and our learning history impact on our ability to cope with stress. All three conditions affect the adaptability of the central nervous system, the autonomic nervous system, the endocrine system, the immune system and peripheral organ function, and finally determine the efficacy of mechanisms participating in stress vulnerability and resilience. Our knowledge on these determinants and their interplay grows from day to day. However, in addition, stress-related disorders are multi-causal, and we cannot expect to find simple mono-causal mechanisms to target efficient treatment strategies.

The tremendous complexity and heterogeneity of mechanisms in stress-related disorders creates another big challenge for neurobehavioral medicine. Theoretically, this points to highly personalized treatment strategies, but practically, it will be simply impossible for a practitioner to oversee and assess the variety of all these factors.

Even if this would all be possible, our present knowledge would not suffice to fully uncover the aetiological mechanisms in a given patient. Finally, we learn day by day about new mechanisms, which are likely to be relevant for stress-related disorders. Does this mean that we are overstrained and have to give up targeting causative treatments?

TRANSLATIONAL REQUIREMENTS

Diagnostic and therapeutic interventions should profit from available knowledge from psychobiology. This challenge is particularly true for stress medicine, since basic research in animals and people from the past decades has profoundly revolutionized our understanding of how stress affects mental and physical health. The Human Genome Project, for example, has stimulated research on how specific genes and gene activities are associated with stress-related disorders, and how pre- and postnatal adversity 'programmes' stress vulnerability in later life. Today, it seems that early adversity and the underlying epigenetic mechanisms are among the strongest determinants of mental and physical health disturbances.

The challenge is how do we deal with the massive amount of information that comes from gene sequencing, gene expression, proteomic data and metabolomics, and connect that to data from a particular patient? Patients with stress-related disorders would surely benefit from such knowledge. Thus, it may be almost mandatory to incorporate translational tools to improve clinical treatment.

THE NEED FOR QUALIFIED TREATMENT ACROSS DIFFERENT MEDICAL DISCIPLINES

Most medical specialties see patients with stress-related disorders, urologists treat interstitial cystitis, gastroenterologists treat irritable bowel syndrome, gynaecologists treat chronic pelvic pain, rheumatologists treat chronic fatigue syndrome and fibromyalgia, psychiatrists treat panic disorder, and so on. Specialists generally treat these patients in relative isolation, without considering the potentially confounding influence(s) of the frequently overlapping comorbid disorders their patients suffer. This is another important challenge for neurobehavioral medicine, since most physicians do not have a specific education and qualification to diagnose and treat the impact of stress. Thus, one has to find strategies to enable physicians across different disciplines to apply adequate diagnostic and therapeutic strategies.

THERAPEUTIC EFFICACY AND COST EFFICACY

Given the challenges for neurobehavioral medicine described above, it is not surprising that patients with stress-related disorders often need years to receive adequate psychotherapeutic treatment (Hoyer et al., 2006; Wittchen and Jacobi, 2006), while pharmacotherapeutic interventions frequently follow the trial and error paradigm (Ellis et al., 1993; Etkin et al., 2005). Even if the impact of stress becomes obvious, both pharmacotherapeutic and psychotherapeutic treatments should be coordinated and adapted to the disease model. If there is no such model, the therapeutic efficacy and the cost-effectiveness will be weak, and this will finally retard the acceptance and a fruitful development of neurobehavioral medicine. Formally, neurobehavioral based diagnostic and treatment strategies have to meet respective admission requirements, which usually include a number of evidence-based studies, demonstrating benefits for intangible, direct and indirect costs, as compared to current gold standards. Only if these criteria are fulfilled, will costs be covered by insurance companies.

In sum, there are several important premises to successfully establish neurobehavioral medicine in clinical routine. Recently, we developed a strategy, which may meet the challenges described above (Hellhammer and Hellhammer, 2008). In the following paragraph, we will briefly introduce this approach.

Diagnostic Assessment of Stress in a Clinical Setting

If physicians want to assess the role of stress in physical or mental disorders of a given patient, they face the challenges described above. To improve this situation, we have now developed a diagnostic tool which seems to enable the physician to diagnose and treat such disorders or diseases adequately. We call this tool 'Neuropattern'. The first version has been evaluated in more than 1,200 patients and probands, and a revised version is currently being evaluated in another sample of 2,000 patients. Our approach can be understood as a first systematic step towards neurobehavioral medicine. While we feel that the strategy is right, the scientific basis is still contemporary and preliminary, but can constantly be improved by an ongoing exchange of information between bench and bedside.

STRATEGY 1: FOCUSING THE CROSSTALK BETWEEN THE BRAIN AND THE BODY

Since we have to expect that each patient has a highly individual constellation of biological and psychological determinants of stress-related disorders, and that these determinants are complex and interact, resulting in secondary or tertiary effects, our first strategy was to reduce complexity and heterogeneity, and to avoid the missing covariance of the psychological and physiological stress response.

Since a reasonable diagnostic assessment of relevant central and peripheral determinants of stress-related disorders would not be manageable in a clinical setting, we decided to focus solely on the interfaces, which participate in the crosstalk between the brain and the (peripheral) body. In other words, we were interested to assess the activity of these interfaces, but not the causes behind them, which would have left us confronting a tremendous complexity and heterogeneity of central and peripheral mechanisms. Thus, we could 1) considerably reduce complexity and heterogeneity and 2) bypass the missing covariance, since monitoring the activity of the interfaces allows us to assess directly stress effects on the brain-body communication.

STRATEGY 2: ASSESSMENT OF THE ACTIVITY OF INTERFACES BY NEUROPATTERNS

The crosstalk between the brain and the body is reflected by the activity of the endocrine system, the immune system, the autonomic nervous system, and the sensory and motor systems. In our first version, we started to focus on the hypothalamus-pituitary–adrenal axis (HPAA) and the autonomic nervous system (ANS), which are primarily involved in the stress response.

The HPAA interfaces include the paraventricular nucleus (PVN), the pituitary, the adrenals, and glucocorticoid receptors, while the ANS interfaces the respective central and peripheral control systems. The challenge was now to generate measures which reflect the activity of each of these interfaces. To do so, we had first to collect the available knowledge, and then to translate this information from animal or human experiments to the clinical situation. Since we are at the threshold of a new era of neurobehavioral medicine, we need to bridge the gap between hypotheses and solid knowledge by reasonable concepts. Such concepts have not only to integrate the heuristic knowledge from very divergent research areas, but also functionally to link these data together. Obviously, these models are speculative and risky. However, the hypotheses derived from these models will be testable.

Concretely, we conceptualized stress dependent states for each interface, thus predicting how stress alters its activity and, consequently, the crosstalk between the brain and the body. Since it will be impossible to apply comprehensive and expensive measures in clinical routines, we had to develop indirect estimates for each respective activity status. Here, we introduced the idea of 'neuropattern'. First, we characterized the activity status of each of the interfaces by describing associated psychological, biological and symptomatic measures. Second, it became evident that simultaneous alterations on all three measures form a specific 'neuropattern', which may reliably reflect the specific activity of such an interface. Thus, neuropatterns are (neuro)endophenotypes, which refer to discrete (neuro)biological systems in the central nervous system, the endocrine and the autonomic nervous system. Thirdly, we then developed measures to assess these biological, psychological and symptom alterations for each of the neuropatterns.

STRATEGY 3: CLINICAL APPLICABILITY

Stress-related disorders are for most family doctors not an area of expertise. It seems to be unrealistic to assume that practitioners could even acquire the necessary expertise, since such an education would be far too comprehensive to be included into curricula from universities or by continuous education. Thus, we developed a strategy, allowing the practitioner to obtain access to and to handle expert knowledge.

In a first step, the physician, who is interested to explore a possible impact of stress in a given patient applies the Neuropattern Test Set (NTS). The NTS contains questionnaires, a small electrophysiological device and tubes for the collection of saliva (see Figure 4.1). In his office, the physician provides master file data, a brief medical history, and takes several measures, such as blood pressure, waist-to-hip-ratio, body mass index, etc. These data are recorded in the NTS.

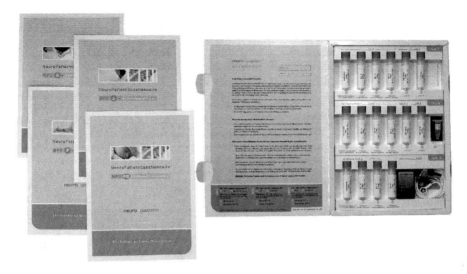

Figure 4.1   Neuropattern Test Set

Note: This includes 16 salivettes for cortisol assessment in saliva, a tablet of 0.25 mg dexamethasone, questionnaires for the patient and the physician, and a portable ECG for analyses of heart rate variability.

In a second step, the patient collects all remaining data at home and at work under naturalistic conditions. She fills out three questionnaires. One questionnaire provides information on early pre- and postnatal development, another one summarizes the pathogenesis and previous symptoms and treatments, while the third collects the specific psychological and symptom variables for the respective neuropatterns. On the evening of the first day, the patient starts physiological recordings of heart rate variability overnight and within the first hour after awakening. The next morning, she performs an orthostatic test. These physiological data provide an estimate of sympathetic and parasympathetic activity respectively. In addition, they provide some information on sleep duration and quality. For HPAA assessment, the patient additionally starts to collect a three-day period of saliva sampling. In the evening of the second day, she takes 0.25 mg dexamethasone, enabling assessment of negative feedback sensitivity of the pituitary–adrenal axis on the subsequent day. After all data have been collected, the patient sends the NTS with all questionnaires, the saliva samples and the electrophysiological device to the central laboratory.

In a third step, this laboratory analyses all the data and performs a comprehensive analysis. The product is a medical report, which includes the results of the diagnosis and suggests possible treatment options. This report is posted to the physician, furthering completion the neuropattern circle (see Figure 4.2).

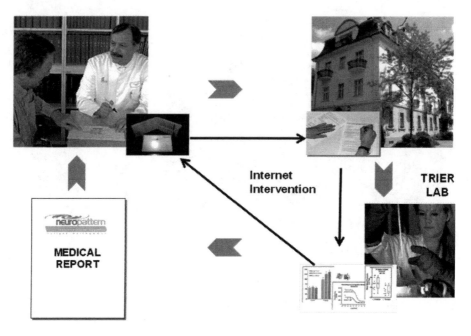

Figure 4.2   The Neuropattern circle

Note: The physician and the patient apply Neuropattern. The physician fills out the anamnestic questionnaire. At home, the patient fills out another three questionnaires, collects saliva, applies the dexamethasone suppression test and takes overnight measures with a portable ECG. Afterwards, the patient sends the Neuropattern Test Set back to the central laboratory in Trier. Here, all data are analysed and integrated into a medical report for the physician. In addition, the physician can encourage his patient to use a personalized web page with individualized self-management modules.

In a fourth step, the physician decides on the basis of this expert report, if and how he will treat the patient with respect to the patient's individual medical conditions. Since the physician can only assign pharmacological treatments, the patient receives additional access to a personal website. This website offers an individualized battery of self-management techniques, allowing the patient to participate actively in the treatment process.

Notably, we presently prepare a stress prevention study with a state institution. Here, the personnel receive free vouchers for an NTS from their employer. Together with their family doctor, they may now detect early symptoms of stress or stress pathology, and, if necessary, assign early treatment.

STRATEGY 4: INDIVIDUALIZED INTERVENTIONS

As it turned out, patients qualify for rather specific constellations of neuropatterns, allowing the physician to assign specific treatments. Burnout, for example, can presently be assessed by psychological questionnaires, but there are no comparable physiological measures. In a pilot study, we applied Neuropattern to a population of 190 teachers, who were enrolled in a study by Brigitte Kudielka in our laboratory, and 49 of them qualified for at least one neuropattern. However, while about half of these subjects presented evidence of a depletion of norepinephrine, data from the other subjects suggest CRF-hypoactivity, serotonin hyperreactivity, adrenal hypoactivity or glucocorticoid receptor resistance. Only subjects qualifying for the norepinephrine depletion pattern are likely to profit from norepinephrine reuptake inhibitors. Internet-based self management for these patients includes rest management and specific dietary recommendations, enabling them to restore depleted norepinephrine. This example illustrates that Neuropattern may enable the discrimination of subtypes, which results in specific individualized indications for pharmacological and psychotherapeutic interventions. Information about benefits for cost efficacy and therapeutic efficacy are not yet available but respective clinical studies are underway.

STRATEGY 5: EXCHANGE AND UPDATE OF DATA

The fact that all information from patients and treatment outcome will be collected and analysed in a central laboratory means a permanent exchange of data between bench and bedside. This will surely be beneficial for both basic research and clinical treatment. Continuous feedback is mandatory to test the clinical efficacy of current concepts and to improve and scientifically update translational concepts and methods. Thus, it seems to be necessary to establish strategies to collect and analyse the data and to elaborate continuous updates.

The five strategies addressed here show how challenges for neurobehavioral medicine can be met practically. Our first experiences with Neuropattern suggest that it is already possible to develop a systematic approach to translate basic research to clinical practice. We are well aware that the compass we use to navigate between bench and bedside is a prototype and not yet very sophisticated. However, a continuous exchange of data will enable the ongoing refinement and calibration of this compass, which will make it increasingly efficient. We believe that our strategies are timely and unavoidable, since the future of neurobehavioral medicine cannot abstain from incorporating and translating information from bench to bedside.

In sum, this strategy permits the transportation of expert knowledge to the practitioner across medical disciplines, and without requiring specific education or expertise in the respective physician.

Clinical Endophenotypes

As mentioned above, the diagnosis and treatment of stress-related disorders may profoundly profit from psychobiological research. First, we are not restricted to psycho-'logical' explanations. Successful treatment implies a correct model of the patients' disorder. Behaviour therapists, for example, try to link symptoms to specific mental or environmental events, to develop a hypothetical aetiological model, which provides guidance for therapeutic decisions. A psychobio-'logical' model, on the other hand, would allow the therapist to extend her model beyond psychological explanations. Second, the model would enable the incorporation of both adequate pharmacological treatment and possibly new and different psychotherapeutic techniques. George Chrousos and his group at the National Institutes of Health (NIH) in Bethesda and now in Athens started very early to develop neurobiological models of stress and to link them to diseases. In a permanent series of updates and reviews (e.g. Chrousos and Kino, 2007; Kyrou et al., 2006; Charmandari et al., 2005; Tsigos and Chrousos, 2002), they enabled researchers and clinicians to follow up with recent advances in the neurosciences. Our neuropatterns are based on such models and are associated with physical and mental health disorders, thus allowing the conceptualization of clinical endophenotypes. Such endophenotypes seem to be valuable tools for the future of neurobehavioral medicine. We will here provide some examples, which may illustrate this vision.

EXAMPLE I: PSYCHOLOGICAL ASSESSMENT ALONE MAY BE MISLEADING

Contra-intuitively, in a major subgroup of infertile men, depression is rather related to improved fertility. Active, dominant and competitive behaviour was found to be associated with low testosterone levels and low sperm count. Accordingly, activity wheel stress in animals resulted in a strong turnover of norepinephrine in many brain areas, accompanied by a vasoconstriction of testicular blood vessels. In consequence, luteinizing hormone could not sufficiently stimulate the synthesis and release of testosterone in Leydig cells, finally resulting in a degeneration of spermatids in testosterone sensitive stages of maturation. In these patients, behavioural therapy turned out to improve coping with stress and significantly increased sperm count and fertility (Hellhammer and Gutberlet, 1988 for an overview). However, at the beginning, these young patients were not interested to see a psychotherapist, since they did not suffer by their stress load and none of them sought stress management. Thus, these patients could neither perceive the negative effects of stress nor receive adequate treatment, unless the andrologist would be able to diagnose the role of stress in the situation. Furthermore, in depressed patients who share this mechanism, an antidepressant may provide relief from depression but it is unlikely to improve fertility. Notably, there are other subgroups in male infertility, one of which is associated with anxiety and depression, higher cortisol and lower testosterone levels, and low sperm count and sperm motility. In these patients antidepressant treatments may well be indicated to improve fertility.

EXAMPLE II: BIOLOGICAL ASSESSMENT ALONE MAY BE MISLEADING

Elevated cortisol levels are considered an important biomarker of stress effects on mental and physical health. Indeed, most patients suffering from depression and anxiety disorders show such dysregulations of HPAA function. On the other hand, there is another subgroup of patients showing stress-related disorders and low cortisol levels. Typically, these patients report three major symptoms: pain, fatigue and irritability. Hypocortisolemic disorders comprehend a spectrum of disorders, such as irritable bowel disease, chronic fatigue syndrome, chronic pelvic pain, fibromyalgia and post-traumatic stress disorders (Heim et al., 2000). It seems that even a small decrease of free cortisol has important consequences, such as a gradual disinhibition of proinflammatory cytokines, of prostaglandine synthesis, and of central nuclei, such as the paraventricular nucleus of the hypothalamus and the locus coeruleus. These can be considered the causes of the symptoms which we previously described as the 'hypocortisolism triad'.

Fries (2008) has recently described the endophenotypes which are associated with hypocortisolism, and which we conceptualized for Neuropattern. Evidently, a lack of CRF, ACTH, cortisol and glucocorticoid receptors all result in slightly different neuropatterns, which allow a discrimination of the possible locus of hypocortisolism. Applying Neuropattern routinely includes data collection on early adversity. As it turned out, pre- and postnatal programming of stress-sensitive systems in the brain and the body may be among the most potent factors of stress vulnerability in later life. This may change our view on the aetiology and pathogenesis of stress-related disorders, as the following example may illustrate.

Quite recently, we found evidence of prenatal programming of hypocortisolism in fibromyalgia (FMS) (Klingmann et al., 2008). In a study with female FMS patients, only those with a shorter gestational length (<38 weeks) showed a lower cortisol awakening response when compared to FMS subjects with a gestational length >38 weeks. Additionally, in the FMS group born before the 38th week of gestation, several stressful events during pregnancy occurred in a larger number than in the healthy comparison group. Thus, it is not unlikely that an adrenal insufficiency can be prenatally determined. Under normal life conditions, the HPAA may adapt and function well. However, if a major life event occurs, as was the case in 72 percent of these FMS patients, the adrenals could be unable to mount sufficient cortisol to dampen the stress response. We currently hypothesize that under these circumstances stress mediators such as catecholamines and proinflammatory cytokines may be disinhibited and affect brain function. This might result in an enhanced responsiveness to external and internal pain- and fatigue-eliciting stimuli, finally promoting a fatigue- and pain memory.

Of course, we do not yet know if this hypothesis is correct. But our example already illustrates that new information from stress research (prenatal glucocorticoid programming in this case) provides new perspectives on mechanisms of diseases, which may have a profound impact on the prevention, diagnosis and treatment of stress-related disorders. Hypothetically, there would be an indication for an intake of glucocorticoids, once a subject at risk is exposed to a major stressor. In addition, it is unlikely that psychotherapy would be efficient. Rather, the patients may profit from neuropsychological treatments. Such hypotheses are testable, particularly in the present situation, where there is a big gap between clinical demands and knowledge on mechanisms behind fibromyalgia.

Conclusions

At present, numerous activities and initiatives can be observed to improve stress medicine by incorporating the rapidly increasing knowledge from the behavioural neurosciences. We are entering a new era of neurobehavioral medicine, which will improve the treatment and prevention of stress-related disorders. Presently, we are faced with a prior task to provide a platform, which facilitates an exchange of knowledge between the bench and the bedside. We can surely not afford to wait for translational tools, if we care about the patient.

Unlike other medical disciplines, neurobehavioral medicine is multidisciplinary and confronted with a complex interplay of aetiological factors. As described above, numerous challenges need to be met. Clearly, we need translational strategies to cope with these challenges. As illustrated here, it is already possible to develop such translational tools. The examples provided above suggest that the strategies applied can be successfully practised, but still need years of continuous updates and development to become part of clinical routine. However, the time will come where state-of-the-art methods in neurobehavioral medicine will be accessible for physicians across different disciplines.

References

Andlin-Sobocki, P., Jonsson, B., Wittchen, H.U. and Olesen, J. (2005). Cost of disorders of the brain in Europe. *Eur J Neurol*, 12(Suppl 1), 1–27.

Charmandari, E., Tsigos, C. and Chrousos, G. (2005). Endocrinology of the stress response. *Annu Rev Physiol*, 67, 259–84.

Chrousos, G.P. and Kino, T. (2007). Glucocorticoid action networks and complex psychiatric and/or somatic disorders. *Stress*, 10, 213–19.

Ellis, C.R., Singh, N.N. and Landrum, T.J. (1993). Pharmacotherapy: I. *Journal of Developmental and Physical Disabilities*, 5, 1–4.

Etkin, A., Pittenger, C., Polan, H.J. and Kandel, E.R. (2005). Toward a neurobiology of psychotherapy: basic science and clinical applications. *J Neuropsychiatry Clin Neurosci*, 17, 145–58.

Fries, E. (2008). Hypocortisolemic disorders. In Hellhammer, D.H. and Hellhammer, J. (eds), *Stress: The Brain-Body Connection* (vol. 174, pp. 60–77). Basel: Karger.

Heim, C., Ehlert, U. and Hellhammer, D.H. (2000). The potential role of hypocortisolism in the pathophysiology of stress-related bodily disorders. *Psychoneuroendocrinology*, 25, 1–35.

Hellhammer, D.H. and Gutberlet, I. (1988). Male infertility: preliminary evidence for two neuroendocrine mediators of stress on gonadal function. In Ferrendelli, J.A., Collins, R.C. and Johnson, E.A. (eds), *Neurobiology of Amino Acids, Peptides and Trophic Factors*. Boston, MA and Dordrecht: Kluwer Academic Publishers.

Hellhammer, D.H. and Hellhammer, J. (2008). *Stress: The Brain-Body Connection* (vol. 174). Basel, Karger.

Hoyer, J., Helbig, S. and Wittchen, H.-U. (2006). Experiences with psychotherapy for depression in routine care: a naturalistic patient survey in Germany. *Clinical Psychology and Psychotherapy*, 13, 414–21.

Klingmann, P.O., Kugler, I., Steffke, T.S., Bellingrath, S., Kudielka, B.M. and Hellhammer, D.H. (2008). Sex-specific prenatal programming: a risk for fibromyalgia? *Ann N Y Acad Sci*, 1148, 446–55.

Kyrou, I., Chrousos, G.P. and Tsigos, C. (2006). Stress, visceral obesity, and metabolic complications. *Ann N Y Acad Sci*, 1083, 77–110.

Lademann, J., Mertesacker, H. and Gebhardt, B. (2006). Psychische Erkrankungen im Fokus der Gesundheitsreporte der Krankenkassen. *Psychotherapeutenjournal*, 5, 123–9.

Tsigos, C. and Chrousos, G.P. (2002). Hypothalamic-pituitary-adrenal axis, neuroendocrine factors and stress. *J Psychosom Res*, 53, 865–71.

WHO (2003). Mental health in the WHO European Region. *Fact sheet EURO*. World Health Organization.

Wittchen, H.-U. and Jacobi, F. (2006). Psychische Störungen in Deutschland und der EU: Größenordnung und Belastung. *Verhaltenstherapie and Psychosoziale Praxis*, 38, 189–92.

PART II
Work and Dispositional Occupation Sources of Health

5

Work Hours, Work Intensity and Work Addiction: Risks and Rewards[1]

Ronald J. Burke and Lisa Fiksenbaum

This chapter reviews the literature on the antecedents and consequences of working hours, work intensity, and work addiction particularly among managers and professionals. The dependent variables associated with these include health-related illnesses, injuries, sleep patterns, fatigue, heart rate and hormone level changes, as well as several work/non-work life balance issues. Motives for working long hours, such as joy in work, avoiding job insecurity or negative sanctions from a superior, and employer demands, are addressed in detail. The chapter suggests a need for more research to better understand the effects of work hours, work intensity, and workaholism, as well as provides a number of implications and organizational and societal suggestions for addressing work hour concerns.

Porter (2004) explored the questions of how and why people work, considering work, the work ethic, and work excess. There were several reasons why people work hard and each reason may have both desirable and undesirable consequences to the individual, the organization, or both. Some people feel compelled towards excess work even when externally imposed demands are absent. Golden (1998) proposes that the actual hours worked are a function of three factors: hours desired by the worker, hours demanded by the employer, and the institutional environment in which working hour decisions are made (legal constraints, workplace norms, the larger economic environment). There

---

[1] Preparation of this chapter was supported in part by York University. Several colleagues participated in the design and conduct of the research program: Zena Burgess, Astrid Richardsen, Stig Matthiesen, and Graeme MacDermid.

are positive reasons for working long hours (more pay, self-actualization, a sense of commitment to colleagues and clients, work enjoyment) and also negative reasons (to avoid sanctions, deal with employment insecurity). Working longer hours may increase one's competitiveness in the short term but may not be sustainable—and perhaps become counterproductive—in the longer term. Long hours may influence physical and mental health and well-being by increasing stress. Can one make a distinction between a healthy work ethic and working to excess? How much work is too much? One can work to have material possessions, to not be left behind (Reich, 2000), to confirm self-worth, and to provide for children.

Although the terms workaholic and work addict encompass all the problems that addiction brings (Oates, 1971), most people believe that work is healthy, desirable, and protective of many illnesses. In support of this view, research has shown that holding multiple roles instead of a single role (e.g., homemaker) generally leads to favorable well-being outcomes among women (Barnett and Marshall, 1992).

The importance of focusing on work hours is multi-faceted. First, a large number of employees are unhappy about the number of hours they work (Clarkberg and Moen, 2001; Dembe, 2005; Jacobs and Gerson, 1998; MacInnes, 2005). Second, the amount of time demanded by work is an obvious and important way in which work affects other parts of one's life (Galinsky, 1999; Shields, 1999). Third, work hours are a widely studied structural output of employment (Adam, 1993). Fourth, the study of work hours and well-being outcomes has produced both inconsistent and complex results (Barnett, 1998).

New technology and job flexibility have facilitated working from home or outside the office, which has contributed to an increase in hours worked in North America (Golden and Figart, 2000a). These alternative work arrangements can be seen as beneficial: for example, a working mother who chooses to spend more time with her children can do so by working from home or working night shifts. In a study of 61 French hospitals, 85 percent of nurses employed had requested the night shift to allow more time to be spent with their young children during the day (Barton, 1994). This accommodates dual income families, presenting an arrangement to allow them to share the child rearing.

Employer demands and the institutionalized nature of work and employment has tended to constrain work hours in established patterns. But these patterns are changing, several contrasting factors influenced working hours in the 2000s. First, the labor union movement for shorter hours in the EEU has lead to a reduction in working hours in some European countries (Rifkin, 2004). Second, the need for organizations to provide 24/7 service has led to the creation of more flexible and non-standard work schedules (Kreitzman, 1999). Third, more employees have also undertaken flexible work schedules to meet their family responsibilities (Hochschild, 1997).

Brett and Stroh (2003) examined the question of why some managers work 61 or more hours per week. They considered four explanations: the work-leisure trade-off, social contagion, work as an emotional respite from home, and work as its own rewards. Data was collected from a sample of 595 male and 391 female MBA alumni of the same university. The males were all married with children at home and a smaller percentage of the females were married and had children. More men than women worked 61 or more hours per week (29 percent versus 11 percent). Men worked 56.4 hours per week and women worked 51.5 hours per week. For males, rewards of work was the only of the four hypotheses to be supported, with hours worked significantly connected with job involvement and intrinsic satisfaction. For females, the work-leisure trade-off and social contagion hypotheses were supported. However, hours worked did not correlate with job involvement, income, or job satisfaction for females.

Hewlett and Luce (2006) examined "extreme jobs," that is, jobs in which incumbents worked 70 hours a week or more, were high wage earners, and had jobs having at least five characteristics of work intensity. These characteristics are listed below.

- unpredictable flow of work;

- fast-paced work under tight deadlines;

- inordinate scope of responsibility that amounts to more than one job;

- work-related events outside regular work hours;

- availability to clients 24/7;

- responsibility for profit and loss;

- responsibility for mentoring and recruiting;

- large amount of travel;

- large number of direct reports;

- physical presence at workplace at least ten hours a day.

They carried out surveys of high wage earners in the United States and high earning managers and professionals working in large multinational organizations. In addition, they conducted focus groups and interviews to better understand the motivations for, and the effects of, working in these jobs.

Their two surveys of high-earning managers and professionals revealed four characteristics that created the most intensity and pressure: unpredictability (cited by 91 percent of respondents), fast pace with tight deadlines (86 percent), work-related events outside business hours (66 percent), and 24/7 client demands (61 percent).

They concluded that managers and professionals were now working harder than ever. Of the extreme job holders, 48 percent said they were now working an average of 16.6 hours per week more than they did five years ago. And 42 percent took 10 or fewer vacation days per year (less than they were entitled to) and 55 percent indicated that they had to cancel vacation plans regularly. Forty-four percent of their respondents felt the pace of their work was extreme.

But extreme job holders (66 percent in the US sample and 76 percent in the global sample) said that they loved their jobs. Several reasons were given for working these long hours: the job was stimulating and challenging (over 85 percent), working with high quality colleagues (almost 50 percent), high pay (almost 50 percent), recognition (almost 40 percent), and power and status (almost 25 percent). In addition, increased competitive pressures, improved communication technologies, downsizings and restructurings resulting in few higher level jobs, flattened organizational hierarchies, and values changes in the broader society supportive of "extremes" also played a role (Wiehert, 2002).

Individuals holding extreme jobs, however, had to let some things go. These included: home maintenance (about 70 percent), relationships with their children (almost 50 percent), relationships with their spouses/partners (over 45 percent), and a satisfying sex life (over 40 percent).

Extreme jobs were more likely to be held by men than women (17 percent versus 4 percent in the US sample; 30 percent versus 15 percent in the global sample). Women were more likely to be in jobs with high demands but working fewer hours. Women were not afraid of jobs having high levels of responsibility. Both women and men in extreme jobs indicated "difficulties" with their children (acting out, eating too much junk food, under-achieving in school, too little adult supervision).

In the US sample, most women (57 percent) in extreme jobs did want to continue working as hard in five years, 48 percent of men felt the same way. Only 13 percent of women and 27 percent of men wanted to continue at this pace. The respective numbers were higher in the global survey: women, 80 percent, men 55 percent; and women, 5 percent and men, 17 percent.

Work Hours and Their Effects

A variety of outcome measures have been examined in connection with working long hours (van der Hulst, 2003). Most studies of long work hours have been conducted in Japan where "karoshi," sudden death due to long hours and insufficient sleep was first observed. The Japanese coined this term to refer to deaths of individuals from overwork or working long work hours, and have actually defined such deaths (Kanai, 2006). Several hypotheses have been advanced to explain the relationship between long work hours and adverse health outcomes. Working long hours affects the cardiovascular system through chronic exposure to increases in blood pressure and heart rate (Buell and Breslow, 1960; Iwasaki, Sasaki, Oka, and Hisanaga, 1998; Uehata, 1991). Working long hours produces sleep deprivation and lack of recovery leading to chronic fatigue, poor health-related behaviors, and ill health (Ala-Mursjula, Vahtera, Kivimaki, Kevin, and Penttij, 2002; Defoe, Power, Holzman, Carpentieri, and Schulikin, 2001; Liu and Tanaka, 2002). Working long hours makes it more difficult to recover from job demands and the stress of long work hours. Finally, working long hours has been associated with more errors and accidents (Gander, Merry, Millar, and Weller, 2000; Loomis, 2005; Nachreiner, Akkermann, and Haenecke, 2000; Schuster and Rhodes, 1985).

More specifically, the literature suggests that long hours are associated with adverse health effects and increased safety risk (Harrington, 1994; 2001; Cooper, 1996; Kirkcaldy, Trimpop, and Cooper, 1997; Spurgeon, Harrington, and Cooper, 1997). Long work hours have been found to be associated with poor psychological health (Kirkcaldy, Levine, and Shephard, 2000; Sparks, Cooper, Fried, and Shirom, 1997; Borg and Kristensen, 1999), excessive fatigue (Rosa, 1995), and burnout (Barnett, Gareis, and Brennan, 1999). Several studies have also reported that long working hours are associated with more work-family conflict (Crouter, Bumpus, Maguire, and McHale, 1999; Crouter, Bumpus, Head, and McHale, 2001; Galambos, Sears, Almeida, and Kolaric, 1995; Galinsky, Bond, Kim, Bachon, Brownfield, and Sakal, 2005; Staines and Pleck, 1984), or fatigue, worrying, and irritability (Grzywicz and Marks, 2000; Kluwer, Heesink, and van den Vliert, 1996; Geurts, Rutte, and Peeters, 1999).

Dembe, Erickson, Delbos, and Banks (2005) examined the impact of overtime and extended working hours on the risk of occupational injuries and illnesses in a representative sample of working adults in the United States. They estimated the relative risk of long working hours per day, extended hours per week, long commute times, and overtime schedules on reporting a work-related injury or illness after controlling for age, gender, occupation, industry, and region. Data were collected from 10,793 workers between 1987 and 2000. After adjusting for these control factors, working in jobs with overtime schedules was associated with a 61 percent higher injury hazard rate compared to jobs without overtime. Working at least 12 hours per day was associated with a 32 percent increased hazard rate and working at least 60 hours per week was associated with a 23 percent increased hazard rate. A strong dose response effect was observed with the injury rate increasing in correspondence with the number of hours per day (or per week) in the worker's customary schedule. Job schedules with long working hours were not more risky because they are concentrated in inherently hazardous industries or occupations, or because people working long hours have more total time at risk for a work injury.

Van der Hulst, van Veldenhoven, and Beckers (2006) considered overtime, work characteristics (job demands, job control), and need for recovery in a large sample (N = 1473) of Dutch municipal administration employees working full-time. The Effort-Recovery model (Meijman and Mulder, 1998) proposes that negative consequences of long working hours for health and well-being depends on the opportunities for recovery during the work day (internal recovery) and after work (external recovery). Working overtime reduces the time available for recovery. In addition, external recovery may be poor due to the spill-over of work demands to one's home life. Finally, overtime is more likely to occur in demanding jobs limiting opportunities for internal recovery. They examined four types of jobs; "low strain"—low demands, high control; "passive"—low demands, low control; "active"—high demands, high control; "high strain"—

high demands, low control. Overtime was common for a majority of employees and in jobs having high demands. While there was no relationship between working overtime and need for recovery in the total sample, there was a significant and positive relationship between overtime hours and need for recovery in high strain jobs (high job demands, low control); there was also a relationship between overtime and need for recovery in active jobs (high demands, high control). Working conditions (high demand jobs) influenced the relationship between overtime and need for recovery.

Caruso, Hitchcock, Dick, Russo, and Schmitt (2004) reviewed the accumulating research evidence on the influence of overtime and extended workshifts on worker health and safety as well as worker errors, considering 52 studies in total. Overtime has increased in the United States from 1970 to 2000 (Rones, Ilg, and Gardner, 1997; Hetrick, 2000). Overtime is defined as working more than 40 hours per week; extended work shifts are defined as shifts longer than 8 hours. They found, in a majority of studies of general health that overtime was associated with poorer perceived general health, increased injury rate, more illness, and increased mortality. A pattern of reduced performance on psychophysiological tests and injuries while working long hours, particularly very long shifts, and when 12-hour shifts combined with over 40 hours of work a week was also noted. When 12-hour shifts were combined with more than 40 hours of work per week, more adverse effects were evident. Haenecke, Tiedemann, Nachreiner, and Grzech-Sukalo (1998), in a study of 1.2 million German workers, found that the risk of workplace accidents increased during the latter portion (after the eighth hour) of a long work shift.

Van der Hulst (2003) found that long work hours was associated with adverse health, particularly cardiovascular disease, disability retirement, self-reported health, and fatigue. She concluded that working more than 11 hours a day was associated with a three-fold risk of coronary heart disease and a four-fold risk of diabetes. In addition, working 60 or more hours a week was associated with a three-fold risk of disability retirement.

Van der Hulst's (2003) review showed that working long hours was associated with poorer physiological recovery, and with fewer hours of sleep. Van der Hulst (2003) suggested two possible pathways between long hours and health: insufficient feelings of recovery from the demands of long hours (a psychological explanation) and poor life-style behaviors (a behavioral life-style explanation). Long work hours are believed to be associated with life-style choices such as smoking, coffee and alcohol consumption, lack of exercise, and a poor (unhealthy) diet. These unhealthy behaviors produce physiological changes (e.g., high blood pressure, high levels of cholesterol, obesity, diabetes) and higher risk of coronary heart disease and poorer health in general. One perspective on why long work hours may be associated with reduced psychological well-being is the Effort-Recovery model (Meijman and Mulder, 1998). Working long hours is associated with short-term psychological costs which are irreversible. Individuals experience recovery when the work hours stop. Excessive work hours and insufficient recovery causes these negative effects to persist for a longer period of time or even become irreversible. Long work hours reduces the time of recovery as well as prolonging persistent and psychological demands (Benson, 2005; Czeisler, 2006).

Rissler (1977) studied the effects of high workload and overtime on heart rate and hormone levels during the rest and work hours. High workload was associated with higher levels of adrenaline and heart rate during evenings at home (rest periods) as well as feelings of fatigue and irritation. His results also indicated an accumulation effect of overtime on adrenaline levels. That is, it takes several weeks to return to normal (resting) values following several weeks of overtime.

Van der Hulst and Geurts (2001), in a study of 525 full-time employees of the Dutch Postal Service, found that working overtime was associated with negative work-home interference. Employees working overtime and reporting low rewards, indicated greater burnout, negative work home interference, and slower recovery. Employees working overtime and experiencing a high pressure to work overtime, coupled with low rewards, had poorer recovery, more cynicism, and negative work-home interference.

Major, Klein, and Erhart (2002), in a study of 513 employees from one firm, found that hours worked per week was significantly related to work-interference with family. Antecedents of hours worked included career identity, service, work overload, organizational expectations, self-reported financial needs, and non-job responsibilities (negatively). Parental demands were unrelated to hours worked; organizational rewards for time spent at work was respectively correlated (but weakly) with hours worked. Hours worked fully or partially related to the effects of many work and family characteristics on work-interfering with family.

Rosa (1995) reported that overtime and fatigue were found to be associated with increases in back injuries, hospital outbreaks of bacterial infection, a three-fold increase in accidents after 26 hours of work, and increased risk of safety violations in nuclear power plants, showing that long work hours does not just negatively affect the worker, it puts a strain on overall workplace safety. Shimomitsu and Levi (1992) found that two thirds of Japanese workers complain of fatigue, with "karoshi" or death from overwork an important social concern. Moruyama, Kohno, and Morimoto (1995) found long work hours associated with poor lifestyle habits such as heavy smoking, poor diet, and lack of exercise. Sparks, Cooper, Fried, and Shirom (1997) undertook a meta-analysis of 21 samples and found small but significant correlations between hours of work and health symptoms, physiological and psychological health symptoms. Qualitative analyses of 12 other studies supported the findings of a positive relationship between hours of work and health.

Addressing Work Hours Concerns

Is working long hours really necessary? Can organizations reduce the need for face time (Brown and Benson, 2005) among employees without affecting their identities and further career opportunities? Can one still get the same personal and psychological rewards but work fewer hours? One solution is to separate face time from performance appraisals and opportunities for more challenging work. A second is to provide models of managers that do outstanding work but work fewer hours (Munck, 2001). Identifying unproductive but time consuming work practices is also useful. Individuals can be encouraged and supported to make small changes in hours—but enough to be noticed—and then have these rewarded. Workers' ability to exert control over work schedules has been shown to have an influence on the effects of work hours on health (Barton, 1994; Smith, Hammond, Macdonald, and Folkard, 1998).

Van der Hulst and Geurts (2001) suggest that compensation may also reduce adverse effects of work hours. In addition, length of vacation and commuting time may affect the relationship of overtime and health and safety. Strategies for preventing work injuries should consider changes in scheduling practices, job redesign, and health promotion programs for people working in jobs involving overtime and extended hours (Golden and Figart, 2000b). More days of vacation allow for more rest and may lessen the impact of overtime; longer commute times may add additional job stressors to the effects of working hours (DeGraaf, 2003).

Cartwright (2000) offers these suggestions for breaking out of the long working-hours culture.

- Schedule meetings only during core hours—no breakfast meetings or meetings after 5:00 p.m;

- Take regular breaks. Take a short walk. Do not work through lunch;

- Take your full vacation time. Plan your work around your holidays not your holidays around your work;

- Do not take work home on a regular basis;

- Say no to unrealistic deadlines. It is better to under-promise but over-deliver than to over-promise but under-deliver;

- Do not work late because others are doing so;

- Monitor the hours you and your staff work. Use this information to make the case for more resources.

There are a number of other initiatives that could be undertaken by societies, organizations and their employees to minimize the potential adverse effects of long work hours. These include:

- encourage governments to regulate the length of work schedules as is already the case in many countries in Europe (Green, 2001; Hayden, 2003);

- changes to the work organization and job design;

- increase worker control of their work hours;

- utilize ergonomic job design;

- increase worker training;

- develop capable supervision;

- establish a workplace culture that promotes health and safety;

- employ more people working fewer hours;

- use more rest breaks (Tucker, Folkard, and Macdonald, 2003);

- redesign work to avoid the need for overtime;

- offer health promotion counseling about the risks of long work schedules; and

- provide medical examinations for at risk workers.

Work Intensity

Work intensity is generally conceptualized as an effort-related activity (Green, 2004a; 2004b; 2005). In this regard, it is very similar to the "work effort" concept discussed by Green (2001:56) as: "the rate of physical and/or mental input to work tasks performed during the working day ... in part, effort is inversely linked to the 'porosity' of the working day, meaning those gaps between tasks during which the body or mind rests." Obviously, it would be difficult to measure such effort objectively; it can only be determined through self-reports, or extraordinarily well-controlled laboratory experiments. Burchell and Fagan (2004) used "speed of work" to mean work intensity, and reported that Europeans were working more intensely (2000 compared to 1991). Green (2001) focused on "effort change" (respondents were asked to compare their current jobs with that of five years previously on items that included "how fast you work," and "the effort you have to put into your job"), and "work effort" ("How much effort do you put into your job beyond what is required?" and "My job requires that I work very hard"). He found that work effort had increased in Britain. While these are good starting points for conceptualizing work intensity, they measure only certain aspects of it. There is no research that attempts to capture a more extensive list of attributes.

Worrall and Cooper (1999), questioning over 1,200 UK managers from 1997 to 1999, found that the pace of change had increased over these years. Managers now saw their jobs as more complex and fragmented. Managers in the 1999 survey had to deal with more information, to acquire a wider range of skills, and managed more staff. Seventy-six percent of these managers felt that the number of hours worked had a negative effect on their health. Clark (2005) comes to similar conclusions in a study of changes in job quality in OECD countries.

Green (2001), using various employee surveys conducted in the UK over almost a 20-year period, concluded that work effort has intensified since 1981. And between 1986 and 1997 there have been increases in the sources of pressure inducing hard work from employees. The most common sources of pressure were: one's own choice, fellow workers or colleagues, clients or customers, supervisors or bosses, pay incentives, and reports and appraisals (see also George, 1997; Gallie, 2005).

Increases in work effort or intensity are represented in employees having less idle time (less time between tasks), having to work harder now, needing more skills (multi-skilling), greater use of performance goals and appraisals, use of total quality management and just-in-time processes, needing to work faster, having more deadlines, and having more responsibility (Green and McIntosh, 2001).

Messenger (2004; 2006) makes the case for "decent working time" to balance the needs of workers and employers. Decent working time is proposed to have five dimensions: working time is healthy and safe, is family-friendly, promotes gender equality, supports organizational productivity, and offers workers some choice and influence in hours of work and when they are worked.

Workaholism and Work Addiction

Workaholism and long working hours have positive connotations such as dedication, commitment, and organizational citizenship behavior as well as negative connotations such as ill health and damaged family relationships (Killinger, 1991). Number of hours worked per week, while obviously an element of workaholism, does not capture one's degree of work involvement, a psychological state or attitude. Hours worked per week, however, is a behavioral manifestation of workaholism (Ng, Sorensen, and Feldman, 2007). Some writers view workaholism positively from an organizational perspective. Machlowitz (1980) conducted a qualitative interview study of 100 workaholics and found them to be very satisfied and productive. Others view workaholism negatively (Fassel, 1990; Killinger, 1991; Oates, 1971). These writers equate workaholism with other addictions and depict workaholics as unhappy, obsessive, tragic figures who are not performing their jobs well and are creating difficulties for their co-workers (Porter, 1996). The former would advocate the encouragement of workaholism; the latter would discourage it.

DEFINITIONS OF WORKAHOLISM

Oates (1971), generally acknowledged as the first person to use the word workaholic, defined it as "a person whose need for work has become so excessive that it creates noticeable disturbance or interference with his bodily health, personal happiness, and interpersonal relationships, and with his smooth social functioning" (Oates, 1971). Killinger (1991) defines a workaholic as "a person who gradually becomes emotionally crippled and addicted to control and power in a compulsive drive to gain approval and success." Robinson (1998) defines workaholism "as a progressive, potentially fatal disorder, characterized by self imposed demands, compulsive overworking, inability to regulate work to the exclusion of most other life activities." Porter (1996) defines workaholism as "an excessive involvement with work evidenced by neglect in other areas of life and based on internal motives of behavior maintenance rather than requirements of the job or organization." Most writers use the terms excessive work, workaholism, and work addiction interchangeably.

TYPES OF WORKAHOLICS

Spence and Robbins (1992) propose three workaholic patterns based on their workaholic triad notion. The workaholic triad consists of three concepts: work involvement, feeling driven to work because of inner pressures, and work enjoyment. Data were collected in this study from 368 social workers holding academic appointments. Profile analysis resulted in the same six profiles for women and men—three workaholic types and three non-workaholic types. These profiles were: Work Addicts (WAs) score high on work involvement, high on feeling driven to work, and low on work enjoyment. Work Enthusiasts (WEs) score high on work involvement, low on feeling driven to work, and high on work enjoyment. Enthusiastic Addicts (EAs) score high on all three workaholism components. Unengaged Workers (UWs) score low on all three workaholism components. Relaxed Workers (RWs) score low on feeling driven to work and work involvement, and high on work enjoyment. Disenchanted Workers (DWs) score high on feeling driven to work, and low on work involvement and work enjoyment.

Research Findings

The following sections of the chapter will review research findings that compare the personal demographics, job behaviors, work outcomes, extra-work outcomes, and psychological health of the three types of workaholics proposed by Spence and Robbins (1992).

PERSONAL DEMOGRAPHIC AND WORK SITUATIONAL CHARACTERISTICS

A critical question involves potential differences between the three workaholism types on both personal demographic and work situation characteristics including hours worked per week. If the workaholism types were found to differ on these (e.g., organizational level, marital status, hours worked per week), these differences would account for any differences found on work and health outcomes.

A number of studies (Spence and Robbins, 1992; Burke, 1999a; Burke, Burgess, and Oberklaid, 2002; Bonebright, Clay, and Ankenmann, 2000) have reported essentially no differences between the three workaholism types on a variety of personal and work situation characteristics. The workaholism types work the same number of hours and extra-hours per week; the workaholism types working significantly more hours per week and more extra-hours per week than the non-workaholism types.

JOB BEHAVIORS

There has been considerable speculation regarding the work behaviors likely to be exhibited by workaholics (see Mudrack, 2006). This list includes hours worked per week, extra hours worked per week, job involvement, job stress, non-delegation of job responsibilities to others, high (or low) levels of job performances, high levels of interpersonal conflict and of lack of trust. There is empirical research that examines some of these hypothesized relationships.

Burke (1999a) considered these relationships in a large sample of Canadian MBA graduates. Comparisons of the three workaholism types on a number of behavioral manifestations provided considerable support for the hypothesized relationships. First, there were no differences between WAs, EAs, and WEs on hours worked per week or extra-hours worked per week; workaholism types working significantly more hours and extra hours per week than did the three non-workaholism types. Second, EAs devoted more time to their jobs in a psychological sense than did both WEs and WAs. Third, WAs reported greater job stress than did EAs, both reporting greater job stress than did WEs. Fourth, both EAs and WEs reported greater job involvement than did WAs. Fifth, WAs had greater inability and unwillingness to delegate than both WEs and EAs. Sixth, EAs were more perfectionistic than were WEs.

Spence and Robbins (1992) found that WAs reported higher levels of job stress, perfectionism, and unwillingness to delegate job duties to others than did WEs. Kanai, Wakabayashi, and Fling (1996), using the Spence and Robbins measures, reported that WAs and EAs scored higher than WEs on measures of job stress, perfectionism, non-delegation, and time committed to job.

ANTECEDENTS OF WORKAHOLISM

Four potential antecedents of workaholism have received some conceptual and research attention. Three of these, family of origin, Type A behavior, and personal beliefs and fears, are the result of socialization practices within families and society at large. The fourth, organizational support for work-personal life imbalance, represents organizational values and priorities.

Family of origin

Robinson (1998) has written about work addiction as a symptom of a diseased family system. Work addiction, similarly to other addictive behaviors, is intergenerational and passed on to future generations through family processes and dynamics. In this view, work addiction is seen as a learned addictive response to a dysfunctional family of origin system.

Personal beliefs and fears

Burke (1999b) examined the relationship of personal beliefs and fears and workaholism. Beliefs and fears are a reflection of values, thoughts and interpersonal styles. Three measures of beliefs and fears developed by Lee, Jamieson, and Earley (1996) were used: "Striving against others", "No moral principles," and "Prove yourself." Burke compared the three workaholism types on these measures of beliefs and fears. WAs scored significantly higher than WEs and EAs on measures of striving against others and no moral principles, as well as on the composite measure. In addition, WAs scored higher on the need to prove oneself than did WEs. Workaholism thus emerges as work behaviors in response to feelings of low self-worth and insecurity. This is best reflected in managers' feelings of being driven to work. Paradoxically these beliefs and fears were also found to be associated with lower levels of work enjoyment.

Kaiser and Kaplan (2006) offer some observations on the well-springs of "overdoing it" at work based on their coaching and consulting work with executives. They emphasize intrapersonal issues, describing how psychological wounds sensitize managers to be anxious about being hurt again. When managers feel threatened, their behavior frequently goes to the extreme, either overdoing or underdoing. Kaiser and Kaplan propose the following sequence: first one's sensitivity becomes activated, this influences (or distorts) one's perceptions of resources and demands in one's environment, precipitating feelings of threat which in turn promote compulsion—overdoing—leading to working extreme hours, striving to prove oneself, impatience with the performance of others, over-controlling, non-delegating, and micromanaging. This list reads like a template for the work addict. Common sensitivities include feelings of intellectual inadequacy, fears of appearing weak, reluctance to depend on others and vulnerability from being criticized. Work addicts need constantly to prove themselves, tend to overcome feelings of low self-worth, and continually increase the performance ante.

Type A behavior

Zhdanova, Allison, Pui, and Clark (2006), using meta-analysis, provided support for Type A behavior as an antecedent of workaholism. Type A behavior has been shown to be associated with levels of job stress, psychological distress, and coronary heart disease. Burke, Richardsen, and Martinussen (2004), in a study of 171 Norwegian owners and senior managers of construction companies, noted that WAs scored higher than WEs on Impatience-Irritation; EAs scored higher than WEs on Achievement Striving, both being dimensions of Type A behavior. Impatience-Irritation has been shown to be predictive of psychological distress.

Organizational values

Burke (1999c) compared perceptions of organization culture values supporting work-personal life imbalance across the three workaholism types. Organizational values encouraging work-family imbalance were measured by scales developed by Kofodimos (1993). WAs reported higher imbalance values than both WEs and EAs. Thus WAs see their workplaces as less supportive of work-personal life balance than the two other workaholism types.

Johnstone and Johnston (2005), using two of the three Spence and Robbins workaholism components (work enjoyment, feeling driven to work because of inner pressures), examined the relationship of these to four aspects of organizational climate: work pressures, involvement, supervisor support, and co-worker cohesion. Data were collected in two occupation groups, business services (law firms, management consultants, accounting firms) and social services (schools, social workers in government agencies, workers in a hospice). Involvement, supervisor support, and co-worker cohesion were positively related to work enjoyment while work pressures was negatively related to work enjoyment. Only work pressures were significantly related (positively) to feeling driven.

WORK OUTCOMES

The relationship between workaholism and indicators of job and career satisfaction and success is difficult to specify. It is likely that different types of workaholics will report varying work and career satisfactions (Scott, Moore and Miceli, 1997).

Burke (1999d) compared levels of work and career satisfaction and success among the workaholism profiles observed by Spence and Robbins (1992). Four work outcomes, all significantly inter-correlated, were used: Intent to Quit, Work Satisfaction, Career Satisfaction, and Future Career Prospects. WAs scored lower than WEs and EAs on Job Satisfaction, Career Satisfaction, and Future Career Prospects, and higher than WEs on Intent to Quit. It should be noted that all three workaholic profiles (WAs, EWs, WEs) worked the same number of hours per week and had the same job and organizational tenure.

WORKAHOLISM TYPES AND FLOW AT WORK

Csikszentmihalyi (1990) uses the term optimal experience to refer to times when individuals feel in control of their actions and masters of their own destinies. Optimal experiences commonly result from hard work and meeting challenges head on. Would the workaholism types differ in the experience of flow? In a study of 211 Norwegian journalists, Burke and Matthiesen (2004) found that journalists scoring higher on work enjoyment and lower on feeling driven to work because of internal needs indicated higher levels of flow or optimal experience at work. In this same study, Burke and Matthiesen found that WEs and EAs indicated higher levels of flow than did WAs.

PSYCHOLOGICAL WELL-BEING

There is considerable consensus in the workaholism literature on the association of workaholism and poorer psychological and physical well-being. In fact, some definitions of workaholism incorporate aspects of diminished health as central elements. It is not surprising that this relationship has received research attention.

Burke (1999e) compared the three workaholism types identified by Spence and Robbins (1992) on three indicators of psychological and physical well-being in a sample of 530 employed women and men MBA graduates: psychosomatic symptoms, lifestyle behaviors, and emotional well-being. Once again, the comparisons of the workaholism types on the three measures of psychological and physical well-being provided considerable support for the hypothesized relationships. WAs had more psychosomatic symptoms than both WEs and EAs and poorer physical and emotional well-being than did WEs.

In a study of 171 Norwegian construction company owners and senior managers, Burke, Richardsen, and Martinussen (2004) found that WAs reported higher levels of emotional exhaustion than both WEs and EAs; the three workaholism types were similar on levels of cynicism and personal efficacy.

EXTRA-WORK SATISFACTIONS AND FAMILY FUNCTIONING

A number of writers have hypothesized that workaholism is likely to impact negatively on family functioning (Killinger, 1991; Porter, 1996; Robinson, 1998). Burke (1999f) considered the relationship of the three workaholism types identified by Spence and Robbins (1992) and three types of extra-work satisfaction: family satisfaction, relationship satisfaction, and community satisfaction. WAs reported less satisfaction on all three extra-work satisfaction measures than did WEs and less satisfaction on one (family) than did EAs.

ADDRESSING WORKAHOLISM

There is a large speculative literature suggesting ways to reduce levels of workaholism. One part of this work focuses on individual and family therapy (Killinger, 1991; Robinson, 1998); a second part emphasizes organizational and managerial interventions.

Individual counseling

Workaholics Anonymous chapters have sprung up in some North American cities. These groups, patterned after Alcoholics Anonymous self-help groups, endorse the 12-step approach common to the treatment of a variety of addictions. Killinger (1991) and Robinson (1998) include chapters outlining actions an individual might pursue to reduce levels of workaholism; Chen (2006) shows how the use of Rational Emotive Behavior Therapy (REBT) can be effective in lessening work-life balance concerns and ameliorating the effects of workaholism.

Family therapy

Robinson and his colleagues, consistent with their clinical and consulting perspective, focus on treatment, both individual and family. This is not surprising given the central role they give to both family of origin and current family functioning in the development maintenance and intergenerational transmission of workaholism. The treatment recommendations Robinson offers (1998) are similar to those offered to alcoholic families.

Thus, denial is common among workaholics and their family members. Family members are reluctant to complain. Workaholics define their behavior and symptoms in a favorable light (Killinger, 1991; Porter, 1996). Parental expectations of children, often unrealistic, must be addressed. Family structures need to be identified. How do family members collude with the workaholic parent? Family members need help in expressing their negative feelings to the workaholic. Families need to learn to set boundaries around the amount they work together and talk about work. Family members can set goals to improve family dynamics (e.g., communication, roles, expression of feelings).

Workplace interventions

How can employers help workaholics and workaholics help themselves? Schaef and Fassel (1988) offer the following ideas. Employers should pay attention to the performance and work habits of employees and be alert to warning signs of workaholism. They should ensure that employees take vacation time away from work. Finally, job insecurity, work overload, limited career opportunities, and lack of control can make employees feel compelled to work longer. If these factors exist, employers should try to minimize their impact on the atmosphere within the organization.

Haas (1991) also highlights the role that managers can play in assisting their workaholic employees to change. Workaholic employees should be referred to an employee assistance program or a recovery program to start treatment processes. Managers should help prioritize projects for employees as long-term and short-term assignments. Workaholics must be encouraged and helped to delegate their work. At the end of each day, the manager should meet with the employee to discuss what has been accomplished during that day and to plan (down to short intervals) for the following day. The employee should be given specific times to take breaks and to leave work. It may also be possible to reduce the negative effects of workaholism, particularly well-being and health consequences, through stress-management training.

The development of workplace values that promote new, more balanced priorities and healthier lifestyles will support those workaholism types that want to change their behaviors (Austin Knight, 1995; Messenger, 2006). More people today want a life beyond work. Employees can work more effectively if they can integrate their work, families, and personal lives in more satisfying ways. This becomes a win-win situation for all involved (Friedman, Christensen, and DeGroot, 1998; Nash and Stevenson, 2004a; 2004b).

Risks and Rewards

> *The gross national product does not allow for the health of our children, the quality of their education, or the joy of their play. It does not include the beauty of our poetry or the strength of our marriages; the intelligence of our public debate or the integrity of our public officials. It measures neither our learning; neither our compassion nor our devotion to our country; it measures everything, in short except that which makes life worthwhile. (Kennedy, 1968)*

As this review has shown, working long hours was associated with both risks and rewards. The risks included lower family satisfaction, disrupted sleep patterns, and psychological distress. The rewards included work satisfaction, upward mobility, and higher incomes (Bunting, 2004). Choose wisely.

References

Adam, B. (1993) Within and beyond the time economy of employment relations: conceptual issues pertinent to research on time and work. *Social Science Information*, 32, 163–84.

Ala-Mursjula, L., Vahtera, J., Kivimaki, M., Kevin, M.V., and Penttij, J. (2002) Employee control over working times: associations with subjective health and sickness absences. *Journal of Epidemiology and Community Health*, 56, 272–8.

Austin Knight (1995) *Long Hour Culture*. London: Austin Knight.

Barnett, R.C. (1998) Towards a review and reconceptualization of the work/family literature. *Genetic Social and General Psychology Monograph*, 124, 125–82.

Barnett, R.C., Gareis, K.C., and Brennan, R.T. (1999) Fit as a mediator of the relationship between work hours and burnout. *Journal of Occupational Health Psychology*, 4, 307–17.

Barnett, R.C. and Marshall, N.L. (1992) Worker and mother roles, spillover effects, and psychological distress. *Women and Health*, 19, 13–41.

Barton, J. (1994) Choosing to work at night: a moderating influence on individual tolerance to shift work. *Journal of Applied Psychology*, 79, 449–54.

Benson, H. (2005) Are you working too hard? *Harvard Business Review*, November, 53–8.

Bonebright, C.A., Clay, D.L., and Ankenmann, R.D. (2000) The relationship of workaholism with work-life conflict, life satisfaction, and purpose in life. *Journal of Counseling Psychology*, 47, 469–77.

Borg, V. and Kristensen, T.S. (1999) Psychosocial work environment and mental health among traveling sales people. *Work and Stress*, 13, 132–43.

Brett, J.M. and Stroh, L.K. (2003) Working 61 plus hours a week: why do managers do it? *Journal of Applied Psychology*, 88, 67–78.

Brown, M. and Benson, J. (2005) Managing to overload? Work overload and performance appraisal processes. *Group and Organization Management*, 30, 99–124.

Buell, P. and Breslow, L. (1960) Mortality from coronary heart disease in Californian men who work long hours. *Journal of Chronic Disease*, 11, 615–26.

Bunting, M. (2004) *Willing Slaves: How the Overwork Culture is Ruling Our Lives*. New York, NY: HarperCollins.

Burchell, B. and Fagan, C. (2004) Gender and the intensification of work: evidence from the European Working Conditions survey. *Eastern Economic Journal*, 30, 627–42.

Burke, R.J. (1999a) Workaholism in organizations: measurement validation and replication, *International Journal of Stress Management*, 6, 45–55.

Burke, R.J. (1999b) Workaholism in organizations: the role of personal beliefs and fears. *Anxiety, Stress and Coping*, 14, 1–12.

Burke, R.J. (1999c) Workaholism in organizations: the role of organizational values. *Personnel Review*, 30, 637–45.

Burke, R.J. (1999d) Are workaholics job satisfied and successful in their careers? *Career Development International*, 26, 149–58.

Burke, R.J. (1999e) Workaholism in organizations: psychological and physical well-being consequences. *Stress Medicine*, 16, 11–16.

Burke, R.J. (1999f) Workaholism and extra-work satisfactions. *International Journal of Organizational Analysis*, 7, 352–64.

Burke, R.J., Burgess, Z., and Oberklaid, F. (2002) Workaholism, job and career satisfaction among Australian psychologists. *International Journal of Management Literature*, 2, 93–103.

Burke, R.J. and Matthiesen, S. (2004) Workaholism among Norwegian journalists: antecedents and consequences. *Stress and Health*, 20, 301–8.

Burke, R.J., Richardsen, A.M., and Mortinussen, M. (2004) Workaholism among Norwegian senior managers: new research directions. *International Journal of Management*, 21, 415–26.

Cartwright, S. (2000) Taking the pulse of executive health in the UK. *Academy of Management Executive*, 14, 16–23.

Caruso, C., Hitchcock, F., Dick, R., Russo, J., and Schmitt, J.M. (2004) *Overtime and Extended Work Shifts: Recent Findings on Illness, Injuries and Health Behaviors*. Publication No. 2004-143. Cincinnati, OH: NIOSH Publications.

Chen, C. (2006) Improving work-life balance: REBT for workaholic treatment. In R.J. Burke (ed.), *Research Companion to Working Time and Work Addiction* (pp. 310–29). Cheltenham: Edward Elgar.

Clark, A.E. (2005) Your money or your life: changing job quality in OECD countries. *British Journal of Industrial Relations*, 43, 377–400.

Clarkberg, M. and Moen, P. (2001) The time squeeze: is the increase in working time due to employer demands or employee preferences? *American Behavioral Scientist*, 44, 1115–36.

Cooper, C.L. (1996) Editorial: working hours and health. *Work and Stress*, 10, 1–4.

Crouter, A.C., Bumpus, M.F., Head, M.R., and McHale, S.M. (2001) Implications of overwork and overload for the quality of men's family relationships. *Journal of Marriage and Family*, 63, 404–16.

Crouter, A.C., Bumpus, M.F., Maguire, M.C., and McHale, S.M. (1999) Working parents, work pressures and adolescents' well-being: insights into dynamics in dual career families. *Developmental Psychology*, 25, 1453–61.

Csikszentmihalyi, M. (1990) *Flow: The Psychology of Optimal Experience*. New York, NY: HarperCollins.

Czeisler, C.A. (2006) Sleep deficit: the performance killer. *Harvard Business Review*, October, 53–9.

Defoe, D.M., Power, M.L., Holzman, G.B., Carpentieri, A., and Schulkin, J. (2001) Long hours and little sleep: work schedules of residents in obstetrics and gynecology. *Obstetrics and Gynecology*, 97, 1015–18.

DeGraaf, J. (2003) *Take Back Your Time: Fighting Overwork and Time Poverty in America*. San Francisco, CA: Berrett-Koehler.

Dembe, A.E. (2005) Long working hours: the scientific bases for concern. *Perspectives on Work*, winter, 20–22.

Dembe, A.E., Erickson, J.B., Delbos, R.G., and Banks, S.M. (2005) The impact of overtime and long work hours on occupational injuries and illnesses: new evidence from the United States. *Occupational and Environmental Medicine*, 62, 588–97.

Fassel, D. (1990) *Working Ourselves to Death: The High Costs of Workaholism, the Rewards of Recovery*. San Francisco, CA: HarperCollins.

Friedman, S.D., Christensen, P., and DeGroot, J. (1998) Work and life: the end of the zero-sum game. *Harvard Business Review*, 76, 119–29.

Galambos, N.L., Sears, H.A., Almeida, D.M., and Kolaric, G. (1995) Parents' work overload and problem behavior in young adolescents. *Journal of Research on Adolescence*, 5, 201–23.

Galinsky, E. (1999) *Ask the Children: What America's Children Really Think About Working Parents*. New York, NY: William Morrow.

Galinsky, E., Bond, J.T., Kim, S.S., Bachon, L., Brownfield, E., and Sakal, K. (2005) *Overwork in America: When the Way Work Becomes Too Much*. New York, NY: Families and Work Institute.

Gallie, D. (2005) Work pressure in Europe 1996–2001: Trends and determinants. *British Journal of Industrial Relations*, 43, 351–75.

Gander, P.H., Merry, A., Millar, M.M., and Weller, J. (2000) Hours of work and fatigue-related error: a survey of New Zealand anaesthetists. *Anaesthetic and Intensive Care*, 28, 178–83.

George, D. (1997) Working longer hours: pressure from the boss or pressure from the marketers? *Review of Social Economy*, 60, 33–65.

Geurts, S., Rutte, C., and Peeters, M. (1999) Antecedents and consequences of work-home interference among medical residents. *Social Science and Medicine*, 48, 1135–48.

Golden, L. (1998) Work time and the impact of policy institutions: reforming the overtime hours law and regulation, *Review of Social Economy*, 55, 33–65.

Golden, L. and Figart, D.M. (2000a) *Work Time: International Trends, Theory and Policy Perspectives*. London: Routledge.

Golden, L. and Figart, D. (2000b) Doing something about long hours. *Challenge*, 43, 15–35.

Green, F. (2001) It's been a hard day's night: the concentration and intensification of work in late twentieth-century Britain. *British Journal of Industrial Relations*, 39, 53–80.

Green, F. (2004a) Why has work effort become more intense? *Industrial Relations*, October.

Green, F. (2004b) Work intensification, discretion, and the decline in well-being at work. *Eastern Economic Journal*, 30, 615–25.

Green, F. (2005) *Demanding Work: The Paradox of Job Quality in the Affluent Economy*. Princeton, NJ: Princeton University Press.

Green, F. and McIntosh, S. (2001) The intensification of work in Europe. *Labour Economics*, May, 291–308.

Grzywicz, J.G. and Marks, N. (2000) Reconceptualizing the work-family interface: an ecological perspective on the correlates of positive and negative spillover between work and family. *Journal of Occupational Health Psychology*, 5, 111–26.

Haas, R. (1991) Strategies to cope with a cultural phenomenon: workaholism. *Business and Health*, 36, 4.

Haenecke, K., Tiedemann, S., Nachreiner, F., and Grzech Sukalo, H. (1998) Accident risk as a function of hour at work and time of day as determined from accident data and exposure models for the German working population. *Scandinavian Journal of Work, Environment and Health*, 24, 43–8.

Harrington, J.M. (1994) Working long hours and health. *British Medical Journal*, 308, 1581–2.

Harrington, J.M. (2001) Health effects of shift work and extended hours of work. *Occupational and Environmental Medicine*, 58, 68–72.

Hayden, A. (2003) Europe's work-time alternatives. In J. de Graaf (ed.), *Take Back Your Time: Fighting Overwork and Time Poverty in America* (pp. 202–10). San Francisco, CA: Berrett-Koehler.

Hetrick, R. (2000) Analyzing the recent upward surge in overtime hours. *Monthly Labor Review*, 123(2), 30–33.

Hewlett, S.A. and Luce, C.B. (2006) Extreme jobs: the dangerous allure of the 70-hour work week. *Harvard Business Review*, December, 49–59.

Hochschild, A. (1997) *The Time Bind*. New York, NY: Henry Holt.

Iwasaki, K., Sasaki, T., Oka, T., and Hisanaga, N. (1998) Effect of working hours on biological functions related to cardiovascular system among salesmen in a machinery manufacturing company. *Industrial Health*, 36, 361–7.

Jacobs, J.A. and Gerson, K. (1998) Who are the overworked Americans? *Review of Social Economy*, 56, 442–59.

Johnstone, A. and Johnston, L. (2005) The relationship between organizational climate, occupational type and workaholism. *New Zealand Journal of Psychology*, 34, 181–8.

Kaiser, R.B. and Kaplan, R.B. (2006) The deeper world of executive development: outgrowing sensitivities. *Learning and Education*, 5, 463–83.

Kanai, A. (2006) Economic and employment conditions: Karoshi work to death and the trend of studies on workaholism in Japan. In R.J. Burke (ed.), *Research Companion to Working Time and Work Addiction*. Cheltenham: Edward Elgar.

Kanai, A., Wakabayashi, M., and Fling, S. (1996) Workaholism among employees in Japanese corporations: an examination based on the Japanese version of the workaholism scales. *Japanese Psychological Research*, 38, 192–203.

Kennedy, R.F. (1968, March 18) Address. University of Kansas, Lawrence, KS.

Killinger, B. (1991) *Workaholics: The Respectable Addicts*. New York, NY: Simon and Schuster.

Kirkcaldy, B.D., Levine, R., and Shephard, R.J. (2000) The impact of working hours on physical and psychological health of German managers. *European Review of Applied Psychology*, 50, 443–9.

Kirkcaldy, B., Trimpop, R., and Cooper, C. (1997) Working hours, job stress, work satisfaction and accident rates among medical practitioners, consultants and allied personnel. *International Journal of Stress Management*, 4, 79–87.

Kluwer, E.S., Heesink, J.A.M., and van den Vliert E. (1996) Marital conflict about the division of household labor and paid work. *Journal of Marriage and the Family*, 58, 958–69.

Kofodimos, J. (1993) *Balancing Act*. San Francisco, CA: Jossey Bass.

Kreitzman, L. (1999) *The 24-Hour Society*. London: Profile Books.

Lee, C., Jamieson, L.F., and Earley, P.C. (1996) Beliefs and fears and Type A behavior: implications for academic performance and psychiatric health disorder symptoms. *Journal of Organizational Behavior*, 17, 151–78.

Liu, Y., Tanaka, H., and The Fukuoka Heart Study Group (2002) Overtime work, insufficient sleep, and risk of non-fatal acute myocardial infarction in Japanese men. *Occupational Environmental Medicine*, 59(7), 447–51.

Loomis, D. (2005) Long work hours and occupational injuries: new evidence on upstream causes. *Occupational and Environmental Medicine*, 62, 585.

Machlowitz, M. (1980) *Workaholics: Living with Them, Working with Them*. Reading, MA: Addison-Wesley.

MacInnes, J. (2005) Work-life balance and the demands for reduction in working hours: evidence from the British Social Attitudes Survey 2002. *British Journal of Industrial Relations*, 43, 273–95.

Major, V.S., Klein, K.J., and Erhart, M.G. (2002) Work time, work interference with family, and psychological distress. *Journal of Applied Psychology*, 87, 427–36.

Meijman, T.F. and Mulder, G. (1998) Psychological aspects of workload. In P. Drenth, H. Thierry, and C. DeWolff (eds), *Handbook of Work and Organizational Psychology*, 2nd edition. Vol. 2. *Work Psychology* (pp. 5–33). Hove: Psychology Press.

Messenger, J.C. (2004) *Working Time and Worker's Preferences in Industrialized Countries: Finding the Balance*. London: Routledge.

Messenger, J.C. (2006) Decent working time: balancing the needs of workers and employers. In R.J. Burke (ed.), *Research Companion to Working Hours and Work Addiction* (pp. 221–41). Cheltenham: Edward Elgar.

Moruyama, S., Kohno, K., and Morimoto, K. (1995) A study of preventive medicine in relation to mental health among middle-management employees. Part 2. Effects of long working hours on lifestyles, perceived stress and working-life satisfaction among white-collar middle-management employees. *Nippon Elseigaku Zasshi [Japanese Journal of Hygiene]*, 50, 849–60.

Mudrack, P. (2006) Understanding workaholism: the case for behavioral tendencies. In R.J. Burke (ed.), *Research Companion to Working Time and Work Addiction* (pp. 108–28). Cheltenham: Edward Elgar.

Munck, B. (2001) Changing a culture of face time. *Harvard Business Review*, November, 3–8.

Nachreiner, F., Akkermann, S., and Haenecke, K. (2000) Fatal accident risk as a function of hours into work. In S. Hornberger, P. Knauth, G. Costa, and S. Folkard (eds), *Shift Work in the 21st Century* (pp. 19–24). Frankfurt: Peter Lang.

Nash, L. and Stevenson, H. (2004a) Success that lasts. *Harvard Business Review*, February, 102–9.

Nash, L. and Stevenson, H. (2004b) *Just Enough: Tools for Creating Success in Your Work and Life*. New York, NY: John Wiley.

Ng, T.W.H., Sorensen, K.L., and Feldman, D.C. (2007) Dimensions, antecedents, and consequences of workaholism: a conceptual integration and extension. *Journal of Organizational Behavior*, 28, 111–36.

Oates, W. (1971) *Confessions of a Workaholic: The Facts about Work Addiction*. New York, NY: World Publishing.

Porter, G. (1996) Organizational impact of workaholism: suggestions for researching the negative outcomes of excessive work. *Journal of Occupational Health Psychology*, 1, 70–84.

Porter, G. (2004) Work, work ethic and work excess. *Journal of Organizational Change Management*, 17, 424–39.

Reich, R.B. (2000) *The Future of Success*. New York: Knopf.
Rifkin, J. (2004) *The European Dream*. New York, NY: Tarcher/Penguin.
Rissler, A. (1977) Stress reactions at work and after work during a period of quantitative overload. *Ergonomics*, 20, 13–16.
Robinson, B.E. (1998) *Chained to the Desk: A Guidebook for Workaholics, Their Partners and Children and the Clinicians Who Treat Them*. New York, NY: New York University Press.
Rones, P.L., Ilg, R.E., and Gardner, J.M. (1997) Trends in hours of work since the mid-1970s. *Monthly Labor Review*, 120, 3–14.
Rosa, B.R. (1995) Extended work shifts and excessive fatigue. *Journal of Sleep Research*, 4, 51–6.
Schaef, A.W. and Fassel, D. (1988) *The Addictive Organization*. San Francisco, CA: Harper Row.
Schuster, M. and Rhodes, S. (1985) The impact of overtime work on industrial accident rates. *Industrial Relations*, 24, 234–46.
Scott, K.S., Moore, K.S., and Miceli, M.P. (1997) An exploration of the meaning and consequences of workaholism. *Human Relations*, 50, 287–314.
Shields, M. (1999) Long working hours and health. *Health Reports*, 11, 33–48.
Shimomitsu, T. and Levi, L. (1992) Recent working life changes in Japan. *European Journal of Public Health*, 2, 76–96.
Smith, L., Hammond, T., Macdonald, I., and Folkard, S. (1998) 12-hr shifts are popular but are they a solution? *International Journal of Industrial Ergonomics*, 21, 323–31.
Sparks, K., Cooper, C., Fried, Y., and Shirom, A. (1997) The effects of hours of work on health: a meta-analytic review. *Journal of Occupational and Organizational Psychology*, 70, 391–409.
Spence, J.T. and Robbins, A.S. (1992) Workaholism: definition, measurement, and preliminary results. *Journal of Personality Assessment*, 58, 160–78.
Spurgeon, A., Harrington, J.M., and Cooper, C. (1997) Health and safety problems associated with long working hours: a review of the current position. *Occupational and Environmental Medicine*, 54, 367–75.
Staines, G.L. and Pleck, J.H. (1984) Non standard work schedules and family life. *Journal of Applied Psychology*, 69, 515–23.
Tucker, P., Folkard, S., and Macdonald, I. (2003) Rest breaks reduce accident risk. *Lancet*, 361, 680.
Uehata, T. (1991) Long working hours and occupational stress-related cardiovascular attacks among middle aged workers in Japan. *Journal of Human Ergonomics*, 20, 147–53.
van der Hulst, M. (2003) Long work hours and health. *Scandinavian Journal of Work, Environment and Health*, 2, 171–88.

van der Hulst, M. and Geurts, S. (2001) Associations between overtime and psychological health in high and low reward jobs. *Work and Stress*, 156, 227–40.

van der Hulst, M., van Veldenhoven, M., and Beckers, D. (2006) Overtime and need for recovery in relation to job demands and job control. *Journal of Occupational Health*, 48, 11–19.

Wiehert, I.C. (2002) Job insecurity and work intensification: the effects on health and well-being. In B.J. Burchell, D. Lapido, and F. Wilkinson (eds), *Job Security and Work Intensification* (pp. 57–74). London: Routledge.

Worrall, L. and Cooper, C.L. (1999) *Quality of Work Life Survey*. London: Institute of Management.

Zhdanova, L., Allison, L.K., Pui, S.Y., and Clark, M.A. (2006) A meta-analysis of workaholism antecedents and outcomes. SIOP conference, Dallas, TX, May.

6

Gender Differences in Burnout: A Literature Review

Ayala Malach-Pines and Sigalit Ronen

Who is more burned out, men or women? Some, mostly men, will argue that men are more burned out. After all, men work in more demanding careers, work longer hours and many of them have the added economic responsibility of supporting a wife and a family. Others, mostly women, will argue that women are more burned out. After all, after a demanding day at work, women return to a "second shift" at home (Hochshield, 1989), where they carry the main physical and emotional responsibility for the care of the home and the family.

Studies of gender differences in burnout reveal inconsistent results (Schaufeli and Enzmann, 1998). Some studies report higher levels of burnout among women (e.g., Etzion, 1984; 1987; Etzion and Pines, 1986; Golembiewski, Scherb, and Boudreu, 1993; Maslach and Jackson, 1986; Pastore and Judd, 1993; Pines and Aronson, 1988; Toker et al., 2005). Some studies report higher levels of burnout among men (e.g., Brake, Bloemendal, and Hoogstraten, 2003; Burke, Greenglass, and Schwarzer, 1996; Cahoon and Rowney, 1984; Greenglass and Burke, 1988; Norvell, Hills, and Murrin, 1993: Zani and Pietrantoni, 2001). And some studies report no gender differences in burnout (e.g., Benbow and Jolley, 2002; Etzion, 1988; Greenglass, 1991; Greenglass, Burke, and Ondrack, 1990; Hakanen, 1999; Izraeli, 1988; Jawahar, Stone, and Kisamore, 2007; Maslach and Jackson, 1985).

The controversy about gender differences in burnout, and the related question about the possible reason or reasons for such gender differences or lack thereof, is related to a much broader question regarding the causes of sex differences in human behavior in general. Theories about the origins of gender differences in human behavior tend to be divided into two major categories:

theories that focus on *biological* explanations for sex differences and *social* theories that focus on social forces as the explanation for most gender differences (Wood and Eagly, 2002). Among the biological theories, the two leading theories are evolutionary theory and psychoanalytic theory. Among the social theories, two leading theories are social role theory and social construction theory.

According to the *evolutionary* theory, during the thousands of years that modern man's ancestors traveled in small hunting and gathering bands, the sexes did different jobs and developed different skills (Buss, 2000; Darwin, 1871). As a result of these prehistoric developments, men are goal directed and tend to place themselves in hierarchies while women have a talent for words, emotional sensitivity, empathy, a gift for networking, and a preference for cooperation (Fisher, 1999).

To feminist *psychoanalytic* theorists, gender differences are the result of different childhood experiences and different developmental tasks that boys and girls face growing up (Chodorow, 1978; Rubin, 1983). Boys, to develop a masculine gender identity, have to suppress their emotional attachment to their mother and shift their identification to their father. As a result, the masculine self is separate and autonomous. Girls do not have to separate from their mother to develop feminine gender identity. As a result, theirs is a "self in relations" (Jordan and Surrey, 1986; Miller, 1987).

To *social role* theory, individuals occupy multiple roles and may change their behavior accordingly. The theory emphasizes the role of social forces such as cultural norms, gender roles, stereotypes, and gender role expectations (Basow, 1992; Deaux and LaFrance, 1998; Eagly, 1987; Spence and Buckner, 2000). Culture is viewed as influencing gender, as evidenced in the variety of gender roles across cultures (Myers, 1999; Triandis, 1994; Williams and Best, 1990).

According to *social construction* theory, reality is socially constructed (Bohan, 1997; Butler, 1990; DeLamater and Hyde, 1998; Gergen and Davis, 1997; Goldner, 1991; 1998; Mednick, 1989). There is no one "reality" that is simultaneously experienced by all people. Different cultures have their own unique understandings of the world. The behavior of men and women is varied across social contexts as a result of the different meanings ascribed to these contexts (e.g., Bohan, 1997; Gergen and Davis, 1997). Further, people tend to divide the world into pairs of opposites: us/them, good/bad, men/women. The same tendency also makes them emphasize the differences between those pairs and hide the fact that the similarity is often greater than the difference (Tavris, 1992).

Social constructionists criticize the views of "cultural feminists" such as Chodorow and Miller as essentialist views that construe gender as residing within the individual and portray men and women as opposites (Butler, 1990: Bohan, 1997). They urge us to be cognizant of the "coercive and regulatory consequences" of a portrayal of women or of men as a homogenous class, a "seamless category" (Butler, 1990: 4). Instead of emphasizing the differences between men and women, social constructionists emphasize the subjective experience of every individual.

Based on the biological perspective, including both evolutionary and psychoanalytic theories, gender differences in burnout can be expected to be large and universal. Based on the social perspective, including both social role and social construction theories, gender differences in burnout can be expected to vary across cultural contexts. In terms of their size, according to social role theory gender differences in burnout can be expected to be small; according to social construction theory individual differences in burnout can be expected to be larger than gender differences.

Following this introduction on the subject of gender, a few words of introduction about burnout seem in order.

Burnout, experienced as a state of physical, emotional, and mental exhaustion (Pines and Aronson, 1988), a lowered sense of accomplishment, and depersonalization (Maslach, 1982; Maslach and Leiter, 1997), has been described as the end result of a process of emotional attrition (e.g., Freudenberger, 1980: 13; Maslach, 1982: 3; Pines, 1993: 386; Pines and Aronson, 1988: 9). Research has shown that exhaustion is the central, dominant, and most significant component of burnout (Burke and Richardsen, 1993; Koeske and Koeske, 1989; Schaufeli and Ven Dierendonck, 1993; Wallace and Brinkeroff, 1991) and its most intrinsic dimension (Evans and Fischer, 1993; Garden, 1987). The exhaustion component represents the individual dimension of burnout. The depersonalization (or cynicism) component represents the interpersonal dimension of burnout. It refers to a negative and extremely detached response to clients, patients or other people with whom the service provider works. The component of reduced accomplishment or efficacy represents the self-evaluation dimension of burnout. It refers to feelings of incompetence, inefficiency, and a lack of achievement and productivity at work.

According to Leiter's (1989) model of burnout, emotional exhaustion is the first critical sign of burnout. Employees respond to emotional exhaustion by developing depersonalization toward their clients, and as commitment to their clients diminishes and exhaustion continues, they a experience loss of their sense of personal accomplishment and develop a full burnout syndrome.

Burnout has been found to be associated with various negative work outcomes such as absenteeism, turnover, low productivity, decreased job satisfaction, and reduced commitment to the job or organization. It has been shown to be associated with both physical illness and mental health problems such as anxiety and depression. For this reason, great theoretical, empirical, and practical efforts have been invested in identifying predictors and correlates of burnout.

Since its introduction into the scientific literature in the mid 1970s and until the turn of the twentieth century, the majority of studies on burnout focused on the burnout of those working with people in the human services (e.g., Farber, 1983; Freudenberger, 1980; Maslach, 1982; Maslach, Schaufeli, and Leiter, 2001; Pines and Aronson, 1988).

There are three characteristics that *human service professionals* who work with people share. First, they frequently perform emotionally taxing work. Second, they share certain characteristics that made them choose a career in the human services. Third, they share a "client centered" orientation. Theses three characteristics are well documented antecedents of burnout (Pines and Aronson, 1988).

In the human service professions, people work with other people in emotionally demanding situations over extended periods of time. The professionals are exposed to their clients' psychological, physical, emotional, social, and economic problems and are expected to be both skilled and professionally concerned.

Another source of stress stems from the special characteristics of the professionals themselves. Most times those who choose to help others as a career are individuals who are particularly sensitive to the needs of others and to their pain and suffering. Occupational identity can be enhanced by the homogeneity of the people selecting a particular occupation. The nature of the tasks involved acts as a screening device, attracting people with particular personality attributes. Most human service professionals are feeling types and are essentially humanitarian. Their dominant motivation is to help people in trouble or in pain and they describe themselves as empathic and understanding.

A third cause of burnout is the "client centered" orientation that characterizes human service professions. In client centered orientation, the focus is on the people receiving the service. The professional's role is defined by the client's needs. Feelings are legitimate only when expressed by the clients. Most human relationships are symmetrical, but the therapeutic relationship (like parenthood) is not; it is complementary: the professional gives and the client receives.

This asymmetry can become stressful for the professional providing help. Its effects are doubled when combined with the emotional intensity characterizing human service work and with the selective group of people who choose a career in the human services. And since all three elements are present in nearly all human service work, they make burnout almost inevitable.

All three antecedents of burnout are particularly prevalent and powerful for women, especially women who carry the double burden of a career and a family.

Women are often drawn to occupations in which they work with people, especially in a helping role. According to Bulan, Erickson, and Wharton (1997), the people oriented nature of service jobs is more closely related to the traditional care-taking role of women and as such, may contribute to feelings of authenticity that can provide women with positive feelings about service work. Because of these feelings of authenticity or because of other reasons, women are disproportionately represented in professions that require contact with people in intense, painful, or emotionally demanding situations such as teaching, nursing, counseling, childcare, social work, and social welfare. In addition, women are also expected to provide this nurturance at home to their children, spouse, and aging parents.

Sex role stereotypes describe women as caring, empathic, and sensitive to the needs of others (Basow, 1992). If this characterization is true for women in general, it is no doubt even truer for women in the human services. Of the self-selected helpers, women are the most pre-determined.

The professions that many women choose are often client centered, just as the role of mother is child oriented. Being child oriented is an endless task: there is always more a "good mother" could do, and this societal norm is a source of guilt and anxiety for many women.

If a woman is sensitive and feeling, her professional struggles as a human service professional can be more frustrating than if she were not. If she is empathic, the pain and helplessness she witnesses are more painful. If she knows herself to be a caring human being, the realization that she has become numb to other people's needs and feelings is more devastating.

Indeed, studies found gender differences in job values. Young women were found to be more concerned with the well being of others, less likely than young men to accept materialism and competition, and more likely to emphasize the importance of finding meaning in life (Beutel and Marini, 1995; Nilsen, 1992) and to favor non materialistic job values (Gooderham et al., 2004).

It should be noted, however, that in recent years, a shift in gender differences related to job values has been demonstrated. The demonstrated shift shows that gender based differences in job related values are decreasing (Marini et al., 1996; Gooderham et al., 2004). The growing similarity between young men and women, which may have many causes, may be reflected in the future in growing similarity in their occupational choices. In the present, however, occupational segregation is the rule rather than the exception.

Women tend to be drawn to occupations that are not only highly demanding but also low in control, like pink or blue collar occupations (e.g., cashiers, tellers, assembly line workers, janitresses and chambermaids). The self-selection of women into these occupations may reflect gender role expectations and cultural norms that are prevalent in certain populations. According to Karasek and Theorell's (1990) demands-control model, high job demands are more harmful and destructive for employees who have little control over their work. It is control that makes the difference in the stressor–strain relationship, because employees with high job demands and high control may also experience job challenge rather than strain alone (Terry and Jimmieson, 1999). Given women's attraction and selection into low control occupations, it can be expected that women will show higher levels of burnout overall. A tentative support for this proposition is offered by Pines and Guendelman's (1995) findings which demonstrated the existence of burnout among blue collar woman. In their sample of Mexican women employed in electronics and garment assembly plants, the main cause for burnout was the fact that work did not enable these women to escape conditions of poverty or to help their families escape these conditions.

Based on everything written so far about the characteristics of work in service occupations, it can be expected that gender differences in burnout will be larger in the service professions and in the human service professions than in professions that do not involve work with people, with women scoring higher on burnout because of their special stresses associated with work in these occupations. It can further be expected that gender differences in burnout will be larger when burnout is measured using instruments that focus on emotional exhaustion than when it is measured using instruments that focus on other aspects of burnout, such as depersonalization.

Starting with the second part of this prediction, several of the studies that reported higher levels of burnout among women (e.g., Etzion, 1984; 1987; Etzion and Pines, 1986; Pines, 1987; Pines and Aronson, 1988) indeed used the Burnout Measure (BM) (Pines and Aronson, 1988; Pines, 2005), a measure that focuses on emotional exhaustion as the central, dominant, and most significant component of burnout (and found to be highly correlated with the emotional exhaustion subscale of the Maslach Burnout Inventory (MBI), Schaufeli and Van Dierendonck, 1993). Other studies also showed women scored significantly higher than men in emotional exhaustion (e.g., Antoniou, Polychroni, and Vlachakis, 2006; Hakan, 2004; Pastore and Judd, 1993). On the other hand, studies in which men were found to be more burned out than women used the MBI and found men scored higher in depersonalization (e.g., Brake, Bloemendal, and Hoogstraten, 2003; Greenglass and Burke, 1988; Hakan, 2004).

However, the use of the BM does not always reveal gender differences in burnout. For example, a study of gender differences in Israelis' responses to the Palestinian uprising, the Intifada, that used the BM, revealed significant differences in burnout among left wingers, right wingers, settlers in the occupied territories, Orthodox Jews, Arabs, and army officers, but no differences in burnout across gender (Pines, 1997). Men and women on the political left responded more similarly to each other than to men and women on the political right. This suggests that it is not necessarily the measure (the BM), but rather the experience that the measure is assessing that is responsible for the gender differences in burnout found in this study.

In addition to the measure of burnout, the structural characteristics of the work involved seem to have an effect on gender differences in burnout. For example, in a recent study by Rupert and Morgan (2005) that explored the influence of work setting on burnout among professional psychologists, it was found that women psychologists experienced higher levels of emotional exhaustion in agency settings but not in either solo or group independent practices. On the other hand, men psychologists experienced higher levels of emotional exhaustion in group independent practices.

Getting to the prediction that gender differences in burnout will be larger in human service professions than in professions that do not involve work with people, two studies reported in Pines and Aronson (1988) enabled an examination of this prediction. The first study involved 220 human service professionals (47 men and 173 women) who participated in a burnout workshop. Their mean burnout was 3.7 (S.D. = .6) (indicating danger signs of burnout). The mean burnout for men was 3.5; the mean for women was 3.8. The second study included 294 undergraduate students at UC Berkeley (106 men and 188 women) who took an elective class in Social Psychology. Their mean burnout was 3.3 (S.D. = .8). The mean burnout for men was 3.2; the mean for women was 3.3. Comparison of the findings of the two studies reveals higher levels of burnout and larger gender differences among the human service workers than among the students (that included, besides psychology students, students from all other university faculties). These findings provide tentative support for the prediction of larger gender differences in burnout in the human service professions and can be explained by the characteristics of these professions as well as the characteristics of women outlined earlier.

However, gender differences in burnout have also been found in non-human service professions. In a recent longitudinal study, Ronen (2008) asked 874 engineering students (67 percent male, 33 percent female) to rate their satisfaction with their chosen profession and the extent to which they expect to be self-actualized as engineers. Female students reported lower levels of both satisfaction in their chosen profession (t = 5.96, p<.00) and expectations for self-actualization (t = 3.79, p<.00) than male students. Fifteen months later, in a sample of 131 employed engineers (61 percent male, 39 percent female) it was found that women's mean burnout (2.79; S.D. = .89) was significantly higher than men's mean burnout (2.40; S.D. = .87). Furthermore, lower satisfaction with the chosen engineering profession and lower expectation for self-actualization at work than 15 months earlier, predicted higher burnout only among women

(-.36, p<.05 and -.48, p<.01 respectively) and explained 27 percent of the variability in their burnout (compared to 3 percent in men).

Another longitudinal study that investigated gender differences in burnout, in coping and in the availability of social support among high-tech engineers (Ronen and Pines, 2008), revealed gender differences in burnout at both Time 1 and 2 (using the BM), with women engineers reporting higher burnout than men. Participants in Time 1 were 284 engineers (56 percent male, 44 percent female). Participants in Time 2 were 118 engineers (48 percent male, 52 percent female). Men's mean burnout at Time 1 was 2.9, women's mean was 3.2 (S.D. = .7 for both). In Time 2, men's mean burnout was 3.0, women's mean was 3.3 (S.D. = .6 for both). These gender differences in burnout were interpreted as related to women's greater tendency to utilize emotion focused coping, their smaller peer support in the engineering profession, and greater work-family conflict.

Some studies compared the influence of gender on burnout to the influence of culture. In one such study, gender differences in burnout and coping of 503 human service professionals in Israel and the United States were compared (Etzion and Pines, 1986). A two-way analysis of variance revealed main effect for gender (women were more burned out than men, $F(1,501) = 25.3$) and an even larger main effect for culture (Americans were more burned out than Israelis, $F(1,501) = 93.4$) but no interaction effect.

Other studies also demonstrated a greater influence of culture on burnout when compared to the influence of gender. For example, Linzer et al. (2002), who examined gender differences in physician burnout in the Netherlands and the United States, discovered that US women experienced more burnout than US men, but the gender difference in burnout among Dutch physicians was not significant. The finding was explained in the fewer work hours and greater work control of women in the Netherlands compared to those in the US.

Within culture, gender division of labor can explain differences in burnout. Hakanen (1999) found a slightly higher number of burnout cases among women in Finland than men, which were explained by the fact that the five industries with the highest incidence of burnout predominantly employed women (hotels and catering, banking, insurance, education, and research).

As a result of such findings, Kulik (2006) argued that employment status has a greater effect on burnout than gender, and Greenglass (1991) suggested that instead of focusing on gender differences in burnout, research should focus on gender related differences in precursors of burnout, because while work sources appear to be the primary precursors of burnout in men, predictors of burnout in women include both work and family variables, such as role conflict.

Getting back to the controversy between the *biological* explanations for sex differences and the *social* explanation for gender differences, we can now examine the evidence presented in light of the contradictory predictions generated by these theories.

The finding that women are employed in high burnout professions (Hakanen, 1999), are drawn to work in human services occupations (Pines and Aronson, 1988), and tend to be more concerned than men with the well being of others (Beutel and Marini, 1995; Nilsen, 1992) can be explained by *evolutionary* theory in the thousands of years of human evolution in which the sexes did different jobs and developed different skills (Buss, 2000; Darwin, 1871), including women's talent for words, emotional sensitivity, and empathic abilities (Fisher, 1999).

These gender differences, which can be viewed as an explanation for the gender differences in burnout, can also be explained by feminist *psychoanalytic* theorists in the different developmental tasks that boys and girls face growing up (Chodorow, 1978; Rubin, 1983), as a result of which women's self is a "self in relations" (Jordan and Surrey, 1986; Miller, 1987).

On the other hand, the findings of cross-cultural differences in burnout (e.g., Linzer et al., 2002), and the finding that cross cultural differences in burnout are greater than gender differences in burnout (e.g., Etzion and Pines, 1986), contradicts the biological theories in support of social theories. According to *social role theory*, culture influences gender roles (Myers, 1999; Triandis, 1994; Williams and Best, 1990) and the result can be gender differences in burnout. An explanation for the findings of no gender differences in burnout is offered by *social construction theory* which views the behavior of men and women as varied across social contexts as a result of the different meanings ascribed to these contexts (e.g., Bohan, 1997; Gergen and Davis, 1997).

Wood and Eagly (2002) reviewed cross-cultural evidence for gender differences in behavior, especially in the activities that contribute to sex-typed divisions of labor. They concluded that sex differences derive from the interaction between the physical specialization of the sexes, especially female reproductive capacity, and the economic and social structural aspects of societies. This chapter concludes, similarly, that gender differences in burnout seem to derive from an interaction between occupational specialization of the sexes (explained by evolutionary, psychoanalytic, and social role theories) and social structural aspects of societies (explained by social role and social construction theories). This explanation can account for the cases in which men reported higher burnout (expressed in depersonalization), cases in which women reported higher burnout (expressed in emotional exhaustion), and cases in which gender differences in burnout were not found (because men and women encountered similar burnout causing stresses).

In short, the answer to the question that opened this chapter—who is more burned out, men or women?—is: it depends, on the culture, the profession, the job, the other stresses encountered, and the measure used for assessing the level of burnout.

References

Antoniou, A.S., Polychroni, F., and Vlachakis, A.N. (2006). Gender and age differences in occupational stress and professional burnout between primary and high school teachers in Greece. *Journal of Managerial Psychology*, 21, 682–90.

Basow, S. (1992). *Gender Stereotypes and Roles*. Pacific Grove, CA: Brooks/Cole.

Benbow, S.M. and Jolley, D.J. (2002). Burnout and stress amongst old age psychiatrists. *International Journal of Geriatric Psychiatry*, 17, 710–14.

Beutel, A.M. and Marini, M.M. (1995). Gender and values. *American Sociological Review*, 60, 436–48.

Bohan, J.S. (1997). Regarding gender: essentialism, constructionism and feminist psychology. In M.M. Gergen and S.N. Davis (eds), *Toward a New Psychology of Gender* (pp. 31–47). New York: Routledge.

Brake, T.H., Bloemendal. E., and Hoogstraten, J. (2003). Gender differences in burnout among Dutch dentists. *Community Dent Oral Epidemiology*, 31, 321–7.

Bulan, H.F., Erickson, R.J., and Wharton, A.S. (1997). Doing for others on the job: the affective requirements of service work, gender, and emotional well-being. *Social Problems*, 44, 235–56.

Burke, R.J., Greenglass, E.R., and Schwarzer, R. (1996). Predicting teacher burnout over time: effects of work stress, social support, and self-doubts on burnout and its consequences. *Anxiety, Stress, and Coping: An International Journal*, 9, 261–75.

Burke, R.J. and Richardsen, A.M. (1993). Psychological burnout in organizations. In R.T. Golembiewski (ed.), *Handbook of Organizational Behavior* (pp. 263–99). New York: Marcel Dekker.

Buss, D. (2000). *The Dangerous Emotion*. New York: The Free Press.

Butler, J. (1990). *Gender Trouble: Feminism and the Subversion of Identity*. London: Routledge.

Cahoon, A.R. and Rowney, J.I.A. (1984). Managerial burnout: a comparison by sex and level of responsibility. *Journal of Health and Human Resources Administration*, 7, 249–63.

Chodorow, N. (1978). *The Reproduction of Mothering*. Berkeley CA: UC Press.

Darwin, C. (1871). *The Descent of Man and Selection in Relation to Sex*. New York: D. Appleton.

Deaux, K. and LaFrance, M. (1998). Gender. In D. Gilbert, S.T. Fiske, and G. Lindzey (eds), *Handbook of Social Psychology* (4th edn). New York: Random House.

DeLamater, J.D. and Hyde, J.S. (1998). Essentialism vs. social constructionism in the study of human sexuality. *Journal of Sex Research*, 35, 10–18.

Eagly, A. (1987). *Sex Differences in Social Behavior: A Social-Role Interpretation*. Hillsdale, NJ: Erlbaum.

Etzion, D. (1984). The moderating effect of social support on the relationship of stress and burnout. *Journal of Applied Psychology*, 69, 615–22.

Etzion, D. (1987). Burning out in management: a comparison of women and men in matched organizational positions. *Israel Social Science Research*. Special issue: Women in Israel, 5, 147–63.

Etzion, D. (1988). The experience of burnout and work/non work success in male and female engineers: a matched pair comparison. *Human Resource Management Journal*, 27, 163–79.

Etzion, D. and Pines, A.M. (1986). Sex and culture in burnout and coping among human service professionals. *Journal of Cross Cultural Psychology*, 17, 191–209.

Evans, B.K. and Fischer, D.G. (1993). The nature of burnout: a study of the three factor model of burnout in human service and non human service samples. *Journal of Occupational and Organizational Psychology*, 66, 29–38.

Farber, B.A. (ed.) (1983). *Stress and Burnout in the Helping Professions*. New York: Pergamon.

Fisher, H. (1999). *The First Sex: The Natural Talents of Women and How They Are Changing the World*. New York: Random House.

Freudenberger, H.J. (1980). *Burn-out: The High Cost of High Achievement*. Garden City, NY: Doubleday.

Garden, A.M. (1987). Depersonalization: a valid dimension of burnout? *Human Relations*, 40, 545–60.

Gergen, M.M. and Davis, S.N. (eds) (1997). *Toward a New Psychology of Gender*. New York: Routledge.

Goldner, V. (1991). Toward a critical relational theory of gender. *Psychoanalytic Dialogues*, 1, 249–72.

Goldner, V. (1998). Theorizing gender and sexual subjectivity: modern and postmodern perspectives. Paper presented at the conference on Gender and Contemporary Perspectives in Psychoanalysis. November 26–28, Israel.

Golembiewski, R.T., Scherb, K., and Boudreu, R.A. (1993). Burnout in cross-national settings: generic and model-specific perspectives. In W. Schaufeli, C. Maslach, and T. Marek (eds), *Professional Burnout: Recent Developments in Theory and Research* (pp. 217–34). Washington DC: Taylor and Francis.

Gooderham, P., Nordhaug, O., Ringdal, K., and Birkelund, G.E. (2004). Job values among future business leaders: the impact of gender and social background. *Scandinavian Journal of Management*, 20, 277–95.

Greenglass, E.R. (1991). Burnout and gender: theoretical and organizational implications. *Canadian Psychology*, 32, 562–74.

Greenglass, E.R. and Burke, R.J. (1988). Work and family precursors of burnout in teachers: sex differences. *Sex Roles*, 18, 215–29.

Greenglass, E., Burke, R.J., and Ondrack, M. (1990). A gender-role perspective of coping and burnout. *Applied Psychology: An International Review*, 39, 5–27.

Hakan, S. (2004). An analysis of burnout and job satisfaction among Turkish special school headteachers and teachers, and the factors effecting their burnout and job satisfaction. *Educational Studies*, 30, 291–306.

Hakanen, J. (1999). Gender-related differences in burnout. *Tiendonvalitys*, Special Issue, 1–6.

Hochshield, A. (1989). *The Second Shift*. New York: Viking Press.

Izraeli, D.N. (1988). Burning out in medicine: a comparison of husbands and wives in dual career couples. *Journal of Social Behavior and Personality*, 3, 329–46.

Jawahar, I.M., Stone, T.H., and Kisamore, J.L. (2007). Role conflict and burnout: the direct and moderating effects of political skill and perceived organizational support on burnout dimensions. *International Journal of Stress Management*, 14, 142–59.

Jordan, J.V. and Surrey, J.L. (1986). The self in relations: empathy and the mother-daughter relationship in the psychology of today's woman. In T. Barn and D.W. Cantor (eds), *New Psychoanalytic Visions* (pp. 81–104). Hillsdale, NJ: Analytic Press.

Karasek, R.A. and Theorell, T.G. (1990). *Healthy Work: Stress, Productivity and the Reconstruction of Working Life*. New York: Basic Books.

Koeske, G.F. and Koeske, R.D. (1989). Construct validity of the Maslach Burnout Inventory: a critical review and conceptualization. *Journal of Applied Behavioral Science*, 25, 131–44.

Kulik, L. (2006). Burnout among volunteers in the social services: the impact of gender and employment status. *Journal of Community Psychology*, 34, 541–61.

Leiter, M.P. (1989). Conceptual implications of two models of burnout: a response to Golembiewski. *Group and Organization Studies*, 14, 15–22.

Linzer, M., McMurray, J.E., Mechteld, R.M.V., Oort, F.J., Smets, E.M.A., and Hanneke, C.J.M.H. (2002). Sex differences in physician burnout in the United States and the Netherlands. *Journal of the American Women's Medical Association*, 57, 191–3.

Marini, M., Pi-Ling Fan, M., Finley, E., and Beutel, A.M. (1996). Gender and job values. *Sociology of Education*, 69, 49–65.

Maslach, C. (1982). *Burnout: The Cost of Caring*. Englewood Cliffs, NJ: Prentice Hall.

Maslach, C. and Jackson, S. (1985). The role of sex and family variables in burnout. *Sex Roles*, 12, 837–51.

Maslach, C. and Jackson, S. (1986). *Maslach Burnout Inventory Manual*. Palo Alto, CA: Consulting Psychologist Press.

Maslach, C. and Leiter, M.P. (1997). *The Truth About Burnout: How Organizations Cause Personal Stress and What To Do About It*. San Francisco, CA: Jossey Bass.

Maslach, C., Schaufeli, W.B., and Leiter, P.M. (2001). Job Burnout. *Annual Review of Psychology*, 53, 397–422.

Mednick, M.T. (1989). On the politics of psychological constructs: stop the bandwagon, I want to get off. *American Psychologist*, 44, 1118–23.

Miller, B.J. (1987). *Toward a New Psychology of Women*. Boston, MA: Beacon Press.

Myers, D. (1999). *Social Psychology*. International Edition. Boston, MA: McGraw Hill.

Nilsen, A. (1992). *Women Ways of Caring: A Life-Course Approach to The Occupational Careers of Three Cohorts of Engineers and Teachers*. Bergen: Department of Sociology, Bergen University.

Norvell, N.K., Hills, H.A., and Murrin, M.R. (1993). Understanding burnout in male and female law enforcement officers. *Psychology of Women Quarterly*, 3, 289–301.

Pastore, D.L. and Judd, M.R. (1993). Gender differences in burnout among coaches of women's athletic teams at 2-year colleges. *Sociology of Sport Journal*, 10, 205–12.

Pines, A.M. (1987). Gender differences in marriage burnout. *Israel Social Science Research*, Special issue: Women in Israel, 5, 60–75.

Pines, A.M. (1993). Burnout. In L. Goldberger and S. Breznitz (eds), *Handbook of Stress* (pp. 386–402) (2nd edn). New York: Free Press.

Pines, A.M. (1997). Gender differences in burnout: Israeli's response to the intifada. *European Psychologist*, 2, 28–34.

Pines, A.M. (2005). The Burnout Measure Short Version (BMS). *International Journal of Stress Management*, 12, 78–88.

Pines, A.M. and Aronson, E. (1988). *Career Burnout: Causes and Cures*. New York: The Free Press.

Pines, A. and Guendelman, S. (1995), Exploring the relevance of burnout to Mexican blue collar women. *Journal of Vocational Behaviour*, 47(1), 1–19.

Ronen, S. (2008). Gender differences in stress, burnout and well-being among engineers: a longitudinal study. Unpublished manuscript.

Ronen, S. and Pines, A.M. (2008). Gender differences in engineers' burnout. *Equal Opportunities International*, 27(8), 677–91.

Rubin, L. (1983). *Intimate Strangers*. New York: Harper and Row.

Rupert, P.A. and Morgan, D.J. (2005). Work setting and burnout among professional psychologists. *Professional Psychology: Research and Practice*, 36(5), 544–50.

Schaufeli, W.B. and Enzmann, D. (1998). *The Burnout Companion to Study and Practice: A Critical Analysis*. London and Philadelphia, PA: Taylor and Francis.

Schaufeli W.B. and Van Dierendonck, D. (1993). The construct validity of two burnout measures. *Journal of Organizational Behavior*, 14, 631–47.

Spence, J.T. and Buckner, C.E. (2000). Instrumental and expressive traits, trait stereotypes and sexist attitudes: what do they signify? *Psychology of Women Quarterly*, 24, 44–62.

Tavris, C. (1992). *The Mismeasure of Women*. New York: Simon and Schuster.

Terry, D.J. and Jimmieson, N.L. (1999). Work control and employee well-being: a decade review. In C.L. Cooper and I.T. Robertson (eds), *International Review of Industrial and Organizational Psychology* (vol. 14, pp. 95–148). Chichester: Wiley.

Toker, S., Shirom, A., Shapira, I., Berliner, S., and Melamed, S. (2005). The association between burnout, depression, anxiety, and inflammation biomarkers: C-reactive protein and fibrinogen in men and women. *Journal of Occupational Health Psychology*, 10, 344–62.

Triandis, H.C. (1994). *Culture and Social Behavior*. New York: McGraw Hill.

Wallace, J. and Brinkeroff, M.B. (1991). The measurement of burnout revisited. *Journal of Social Service Research*, 14, 85–111.

Williams, J.E. and Best D.L. (1990). *Sex and Psyche: Gender and Self Viewed Cross-Culturally*. Newbury Park, CA: Sage.

Wood, W. and Eagly, A.H. (2002). A cross-cultural analysis of the behavior of women and men: implications for the origins of sex differences. *Psychological Bulletin*, 128, 699–727.

Zani, B. and Pietrantoni, L. (2001). Gender differences in burnout, empowerment and somatic symptoms among health professionals: moderators and mediators. *Equal Opportunities International*, 20, 39–48.

7

American Adolescents in the Workplace: Exploration of Health-Related Psychosocial Issues

Donald E. Greydanus, Helen D. Pratt and Dilip R. Patel

Introduction

A review of the literature on adolescents, stress, and work yields sparse research on the impact of employment on adolescents or the role of work-related stress in the life of teenagers (Cooper, 2005). Most literature on working adolescents has been focused on determining the types of adolescents who work and what safety issues exist. Very limited attention has been given to the psychosocial impact of work for these youth. When stress was addressed, researchers studied the presence or absence of diagnosable mental health disorders (including post traumatic stress disorders, anxiety disorders, and depression). This chapter will focus on what we do know about adolescents who work and the role of stress in their lives. Emphasis is placed on helping youth correct depression and substance abuse that may be precipitated or worsened by their employment experiences.

Defining Work

Employment data on youth aged 12 to 23 years is focused on those who self-report working in at least some capacity for which they are paid during any given year. The time periods are divided into; a) academic year, b) summer, and c) full-year employment. Youth who report any hours of work are included in this report. The United States federal laws govern when, where, and how many hours an adolescent can work. Youth aged 14 to 18 years (or who have not graduated high school) are only allowed to work up to 20 hours per week during the academic/school year.

Prevalence

The majority of youth in the United States, Europe, and Canada have part-time work while in school (Dupré et al., 2006). There were 17.2 million high-school youth (aged 14 to 17 years) in the United States in 2006 (US Census Bureau 2007). About a quarter of that number (4.25 million) work in some capacity during any given year. It was reported that between April and July of 2006, 21.9 million 16 to 24 year olds were employed in some capacity; with more youth employed during summer months than during the school year (Bureau of Labor Statistics, 2006). A national report on youth labor in the United States concluded that in 2000, 40 to 57 percent of youth aged 13–15 years worked part of any given year (National Institute for Occupational Safety and Health [NIOSH], 2006). Between 57 to 64 percent of youth aged 14 and 15 years worked in 1999 (Herman, 2000). Approximately 44 percent of youth aged 16–17 years are generally employed each year. That translates into 2.3 million (in 2005) and 2.4 million (in 2006) adolescents aged 16 to 17 years who worked in the United States (NIOSH, 2006).

Types of Employment

The National Research Council and Institute of Medicine (1999) reported that approximately half of working youth (ages 15–17 years) are employed in the retail sector (i.e., restaurants, fast-food outlets, grocery stores, and other retail stores). The Council also reported that a quarter of employed youth worked in the service sector (e.g., health care settings such as nursing homes). Almost one eighth work in agriculture and the rest are employed in a variety of other jobs including babysitting, cleaning houses, lawn work, clerical work, computers, construction work, and others.

Benefits of Employment for Adolescents

The National Research Council and Institute of Medicine (1999) also reported that there is strong evidence showing positive links between working during high school and subsequent vocational outcomes. This report concluded that work experience during high school leads to less unemployment, a longer duration of employment after completing schooling, and higher subsequent earnings, and promotes postsecondary educational attainment. These youth also gain other benefits such as being able to build self-esteem, develop a stronger sense of personal efficacy, learn job skills, obtain an opportunity to prepare for adult wage earning, learn responsibility, develop an orientation to occupational achievement, and develop increased physical activity in leisure time with increased working (Carrière, 2005).

Although these benefits are based on employment that is limited in intensity (usually defined as 20 hours or less per week) during the high school year (McCreary et al., 2004; National Research Council and Institute of Medicine, 1999), work experience as an adolescent can promote resilience for the later transition to young adulthood (Mortimer and Staff, 2004). While some youth work to pay for basic needs (i.e., food, clothing, school supplies), others work to earn money for extras (e.g., gas, car insurance, more expensive clothing, or a greater variety of clothing); others work to save money to purchase a car or to pay for their college expenses such as books, housing, and tuition (National Research Council and Institute of Medicine, 1999).

Risks of Employment for Adolescents

Youth who work are at risk of injury and, although rare, death while at work (Occupational Safety and Health Administration [OSHA], 2007). There are over 200,000 injuries among 14 to 17 year olds each year while at their jobs (Delp et al., 2005). There is a 20 percent increase in deaths at work among Hispanic youth (versus Caucasian and African-American youth) with the highest death rates noted in those involved in construction work (Delp et al., 2005). Agriculture has also been documented to be one of the most hazardous work environments for both adults and children (Cooper, 2005). Non-death injuries at work are higher for African American youth from families of low income (i.e., under $20,000 per year), and factors regarding these injuries are often poorly investigated (Delp et al., 2005).

High-intensity work (usually defined as more than 20 hours per week) is associated with unhealthy and problem behaviors, including low grades, low college aspirations, decreased eventual educational attainment, substance use/ abuse (e.g., cigarettes, alcohol, and marijuana), insufficient sleep and exercise, and limited time spent with families (Bachman et al., 2003; Herman, 2000; National Research Council and Institute of Medicine, 1999; OSHA, 2007).

Largie et al. (2001) examined emotional or mental health linkages for working youth and found that working was related to: 1) higher depression scores; 2) poorer relationships with parents (including fewer conversations and of poorer quality) and best friend; 3) less touch (or physical affection) with parents; 4) less time spent with family (but not friends); 5) more hours spent doing chores; 6) lower grade point average; and 7) more frequent smoking. Paternoster et al. (2003) supported these findings in their research that examined data from the National Longitudinal Survey of Youth (NLSY).

Researchers have theorized that youth are prone to injury because of several developmental factors related to whether or not an adolescent has well developed: a) cognitive abilities (i.e., abstract thinking, problem solving, and predictive skills), b) integrated thinking skills, c) motor coordination and skills, d) overall integrated adaptive skills, and d) interpersonal relationship skills. These skills are generally present in the 17–23 year old age group who has experienced a normal (i.e., no trauma or deficits) matriculation from childhood to adulthood (Greydanus et al., 2007; Pratt and Greydanus, 2006).

However, Westaby and Lowe (2005) contend that despite a youth's susceptibility to social influence, little research has examined the extent to which social factors impact a youth's risk-taking orientation and injury at work. They did conclude, however, that the working adolescent's co-worker's risk-taking was a relatively strong predictor of their personal risk-taking orientation at work. Paschall et al. (2002; 2004) describe increased alcohol use in youth working over 10 hours per week because of exposure to peers and adults who are using alcohol; other factors include demographic differences in employed and unemployed adolescents and increased access to alcohol. Carrière (2005) notes an association between increased working in youth and alcohol as well as cigarette use while Wu et al. (2003) also link work in youth with illicit drug use and increased mental health problems. The frequency of smoking and presence of nicotine dependence in the workplace also influences the ability of working teens to stop smoking (Fagan et al., 2003). Johnson (2004) lists being Caucasian as a risk factor for working youth to use drugs. Furthermore, as teenagers transition to young adulthood, unemployment in young adults increases the risk for daily smoking in females (Weden et al., 2006).

Stress and Adolescents

Occupational stress is an issue for adolescents and adults (Zimmerman et al., 2004; Fitzgerald et al., 2005). One way to measure work stress is with the Emotions at Work Scale using a 19-item scale (deCastro et al., 2006). Emotional disorders or symptoms, behavior problems, substance use or abuse are frequently thought to be behavioral manifestations of stress for both adults and adolescents. Mortimer et al. (1992a; 1992b) studied working youth with a focus on the role of stress. Results from their two studies make it clear that although stress is a normal and natural part of the human experience, prolonged stress can have serious health consequences and impair social and emotional functioning.

Work related stress is manifested differently in males and females. Reported gender differences on the impact of stress stated that the duration of an adolescent's work history had no adverse outcomes for either gender; however, the intensity of work for girls was found to be linked to school problem behavior, alcohol use, and smoking. Complexity of work for girls is also related to school problem behavior. Intensity of past work was related to boys' substance use and a decrease in their internal control (Mortimer et al., 1992a; 1992b). Dupré et al. (2006) noted that adolescents demonstrate aggressive behavior toward supervisors much as adults can, if they feel a sense of injustice from them. Their aggressive behaviors can include damaging property, punching, and verbal insults. Youth who depend financially on their jobs are more likely to engage in such acting out behavior if subjected to abuse at work (Dupré et al., 2006).

Melman et al. (2007) examined the effects of employment on the mental health of ninth graders (13–14 year olds). Findings supported that for youth who viewed their jobs as providing useful skills for their future reported experiencing psychological benefit from their employment. However, results also indicated that the greater the amount of time students reported participating in activities (i.e., work, sports, others), the higher their self-reported level of anxiety, but not for symptoms of depression or somatization. Finally, the authors concluded that boys who reported more stress at work also manifested more depressive affect, self-derogatory behaviors, and an orientation towards a more external locus of control.

McCreary et al. (2004) compared working to non-working youth and found that youth employment was associated with: 1) greater depression (especially for girls), 2) inferior relationships with parents and best friend, including less time and physical contact with parents, 3) lower grade point averages, 4) smoking, 5) substance use, and 6) negative aspects of psychological, behavioral, and social well-being when compared to their research cohorts.

Weller et al. (2003) supported these findings and also concluded that the negative effects of school-year work on academic factors and health behaviors differed by grade, but not by race/ethnicity or parent education. Next, they found that working long hours during the school year both decreased performance/engagement in school and satisfaction with amount of leisure time, and increased health risk behaviors and psychological stress.

Helping Working Adolescents Manage Stress

OSHA (2007) posted helpful hints for managing stress levels in working adolescents. OSHA suggests that adolescents, parents, teachers, and employers watch youth for signs that their jobs are extracting too much physical or mental energy. Those signs include a drop in academic performance, loss of interest in school or other pleasurable activities, a loss of energy to complete normal routines, or manifestations of anxiety (e.g., irritability, hyper- or hypoactivity, fatigue, depression, increased use of substances) (OSHA, 2007). By using a model of cooperation between the local university, schools, and community, youth leaders can be educated to encourage policies to improve work related stress in teenagers (Delp et al., 2005). It is also recommended that substance abuse preventive programs be established at work, especially for young adolescent workers (Wu et al., 2003).

DEPRESSION

Sadness is a basic emotion brought on by a current or past negative event, such as loss of a friend or family member, moving away from an established home, flunking school, or others. *Depression* is sustained sadness due to negative events of life and/or a condition that may develop on a spontaneous basis. During adolescence, depression can arise as a common mental health disorder with a prevalence of 3 to 8 percent which can interfere with day to day life and be a risk factor in suicide (Calles, 2007; Costello et al., 2003; Elliott and Smiga, 2006; Greydanus et al., 2008; Zalsman et al., 2006). A variety of mood disorders have been described by the American Academy of Psychiatry's *Diagnostic and Statistical Manual of Mood Disorders*, as listed in Table 7.1 (American Psychiatric Association, 2000).

Depression can be precipitated or worsened by stress noted in the workplace of an adolescent who is employed. Depression can also be comorbid with a variety of disorders or a variety of disorders can be worsened because of depression. These disorders include anxiety, attention-deficit/hyperactivity disorder (ADHD), oppositional defiant disorder (ODD), conduct disorder, and substance abuse disorder (including nicotine and alcohol use or abuse). Management of depressed youth includes a variety of therapies (Table 7.2) and possible psychopharmacology, such as the use of selective serotonin reuptake inhibitors (SSRIs) (Greydanus, 2006; Greydanus and Patel, 2006; Greydanus and Reed, 2006, Greydanus and Yadav, 2006; Greydanus et al., 2008). Removal from employment may be an important management tool in depression of youth with depression precipitated or worsened by events at the workplace.

Table 7.1   Types of mood disorders

Adjustment disorder with depressed mood
Bipolar disorder
Depressive disorder not otherwise specified (NOS)
Dysthymic disorder
Major depressive disorder
Mood disorder due to a general medical condition
Substance induced mood disorder

Table 7.2   Psychological therapies for depression

Individual therapy
Group therapy
Family therapy
Social skills therapy
Others

SUBSTANCE ABUSE

Tobacco

Tobacco use among adolescents is a frequently implicated drug used by adolescents who are working. One of the underlying factors in this use is the widespread use and abuse of tobacco in general society, including adolescents and young adults around the world (Eaton et al., 2006; Greydanus, 2006; Greydanus and Patel, 2006; Greydanus and Reed, 2006, Greydanus and Yadav, 2006; Heyman, 2000; Hogan, 2000; Johnston et al., 2006; WHO, 2000). Tobacco is the most frequent drug used on a daily basis by youth and this often leads to a lifetime addiction to this drug.

Nicotine is an important component in tobacco and results in the addiction quality of tobacco. Nicotine is absorbed over multiple sites, including the lungs, skin, gastrointestinal tract, and buccal mucosa. One cigarette contains about 10 mg of nicotine and smoking a typical cigarette delivers 1.0 to 3.0 mg to the central nervous system that contains many nicotine acetylcholine receptors. Introduction of smoking at the work place reinforces the tolerance to tobacco teens may acquire in other areas of their lives. They are exposed to various chemicals in the cigarette, including tar, benzopyrene, carbon monoxide, arsenous oxide, radioactive polonium, and others in addition to the nicotine (Greydanus, 2006; Greydanus and Patel, 2006; Greydanus and Reed, 2006; Greydanus and Yadav, 2006). Even exposure to tobacco in passive smoking can be dangerous. Adults addicted to tobacco (i.e., nicotine) are at significantly increased risk to eventual premature death due to lung cancer, emphysema, heart disease, oral cancer (from chewing tobacco), and other complications.

All adolescents, whether working or not, should be asked about smoking and if they do smoke, taught about the dangers of tobacco use and ways of stopping. Youth at high risk of smoking, such as through exposure in the workplace, should be screened and educated in this manner. From a public health viewpoint, advertisements encouraging and glorifying tobacco use should not be allowed, whether in movies, on television, in magazines, or elsewhere (Bauer et al., 2000). From a personal patient viewpoint, teens at work should be screened for tobacco use and offered treatment plans to quit smoking before a lifelong pattern of addiction emerges.

A variety of effective nicotine therapies are now available for these youth and primary care clinicians can be very useful in helping their adolescent patients give up smoking (Covey et al., 2000; Fiore et al., 2000; Lancaster and Stead, 2000a; 2000b; Lillington et al., 2000; Greydanus et al., 2008; Patel and Greydanus, 2000). Nicotine replacement (NT) products include the nicotine patch, gum, nasal spray, and inhaler. These NT products can double the successful cessation rates of those who seek to stop smoking without the use of medication. Though it is recommended that NT products not be taken while actively smoking, severe adverse effects (such as cardiac arrhythmias) have not been reported with the combination of both.

The nicotine patch is used for eight weeks, first of a higher strength and in four weeks, of the lower strength (Fiore et al., 2000; Greydanus et al., 2008). If local dermatologic reactions arise from the patch, patch rotation and the application of hydrocortisone cream usually corrects the problem. If vivid dreams or insomnia develop, the patch is worn only when awake. Nicotine gum (nicotine polacrilex) is not a popular vehicle for adolescents who tend not to like its bitter taste or other side effects, such as mouth soreness, jaw ache, hiccups, or dyspepsia. Some youth or young adults, however, use a gum and patch combination.

The nicotine nasal spray induces a rapid rise in serum nicotine levels and is preferred by some smokers who want to quit using tobacco. It is not used in those with asthma since the spray can stimulate bronchospasm. Other adverse effects include nasal irritation, coughing, sneezing, watery eyes, and a clear nasal discharge. The nicotine inhaler mimics the hand-to-mouth behavior of smokers and induces a low serum level of nicotine. It is used for three months on a regular basis and then gradually stopped over three months. Side effects include nasal irritation, coughing, mouth-throat irritation, and dyspepsia.

A variety of medications have been used to treat nicotine addiction in adults (see Table 7.3) (Fiore et al., 2000; Greydanus et al., 2008). Varenicline is a newer product used to block nicotine receptor sites and reduce the pleasure in smoking (Greydanus et al., 2008). Bupropion has been used to improve cessation rates of tobacco abuse to 40 percent, versus 30 percent with nicotine replacement therapy in adults. Sustained-release bupropion is prescribed in a daily oral dose of 150 mg for three days and then increased to 150 mg twice a day for 12 weeks (Shiffman et al., 2000). There should be at least eight hours between doses and a daily dose of 300 mg should not be exceeded, to reduce the risk of seizures. Bupropion may reduce nicotine cravings while improving problems of depression and weight gain noted with attempts to quit smoking. It is not given to those with epilepsy, eating disorders, neoplasm of the central

Table 7.3   **Medications used to treat adult nicotine addiction**

Bupropion
Bupspirone
Doxepin
Naltrexone
Clonidine
Nortriptyline
Mecamylamine
Oral destrose
Varenicline tartrate

nervous system, or medication that reduces the seizure threshold. Adverse effects include headaches, dry mouth, tremors, and insomnia.

Alcohol

Another drug that working youth are at risk of using is alcohol, one of the most widely consumed and abused chemicals in youth and adults around the world. Over 80 percent of 17–18 year olds in the United States have a lifetime prevalence of alcohol use, over 50 percent note they have used it over the previous month of being surveyed, and 4 percent use it on a daily basis (Eaton et al., 2006; Greydanus et al., 2008; Johnston et al., 2006). The average age of first use is 12 years in the United States and youth are encouraged to consume this chemical by all levels of the media. Thus, exposure to alcohol in the workplace becomes one more risk factor in the consumption of alcohol by adolescents that clinicians must ask about and deal with if found. Familiarity with using alcohol and misunderstanding about its serious adverse effects can lead these youth to daily drinking, binge drinking, driving a car or motorcycle while intoxicated, drinking while pregnant (i.e., fetal alcohol syndrome) or even overt alcoholism (Greydanus, 2006; Greydanus and Patel, 2006; Greydanus and Reed, 2006, Greydanus and Yadav, 2006; Greydanus et al., 2008) (Table 7.4). Some youth are genetically programmed to consume excess alcohol after learning about it from peers and the media. And some youth who consume excess alcohol may develop various abnormal laboratory results, including anemia, elevated liver enzymes (serum gamma glutamyl transpeptidase, glutamic-oxaloacetic or pyruvic transaminases, and alkaline phosphatase, bilirubin), elevated uric acid levels, and other conditions (Greydanus, 2006; Greydanus and Patel, 2006; Greydanus and Reed, 2006, Greydanus and Yadav, 2006; Greydanus et al., 2008).

Table 7.4 Consequences of adolescent alcohol consumption

Daily drinking pattern
Drinking while driving (leading to motor vehicle accidents, injury, death)
Drinking while pregnant (fetal alcohol syndrome)
Medical complications:
    Intoxication
    Gastritis
    Pancreatitis
    Toxic psychosis
    Worsening of medical conditions (e.g., diabetes, epilepsy, others)
Alcohol withdrawal syndrome (tremors, hallucinations, seizures, delirium tremens)
Alcoholism
Others

Adolescents may progress from experimentation with alcohol to more serious consumption patterns that may be encouraged by peers and others at school and work. As their alcohol consumption worsens, the adolescent becomes more and more preoccupied with becoming "high" and life can become out of control with difficulty at school and at work. There may be increased moodiness, overt depression, acting out behaviors, and lethargy. Consequences of such behavior may be flunking out of school, loss of a job, worsening depression, violence, and suicide.

Management of alcohol abuse in youth begins with the recognition that many youth are misusing alcohol, and hence screening all youth for alcohol use and misuse is important for clinicians caring for adolescents and young adults. Youth who work, especially those employed over 20 hours per week, are at risk for alcohol use and abuse. Society must avoid the concept that "everyone drinks alcohol and it is OK!" Clinicians should carefully screen for alcohol misuse and depression in youth who state they work outside their school time. Education of the potential dangers of alcohol consumption is also important for clinicians to include in their regular practice routines. If depression is identified, psychological and pharmacologic therapies may be helpful, as previously considered (Table 7.2). Further, a number of medications have been used to treat alcohol withdrawal syndrome and alcohol dependence (see Table 7.5). They are not approved for use in adolescents, but some are used by alcohol experts for this

Table 7.5   Medications used to treat adult alcoholics

Alcohol withdrawal syndrome
Clorazepate
Lorazepam
Chlordiazepoxide
Diazepam
Various antipsychotics
Alcohol dependence
Acamprosate
Calcium carbimide
Disulfiram
Naltrexone
Tiapride
Bromocriptine
Buspirone
Carbamazepine
Nalmefene
Selective serotonin reuptake inhibitors (SSRIs)
Tricyclic antidepressants (TCAs)

Source: Swift, 1999; Greydanus et al., 2008.

age group (Greydanus et al., 2008). Self-help groups, such as Alcohol Anonymous (AA), can also be very beneficial for youth who are alcoholics. The ultimate aim, therefore, is that youths should not be allowed to abuse alcohol and become depressed because of the stresses faced in the workplace and at school.

References

American Psychiatric Association (2000). *Diagnostic and Statistical Manual of Mental Disorders, Text Revision*, 4th edn. Washington, DC: American Psychiatry Association.

Bachman, J.G., Safron, J., Sy, S., and Schulenberg, J. (2003). Wishing to work: new perspectives on how adolescents' part-time work intensity is linked to educational disengagement, substance use, and other problem behaviours. *International Journal of Behavioral Development*, 27(4): 301–16.

Bauer, U.E., Johnson, T.M., Hopkins, R.S., et al. (2000). Changes in youth cigarette use and intentions following implementation of a tobacco control program: findings from the Florida Youth Tobacco Survey, 1998–2000. *JAMA*, 284(6): 723–8.

Bureau of Labor Statistics (2006). *Employment and Unemployment among Youth— Summer 2006*. News release, Friday, August 25. Washington DC: United States Department of Labor.

Calles, J.L. (2007). Depression in children and adolescents. *Prim Care: Clinics in Office Practice*, 34(2): 243–58.

Carrière, G. (2005). Weekly work hours and health-related behaviors in full time students. *Health Rep*, 16: 11–22.

Cooper, S.R. (2005). Nontraditional work factors in farm worker adolescent populations: implications for health research and interventions. *Public Health Reports*, 120(6): 622–9.

Costello, E.J., Mustillo, S., Erkanli, A., et al. (2003). Prevalence and development of psychiatric disorders in childhood and adolescence. *Arch Gen Psychiatry*, 60(8): 837–44.

Covey, L.S., Sullivan, M.A., Johnston, J.A., et al. (2000). Advances in non-nicotine pharmacotherapy for smoking cessation. *Drugs*, 59(1): 17.

deCastro, A.B., Curbou, S., Agnew, J., et al. (2006). Measuring emotional labor among young workers: refinement of the Emotions at Work Scale. *AADHN J*, 54: 201–9.

Delp, L., Brown, M., and Domenzain, A. (2005). Fostering youth leadership to address work place and environmental health issues: a university-school-community partnership. *Health Promotion Practice*, 6: 270–85.

Dupré, K.E., Inness, M., Connelly, C.E., et al. (2006). Workplace aggression in teenage part-time employees. *J Appl Psychol*, 91: 987–97.

Eaton, D.K., Kann, L., Kirchen, S., et al. (2006). Youth risk behavior surveillance: United States, 2005. *MMWR*, 55(SS-5): 1–108.

Elliott, G.R. and Smiga, S.M. (2006). Mood disorders in children and adolescents. In D.E. Greydanus, D.R. Patel, and H.D. Pratt (eds), *Behavioral Pediatrics*, 2nd edn (pp. 589–617). Lincoln, NE and New York: iUniverse Publishers.

Fagan, P., Eisenberg, M., Frazier, L., et al. (2003). Employed adolescents and beliefs about self efficacy to avoid smoking. *Addic Behav*, 28: 613–26.

Fiore, M.C., Bailey, W.C., Cohen, S.J., et al. (2000). *Treating Tobacco Use and Dependence: Clinical Practice Guideline*. Rockville, MD: US Department of Health and Human Services.

Fitzgerald, S.T., Brown, K.M., Sonnega, J.R., and Ewart, C.K. (2005). Early antecedents of adult work stress: social-emotional competence and anger in adolescence. *Journal of Behavioral Medicine*, 28(3): 223–30.

Greydanus, D.E. (2006). Psychopharmacology in the adolescent. In S.Y. Bhave, M.K.C. Nair, A. Parthasarathy, P.S.N. Menon, and D.E. Greydanus (eds), *Bhave's Textbook of Adolescent Medicine* (pp. 812–25). New Delhi: Jaypee Brothers Medical Publishers.

Greydanus, D.E., Calles, J., and Patel, D.R. (2008). *Pediatric and Adolescent Psychopharmacology*. Cambridge: Cambridge University Press.

Greydanus, D.E. and Patel, D.R. (2006). Substance abuse disorders in the adolescent. In D.E. Greydanus, D.R. Patel, and H.D. Pratt (eds), *Essential Adolescent Medicine* (pp. 695–713). New York: McGraw-Hill Medical Publishers.

Greydanus, D.E., Pratt, H.D., and Patel, D.R. (2007). Attention deficit hyperactivity disorder across the life span. *Disease of the Month*, 53(2): 65–128.

Greydanus, D.E. and Reed, W.J. (2006). Substance use and abuse in adolescents. In D.E. Greydanus, D.R. Patel, and H.D. Pratt (eds), *Behavioral Pediatrics*, 2nd edn (pp. 812–55). New York and Lincoln, NE: iUniverse Publishers.

Greydanus, D.E. and Yadav, S. (2006). Substance abuse disorders. In S.Y. Bhave, M.K.C. Nair, A. Parthasarathy, P.S.N. Menon, and D.E. Greydanus (eds), *Bhave's Textbook of Adolescent Medicine* (pp. 800–805). New Delhi: Jaypee Brothers Medical Publishers.

Herman, A.M. (2000). *Report on the Youth Labor Force*. Washington, DC: US Department of Labor.

Heyman, R.B. (2000). Tobacco and the 21st century. *State of the Art Reviews: Adolescent Medicine*, 11(1): 69–78.

Hogan, M.J. (2000). Diagnosis and treatment of teen drug use. *Med Clin No Amer*, 84(4): 927–66.

Johnson, M.K. (2004). Further evidence on adolescent employment and substance use: differences by race and ethnicity. *J Health and Soc Behav*, 45: 187–97.

Johnston, L.D., O'Malley, P.M., Bachman, J.G., and Schulenberg, J.E. (2006). *Monitoring the Future National Results on Adolescent Drug Use: Overview of Key Findings* (NIH Publication No. 07-6202). Bethesda, MD: National Institute on Drug Abuse.

Lancaster, T. and Stead, L.F. (2000a). Individual behavioral counseling for smoking cessation: Cochrane review. In *The Cochrane Library*, Issue 2. Oxford: Update Software Ltd.

Lancaster, T. and Stead, L.F. (2000b). Self-help interventions for smoking cessation: Cochrane review. In *The Cochrane Library*, Issue 2. Oxford: Update Software Ltd.

Largie, S., Field, T., Hernandez-Reif, M., Sanders, C.E., and Diego, M. (2001). Employment during adolescence is associated with depression, inferior relationships, lower grades, and smoking. *Adolescence*, 36(142): 395–402.

Lillington, G.A., Leonard, C.T., and Sachs, D.P.L. (2000). Smoking cessation: techniques and benefits. *Clinics in Chest Medicine*, 21(1): 199.

McCreary, B.T., Joiner, T.E., Schmidt, N.B., and Ialongo, N.S. (2004). Stressors and child and adolescent psychopathology: measurement issues and prospective effects. *Journal of Clinical Child and Adolescent Psychology*, 33(2): 412–25.

Melman, S., Little, S.G., and Akin-Little, K.A. (2007). Adolescent over scheduling: the relationship between levels of participation in scheduled activities and self-reported clinical symptomology. *High School Journal*, 90(3): 18–30.

Mortimer, J.T., Finch, M., Shanahan, M., and Ryu, S. (1992a). Adolescent work history and behavioral adjustment. *Journal of Research on Adolescence*, 2(1): 59–80.

Mortimer, J.T., Finch, M., Shanahan, M., and Ryu, S. (1992b). Work experience, mental health, and behavioral adjustment in adolescence. *Journal of Research on Adolescence*, 2(1): 25–57.

Mortimer, J.T. and Staff, J. (2004). Early work as a source of developmental discontinuing during the transition to adulthood. *Development and Psychopathology*, 16: 1047–70.

National Institute for Occupational Safety and Health (NIOSH) (2006). *Safety and Health Topic: Young Worker Safety and Health*. Washington, DC: NIOSH.

National Research Council and Institute of Medicine (1999). Adolescents taking their place in the world. In Michele D. Kipke (ed.), *Risks and Opportunities: Synthesis of Studies on Adolescence* (pp. 43–50). Washington, DC: National Academy Press. Available at: http://books.nap.edu/html/risks_opportunities/notice.html [Accessed: December 21, 2010].

Occupational Safety and Health Administration (OSHA) (2007). Teen Workers home page. Washington, DC: OSHA. [Online] Available at: http://www.osha.gov/SLTC/teenworkers/parents.html [Accessed: December 21, 2010].

Paschall, M.J., Flewelling, R.L., and Russell, T. (2004). Why is work intensity associated with heavy alcohol use? *J Adolesc Health*, 34: 79–87.

Paschall, M.J., Ringwalt, C.L., and Flewelling, R.L. (2002). Explaining higher levels of alcohol use among working adolescents: an analysis of potential explanatory variables. *J Stud Alcoh*, 63: 169–78.

Patel, D.R. and Greydanus, D.E. (2000). Office interventions for adolescents smokers. *State of the Art Reviews: Adolescent Medicine*, 11(3): 1–11.

Paternoster, R., Bushway, S., Brame, R., and Apel, R. (2003). The effect of teenage employment on delinquency and problem behaviors. *Social Forces*, 82(1): 297–335.

Pratt, H.D. and Greydanus, D.E. (2006). Normal psychological development. In D.E. Greydanus, D.R. Patel, and H.D. Pratt (eds), *Behavioral Pediatrics*, 2nd edn (pp. 5–36). New York and Lincoln, NE: iUniverse Publishers.

Shiffman, S., Johnston, J.A., Khayrallah, M., et al. (2000). The effect of bupropion on nicotine craving and withdrawal. *Psychopharmacology*, 148: 33.

Swift, R.M. (1999). Drug therapy for alcohol dependence. *N Engl J Med*, 340(19): 1482–90.

United States Census Bureau (2007). *Minority Population Tops 100 Million*. US Census Bureau News. Washington, DC: US Department of Commerce.

Weden, M.M., Astone, N.M., and Bishari, D. (2006). Racial, ethnic, and gendered differences in smoking cessation associated with employment and joblessness through young adulthood in US *Soc Sci and Med*, 52: 303–16.

Weller, N.F., Cooper, S.P., Basen-Engquist, K., Kelder, S.H., and Tortolero, S.R. (2003). School-year employment among high school students: effects on academic, social, and physical functioning. *Adolescence*, 38(151): 441–58.

Westaby, J.D. and Lowe, J.K. (2005). Risk-taking orientation and injury among youth workers: examining the social influence of supervisors, coworkers, and parents. *Journal of Applied Psychology*, 90(5): 1027–35.

WHO (2000). *The World Health Report 1999: Combating the Tobacco Epidemic*. Geneva: WHO.

Wu, L.T., Schlenger, W.E., and Galvin, D.M. (2003). The relationship between employment and substance abuse among students aged 12 to 17. *J Adolesc Health*, 32: 5–15.

Zalsman, G., Brent, D.A., and Weersing, V.R. (2006). Depressive disorders in childhood and adolescence: an overview. Epidemiology, clinical manifestation and risk factors. *Child Adolesc Psychiatric Clin N Am*, 15: 827–41.

Zimmerman, F.J., Christakis, D.A., and Vander Stoep, A. (2004). Tinker, tailor, soldier, patient: work attributes and depression disparities among young adults. *Soc Sci and Med*, 58: 1889–901.

8

Emotional Intelligence as a Personality Trait

Konstantinos V. Petrides

Emotional Intelligence as a Personality Trait

Although emotional intelligence (EI) has been the subject of much attention, both in the popular as well as in the academic literatures, only now are we beginning to answer some of the fundamental questions that have emerged in the field. The aim of the present chapter is to review the status of the field with reference to the distinction between ability EI and trait EI (Petrides and Furnham, 2000) and with particular emphasis on the latter of the two constructs.

The distal roots of EI can be traced back to E.L. Thorndike's (1920) 'social intelligence', which concerned the ability to understand and manage people and to act wisely in human relations. Its proximal roots lie in Gardner's (1983) work on multiple intelligences and, more specifically, his concepts of intrapersonal and interpersonal intelligence. According to Gardner (1999: 43) '*Interpersonal intelligence* denotes a person's capacity to understand the intentions, motivations, and desires of other people and, consequently, to work effectively with others', while '*Intrapersonal intelligence* involves the capacity to understand oneself, to have an effective working model of oneself – including one's own desires, fears, and capacities – and to use such information effectively in regulating one's own life.'

As a term, 'emotional intelligence' appeared several times in the literature (Greenspan, 1989; Leuner, 1966) before the first models and definitions were introduced (Payne, 1986; Salovey and Mayer, 1990). Goleman's (1995) seminal book popularized the idea beyond all expectations and also influenced most subsequent conceptualizations of EI. Subsequently, several different models of EI emerged. However, it would be fair and accurate to say that the correspondence between models and data has been generally weak, with most models dissociated from empirical evidence and most studies carried out in a theoretical vacuum.

Trait EI versus Ability EI

In the rush to create measures of the new construct, researchers and theorists overlooked the fundamental difference between *typical* versus *maximal* performance (e.g. Cronbach, 1949; Hofstee, 2001). Thus, while some researchers started to develop and use self-report questionnaires, others embarked on the development of maximum-performance tests of EI. All of them, however, assumed they were operationalizing the same construct. Unsurprisingly, this led to conceptual confusion and numerous seemingly conflicting findings.

It must be understood that the way in which individual differences variables are measured (self-report versus maximum-performance) has important and wide-ranging implications for their operationalization. In recognition of this basic fact, Petrides and Furnham (e.g. 2000; 2001) distinguished between *trait EI* (or 'trait emotional self-efficacy') and *ability EI* (or 'cognitive-emotional' ability). The former is measured through self-report questionnaires, whereas the latter ought to be measured through maximum performance tests. It is important to realize that trait EI and ability EI are two *different* constructs, a position which we have maintained for many years and which has been fully supported by empirical findings (e.g. Brannick, Wahi, Arce and Johnson, 2009; Freudenthaler, Neubauer and Haller, 2008; Warwick and Nettelbeck, 2004). The differences between the two EI constructs are summarized in Table 8.1.

It is hopefully clear that the distinction between trait EI and ability EI is predicated on the method used to measure the construct and *not* on the elements (facets) that the various models are hypothesized to encompass. As such, it is unrelated to the distinction between 'mixed' and 'ability' models of EI (Mayer, Salovey and Caruso, 2000), which is based on whether a theoretical model 'mixes' cognitive abilities and personality traits or not. Unlike the distinction between trait EI and ability EI, that between 'mixed' and 'ability' models pays no heed to the most crucial aspect of construct operationalization (i.e., the method of measurement) and explicitly proposes that cognitive abilities may be measured via self-report (see Mayer, Salovey and Caruso, 2000; Tapia, 2001). In short, the distinction between mixed versus ability models is at variance both

Table 8.1 Trait EI versus ability EI

Construct	Measurement	Conceptualization	Expected relationship to g	Construct validity evidence	Example measures	Properties of measures
Trait EI	Self-report	Personality trait	Orthogonal (i.e. uncorrelated)	Good discriminant and incremental validity vis-à-vis personality Good concurrent and predictive validity with many criteria	TEIQue	Easy to administer Standard scoring procedures Good psychometric properties
Ability EI	Performance-based	Cognitive ability	Moderate to strong correlations	Limited concurrent and predictive validity Lower than expected correlations with IQ measures	MSCEIT	Difficult to administer Atypical scoring procedures Weak psychometric properties

Note: g = general cognitive ability; TEIQue = Trait Emotional Intelligence Questionnaire (e.g. Petrides, 2009); MSCEIT = Mayer-Salovey-Caruso Emotional Intelligence Test (e.g. Mayer, Salovey and Caruso, 2002).

with established psychometric theory as well as with all available empirical evidence (for a discussion, see Petrides, 2009).

Measurement of Ability EI

The most prominent measures of ability EI are the Multifactor Emotional Intelligence Scale and its successor the Mayer-Salovey-Caruso Emotional Intelligence Test (MSCEIT; Mayer, Salovey and Caruso, 2002). The problem that ability EI tests have to tackle is the inherent subjectivity of emotional experience (e.g. Robinson and Clore, 2002; Watson, 2000). Unlike standard cognitive ability tests, tests of ability EI cannot be objectively scored because in the vast majority of emotion-related domains there are no clear-cut criteria for what may constitute a veridically correct response.

Ability EI tests have attempted to bypass this problem by relying on alternative scoring procedures, which had also been used in the past for addressing similar difficulties in the operationalization of social intelligence (e.g. 'consensus' and 'expert' scoring), but without marked success (see O'Sullivan and Ekman, 2004; Matthews, Zeidner and Roberts, 2002). It is perhaps still too early to pass final judgment on the effectiveness of these procedures and it should be noted that some progress has been achieved over the many iterations that the best of these tests have undergone (e.g. Mayer, Salovey and Caruso, 2002). However, the fact that ability EI tests, after 15 years of development, continue to grapple with questions about internal consistency and factor structure does not augur well for their future (see Brody, 2004; and Keele and Bell, 2009).

Measurement of Trait EI

The large number of trait EI measures has perhaps created an impression that the construction of psychometrically sound questionnaires is an easy business. Anyone cognizant of even the basic elements of psychometrics, particularly those relating to the validation process, knows that this could hardly be further from the truth. The fact is that very few trait EI measures have been developed within a clear theoretical framework and even fewer have any empirical foundation worth reviewing. Indicative of the confused state of the field is that virtually all self-report measures purport to provide cognitive ability operationalizations of EI.

In an effort to address the limitations of extant trait EI measures,[1] we have created the Trait Emotional Intelligence Questionnaire (TEIQue). Over the past 12 years, the various forms and translations of the TEIQue have being developed, adapted, and validated within the context of our academic research programme on trait emotional intelligence (Petrides, 2009). The TEIQue is predicated on the trait EI theory and model, which conceptualizes emotional intelligence as a constellation of emotional self-perceptions located at the lower levels of personality hierarchies (Petrides, Pita and Kokkinaki, 2007). The latest version of the long form of the TEIQue comprises 153 items, providing scores on 15 facets, four factors, and global trait EI. It is the only inventory that covers the trait EI sampling domain (see Table 8.2) comprehensively and one of few psychological measurement instruments embedded within academic research programmes of international calibre. Hitherto, the TEIQue has been translated into 15 languages (see www.psychometriclab.com).

Table 8.2   The sampling domain of trait EI

Facets	High scorers perceive themselves as ...
Adaptability	... flexible and willing to adapt to new conditions.
Assertiveness	... forthright, frank and willing to stand up for their rights.
Emotion perception (self and others)	... clear about their own and other people's feelings.
Emotion expression	... capable of communicating their feelings to others.
Emotion management (others)	... capable of influencing other people's feelings.
Emotion regulation	... capable of controlling their emotions.
Impulsiveness (low)	... reflective and less likely to give in to their urges.
Relationships	... capable of having fulfilling personal relationships.
Self-esteem	... successful and self-confident.
Self-motivation	... driven and unlikely to give up in the face of adversity.
Social awareness	... accomplished networkers with excellent social skills.
Stress management	... capable of withstanding pressure and regulating stress.
Trait empathy	... capable of taking someone else's perspective.
Trait happiness	... cheerful and satisfied with their lives.
Trait optimism	... confident and likely to 'look on the bright side' of life.

1   It is important to note that the authors of these questionnaires view their products as measures of 'emotional intelligence', not trait EI. Without exception, these questionnaires are conceptually and psychometrically flawed, not least because they are not assessing cognitive abilities of any kind.

In most cases, the existence of alternative measures for a single construct is a sign of research progress. We suspect the main reason why this is not yet the case with trait EI is that the field remains stuck in a pre-paradigmatic state in which questionnaires are being 'developed' without any reference to underlying theory, psychometric or substantive. Indeed, most authors and users of these instruments are still under the impression that EI is a unitary construct that can be measured via self-report questionnaires or via maximum-performance tests or via makeshift tasks, without any implications for its conceptualization, or for its nomological network, or for the interpretation of the resultant findings.

A related problem concerns the sampling domain on which the various EI measures (trait and ability) are based. The first step in the operationalization of any psychological construct entails defining its sampling domain, that is, the facets or elements that the construct is hypothesized to encompass (e.g. Cattell, 1973). Virtually all EI models, questionnaires and tests have bypassed this step, providing arbitrarily defined sampling domains. In the vast majority of cases, the inclusion or exclusion of facets in a model is the result of unstated or arbitrary processes.

With respect to the elements they encompass, the various models of EI tend to be complementary rather than contradictory (Ciarrochi, Chan and Caputi, 2000). Moreover, salient EI models tend to share a large number of core facets (elements), even though most of them also include isolated facets that are *prima facie* irrelevant to emotion and cognitive ability. The commonalities between the various models provided the basis for the first sampling domain of trait EI, which included shared facets and excluded isolated ones (Petrides and Furnham, 2001). The TEIQue is modelled on this sampling domain, which is presented in Table 8.2, along with a brief description of each of its different elements. The higher-order structure of the TEIQue is empirically derived, rather than arbitrarily organized into preconceived dimensions that fail to emerge in statistical analyses (Palmer, Manocha, Gignac and Stough, 2003).

Conclusion

The almost chaotic state of the EI field is set to perpetuate, especially as commercial considerations continue to necessitate quick fixes, until a sound theory, predicated on robust psychometric data, prevails. In light of the empirical evidence, such a theory may be developed only with reference to the distinction between trait EI and ability EI, with all the implications that this entails. We believe that the conceptualization flaws and operationalization dead-ends that plague ability EI will soon leave the trait emotional self-efficacy (trait EI) framework as the only genuinely scientific alternative in the field of emotional intelligence.

References

Brannick, M.T., Wahi, M.M., Arce, M. and Johnson, H.A. (2009). Comparison of trait and ability measures of emotional intelligence in medical students. *Medical Education*, 43, 1062–8.

Brody, N. (2004). What cognitive intelligence is and what emotional intelligence is not. *Psychological Inquiry*, 15, 234–8.

Cattell, R.B. (1973). *Personality and Mood by Questionnaire*. San Francisco, CA: Jossey-Bass.

Ciarrochi, J.V., Chan, A.Y.C. and Caputi, P. (2000). A critical evaluation of the emotional intelligence construct. *Personality and Individual Differences*, 28, 539–61.

Cronbach, L.J. (1949). *Essentials of Psychological Testing*. New York: Harper and Row.

Freudenthaler, H.H., Neubauer, A.C. and Haller, U. (2008). Emotional intelligence: instruction effects and sex differences in emotional management abilities. *Journal of Individual Differences*, 29, 105–15.

Gardner, H. (1983). *Frames of Mind: The Theory of Multiple Intelligences*. New York: Basic Books.

Gardner, H. (1999). *Intelligence Reframed: Multiple Intelligence for the 21st Century*. New York: Basic Books.

Goleman, D. (1995). *Emotional Intelligence*. New York: Bantam Books.

Greenspan, S.I. (1989). Emotional intelligence. In K. Field, B.J. Cohler and G. Wool (eds), *Learning and Education: Psychoanalytic Perspectives* (pp. 209–43). Madison, CT: International Universities Press.

Hofstee, W.K.B. (2001). Intelligence and personality: do they mix? In J. Collis and S. Messick (eds), *Intelligence and Personality: Bridging the Gap in Theory and Measurement* (pp. 43–60). Mahwah, NJ: Erlbaum.

Keele, S.M. and Bell, R.C. (2009). Consensus scoring, correct responses and reliability of the MSCEIT v.2. *Personality and Individual Differences*, 47, 740–47.

Leuner, B. (1966). Emotionale intelligenz und emanzipation [Emotional intelligence and emancipation]. *Praxis der Kinderpsychologie und Kinderpsychiatry*, 15, 196–203.

Matthews, G., Zeidner, M. and Roberts, R.D. (2002). *Emotional Intelligence: Science and Myth*. Cambridge, MA: MIT Press.

Mayer, J.D., Salovey, P. and Caruso, D.R. (2000). Competing models of emotional intelligence. In R.J. Sternberg (ed.), *Handbook of Human Intelligence* (pp. 396–420). New York: Cambridge University Press.

Mayer, J.D., Salovey, P. and Caruso, D.R. (2002). *The Mayer-Salovey-Caruso Emotional Intelligence Test (MSCEIT): User's Manual*. Toronto: Multi-Health Systems.

O'Sullivan, M. and Ekman, P. (2005). Facial expression recognition and emotional intelligence. In G. Geher (ed.), *Measuring Emotional Intelligence: Common Ground and Controversy*. Hauppauge, NY: Nova Science Publishing.

Palmer, B.R., Manocha, R., Gignac, G. and Stough, C. (2003). Examining the factor structure of the Bar-On Emotional Quotient Inventory with an Australian general population sample. *Personality and Individual Differences*, 35, 1191–210.

Payne, W.L. (1986). A study of emotion: developing emotional intelligence, self-integration, relating to fear, pain, and desire. *Dissertation Abstracts International*, 47, 203.

Petrides, K.V. (2009). *Technical Manual for the Trait Emotional Intelligence Questionnaires (TEIQue)*. London: London Psychometric Laboratory.

Petrides, K.V. and Furnham, A. (2000). On the dimensional structure of emotional intelligence. *Personality and Individual Differences*, 29, 313–20.

Petrides, K.V. and Furnham, A. (2001). Trait emotional intelligence: psychometric investigation with reference to established trait taxonomies. *European Journal of Personality*, 15, 425–48.

Petrides, K.V., Pita, R. and Kokkinaki, F. (2007). The location of trait emotional intelligence in personality factor space. *British Journal of Psychology*, 98, 273–89.

Robinson, M.D. and Clore, G.L. (2002). Belief and feeling: evidence for an accessibility model of emotional self-report. *Psychological Bulletin*, 128, 934–60.

Salovey, P. and Mayer, J.D. (1990). Emotional intelligence. *Imagination, Cognition and Personality*, 9, 185–211.

Tapia, M. (2001). Measuring emotional intelligence. *Psychological Reports*, 88, 353–64.

Thorndike, E.L. (1920). Intelligence and its uses. *Harper's Magazine*, 140, 227–35.

Warwick, J. and Nettelbeck, T. (2004). Emotional intelligence is …? *Personality and Individual Differences*, 37, 1091–100.

Watson, D. (2000). *Mood and Temperament*. New York: Guilford.

9

Self-Efficacy as a Central Psychological Capacity within the Construct of Positive Organizational Behavior: Its Impact on Work

Magdalini Koutsoumari and Alexander-Stamatios Antoniou

Positivity as a Focus Area in Psychology and Organizational Behavior

THE GROWTH OF POSITIVE PSYCHOLOGY AND ITS RELATION WITH WORK

Positive psychology began as a new field of psychology in 1998, with Martin Seligman being the father of the modern positive psychology movement. The value of the term "positive psychology" lies in its uniting of what had previously been scattered lines of theory and research regarding what makes life most worth living (Peterson and Park, 2003). With its focus on optimal functioning and broadly on factors that add value in life, positive psychology offers a considerable additional prospect concerning the efforts for progress in the fields of leadership and human resources, recruiting and selection. The above is mainly achieved in terms of a better understanding of the critical role that peoples' strengths and positive emotions play in terms of performance in the workplace. Moreover, the way employees feel about themselves, their work, and the people in their environment proves of great importance for their performance (Cartwright and Holmes, 2006). Psychology has focused primarily on negative aspects of human behavior, such as dysfunctions, weaknesses, and pathology (Schaufeli and Salanova, 2007). On the contrary, the increasing interest in positive psychology is related to a focus on personal strengths, optimal functioning, and well-being (Seligman and Csikszentmihalyi, 2000).

The goal of this new field of study is to investigate and understand the positive aspects of life and human disposition. At the mental process level, it is concerned with subjective experiences such as well-being, pleasure, and satisfaction (in relation to the past), hope and optimism (in relation to the future), and flow and happiness (in relation to the present) (Seligman and Csikszentmihalyi, 2000). Seligman pointed out the importance of a meaningful life which provides the highest level of attainment, since happiness originates from utilization of strengths, with the aim of serving a target that exceeds and goes beyond the individual (Seligman, Parks, and Steen, 2004). In their literature review, Seligman, Parks, and Stern (2004) investigated happiness components, and concluded that included among these were elements of pleasure (or positive emotion), engagement, and meaning, with meaning considered to be the most fulfilling path towards happiness.

It can be said that positive psychology offers a perspective that supplements the traditional focus of psychology on psychopathology, illness, and dysfunction. Thanks to the development of this new concept, more and more studies in the field of occupational health psychology (OHP) include positive aspects of health and well-being. The concept of work engagement is an example, as it forms the theoretical antipode of the extensively studied concept of "burnout." Empirical evidence shows that employees who display the syndrome of burnout feel exhausted and cynical, while their engaged co-workers feel vigorous and enthusiastic about their work (Schaufeli and Bakker, 2003).

Positive psychology is, in short, the scientific study of normal human capacities and virtues. It is about a revision or re-examination of the "average person" with interest in what is functional, right, and improving (Sheldon and King, 2001). It is an investigation of the nature of the individual who functions effectively, adapts successfully in an advanced way, and applies accustomed skills. Additionally, it attempts to explain the way in which most people manage to preserve their sense of dignity and purpose, despite any difficulties they meet in life. Sheldon and King (2001), have suggested that positive psychology simply describes the common structure and normal function of human behavior and personality. In other words, it is an attempt to adopt a broader view of human potential, motives, and capacities.

In their book *Character Strengths and Virtues: A Handbook and Classification*, Peterson and Seligman (2004) proceeded to a description and classification of the 24 strengths and virtues which allow human development and progress. Strengths theory application has been expanded to the organizational field, and strengths-based development consists of one of these applications. In particular, it focuses on human strengths' development through talent identification and talent improvement via knowledge and skills (Hodges and Clifton, 2000). At the individual level, strengths-based development involves three stages: identification of talent, qualification of the way one views himself or herself, and behavioral change (Clifton and Harter, 2003). Traces of talent can be identified in several ways, including spontaneous reactions, yearnings, rapid learning, and satisfaction (Buckingham and Clifton, 2001). Another classification system is offered by Snyder and Lopez (2002), who categorize positive psychological approaches as emotion focused (e.g., well being, flow), cognitive focused (e.g., self-efficacy, goal-setting), self based (e.g., authenticity, humility), interpersonal (e.g., forgiveness, empathy), biological (e.g., toughness), and coping approaches (e.g., humor, spirituality).

Research shows that the use of strengths can facilitate goal attainment, develop employee engagement, increase overall well-being and vitality, and determine competitive advantages (Stefanyszyn, 2007). Strengths-based development has been linked to an increase in employee engagement, which is related to business outcomes such as profitability, turnover, safety, and customer satisfaction (Harter, Schmidt, and Hayes, 2002). Other studies have demonstrated increases in positive organizational capacities, such as hope, subjective well-being, and confidence (a construct that draws heavily from Bandura's [1982] work with self-efficacy).

POSITIVE ORGANIZATIONAL BEHAVIOR (POB)

The interest in optimal function has also been increased in the field of organizational psychology, as studies of positive organizational behavior (POB) demonstrate. POB is actually an application of positive psychology in the workplace among other concepts, namely positive organizational scholarship (POS) and psychological capital (Luthans and Youssef, 2007). According to Luthans, POB is defined as "the study and application of positively oriented human resource strengths and psychological capacities that can be measured, developed, and effectively managed for performance improvement in today's workplace" (2002: 59).

POB acknowledges the existence of many positive theoretical concepts in organizational research today. Such positive concepts include those of positive affectivity, positive reinforcement, procedural justice, job satisfaction, job commitment, organizational citizenship behaviors, core self-evaluations (Youssef and Luthans, 2007). Therefore, POB attempts to offer a renewed emphasis on the importance of a positive approach. It is the added value of the positive over the negative that must be demonstrated, in order for POB's contribution to be substantive. Tetrick (2002) argued that it is very unlikely that the same mechanisms that underlie employee illness and malfunctioning constitute the opposite states of employee health and optimal functioning. It seems that POB best contributes by supplementing the traditional negative model, adopting a comprehensive perspective of the positive as well as of the negative aspects, so that criticisms of POB's one-sided positivity bias can be counteracted (Fineman, 2006).

In order for a positive psychological capacity to be included in POB, some criteria must be met, and more specifically the capacity must be characterized as positive, should hold profound theoretical foundations, extensive research basis and valid measurement tools. Additionally, the capacity must be "state-like," as in open to change and development, and have a proven effect on employees' performance. A "state-like" capacity is opposed to what is called "trait-like" capacity or characteristic, as the latter is mainly based on dispositional and relatively stable attributes. In this case, any development usually occurs a) over time, across one's life span, b) through the presence of the appropriate enabling factors and the absence of inhibiting factors, or c) through long-term professional interventions and intensive treatments (Linley and Joseph, 2004). Concerning inclusion criteria, Wright (2003) added that the mission of POB must also include the pursuit of employee happiness and health as viable goals themselves. Employee health and well-being is becoming a business value of strategic importance (Zwetsloot and Pot, 2004). Furthermore, as far as other positive approaches are concerned, we should mention that "state-like" POB is differentiated from positive emotions coming from evolutionary and neuropsychology (see Nicholsen, 1998) and the strength-based approach resulting from Gallup's concern for natural talent (Buckingham and Coffman, 1999).

Research data indicates that traits related to the character (e.g., intelligence, personality) demonstrate almost perfect test–retest correlations. On the other hand, former studies show that positive "state-like" capacities demonstrate lower, although significant, test–retest correlations than "trait-like" dimensions of personality and core self-evaluations (Luthans, Avolio, Avey, and Norman, 2007). Aside from the above available data concerning test–retest correlations, there is also evidence regarding the development of positive organizational behavior capacities through short comprehensive educational interventions.

Empirical evidence at the current time supports the claim of positive situations, like positive emotions, and "state-like" concepts such as a certain kind of self-efficacy, being related to organizational behaviors and organizational effects, and moreover having an effect on them (Stajkovic and Luthans, 1998). The main reason that the above variables may often be altered due to the influence of occasional factors is the tendency these situations have to develop independently and autonomously. The fact is that humans' positive traits, as well as "state-like" characteristics, may predict more temporary positive situations. However, those characteristics affect organizational behaviors and performance in an indirect way through interaction with the direct impact that positive situations have. Based on related empirical findings, Wright (1997; 2007) focuses on time as a main effect variable in organizational behavior research, and proposes stability over six months as an operationalization of the temporal demarcation between traits and states.

Beyond the contribution of positive characteristics theory to recruitment, strengths or POB characteristics have a further impact on today's workplace. As Luthans (2002) states, POB capacities are situations and can be changed through learning, development, change, and management in the workplace, and can also evolve through educational programs. Such capacities, considered as meeting the criteria for inclusion in POB, are namely the "state-like" capacities of self-efficacy, hope, optimism, and resiliency. These capacities, when combined, form the wider concept of psychological capital or PsyCap. PsyCap is a better indicator of performance and satisfaction than any of the individual factors alone. The critical difference of PsyCap from most other positive approaches is the "state-like," open to development criterion and until today there is both conceptual (e.g., Luthans, Avey, Avolio, Norman, and Combs, 2006) and early empirical evidence that PsyCap can be developed in short training interventions (Avey, Luthans, and Mhatre, 2008). According to Luthans et al. (2007), published research regarding PsyCap demonstrate its relation with performance in the workplace, with fewer absences, lower employee cynicism and turnover, higher job satisfaction, commitment, and citizenship behaviors.

Self-Efficacy as an Important "State-Like" Capacity

The positive concept of self-efficacy is placed among some of the best known theoretical concepts, followed by an extensive theoretical background and empirical support, however, it is not often included in positive psychology reports. This is mostly attributed to the fact that many studies of positive psychology are related to the individuals' personality characteristics, meaning "trait-like" characteristics, or personal resources connected with evolution and genetic factors such as positive emotions. However, as described above, states and not traits suit best the concept of positivity in organizations and work in general. It is exactly this "state-like" nature of self-efficacy that defines it as a concept totally induced in POB.

When we refer to self-efficacy, we mainly look up to Bandura's definition and social cognitive theory. A broad definition applicable to POB is that of Stajkovic and Luthans (1998) (in Luthans, 2002), according to which "Self-efficacy refers to an individual's conviction (or confidence) about his or her abilities to mobilize the motivation, cognitive resources, and courses of action needed to successfully execute a specific task within a given context." Therefore, a self-efficacy belief is not independent of the environment, on the contrary it is determined by the given context and task. This is why as a concept it is applicable to many different specified situations and activities and can be measured and developed accordingly.

SELF-EFFICACY AS A POB CAPACITY

Self-efficacy meets the criteria for inclusion in POB in a very satisfying way. Specifically the crucial factors that are unique for the concept of self-efficacy and make it particularly relevant to POB according to Luthans and Youssef (2007) are:

1. It has the best established theoretical foundation and the most extensive research support compared to the other concepts.

2. Self-efficacy has been supported and measured only as a state, unlike hope, optimism, and resilience that have been studied, measured, and tested both as traits as well as states. Self-efficacy is "state-like" in nature not only because it can be increased and developed, but also because it is specified in certain domains. High self-efficacy in one domain doesn't necessarily lead to high self-efficacy in other domains nor is its absence in one field of activity transferred to other fields.

3. There is an established correlation between self-efficacy and various job performance dimensions. These desirable consequences have been accumulated by Luthans and Youssef (2007) in a review of relevant studies and include work behaviors across cultures, leadership effectiveness, moral or ethical decision making, creativity, participation, career decision making, learning, entrepreneurship, and work-related performance as well.

THE CONSTRUCT OF SELF-EFFICACY

Due to the significance of control in people's lives, many theories have been developed regarding this issue. Motives, emotional states, and the actions of people are mostly based on what they believe is true, rather on how things are objectively. Therefore, it is a person's belief in his/her own abilities which is the main issue to be studied (Bandura, 1995). The concept of self-efficacy has received wide and constant empirical support as a cognitive factor motivating human behavior. Fitzgerald and Harmon, in the symposium of the American Psychology Association in 1998, described self-efficacy as the most important new concept in consulting psychology in the past 25 years (Betz, 2000).

Knowledge, transformative functions, and skills are necessary, but in themselves inadequate for the complete execution of tasks. It is a fact that individuals often do not behave effectively, although they know very well what to do. This happens because self-referential thoughts intervene in the relationship between knowledge and action (Bandura, 1982). In the past few years, there has been a growing convergence between theory and research in what concerns the role of self-referential thoughts in the psychological function. Although research is conducted according to a series of various aspects with various names, the basic phenomenon examined by these studies focuses on the individuals' perception of their personal efficacy to produce and regulate events in their life.

Self-efficacy is a concept developed by Albert Bandura within the framework of social cognitive theory and was published as a theory for the first time in 1977. Bandura himself defines self-efficacy as "the belief in one's capabilities to organize and execute the courses of action required to manage prospective situations" (Bandura, 1995), or as a concept which refers to a person's "capabilities to produce designated levels of performance" (Bandura, 1997). It is a concept referring to a person's expectations in relation to his or her ability to activate the necessary resources for managing the requirements of a situation and not the differentiations regarding the anticipated results. Efficacy expectations determine whether an individual is going to initialize a behavior, how much effort he or she will contribute to the accomplishment of the task, and how long he or she will persist in this effort despite any evidence of disproof. Individuals who have a high sense of efficacy make a sufficient effort which, if executed well, produces successful results, while individuals with a low sense of efficacy, are more likely to stop trying and thus fail in executing a task (Bandura, 1997).

Often connected with self-confidence (Luthans and Youssef, 2007), self-efficacy is the variable manipulated in terms of assigning competitive goals to oneself, motivating oneself, generously investing in an effort, mobilizing towards achieving and completing the goal, and persevering when facing obstacles (Stajkovic and Luthans, 1998). Such initiatives driven by the individual reflect the pro-active creation of difference or opposition, despite the responsive reduction of difference or opposition, which less confident people can demonstrate passively, as they respond to challenges of their external environment. Therefore, less efficient people are those that are more prone to failures, desperation, and loss of self-confidence when facing negative feedback, social deprecation, obstacles, and setbacks or even difficulties that a person creates alone, such as self-doubt, skepticism, or negative perceptions and attributions (Bandura and Locke, 2003).

The concept of self-efficacy has been examined in various fields of study and has been found to be related with clinical problems such as fear, addiction, depression, and also with social skills as well as dogmatism. Moreover, it is related to stress in various contexts, smoking, pain control, health, and sports performance. Although research often does not differentiate between generalized and specific efficacy beliefs, previous available evidence supports the use of specific measures of efficacy beliefs in specific domains since this way, the produced results are more robust (Llorens, Schaufeli, Bakker, and Salanova, 2007). As argued by Betz (2000), self-efficacy beliefs are mainly behaviorally specified and not generalized. This means that we can refer to self-efficacy beliefs regarding mathematics, the initiation of social interactions, financial investments, or the repair of a machine. Therefore, the types of self-efficacy expectations are as many as the possible areas of behavior that can be determined.

OCCUPATIONAL SELF-EFFICACY

Self-efficacy has been conceptualized and measured as a personality concept, generalized for various domains, as a specific variable (e.g., expectations for dangerous behavior), and as a task specific variable (e.g., managing a certain fear or solving mathematical problems). Occupational self-efficacy focuses on the work sector and is defined by Schyns and von Collani (2002) as "one's belief in one's own ability and competence to perform successfully and effectively in different situations and across different tasks in a job." This is a rather wide perception of self-efficacy, so that other types of professions can also be compared. On the other hand, it is specific enough to become a solid antecedent in the occupational domain (Schyns, Torka, and Gossling, 2007).

Schyns and von Collani (2002) have created a measurement tool for occupational self-efficacy (Occupational Self-efficacy Scale — OCCSEFF) aiming to create a general scale of self-efficacy which relates to the occupational domain. Contrary to other measurements of self-efficacy, such as those focused on the task (e.g., the professional career self-efficacy developed by Betz and Hackett in 1981), this measurement concerns work more widely, so that a greater range of workers from various professions can be compared. This way it is possible to investigate personal differences in self-efficacy between various occupations (Schyns and von Collani, 2002).

Self-Efficacy's Motivational and Behavioral Outcomes

Empirical research has generated a great number of studies that demonstrate the positive relationship between self-efficacy and different motivational and behavioral outcomes in clinical, educational, and organizational settings. A strong self-efficacy belief reinforces human achievement and capabilities as well as personal well-being in many ways. People who believe in their potential and abilities approach difficult tasks as challenges that should be arranged or attained and not as threats needed to be avoided (Bandura, 1994). Betz (2000) summarizes the effects of self-efficacy beliefs on behavior as follows: a) approach behaviors opposed to avoidance behaviors, b) quality performance behaviors aimed at the target field, and c) persistence in cases where obstacles or frustrating experiences occur.

Accordingly, low self-efficacy expectations in relation to a certain behavior or domain of activity will inevitably lead to the avoidance of these behaviors, lower performance, and to a tendency for resignation when the individual is confronted with discouragement or failure. On the other hand, a sense of personal efficacy in mastering challenges can generate greater interest in the activity than self-perceived inefficacy in producing competent performances (Bandura and Schunk, 1981). The notional dipole of approach opposed to avoidance is one of the simplest, referring to the whole study spectrum of psychology; however, its impact is one of the most crucial.

Human action in general is affected by self-efficacy perceptions in various ways, all related to the above broader effects. According to Bandura (1986) some of these can be categorized as follows:

1. Decision making: people have a tendency to avoid tasks for which they believe their efficacy is low while they undertake those for which they believe their efficacy is good. It is also important that people make accurate estimations regarding self-efficacy. For the condition high perceived efficacy/low ability, the consequences are negative leading to irreparable damage. On the other hand, for the condition low perceived self-efficacy/high ability, the effect is restriction, meaning no development. There is evidence that eventually the most functional efficacy judgments are those which exceed slightly what someone can achieve at a given moment.

2. Effort and persistence: high self-efficacy also relates to stronger and more persistent effort. Additionally, as far as learning is concerned, self-doubt is followed by an urge for a learning process; however the use of already acquired skills is prohibited. In other words, high self-efficacy can be an advantage as well as a disadvantage, since individuals with high self-efficacy may not feel the need for high preparatory effort investment.

3. Thought patterns and emotional reactions: individuals with low self-efficacy tend to believe that conditions are more difficult than they really are. Consequently, they feel stressed and adopt a superficial view of reality. On the contrary, high self-efficacy leads to attention and action depending on the requirements of any given situation, while obstacles produce the required motivation so that more effort is made. Self-efficacy beliefs also relate to causal attribution thought. In the case of high self-efficacy, failure is attributed to inadequate effort, while in the case of low self-efficacy, failure is attributed to lack of ability.

4. Although originally conceived as a task-specific variable, general self-efficacy as a dispositional characteristic has also been supported as a factor predicting individual behavior across situations (Lennings, 1994). Schunk (1983) noted that self-efficacy is salient in a crisis situation. For example, in the context of fire rescue operations, we expect that under those critical and unique situations expectancies created by past experiences will influence the individual's expectations of mastery in the new situations (Sherer et al., 1982).

IMPACT OF SELF-EFFICACY WITHIN WORK AND ORGANIZATIONAL SETTINGS

According to Luthans (2002) Bandura's theory on self-efficacy is a positive approach as is the one by Seligman, and other researchers also believe that self-efficacy is a POB skill. Luthans claims that Bandura's rich theory and considerable research support clearly indicates that a confident individual:

- is more likely to make a choice to really get into the task and welcome the challenge;

- will give more effort and will be motivated to successfully accomplish the task;

- will persist for a longer time when obstacles are encountered or even when there is initial failure.

During the first years of study of self-efficacy in relation to organizational settings, only a few studies were conducted, which demonstrated self-efficacy's low correlation with job search and research productivity of university faculty members (Stajkovic and Luthans, 1998). Following studies demonstrated a correlation between self-efficacy and a number of other measures related to job performance, such as adaptability to advanced technology (Hill, Smith, and Mann, 1987), coping with career related events (Stumpf, Brief, and Hartman, 1987), managerial idea generating (Gist, 1987), managerial performance (Wood, Bandura, and Bailey, 1990), skill acquisition (Mitchell, Hopper, Daniels, George-Falvy, and James, 1994), and newcomer adjustment to an organizational setting (Saks, 1995) (in Stajkovic and Luthans, 1998).

Especially in relation to job performance, self-efficacy has been proven to have a strong connection. In fact, the correlation is generally stronger than that of self-efficacy with other organizational behavior concepts such as goal setting, feedback, job satisfaction, and personality characteristics based on the Big Five personality theory (Luthans, 2002). In addition, the correlation of self-efficacy with job performance has been supported through studies concerning core self-evaluations, a theory in which the concept of generalized self-efficacy is contained, along with self-esteem, locus of control, and emotional stability. Judge and Bono (2001), in their meta-analysis based on 274 correlations, concluded that these four personality characteristics constituting core self-evaluations are placed among the strongest dispositional antecedents of job satisfaction and job performance.

Furthermore, leaders use self-efficacy in order to influence their followers and increase their performance. Studies have shown that transformational and charismatic leaders primarily use the motivational mechanism of enhancing their follower's self-efficacy and self-worth in order to influence them, and once self-efficacy is established, followers will begin to trust the leader, a situation which, in turn, increases their commitment to the leader and organization (see Pillai and Williams, 20003). Eden (1992) argued that leadership is the mechanism through which self-efficacy can be enhanced, which, in turn, increases performance.

Self-efficacy is also positively linked with initiative taking. In the framework of organizational change, the relationship between taking initiatives and self-efficacy is confirmed by Morrison and Brantner (1992), who focused on the study of factors that enhance or hinder learning when in a new job position. Self-efficacy was found to be a favorable factor; therefore it possibly influences the processes prior to organizational change. Heuven et al. (2006), studied the role of self-efficacy in performing emotion work, and concluded that self-efficacy buffers the relationship between emotional job demands and emotional dissonance, as well as the relationship between emotional dissonance and work engagement, having a moderating influence on these relationships.

Noe and Wilk (1993) included self-efficacy in their study on developmental activities, and identified a positive correlation. Thus, it seems that employees with a high sense of self-efficacy are more likely to invest in their career, pursuing projects with high requirements. There is also a positive effect on what concerns processes of organizational change, as people with high self-efficacy beliefs are more likely to be stable and persistent in the face of setbacks or new data brought about by change, while their performance remains stable even after change in the content of their job (Schyns, Torka, and Gossling, 2007).

McDonald and Siegall (1992) have investigated the effect of self-efficacy on attitudes towards work, by studying the behavior and performance of employees in technical agricultural tasks whose occupation had undergone significant changes. Their self-efficacy (in particular, their technological self-efficacy) was found to be positively related to satisfaction, commitment, and work quality, while it was negatively related to delays and absences.

SELF-EFFICACY'S IMPACT ON WORK ENGAGEMENT: A RELATED CONDUCTED RESEARCH

Work engagement has been conceptualized as the positive antipode of burnout (Schaufeli and Bakker, 2004). Many researchers have claimed that work engagement is an antecedent of employee's outcomes, organizational success, and financial performance (Saks, 2006). It is a concept that has been defined in many ways, for example, as an emotional and intellectual commitment to the organization (Baumruk, 2004), or as the amount of effort that an employee chooses to put into his or her work (Frank, Finnegan, and Taylor, 2004).

One of the main approaches for work engagement is that of Schaufeli, Salanova, Gonzalez-Roma, and Bakker (2002), who define engagement as a construct independent to burnout (although negatively related), namely as a positive, fulfilling, work-related state of mind, that is characterized by vigor, dedication, and absorption. Engaged employees demonstrate high levels of energy, are enthusiastic about their work, and are often fully immersed in their work so that time passes quickly (Bakker and Demerouti, 2008).

Related studies investigating the role of self-efficacy as a factor that determines engagement lead to the conclusion that a mutual dependence circle exists. Self-efficacy may precede or follow engagement, meaning that the dependence circle is ascending, since self-efficacy reinforces engagement which reinforces self-efficacy and so on (Schaufeli and Salanova, 2007). Additionally, self-efficacy beliefs have been observed to mediate the relationship between positive emotions (e.g., excitement, satisfaction, relief) and work engagement (Salanova, Agut, and Peiro, 2005). Xanthopoulou et al. (2007), in their study on a sample of German technicians, investigated the role of personal resources (self-efficacy, self-confidence, and optimism) in work engagement prediction.

Results showed that engaged employees attain high levels of self-efficacy and are able to cope with the demands occurring in a wide range of contexts.

Our study investigates the impact of occupational self-efficacy and job resources-demands on work engagement. The sample consisted of 120 employees from a wide range of positions in 18 organizations of the private sector in Greece. These organizations were from a broad range of industries that included advertising, publishing, manufacturing, consulting, and other services. The organizations varied widely in size.

Work engagement was measured using the Utrecht Engagement Scale (UWES) developed by Schaufeli et al. (2002), and more specifically the 17-item standardized Greek version (Schaufeli and Bakker, 2003). The scale measures separately the three dimensions of work engagement: Vigor, Dedication, and Absorption. Occupational self-efficacy was assessed with the 20-item Occupational Self-efficacy Scale (OCCSEFF) developed by Schyns and von Collani (2002) which was translated into the Greek language for the purpose of this study. Finally, job characteristics (job resources-demands) were assessed by the Job Content Questionnaire (JCQ) (Karasek et al., 1998). The version used had been translated and standardized in the Greek language, and we chose to utilize the main scales of Decision Latitude (Skill Discretion + Decision Authority), Psychological Job Demands, and Social Support (Supervisor Support + Co-worker Support) which measure the high-demand/low control/low-support model of job strain development, along with the Job Insecurity Scale.

Participants were 26.7 percent male and 73.3 percent female and their ages ranged from 22 to 53 years (M = 31.8, SD = 5.96). 14.2 percent were high school graduates, 29.2 percent had a technical education, 25.8 percent had a university degree, 27.5 percent had a master's or PhD degree, and 3.3 percent were of another education level. The majority of the sample had been working in the given position for 1–5 years (51.7 percent), 24.2 percent were working less than a year in the given position, 15.8 percent for 5–10 years, 5 percent for 10–15 years, 2.5 percent for 15–20 years and 0.8 percent for over 20 years.

The sample consisted of employees working in positions related to accounting (N = 37), office work/client service (N = 33), the editing/creative field (N = 15), sales/marketing (N = 15), administration (N = 12), information engineering (N = 5), and technical/manual work (N = 3). Regarding turnover, 49.2 percent of the sample reported intention to remain in the current job, 28.3 percent were undecided, and 22.5 percent reported intention to leave.

Theoretical foundation and prior empirical results drove the below-stated hypotheses concerning the construct of occupational self-efficacy:

- Hypothesis 1: occupational self-efficacy will be positively related to work engagement and more specifically self-efficacy will function as an antecedent of work engagement.

- Hypothesis 2: job resources (decision latitude, co-worker support, supervisor support) will be positively related to occupational self-efficacy.

- Hypothesis 3: each one of the job resources (decision latitude, co-worker support, supervisor support) will contribute additional unique variance in relation to occupational self-efficacy.

- Hypothesis 4: occupational self-efficacy will correlate stronger with two of the three dimensions contributing to work engagement, namely Vigor and Absorption.

As shown at the intercorrelations tables (Tables 9.1 and 9.2), positive correlations between study variables provided initial support for hypothesis 1 and support for hypothesis 4. Occupational self-efficacy and work engagement were significantly positively correlated ($r = 0.20$, $p = 0.026$) as expected. Occupational self-efficacy was related with only two of the three engagement dimensions, and was particularly strongly related to vigor ($r = 0.30$, $p = 0.001$) with a moderate relationship to absorption ($r = 0.20$, $p = 0.032$). The above supported our fourth hypothesis, which was based on the notion that self-efficacy is mainly related to action, as indicated by its definition, rather than to affective states. Vigor is the work engagement dimension most connected to action, while absorption mainly consists of both active and cognitive aspects.[1]

Stepwise multiple regression analysis provided additional support for the second scale of hypothesis 1, since occupational self-efficacy made a significant unique contribution (20.3 percent) to the prediction of work engagement (B = 0.34, β = 0.203, $p = 0.026$). Hypothesis 3 was not supported since no

---

[1] *Vigor* refers to high levels of energy and mental resilience while working, the willingness to invest effort in one's work, the ability to not be easily fatigued, and persistence in the face of difficulties. *Dedication* refers to a strong involvement in one's work, accompanied by feelings of enthusiasm and significance, and by a sense of pride and inspiration. *Absorption* refers to a state in which individuals are fully concentrated on and engrossed in their activities, whereby time passes quickly and they have difficulties in detaching themselves from work (Llorens at al., 2007).

Table 9.1   Intercorrelations among study variables

Variable	Occupational self-efficacy	Decision latitude	Job demands	Co-worker support	Supervisor support	Job insecurity
Work engagement	0.20*	0.66**	0.08	0.32**	0.53**	-0.34**
Occupational self-efficacy		0.18	0.15	0.02	0.07	-0.35**

Note: *p<0.05; **p<0.01.

Table 9.2   Intercorrelations among occupational self-efficacy and work engagement dimensions

Variable	Vigor	Dedication	Absorption
Occupational self-efficacy	0.30**	0.09	0.20*

Note: *p<0.05; **p<0.01.

significant contribution of any of the job resources variables (decision latitude, co-worker support, supervisor support) to occupational self-efficacy was observed. Consequently, the research results did not support the existence of the positive gain spiral of resources, efficacy beliefs, and engagement,[2] as one term of this relationship (high job resources enhance self-efficacy beliefs) was not confirmed. These results are shown in Table 9.3.

It is possible that this specific result could be attributed to the type or quality of the resources provided, which may not have been sufficient enough to affect a personal resource such as occupational self-efficacy. Considering that the sample mean for occupational self-efficacy was high, we can assume that employees' occupational efficacy beliefs are more or less formed independently of organizational variables (e.g., by previous work experience, work outcomes, etc.), due to the prevalent conditions of the given labor market, where work benefits provision is inflexible and most organizations, that are small or medium sized, lack motivational strategies and methods.

---

2   Initially the theory was supported by Bandura (1977), who claimed that job resources lead indirectly to engagement through enhancing employees' self-efficacy. The mediating role of self-efficacy among job resources and engagement has been investigated in many recent studies.

Table 9.3   Summary of stepwise regression analyses for variables predicting work engagement and occupational self-efficacy

Variable	B	b	95% Confidence Interval for B Lower bound	Upper bound
Work engagement				
Occupational self-efficacy	0.34	0.20*	-0.64	0.04
Occupational self-efficacy				
Decision latitude	0.00	0.21	-0.19	0.00
Co-worker support	0.02	0.07	-0.05	0.08
Supervisor support	0.00	0.00	-0.05	0.05

Conclusions and Implications

The role of self-efficacy in the workplace is that of a concept whose nature is "state-like," and can therefore be developed and effectively trained. Empirical evidence demonstrates the value of such an effort, namely to develop beliefs of high self-efficacy, or specifically occupational self-efficacy, for individuals in working environments. We have already examined some of its most important effects on organizational behavior and job performance, consequently any variables predicting occupational self-efficacy need to be specified. Bandura (1997) has introduced four ways through which the positive concept of self-efficacy can be developed. In order of importance these are: a) mastery experiences or performance attainments, b) vicarious learning or modeling, c) positively oriented persuasion or feedback, and d) physiological or psychological arousal.

Crucial, however, are some of the remarks Bandura makes regarding the above statements. For example, the way an individual interprets a previous success may alter its impact on self-efficacy since it can be attributed either to hard work or to factors related to chance and external aid. In the case of modeling (the observation of others succeeding in similar tasks or activities), positive effects on self-efficacy can only be achieved if the other person is someone that the observer can relate to and/or identify with. In other cases positive situations or conditions may have a moderate effect, while negative ones may cause great damage to self-efficacy beliefs (e.g., positive feedback opposed to negative feedback or psychological health opposed to a psychological disorder or burnout). As an overall presumption, the point of interest is concerned with the processes influencing self-efficacy, its task-specific or generalized impacts, its relation with other constructs and measures, and the applicable interventions in the workplace context enhancing it. In a modern working environment, oriented towards positivity and human virtues and strengths, the role of self-efficacy or confidence is proven to be multiple in nature.

References

Avey, J.B., Luthans, F., and Mhatre, K.H. (2008). A call for longitudinal research in positive organizational behavior. *Journal of Organizational Behavior*, (www.interscience.wiley.com) DOI: 10.1002/job.517.

Bakker, A.B. and Demerouti, E. (2008). Towards a model of work engagement. *Career Development International*, 13(3), 209–23.

Bandura, A. (1977). Self-efficacy: toward a unifying theory of behavioral change. *Psychological Review*, 84, 191–215.

Bandura, A. (1982). Self-efficacy mechanism in human agency. *American Psychologist*, 37(2), 122–47.

Bandura, A. (1986). *Social Foundations of Thought and Action: A Social Cognitive Theory*. Englewood Cliffs, NJ: Prentice-Hall.

Bandura, A. (1994). Self-efficacy. In V.S. Ramachaudran (ed.), *Encyclopedia of Human Behavior*, 4 (pp. 71–81). New York: Academic Press. Available at: http://www.des.emory.edu/mfp/BanEncy.html [Accessed: 15 January 2010].

Bandura, A. (1995). Exercise of personal and collective efficacy in changing societies. In A. Bandura (ed.), *Self-efficacy in Changing Societies*. Cambridge: Cambridge University Press.

Bandura, A. (1997). *Self-efficacy: The Exercise of Control*. New York: Freeman.

Bandura, A. and Locke, E. (2003). Negative self-efficacy and goal effects revisited. *Journal of Applied Psychology*, 88, 87–99.

Bandura, A. and Schunk, D.H. (1981). Cultivating competence, self-efficacy, and intrinsic interest through proximal self-motivation. *Journal of Personality and Social Psychology*, 41(3), 586–98.

Baumruk, R. (2004). The missing link: the role of employee engagement in business success. *Workspan*, 47, 48–52.

Betz, N.E. (2000). Self-efficacy theory as a basis for career assessment. *Journal of Career Assessment*, 8(3), 205–22.

Buckingham, M. and Clifton, D.O. (2001). *Now, Discover Your Strengths*. New York: The Free Press.

Buckingham, M. and Coffman, C. (1999). *First, Break All the Rules*. New York: Simon and Schuster.

Cartwright, S. and Holmes, N. (2006). The meaning of work: the challenge of regaining employee engagement and reducing cynicism. *Human Resource Management Review*, 16, 199–208.

Clifton, D.O. and Harter, J.K. (2003). Strengths investment. In K.S. Cameron, J.E. Dutton, and R.E. Quinn (eds), *Positive Organizational Scholarship* (pp. 111–21). San Francisco, CA: Berrett-Koehler.

Eden, D. (1992). Leadership and expectations: Pygmalion effects and other self-fulfilling prophecies in organizations. *The Leadership Quarterly*, 3(4), 271–305.

Fineman, S. (2006). On being positive: concerns and counterpoints. *Academy of Management Review*, 31, 270–91.

Frank, F.D., Finnegan, R.P., and Taylor, C.R. (2004). The race for talent: retaining and engaging workers in the 21st century. *Human Resource Planning*, 27(3), 12–25.

Gist, M.E. (1987). Self-efficacy: implications for organizational behavior and human resource management. *Academy of Management Review*, 12, 472–85.

Harter, J.K., Schmidt, F.L., and Hayes, T.L. (2002). Business-unit-level relationship between employee satisfaction, employee engagement, and business outcomes: a meta-analysis. *Journal of Applied Psychology*, 87, 268–79.

Heuven, E., Bakker, A.B., Schaufeli, W.B., and Huisman, N. (2006). The role of self-efficacy in performing emotion work. *Journal of Vocational Behavior*, 69, 222–35.

Hill, T., Smith, N.D., and Mann, M.F. (1987). Role of efficacy expectations in predicting the decision to use advanced technologies. *Journal of Applied Psychology*, 72, 307–14.

Hodges, T.D. and Clifton D.O.C. (2000). Strengths-based development in practice. In P.A. Linley and S. Joseph, *International Handbook of Positive Psychology in Practice: From Research to Application*. Hoboken, NJ: Wiley and Sons. Available at: http://www.strengthsquest.com/content/File/111412/Hodges_Clifton_SBD_in_Practice.pdf [Accessed: 15 January 2010].

Judge, T.A. and Bono, J.E. (2001). Relationship of core self-evaluations traits – self-esteem, generalized self-efficacy, locus of control, and emotional stability – with job satisfaction and job performance: a meta-analysis. *Journal of Applied Psychology*, 86(1), 80–92.

Karasek, R., Brisson, C., Kawakami, N., Houtman, I., Bongers, P., and Amick, B. (1998). The Job Content Questionnaire (JCQ): an instrument for internationally comparative assessments of psychosocial job characteristics. *Journal of Occupational Health Psychology*, 3(4), 322–55.

Lennings, C.J. (1994). An evaluation of a generalized self-efficacy scale. *Personality and Individual Differences*, 16(5), 745–50.

Linley, P. and Joseph, S. (eds) (2004). *Positive Psychology in Practice*. New York: John Wiley.

Llorens, S., Schaufeli, W., Bakker, A., and Salanova M. (2007). Does a positive gain spiral of resources, efficacy beliefs and engagement exist? *Computers in Human Behavior*, 23, 825–41.

Luthans, F. (2002). The need for and meaning of positive organizational behavior. *Journal of Organizational Behavior*, 23, 695–706.

Luthans, F., Avey, J.B., Avolio, B.J., Norman, S.M., and Combs, G.M. (2006). Psychological capital development: toward a micro-intervention. *Journal of Organizational Behavior*, 27, 387–93.

Luthans, F., Avolio, B., Avey, J., and Norman, S. (2007). Psychological capital: measurement and relationship with performance and satisfaction. *Personnel Psychology*, 60, 541–72.

Luthans, F. and Youssef, C.M. (2007). Emerging positive organizational behavior. *Journal of Management*, 33(3), 321–49.

McDonald, T. and Siegall, M. (1992). The effects of technological self-efficacy and job focus on job performance, attitudes, and withdrawal behaviors. *Journal of Psychology*, 126, 465–75.

Mitchell, T.R., Hopper, H., Daniels, D., George-Falvy, J., and James, L.R. (1994). Predicting self-efficacy and performance during skill acquisition. *Journal of Applied Psychology*, 79, 506–17.

Morrison, R.F. and Brantner, T.M. (1992). What enhances or inhibits learning a new job? A basic career issue. *Journal of Applied Psychology*, 77, 926–40.

Nicholsen, N. (1998). How hardwired is human behavior? *Harvard Business Review*, July–August, 135–47.

Noe, R.A. and Wilk, S.L. (1993). Investigation of the factors that influence employees' participation in development activities. *Journal of Applied Psychology*, 78, 291–302.

Peterson, C. and Park, N. (2003). Positive psychology as the evenhanded positive psychologist views it. *Psychological Inquiry*, 14, 141–6.

Peterson, C. and Seligman, M.E.P. (2004). *Character Strengths and Virtues: A Handbook and Classification*. Washington, DC: American Psychological Association.

Pillai, R. and Williams, E.A. (2003). Transformational leadership, self-efficacy, group cohesiveness, commitment, and performance. *Journal of Organizational Change Management*, 17(2), 144–59.

Saks, A.M. (1995). Longitudinal field investigation of the moderating and mediating effects of self-efficacy on the relationship between training and newcomer adjustment. *Journal of Applied Psychology*, 80, 211–25.

Saks, A.M. (2006). Antecedents and consequences of employee engagement. *Journal of Managerial Psychology*, 21(7), 600–619.

Salanova, M., Agut, S., and Peiro, J.M. (2005). Linking organizational resources and work engagement to employee performance and customer loyalty: the mediation of service climate. *Journal of Applied Psychology*, 90(6), 1217–27.

Schaufeli, W.B. and Bakker, A.B. (2003). UWES – Utrecht work engagement scale: test manual. Department of Psychology, Utrecht University, Utrecht.

Schaufeli, W.B. and Bakker, A.B. (2004). Job demands, job resources, and their relationship with burnout and engagement: a multi-sample study. *Journal of Organizational Behavior*, 25, 293–315.

Schaufeli, W.B. and Salanova, M. (2007). Efficacy or inefficacy, that's the question: burnout and work engagement, and their relationships with efficacy beliefs. *Anxiety, Stress, and Coping*, 20(2), 177–96.

Schaufeli, W.B., Salanova, M., Gonzalez-Roma, V., and Bakker, A.B. (2002). The measurement of burnout and engagement: a confirmatory factor analytic approach. *Journal of Happiness Studies*, 3, 71–92.

Schunk, D.H. (1983). Progress self-monitoring: effects on children's self-efficacy and achievement. *Journal of Experimental Education*, 51(2), 89–93.

Schyns, B., Torka, N., and Gossling, T. (2007). Turnover intention and preparedness for change: exploring leader-member exchange and occupational self-efficacy as antecedents of two employability predictors. *Career Development International*, 12(7), 660–79.

Schyns, B. and von Collani, G. (2002). A new occupational self-efficacy scale and its relation to personality constructs and organizational variables. *European Journal of Work and Organizational Psychology*, 11(2), 219–41.

Seligman, M.E.P. and Csikszentmihalyi, M. (2000). Positive psychology: an introduction. *American Psychologist*, 55, 5–14.

Seligman, M.E.P., Parks, A.C., and Steen, T. (2004). A balanced psychology and a full life. *Phil. Trans. R. Soc. Lond. B.*, 359, 1379–81.

Sheldon, K.M and King, L. (2001). Why positive psychology is necessary. *American Psychologist*, 56, 216–17.

Sherer, M., Maddux, J.E., Mercandante, B., Prentice-Dunn, S., Jacobs, B., and Rogers, R. (1982). The self-efficacy scale: construction and validation. *Psychological Reports*, 51(2), 663–71.

Snyder, C.R. and Lopez, S. (eds) (2002). *Handbook of Positive Psychology*. Oxford: Oxford University Press.

Stajkovic, A. and Luthans, F. (1998). Self-efficacy and work-related performance: a meta-analysis. *Psychological Bulletin*, 124, 240–61.

Stefanyszyn, K. (2007). Norwich Union changes focus from competencies to strengths. *HR at Work*, 7(1), 10–11.

Stumpf, S.A., Brief, A.P., and Hartman, K. (1987). Self-efficacy expectations and coping with career related events. *Journal of Vocational Behavior*, 31, 91–108.

Tetrick, L.E. (2002). Individual and organizational health. In D. Ganster and P.L. Perrewe (eds), *Research in Organizational Stress and Well-being* (vol. 3, pp. 107–41). Greenwich, CN: JAI Press.

Wood, R., Bandura, A., and Bailey, T. (1990). Mechanisms governing organizational performance in complex decision-making environments. *Organizational Behavior and Human Decision Processes*, 46, 181–201.

Wright, T.A. (1997). Time revisited in organizational behavior. *Journal of Organizational Behavior*, 18, 201–4.

Wright, T.A. (2003). Positive organizational behavior: an idea whose time has truly come. *Journal of Organizational Behavior*, 24, 437–42.

Wright, T.A. (2007). A look at two methodological challenges for scholars interested in positive organizational behavior. In D.L. Nelson and C.L. Cooper (eds), *Positive Organizational Behavior: Accentuating the Positive at Work* (pp. 177–90). Thousand Oaks, CA: Sage.

Xanthopoulou, D., Bakker, A.B., Demerouti, E., and Schaufeli, W.B. (2007). The role of personal resources in the job demands-resources model. *International Journal of Stress Management*, 14, 121–41.

Youssef, C.M. and Luthans, F. (2007). Positive organizational behavior in the workplace: the impact of hope, optimism and resilience. *Journal of Management*, 33(5), 774–800.

Zwetsloot, G. and Pot, F. (2004). The business value of health management. *Journal of Business Ethics*, 55, 115–24.

10

Professional Efficacy and Social Support in Nurses During the SARS Crisis in Canada and China

Esther R. Greenglass, Zdravko Marjanovic, Lisa Fiksenbaum, Sue Coffey, Kan Shi, and Xue Feng Chen

In the period between March and June, 2003, severe acute respiratory syndrome (SARS), a contagious illness caused by a recently identified form of the coronavirus (CoV), infected approximately 8,450 people worldwide and resulted in over 800 deaths (Fleck, 2003; World Health Organization, 2004). Of approximately 30 countries that were directly impacted by the SARS outbreak, SARS had especially adverse effects on China and Canada. In China, the brunt of the impact was felt in the cities of Guangdong and Beijing where 4,033 people were infected and 250 died as a result of SARS (Fleck, 2003). In Canada during this time, SARS' greatest impact was in Toronto and surrounding areas where 247 probable cases of SARS were identified and resulted in the deaths of 44 people (McDonald et al., 2004). The SARS outbreak wreaked chaos on Toronto's healthcare system (Fowler et al., 2003; Peng et al., 2003), businesses and the tourism industry (Mason et al., 2005), and it caused widespread fear and uncertainty among residents (Cheng and Cheung, 2005; Fowler et al., 2003; Maunder et al., 2003). Relative to China, the impact of SARS in Canada was less severe. Nevertheless, 69 percent of adults surveyed in Ontario from April to June 2003 expressed concerns about their vulnerability to SARS contagion, commensurate with rates found in Chinese population surveys (e.g., Lau et al., 2005; Tang and Wong, 2003). Moreover, the fear and anxiety Ontarians felt about SARS was significantly greater than the expressed concerns of Canadians in other provinces (57 percent) and American samples (32 percent) (Blendon et al., 2004).

The SARS outbreak was distinct from other pathogenic outbreaks because of its disproportionately high levels of infection in healthcare workers, particularly in nurses (Masur et al., 2003; McDonald et al., 2004). Nurses spent greater amounts of time in environments where SARS exposure was high, such as hospitals and clinics, and had closer proximal contact with infected SARS patients and their respiratory fluids (Hall et al., 2003; Maunder et al., 2003). Given that respiratory droplets were the primary means of transmitting the SARS-CoV (Peng et al., 2003), greater contact with infected patients increased the probability of becoming infected. In both China and Canada, several researchers have found a relationship between contact with SARS patients and heightened psychological distress (e.g., Chen et al., 2005).

Quarantining was a related factor that was associated with negative psychological outcomes for nurses in both countries. In Canada, Robertson et al. (2004) found that nurses who were quarantined reported greater levels of anger, frustration, loss of control, and perceived stigmatization than nurses who were not quarantined. Other research has found consistently negative outcomes associated with quarantined nurses, such as self-reported post traumatic stress, depression, avoidance, anxiety, social isolation, interpersonal rejection, and fear of infecting others (Bai et al., 2004; Hawryluck et al., 2004; Maunder et al., 2003; Nickell et al., 2004).

Given that nurses experienced high levels of distress due to SARS, it is likely that their perceived professional efficacy and their perceptions of the effectiveness of their services were diminished. Burnout in nurses may result from strain due to excessive workload and uncertainty associated with one's work environment. According to Schaufeli et al. (1996), burnout consists of three dimensions: emotional exhaustion, cynicism, and reduced professional efficacy that are assessed using the MBI-General Survey (MBI-GS). The focus of the present study is nurses' professional efficacy which is defined as expectations of continued effectiveness at work.

Factors Affecting Professional Efficacy

Previous research has shown that diminished efficacy in one's professional role appears to be an erosion of one's self efficacy, resulting from an impoverishment of people's perceptions of themselves in their work role, particularly as a service provider (Lee and Ashforth, 1990). This may explain in part previous work demonstrating that professional efficacy is particularly affected by an individual's resources including their perceived social support and their coping strategies. There is evidence that individual skills, such as coping ability, affect the degree of professional efficacy in nurses. Thus, nurses who use higher levels of control coping in dealing with stress have higher professional efficacy than their counterparts who use control coping less (Greenglass and Burke, 2000). Therefore, to the extent that nurses employed coping, which depended on their own efforts to change the situation (control coping), they were more likely to have positive feelings about their professional accomplishments. The finding that control coping predicted positively and significantly to professional efficacy parallels Leiter (1991), who found that control coping strategies, used by mental hospital employees, were related to more positive assessments of their personal accomplishments.

Coping, Social Support, and Burnout

Additional research suggests that coping strategies appear to be influenced directly by social support. In the past, research on coping and social support has tended to be separate, conceptually and empirically. However, research findings indicate that social support and coping are linked. For example, DeLongis and O'Brien (1990), in their treatment of how families cope with Alzheimer's disease, discuss how interpersonal factors may be important as predictors of an individual's ability to cope with a situation. Hobfoll et al. (1994) also address the interpersonal, interactive nature of coping and social resource acquisition. Greenglass (1993) reports that social support at work and at home contributed to preventive and instrumental coping strategies used by managers.

Perceived organizational support is an important variable that has been identified in the organizational behavior literature as being associated with decreased stress, particularly in dealing with distress due to SARS (Rhoades and Eisenberger, 2002; Tam et al., 2004). Social support may take the form of practical assistance, emotional support, or an informational resource which serves to disseminate and increase knowledge. Additional data suggest that lack of knowledge about SARS should reduce nurses' ability to cope effectively (Cheng and Cheung, 2005; Gan et al., 2004). Organizational support that includes information is expected to be an important factor contributing to nurses' coping with SARS. Informational support should increase a nurse's sense of controllability at a time of high uncertainty by providing important and relevant knowledge.

Underlying organizational support is the valence of feedback that nurses received from doctors, their co-workers, patients, and healthcare administrators regarding their professional performance during the SARS outbreak. Greater performance feedback has been shown to increase employee perceptions of perceived organizational support (Hutchison and Garstka, 1996), and increased glove wearing among nurses working with HIV/AIDS patients (DeVries et al., 1991), an important preventive measure when working with contagious individuals.

In a qualitative study of nurses' daily workplace stressors, researchers found that a lack of feedback from supervisors related to nurses' feelings of powerlessness, frustration, hopelessness, and professional inadequacy (Olofsson et al., 2003). Since lack of knowledge hinders an individual's ability to apply appropriate coping strategies to stressful situations (e.g., Cheng and Cheung, 2005; Gan et al., 2004), low information support (particularly about SARS) from the organization should reduce nurses' ability to cope effectively with SARS stress.

SARS research has focused on the relationship between SARS threat and nurses' preventive behaviors, such as maintaining personal hygiene (e.g., Cheng and Cheung, 2005; Blendon et al., 2004; Wong and Tang, 2005). However, outcomes involving nurses' utilization of preventive coping strategies have yet to be explored. *Preventive coping* is conceptualized as a long-term cognitive anticipation of potential future stressors, aimed at developing general resistance resources to help lessen the severity of stressors should they occur (Schwarzer and Taubert, 2002). In preventive coping, the nature of the stressor that one prepares for is ambiguous and looms in the distant future (Schwarzer and Knoll, 2003). Preventive coping differs from traditional forms of reactive coping (e.g., problem-focused or emotion-focused coping) because the stressor or critical event happens in the future as opposed to the past. Thus, we opine that a preventive coping strategy was theoretically ideal for nurses during the SARS outbreak because of the environmental circumstances in which they worked (e.g., the crisis was novel, and its duration and course were uncertain at the time).

Greenglass (1993) found that low levels of preventive coping were related to higher levels of job anxiety, somatization, and depression in 114 government supervisors; high levels of preventive coping were related to high job satisfaction. Ogus (1992) compared the coping strategies of 128 nurses working in medical and surgical units and found that higher levels of preventive coping were related to lower burnout in nurses. Extrapolating from these studies, we suggest that higher levels of preventive coping should relate positively to nurses' feelings of professional efficacy for two reasons. First, preventive coping should increase nurses' feelings of control and thereby their efficacy on the job, and secondly, preventive coping should mediate the effects of organizational support on professional efficacy.

The Present Study

The present study was conducted in order to examine the relationship between professional efficacy in nurses working during the SARS crisis, preventive coping, organizational support, and feedback. Given that professional efficacy is critical to nurses, particularly during a crisis such as the SARS outbreak, we designed a theoretical model predicting to professional efficacy which combined both psychosocial and individual variables. Since nurses in Canada and China were negatively affected by the SARS outbreak, it is appropriate to conduct cross-national research on SARS. Having two national sources of data enabled us to test the model empirically in culturally different samples, thus allowing for increased validity of our model.

According to our predictions, greater levels of reported positive feedback from others in the same work environment should predict an increase in perceived organizational support. Support, in turn, is seen as predicting to higher levels of preventive coping, defined as precautionary efforts to protect against getting SARS. Preventive coping should lead to higher levels of professional efficacy. Reports of no feedback should lead to lower organizational support. Positive feedback should be negatively related to no feedback (see Figure 10.1 for the theoretical model). The model was tested in nurses working both in Canada and China.

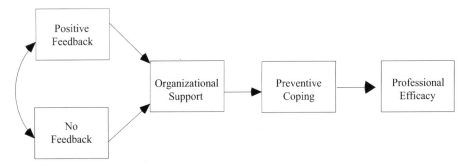

Figure 10.1 Theoretical model of the relationship among organizational support, perceived feedback, preventive coping, and professional efficacy

METHOD

Participants

Table 10.1 presents demographic variables for Canadian and Chinese nurses (n = 541). The Canadian sample was recruited in the province of Ontario: the majority worked in Toronto and surrounding regions during the SARS outbreak (83.6 percent). The Canadian sample consisted of 374 nurses (M = 43.24 years old, SD = 10.02), most of whom were women (94.9 percent) and registered (95.7 percent). Close to three quarters of the sample worked full-time (73.7 percent) and had worked for only one other healthcare organization prior to the SARS outbreak (75.1 percent). Approximately 51 percent of the sample worked as staff nurses. Two percent of the Canadian sample had been diagnosed with suspected or probable SARS. Close to two thirds of the sample worked in the following areas: public health/community health, medical/surgical, emergency, intensive care, long-term care/geriatrics, and mental health.

The Chinese sample was collected in Guangzhou, the capital city of *Guangdong* Province in southern China where the SARS virus originated. These nurses worked in a governmentally designated hospital for the care of SARS patients. It consisted of 167 nurses (M = 28.11 years old, SD = 6.36), most of whom were women (99.4 percent) and registered nurses (93.5 percent). A little more than one half of the sample worked full-time (57.2 percent) and almost all had worked for only one other healthcare organization prior to the SARS outbreak (97.5 percent). Approximately 72 percent of the Chinese sample worked as staff nurses. Twenty-three percent of the Chinese sample had been diagnosed with suspected or probable SARS. Two thirds of the Chinese nurses worked in the following areas: medical/surgical, intensive care, long term care/geriatrics, and emergency. A t-test on age in the two samples indicated that Canadian nurses were significantly older than Chinese nurses (t [440.17] = 20.92, p <.001).

Measures

- *Professional efficacy* (α = .84 and .81, Canadian and Chinese samples, respectively). Professional efficacy was assessed using the 6-item professional efficacy subscale of the *Maslach Burnout Inventory-General Survey* (*MBI-GS*) (Schaufeli et al., 1996) and is defined as satisfaction with work accomplishments and expectations of continued effectiveness at work. Response alternatives ranged

Table 10.1 Canadian and Chinese nurses' area and role during the SARS crisis

	Sample			
	Canadian (*n* = 374)		Chinese (*n* = 167)	
Area and Role	*n*	%	*n*	%
Nursing Area*				
Emergency	29	7.8	16	9.6
Intensive care	29	7.8	32	19.2
Long term care/Geriatrics	24	6.4	19	11.4
Medical/Surgical	44	11.8	38	22.8
Mental health	25	6.7	2	1.2
Obstetrics	13	3.5	0	0
Operating/Recovery	10	2.7	0	0
Pediatrics	28	7.5	0	0
Public health/Community health	64	17.1	1	0.6
Other	108	28.9	32	19.2
Nursing Role**				
Staff nurse	191	51.1	120	71.9
Case manager	19	5.1	5	3.0
Manager	47	12.6	13	7.8
Educator	31	8.3	0	0
Other	86	23.0	17	10.2

Note: *n* = 541; * 27 Chinese nurses did not indicate their nursing area; ** 12 Chinese nurses did not indicate their nursing role.

from 0 = *never* to 6 = *everyday*. Higher values indicate greater levels of professional efficacy. A sample item is, "I could effectively solve the problems that arose in my work."

- *Preventive coping* (α = .68 and .54, Canadian and Chinese samples, respectively). This 5-item scale assessed extent of preventive efforts such as keeping informed about nursing practices and thinking ahead in order to avoid SARS contagion. Response alternatives ranged between 1 = *not at all true* to 4 = *completely true*. Higher values indicate greater levels of preventive coping. A sample item is, "I did what I could so that I would not get SARS."

- *Organizational support* (α = .89 and .84, Canadian and Chinese samples, respectively). Adapted from Eisenberger et al.'s (1986) Survey of Perceived Organizational Support (SPOS), this 5-item scale measured the level of information about SARS that nurses perceived was made available to them by supervisor and hospital administrator sources as well as emotional support. Response alternatives ranged from 1 = *strongly agree* to 5 = *strongly disagree*. Higher values indicate *lower* levels of perceived organizational support. A sample item is, "Nursing supervisors held information and support sessions with nursing staff related to SARS on a regular basis."

- *No feedback and positive feedback*. This 4-item scale was created for the purpose of this study. It assessed nurses' perceived quality and quantity of feedback from doctors, patients, co-workers, and healthcare organizations. The overarching statement read, "Please read each statement and select the response next to each item that most closely describes any feedback you received on your nursing performance during the SARS outbreak," and was followed by items which tapped into each of the above sources of feedback. For each source of feedback, respondents indicated whether they received positive, negative, neutral, or no feedback. A total of each of these types of feedback was computed by summing over responses to the four different feedback sources. For this study, only measures of positive feedback and no feedback were used. A score of 1 was assigned to "no feedback" and a score of 2 was assigned to "positive feedback."

Procedure

Data were collected using a self-report questionnaire in which SARS threat, organizational support, preventive coping, and demographics were some of the variables that were assessed. The English version of the questionnaire was developed for use in Canada and was subsequently translated into Chinese for use in China. In Canada, the questionnaire was posted on an Ontario registered nurses' website where nurses responded anonymously on the Internet. The integrity of the nursing sample was safeguarded against non-nurse respondents by requiring individuals who visited the website to enter a valid member's username and password before accessing the SARS questionnaire. Prior to being able to access the questionnaire, nurses were asked to read an informed consent webpage that conveyed relevant information about the project and matters of confidentiality. At the bottom of the webpage, nurses were asked either to click on an icon that read "I consent to participate," which then led them to the questionnaire, or to not agree and leave the site.

In China, the questionnaire was administered in the standard paper-and-pencil format. Two hundred questionnaires were sent out to nurses by mail of which 167 were returned; a response rate of 84 percent. All of the questionnaires were completed anonymously.

RESULTS

Part 1: Feedback, organizational support, preventive coping, and professional efficacy

A t-test on nurses' perceived feedback indicated that Chinese nurses ($M = 2.57$, $SD = 1.50$) received more positive feedback than their Canadian counterparts ($M = 2.07$, $SD = 1.24$; $t[284.61] = -3.70$, $p < .001$). Organizational support was also significantly higher in Chinese nurses ($M = 1.48$, $SD = 0.49$) than in Canadian nurses ($M = 2.89$, $SD = 1.08$; $t[542.97] = 21.24$, $p < .001$). (Lower numerical values indicated *higher* levels of organizational support.) Conversely, preventive coping was significantly higher in Canadian nurses ($M = 3.81$, $SD = 0.32$) than Chinese nurses ($M = 3.02$, $SD = 0.52$; $t[230.66] = 18.24$, $p < .001$). Canadian nurses ($M = 4.95$, $SD = 0.99$) reported significantly higher levels of professional efficacy than Chinese nurses ($M = 4.65$, $SD = 1.23$; $t[279.86] = 2.71$, $p = .007$). Canadian nurses ($M = 1.18$, $SD = 1.19$) reported significantly higher levels of no feedback than Chinese nurses ($M = 0.60$ $SD = 1.15$; $t[539] = 5.37$, $p < .001$).

Part 2: Testing the model predicting professional efficacy in Canadian nurses

Table 10.2 presents means, standard deviations, and intercorrelations for the variables measured in the study. Negative relationships were found between no feedback and preventive coping, professional efficacy, and positive feedback. No feedback correlated significantly with organizational support. That is, the more nurses reported receiving no feedback (as indicated by higher values), the *lower* their organizational support (as indicated by higher values on the

Table 10.2 Means, standard deviations, and intercorrelation matrix of variables

Canadian Nurses

Variable	1	2	3	4	M	SD
1. No Feedback					1.18	1.19
2. Positive Feedback	-.63***				2.07	1.24
3. Organizational Support[†]	.19***	-.18***			2.89	1.08
4. Preventive Coping	-.14**	.18***	-.20***		3.81	0.32
5. Professional Efficacy	-.12*	.26***	-.23***	.17**	4.95	0.99

Chinese Nurses

Variable	1	2	3	4	M	SD
1. No Feedback					0.60	1.15
2. Positive Feedback	-.60***				2.57	1.50
3. Organizational Support[†]	.17*	-.24**			1.48	0.49
4. Preventive Coping	-.06	.11	-.32***		3.02	0.52
5. Professional Efficacy	-.23**	.33***	-.15	.20*	4.65	1.23

Note: [†] Low values indicate greater organizational support; *** $p < .001$; ** $p < .01$; * $p < .05$.

POS scale). In contrast, positive feedback was positively related to greater preventive coping and greater professional efficacy, and to organizational support. That is, the higher the positive feedback reported by nurses, the higher the reported organizational support. Higher levels of organizational support were related to greater use of preventive coping and increased professional efficacy. Preventive coping and professional efficacy were positively related.

Path analysis using structural equation techniques (SEM) was used to explore the relationships among positive and no feedback, organizational support, preventive coping, and professional efficacy. The statistical package AMOS version 5.0 (Arbuckle, 2003) was used to provide path coefficients and tests of the overall goodness of fit of the model. The maximum likelihood method of parameter estimation was utilized. The independence chi-square ($\chi^2[10] = 276.20$, $p < .001$) confirmed the presence of intercorrelations in the data and, therefore, its suitability for SEM analysis. The χ^2 goodness of fit statistic ($\chi^2[5] = 45.127$, $p < .001$) and the ratio of chi-square to degrees of freedom (9.0254) failed to support the theoretical model. However, it has been suggested that the χ^2 goodness of fit statistic may be misleading, as it is influenced by sample size (Bollen, 1989).

In an attempt to develop a better fitting model, a modification index was considered (i.e., a path from positive feedback to professional efficacy was added). The modified model improved the fit of the data to the model; however the root mean square error of approximation (RMSEA) was slightly higher than the cut-off value (RMSEA = .08) suggested by Browne and Cudeck (1993). Table 10.3 displays the goodness of fit indices for the initial and modified model. A chi-square difference test was calculated between the original model and modified model, in order to determine whether the modified model was a significant improvement over the initial model. The findings indicated a significant χ^2 difference between models (χ^2 [1] = 20.397, $p < .05$); thus, the modified model was a significant improvement in fit.

Table 10.3   Goodness of fit indices for models

Canadian Nurses

Model	Chi-square	df	p	GFI	AGFI	CFI	RMSEA	PCLOSE
Initial model	45.127	5	.000	.957	.871	.849	.147	.000
Modified model	24.730	4	.000	.975	.908	.926	.116	.007

Chinese Nurses

Model	Chi-square	df	p	GFI	AGFI	CFI	RMSEA	PCLOSE
Initial model	18.643	5	.002	.959	.878	.885	.128	.018
Modified model	.699	4	.951	.998	.994	1.00	.000	.977

Note: GFI = Goodness of fit; AGFI = Adjusted goodness of fit; CFI = Comparative fit index; RMSEA = Root mean square error of approximation.

As indicated in Figure 10.2, positive feedback was directly and positively related to professional efficacy (β = .24), whereas no feedback was related to lower perceived organizational support (β = .13). That is, the more respondents reported getting no feedback, the less organizational support they received. As hypothesized, higher perceived organizational support was related to greater use of preventive coping strategies (β = -.20). Preventive coping, in turn, predicted increased feelings of professional efficacy (β = .13). Thus, organizational support had an indirect effect on professional efficacy through preventive coping (β = -.20 × β = .13) Positive feedback was negatively related to no feedback (r = -.63).

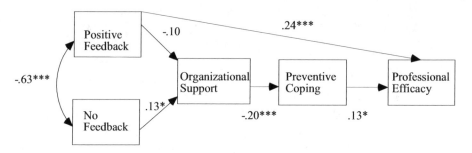

Figure 10.2 Model relating organizational support, perceived feedback, preventive coping, and professional efficacy in Canadian nurses

Note: * p < .05; ** p < .01; *** p < .001.

TESTING THE MODEL PREDICTING PROFESSIONAL EFFICACY IN CHINESE NURSES

Descriptive statistics and correlations among the variables assessed in the study are presented in Table 10.2. Negative relationships were found between no feedback and positive feedback, and professional efficacy. That is, the more no feedback was received, the less positive feedback and the lower the nurse's professional efficacy. No feedback correlated positively with organizational support. Thus, the higher the level of no feedback, the lower the organizational support (given that higher values indicate lower support). Conversely, positive feedback was positively related to professional efficacy, and negatively related to organizational support. Thus, the higher the positive feedback, the higher the participants reported receiving support. Higher levels of organizational support were related to greater use of preventive coping. Preventive coping and professional efficacy were positively related.

SEM was again used to explore the relationships among positive and no feedback, organizational support, preventive coping, and professional efficacy. The independence chi-square ($\chi^2[10] = 128.262, p < .001$) confirmed the presence of inter-correlations in the data and, therefore, its suitability for SEM analysis. The χ^2 goodness of fit statistic ($\chi^2[5] = 18.643, p = .002$) and the ratio of degrees of freedom to chi-square (3.729) failed to support the theoretical model.

In an attempt to develop a better fitting model, an AMOS modification index was considered (i.e., a path modification from positive feedback to professional efficacy was added to the model). The modified model improved the fit of the data to the model. Table 10.3 displays the goodness of fit indices for the initial and modified model. A chi-square difference test indicated a significant χ^2

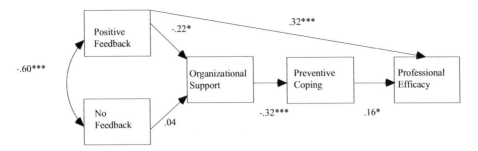

Figure 10.3 Model relating organizational support, perceived feedback, preventive coping, and professional efficacy in Chinese nurses

Note: * p < .05; ** p < .01; *** p < .001.

difference between models (χ^2 [1] = 17.944, p < .05); thus, the modified model was a significant improvement in fit.

As indicated in Figure 10.3, positive feedback was directly and positively related to professional efficacy (β = .32). As hypothesized, positive feedback was related to higher perceived organizational support (β = -.22). In turn, as hypothesized, higher perceived organizational support was related to greater use of preventive coping strategies (β = -.32). Preventive coping, in turn, predicted increased feelings of professional efficacy (β = .16). Thus, organizational support had an indirect effect on professional efficacy through preventive coping (β = -.32 × β = .16). Positive feedback was negatively related to no feedback (r = -.60).

In summary, results obtained with Canadian and Chinese nurses show that Canadian nurses indicated significantly greater levels of no feedback, preventive coping, and professional efficacy than Chinese nurses. In contrast, Chinese nurses reported greater levels of positive feedback and perceived organizational support. Results of the path analysis were similar in both samples, with the exception of the paths from feedback to perceived organizational support. In Canadian nurses, the path from positive feedback to organizational support was not significant and the path from no feedback to organizational support was significant. Thus, in the Canadian sample, the more nurses reported no feedback, the *lower* their organizational support. The opposite was found in the Chinese sample. That is, the more Chinese nurses reported positive feedback, the higher their organizational support. The fit statistics of the model (see Table 10.3) indicate that the data provided a good fit to the model in both samples.

Overall, the data in both samples suggest that the valence of feedback from others in the workplace (e.g., administrators, doctors, nurses) related to levels of organizational support differently in both samples. However, the relationships from positive feedback to professional efficacy, and from organizational support to preventive coping, and from preventive coping to professional efficacy, are robust for both samples of nurses. This suggests that the relationship from feedback to perceived organizational support may be influenced by differences associated with the two samples.

Discussion

The present study was conducted to examine the relationship between professional efficacy in nurses working during the SARS crisis, preventive coping, organizational support, and feedback. A model was developed predicting to professional efficacy and was tested in two samples of nurses working with SARS patients in Canada and in China. To date, there are considerable data indicating that nurses experienced high levels of distress and burnout due to SARS. The present study focused on one component of burnout, professional efficacy, since it was possible that, with increased stress, nurses' perception of their efficacy may have been diminished. In particular, the model put forth here posited individual and social resources as predictors of professional efficacy. According to our predictions, greater levels of reported positive feedback from others in the same work environment were hypothesized to lead to an increase in perceived organizational support. Support, in turn, predicted to higher levels of preventive coping, and preventive coping was hypothesized to lead to higher levels of professional efficacy.

Results of path analysis using SEM techniques indicated that preventive coping related directly to professional efficacy in both samples. Preventive coping also mediated the effects of organizational support on professional efficacy, as expected. In this study, preventive coping consisted of efforts such as keeping informed about nursing practices and thinking ahead in order to avoid SARS contagion and thus, could be seen as also developing resources to deal with the cognitive anticipation of potential future stressors As expected, these kinds of efforts led directly to greater feelings of efficacy in one's role as a nurse probably because of the greater sense of control it gave nurses as well as the fact that nurses were using their knowledge as professionals to enhance their own well being. Secondly, in both samples, the greater the reported support from their organization, the more nurses employed coping strategies that relied on preventive measures. In this study, organizational support indicated the level of information about SARS that nurses perceived was provided to them by supervisor and hospital administrator sources as well as emotional support. Moreover, having knowledge helps an individual to cope appropriately with stressful situations (e.g., Cheng and Cheung, 2005; Gan et al., 2004); consequently, more informational support (particularly about SARS) from one's organization should increase nurses' ability to cope effectively with SARS stress. Further, the positive relationship between organizational support and preventive coping in nurses parallels previous findings reported by Greenglass (1993) that social support at work contributes positively to preventive coping strategies used by managers. At the same time, present results suggest that informational support should increase a nurse's sense of controllability at a time of high uncertainty by providing important and relevant knowledge.

Although not originally predicted, results of SEM in both samples indicated that positive feedback predicted positively to professional efficacy. Nurses who received positive feedback regarding their nursing performance reported greater levels of professional efficacy. Therefore, nurses' feelings of competence in their job are bolstered when they receive positive feedback validating their job performance or efficacy on the job. This interpretation is consistent with Lee and Ashforth (1990) who argue that one's professional role is related to self-efficacy, which results from self-perceptions in a work role. Additional results indicate a significant negative relationship between positive feedback and no feedback in both samples; thus, the greater the perception of positive feedback, the lower the perception of no feedback. These results are expected.

Additional findings from the SEM analyses showed that the relationship between organizational support and feedback was different in the two samples. For example, positive feedback was a significant and positive contributor to organizational support in Chinese nurses only; more positive support was associated with greater reports of organizational support by Chinese nurses. This path was not significant in Canadian nurses. These findings suggest that there was an integral relationship between positive feedback and support in Chinese nurses that was not significant in their Canadian counterparts. This may be related to differences in working conditions in the two samples. For example, the 167 nurses in the Chinese sample worked in a government designated hospital for the care of SARS patients. This may have led to a closer knit working environment (hospital) in China consisting of nurses, doctors, and their co-workers. Working in the same hospital and looking after SARS patients may have contributed to greater feelings of cohesion and mutual interdependency that were not present in the Canadian sample. Moreover, as reported earlier, Chinese nurses also reported significantly *more* positive feedback and organizational support than their Canadian counterparts, results that support the above interpretation. The Canadian sample, in contrast, consisted of nurses from all over Ontario, who worked in hospitals of varying sizes that were general hospitals and were not devoted exclusively to the care of SARS patients. Thus, nurses in these work settings may have been less likely to bond with others as did the nurses in the Chinese sample and, in comparison, may have felt isolated as they struggled to cope with the added distress of caring for SARS patients. In the Canadian sample only, results indicate that no feedback from co-workers and patients contributed to lower organizational support. Canadian nurses also reported more no feedback and less organizational support than Chinese nurses. Taken together, these data suggest that Canadian nurses were working in a less supportive environment that was less responsive to positive feedback than the environment of Chinese nurses. Thus, Canadian nurses may have been more vulnerable to the effects of perceiving no feedback.

These data suggest that, in times of crisis, hospitals could introduce interventions that promote a collegial and supportive environment by providing positive feedback to their staff, which increases levels of perceived organizational support and professional efficacy. These in turn will improve nurses' perceptions of their own efficacy, thus resulting in improved nurse and patient morale. In summary, the findings of this study underscore the integral relationship between nurses' health, their professional efficacy and the well-being of their patients. To the extent that organizational administrations can introduce interventions that will ensure the health and welfare of its nursing staff, they are also able to increase the morale and well-being of their patients.

Some limitations of this study should be noted. The samples in the two countries were not completely comparable: the Chinese nurses were significantly younger than their Canadian counterparts; the Chinese nurses worked in a governmentally designated hospital for the care of SARS patients, whereas the Canadian nurses were employed in a variety of general care hospitals; and close to one-quarter of the Chinese sample had been diagnosed with suspected or probable SARS, while in Canadian nurses, this figure was much lower (2 percent). Thus, for Chinese nurses, the SARS threat was both more personal and more immediate than for the Canadian nurses. Additional data showed that, in both samples, nurses tended to work in similar units such as the emergency, medical/surgical, intensive care, and long term care/

geriatrics. But in the Canadian sample, more nurses were found in public health areas. Finally, although the questionnaire was identical in both samples, data collection differed in the two samples. The Canadian data were collected over the Internet and the Chinese data were gathered by a paper-and-pencil format. Despite these differences, our model predicting to professional efficacy in nurses was similar in both samples; thus, lending increased external validity to the results.

References

Arbuckle, J.L. (2003). *AMOS* (Version 5.0) [Computer software]. Chicago, IL: SPSS.

Bai, Y., Lin, C.C., Lin, C.Y., Chen, J.Y., Chue, C.M., and Chou, P. (2004). Survey of stress reactions among health-care workers involved with the SARS outbreak. *Psychiatric Services*, 55, 1055–7.

Blendon, R.J., Benson, J.M., DesRoches, C.M., Raleigh, E., and Taylor-Clark, K. (2004). The public's response to severe acute respiratory syndrome in Toronto and the United States. *Clinical Infectious Diseases*, 38, 925–31.

Bollen, K.A. (1989). *Structural Equations with Latent Variables*. New York: Wiley.

Browne, M.W. and Cudeck, R. (1993). Alternative ways of assessing model fit. In K.A. Bollen and J.S. Long (eds), *Testing Structural Equation Models* (pp. 136–62). Newbury Park, CA: Sage.

Chen, C.S., Yang, P., Yen, C.F., and Wu, H.Y. (2005). Validation of Impact of Events Scale in nurses under threat of contagion by severe acute respiratory syndrome. *Psychiatry and Clinical Neurosciences*, 59, 135–9.

Cheng, C. and Cheung, M.W.L. (2005). Psychological responses to outbreak of severe acute respiratory syndrome: a prospective, multiple time-point study. *Journal of Personality*, 73, 261–85.

DeLongis, A. and O'Brien, T. (1990). An interpersonal framework for stress and coping: an application to families of Alzheimer's patients. In M.H. Stephens, J.H. Crowther, S.E. Hobfoll, and D.L. Tennenbaum (eds), *Stress and Coping in Later Life Families* (pp. 221–39). New York: Hemisphere Publishing.

DeVries, J.E., Burnette, M.M., and Redmon, W.K. (1991). AIDS prevention: improving nurses' compliance with glove wearing through performance feedback. *Journal of Applied Behavior Analysis*, 24, 705–11.

Eisenberger, R., Huntington, R., Hutchison, S., and Sowa, D. (1986). Perceived organizational support. *Journal of Applied Psychology*, 71, 500–507.

Fleck, F. (2003). How SARS changed the world in less than six months. *Bulletin of the World Health Organization*, 81, 625–6.

Fowler, R.A., Lapinsky, S.E., Hallett, D., Detsky, A.S., Sibbald, W.J., Slutsky, A.S., et al. (2003). Critically ill patients with severe acute respiratory syndrome. *Journal of the American Medical Association*, 290, 367–73.

Gan, Y., Liu, Y., and Zhang, Y. (2004). Flexible coping responses to severe acute respiratory syndrome-related and daily life stressful events. *Asian Journal of Social Psychology*, 7, 55–66.

Greenglass, E.R. (1993). The contribution of social support to coping strategies. *Applied Psychology: An International Review*, 42, 323–40.

Greenglass, E.R. and Burke, R.J. (2000). The relationship between hospital restructuring, anger, hostility and psychosomatics in nurses. *Journal of Community and Applied Social Psychology*, 10, 155–61.

Hall, L.M., Angus, J., Peter, E., O'Brien-Pallas, L., Wynn, F., and Donner, G. (2003). Media portrayal of nurses' perspectives and concerns in the SARS crisis in Toronto. *Journal of Nursing Scholarship*, 35, 211–16.

Hawryluck, L., Gold, W.L., Robinson, S., Pogorski, S., Galea, S., and Styra, R. (2004). SARS control and psychological effects of quarantine, Toronto, Canada. *Emerging Infectious Diseases*, 10, 1206–12.

Hobfoll, S.E., Dunahoo, C.L., Ben-Porath, Y., and Monnier, J. (1994). Gender and coping: the dual-axis model of coping. *American Journal of Community Psychology*, 22, 49–82.

Hutchison, S. and Garstka, M. (1996). Sources of perceived organizational support: goal setting and feedback. *Journal of Applied Social Psychology*, 26, 1351–66.

Lau, J.T.F., Yang, X., Pang, E., Tsui, H.Y., Wong, E., and Wing, Y.K. (2005). SARS-related perceptions in Hong Kong. *Emerging Infectious Diseases*, 11(3), 417–24.

Lee, R.T. and Ashforth, B.E. (1990). On the meaning of Maslach's three dimensions of burnout. *Journal of Applied Psychology*, 75, 743–7.

Leiter, M.P. (1991). Coping patterns as predictors of burnout: the function of control and escapist coping patterns. *Journal of Organizational Behavior*, 12, 123–44.

Mason, P., Grabowski, P., and Du, W. (2005). Severe acute respiratory syndrome, tourism and the media. *International Journal of Tourism Research*, 7, 11–21.

Masur, H., Emanuel, E., and Lane, H.C. (2003). Severe acute respiratory syndrome: providing care in the face of uncertainty. *Journal of the American Medical Association*, 289, 2861–3.

Maunder, R., Hunter, J., Vincent, L., Bennett, J., Peladeau, N., Leszcz, M., et al. (2003). The immediate psychological and occupational impact of the 2003 SARS outbreak in a teaching hospital. *Canadian Medical Association Journal*, 168, 1245–51.

McDonald, L.C., Simor, A.E., Su, I.J., Maloney, S., Ofner, M., Chen, K.T., et al. (2004). SARS in healthcare facilities, Toronto and Taiwan. *Emerging Infectious Diseases*, 10, 777–81.

Nickell, L.A., Crighton, E.J., Tracy, C.S., Al-Enazy, H., Bolaji, Y., Hanjrah, S., et al. (2004). Psychological effects of SARS on hospital staff: survey of a large tertiary care institution. *Canadian Medical Association Journal*, 170, 793–8.

Ogus, E.D. (1992). Burnout and coping strategies: a comparative study of ward nurses. *Journal of Social Behavior and Personality*, 7, 111–24.

Olofsson, B., Bengtsson, C., and Brink, E. (2003) Absence of response: a study of nurses' experience of stress in the workplace. *Journal of Nursing Management*, 11, 351–8.

Peng, P.W.H., Wong, D.T., Bevan, D., and Gardam, M. (2003). Infection control and anesthesia: lessons learned from the Toronto SARS outbreak. *Canadian Journal of Anesthesia*, 50, 989–97.

Rhoades, L. and Eisenberger, R. (2002). Perceived organizational support: a review of the literature. *Journal of Applied Psychology*, 87, 698–714.

Robertson, E., Hershenfield, K., Grace, S.L., and Stewart, D.E. (2004). The psychosocial effects of being quarantined following exposure to SARS: a qualitative study of Toronto health-care workers. *Canadian Journal of Psychiatry*, 49, 403–7.

Schaufeli, W.B., Leiter, M.P., Maslach, C., and Jackson, S.E. (1996). Maslach Burnout Inventory-General Survey (MBI-GS). In C. Maslach, S.E. Jackson, and M.P. Leiter (eds), *MBI Manual*, 3rd edn. Palo Alto, CA: Consulting Psychologists Press.

Schwarzer, R. and Knoll, N. (2003). Positive coping: mastering demands and searching for meaning. In S.J. Lopez and C.R. Snyder (eds), *Positive Psychological Assessment: A Handbook of Models and Measures* (pp. 393–409). Washington, DC: American Psychological Association.

Schwarzer, R. and Taubert, S. (2002). Tenacious goal pursuits and striving toward personal growth: proactive coping. In E. Frydenberg (ed.), *Beyond Coping: Meeting Goals, Visions and Challenges* (pp. 19–35). London: Oxford University Press.

Tam, C.W.C., Pang, E.P.F., Lam, L.C.W., and Chiu, H.F.K. (2004). Severe acute respiratory syndrome (SARS) in Hong Kong in 2003: stress and psychological impact among frontline healthcare workers. *Psychological Medicine*, 34, 1197–204.

Tang, C.S.K. and Wong, C. (2003). An outbreak of the severe acute respiratory syndrome: predictors of health behaviors and effect of community prevention measures in Hong Kong, China. *American Journal of Public Health*, 93, 1887–8.

Wong, C.Y. and Tang, C.S.K. (2005). Practice of habitual and volitional health behaviors to prevent severe acute respiratory syndrome among Chinese adolescents in Hong Kong. *Journal of Adolescent Health*, 36, 193–200.

World Health Organization (2004). *Cumulative Number of Reported Probable Cases of Severe Acute Respiratory Syndrome (SARS): Summary of Probable SARS Cases with Onset of Illness from Nov 1 2002 to 31 July 2003*. [Online]. Available at https://www.who.int/csr/sars/country/table2004_04_21/en/index.html [Accessed November 15, 2005].

PART III
Health, Management and Organizational Effectiveness

11

An Integrative Framework of Supervisor Responses to Workgroup Conflict

Kirsten Way, Nerina L. Jimmieson, and Prashant Bordia

Introduction

It is well-established that prolonged exposure to workplace conflict, as a work stressor, is linked to physical illness and psychological dysfunction in employees (see Spector and Jex, 1998; Romanov, Appelberg, Honkasalo, and Koskenvuo, 1996; Skogstad, Einarsen, Torsheim, Aasland, and Hetland, 2007). In addition to the negative implications for physiological and psychological health, workplace conflict has been shown to influence employee behaviors that have consequences for organizational effectiveness (e.g., turnover and impaired performance; see Bowling and Beehr, 2006; De Dreu and Weingart, 2003). Further, research suggests that managers spend approximately 20 percent of their time managing conflict (Thomas, 1992; Baron, 1989). There also are substantial financial implications associated with workplace conflict. For example, in the United Kingdom, costs at the national level for sickness absence and replacement costs has been estimated to be close to £2 billion per annum (Hoel, Sparks, and Cooper, 2001).

When considered together, these research findings point to the potential for harm from conflict at work, not only for individuals involved, but also for managers, workplaces, and the economy as a whole. Thus, a major challenge for researchers is to increase the capacity of employers to identify and manage workgroup conflict. To achieve this aim, we present a theoretical model of workgroup conflict and employee adjustment that takes into account the important role of supervisors and their conflict handling methods as a stress-buffering or stress-exacerbating mechanism. Supervisors were chosen as a focus for the model as their organizationally sanctioned role is often to enforce rules and expectations about employee behaviors in work contexts. This can place them in a pivotal position from which they can influence how conflict plays out within workgroups. While it must be acknowledged that there are significant bodies of research on third-party mediation, conciliation, and how individuals respond in conflict situations, what appears to be more incomplete is research on the third-party role of supervisors in conflict management when formal conflict resolution processes are not utilized. To add to this limited body of literature, we develop an integrative framework of supervisor behaviors that further builds on the notion that leaders occupy a pivotal role in linking organizational factors with organizational and health outcomes (Quick, Marik-Frey, and Cooper, 2007; Skogstad et al., 2007).

The proposed model brings together several areas of literature, including health and safety risk management, occupational stress and coping, conflict management, and organizational justice. While having clear implications for our understanding of the management of work stressors, these literatures have not been integrated in this way before. Further, most studies in these areas have operationalized variables at the individual level, thereby limiting investigation of how contextual or group-level independent variables may be affecting individual-level employee outcomes. Multi-level research in this area will fill an important gap in the academic literature, answering a call for a multi-level approach to occupational stress research (Bliese and Jex, 1999), while providing practical information to organizations, and their players, that will assist in a number of ways. At the organizational and societal levels, identifying and managing conflict-related risk has the potential to improve organizational effectiveness and reduce conflict-associated costs to employers and the economy as a whole. At the supervisor-level, it provides processes and signposts to navigate the difficult interactions associated with workgroup conflict, thereby allowing supervisors to better manage this potentially emotive workplace phenomenon. This, in turn, has benefits at the worker level, as the individual experience of injustice and strain associated with conflict will be reduced, rather than exacerbated, by the actions or inactions of their supervisor.

Proposed Theoretical Model

Our proposed theoretical model, as depicted in Figure 11.1, represents several main, moderated, and mediated relationships among the variables of interest, modeled at the level of the individual and the workgroup. Specifically, in this model, it is postulated that it is the *workgroup-level* perceptions of conflict, supervisor behavior, and justice that is related to *individual-level* adjustment, where a workgroup is defined as a team to which workers are assigned, that they identify with, and the members of which regularly interact in order to perform tasks related to a common work goal (Anderson and West, 1998). Taking a multi-level perspective on the relationships of interest is theoretically relevant as many aspects of organizational and group processes, including conflict and responses to it, can be argued to have their basis in the thoughts, emotions, and behaviors of individuals which, through social interactions, have characteristics that manifest at the group-level. This has been described by some as being the bottom up or isomorphic nature of many workgroups and departments (Kozlowski and Klein, 2000). Researchers in a number of areas, including organizational justice climate (e.g., Naumann and Bennett, 2000), have argued that workgroups can develop shared perceptions or affective reactions. Research aimed at identifying interventions at the group or departmental level have the added advantage that they can bring about improvements for a large number of employees at the same time (as opposed to interventions aimed at the individual level which can be a lot more costly to implement; see Bliese and Jex, 1999).

As well as using occupational stress theory to explain relationships between workgroup-level perceptions of conflict and individual-level employee adjustment, we draw on risk management and the conflict management literature to more clearly describe the types of behaviors that supervisors may engage in when managing task and relationship conflict among workgroup members. Structurally, the model is based on health and safety risk management frameworks, where risks to employee health are 1) identified, 2) assessed, and 3) controlled through implementing risk control measures (Queensland Government, 2007). Specifically, it is suggested that at the level of the workgroup, employees will have a shared perception of supervisor behaviors, and that supervisors may be perceived as 1) identifying or failing to identify conflict, 2) accurately or inaccurately assessing the severity of conflict, 3) intervening in conflict at the individual and/or organizational levels, and 4) as a third party, using a number of different conflict management styles to respond to the conflict. These supervisor responses will have direct positive effects on workers' shared perceptions of justice (i.e., justice climate) and individual-level employee adjustment, as well moderating the extent to which workgroup conflict influences individual-level employee adjustment. In an attempt to explain why supervisory behaviors may have stress-buffering or stress-exacerbating properties, we argue that justice climate is likely to mediate the interactive effects of workgroup conflict and supervisor responses on individual-level employee adjustment.

It has been argued that both task and relationship subsets of conflict are emotional in nature as they involve perceptions of threats to goals (Jordan and Troth, 2004) and for this reason, emotional intelligence theory (Mayer and Salovey, 1997) provides an important theoretical contribution to the first two categories of supervisor responses in the proposed model. Specifically, it is argued that, for supervisors to respond effectively to conflict in their workgroup, they must have aptitude in several of the constructs of emotional intelligence, and that these will enable them to identify conflict and accurately assess its severity. The importance of emotional intelligence (or emotional competence) in leaders, and its potential relationship with individual and organizational health also was proposed by Quick et al. (2007) and by Yarker, Lewis, Donaldson-Feilder, and Flaxman (2007). Indeed, Yarker et al. (2007) proposed that "managing conflict" and "expressing and managing emotions" are 2 of the 19 management competencies for reducing or preventing work-related stress.

When conceptualizing the third category of supervisor responses to conflict, de Frank and Cooper's (1987) framework of worksite stress management interventions is utilized (i.e., with interventions being targeted at the individual and/or organizational levels). Underpinning the final category—supervisors' conflict handling style—is the Conflict Management Taxonomy/Grid (Blake and Mouton, 1964) and the Dual Concern Theory (Pruitt and Rubin, 1986; Thomas, 1992), where supervisors may handle conflict in their workgroup by contending, conceding, avoiding, collaborating, or compromising. Integrating this well-established conflict management taxonomy into the proposed model addresses a concern raised by De Dreu and Beersma (2005) that the conflict management literature has been isolated from broader issues in organizational psychology, and more needs to be understood about how specific supervisory behaviors influence employees and their stress responses.

These propositions will be discussed in further detail below, and if they hold true, this knowledge will provide theoretically and practically useful insights into the role of supervisors in stress management in organizations, as well as presenting a series of empirically testable hypotheses for future research.

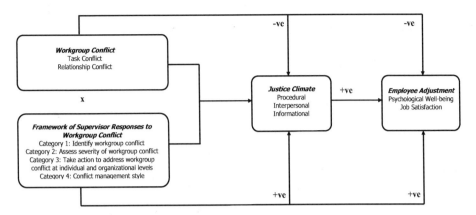

Figure 11.1   An integrative framework of supervisor responses to workgroup conflict

Workgroup Conflict as a Work Stressor

THE STRESSOR-ADJUSTMENT PROCESS

Work stressors can be defined as external demands in the workplace that are perceived by employees as threatening (e.g., aggressive culture, certain managerial practices and communication styles, specific task and role properties, and conflict), whereas strains refer to the negative reactions that are elicited when such demands exceed the coping resources of employees (Koslowsky, 1998). Accordingly, the notion of "stress" is a dynamic process represented by a perceived imbalance between the individual's environment and their ability to deal with such demands. This imbalance brings about a change in either the physical or psychological condition of the individual such that they are forced to deviate from normal functioning. Most theoretical models of the occupational stress process conceptualize this relationship as a causal flow from environmental conditions to employee outcomes or, in other words, from work stressors to strains or adjustment (Lazarus, 1990; Lazarus and Folkman, 1984; Spector, Chen, and O'Connell, 2000). In the present chapter, we focus on two central components of adjustment specific to the mental health of employees; namely, psychological well-being (ranging on a continuum from feeling bad to feeling good) and job satisfaction (ranging from displeased to pleased), as defined by Warr (1991) in his discussion of work adjustment theory. Conceptualizing the stressor-adjustment relationship in this fashion has allowed researchers to study and analyze this phenomenon by modeling it as a process with observable and measurable antecedents (stressors) and outcomes (adjustments).

Conflict, as one type of work stressor, is defined as the tension among employees due to real or perceived differences (Wall and Callister, 1995). Workplace conflict can be classified into the two subsets of task conflict and relationship conflict (Guetzkow and Gyr, 1954; Jehn and Mannix, 2001). Task conflict refers to conflict about allocation and distribution of resources, differences in views about procedures and policies, or disagreements in judgments and interpretation of facts (De Dreu and Van de Vliert, 1997). Relationship conflict, on the other hand, refers to conflict about interpersonal attributes or personal taste, disagreements about political preferences, or opposing values (De Dreu and Van de Vliert, 1997). It has been argued that groups who are exposed to task conflict make better decisions as this type of conflict encourages greater cognitive understanding of the issue being considered. Relationship conflict, on the other hand, is believed to limit the information processing ability of the group as group members spend more cognitive time on each other than on the task. It is important to note, however, that what was originally proposed by Jehn (1995) was a curvilinear relationship between task conflict and performance, meaning that both too little and too much would be related to performance decrements. In addition, relationship conflict may include the more extreme form of conflict described as "workplace bullying" or "workplace harassment." Bullying has been defined as "repeated and persistent acts towards one or more individuals which involve a perceived power imbalance and create a hostile work environment" (Salin, 2003: 1214–15). Jex (1998) noted that the relationship between conflict and distress can be explained from an occupational stress framework. First, conflict brings obstruction in one's goal directed actions which may trigger feelings of increased uncertainty and reduced control, conditions that act as prerequisites for a stress response (Quick, Quick, Nelson, and Hurrell, 1997). Second, conflicts are a causal antecedent for negative emotions which can affect self-esteem, self-worth, sense of self, and similarity with others, and subsequently, be related to physiological and psychological strain (De Dreu, Van Dierendonck, and De Best-Waldhober, 2003; Frone, 2000).

EFFECTS OF WORKGROUP CONFLICT ON EMPLOYEE ADJUSTMENT

Jex and Beehr (1991) specified that interpersonal stressors (a broader construct encompassing both task and relationship conflict) are one of the more detrimental stressors at work (see also Jex, 1998; Smith and Sulsky, 1985). Bolger, DeLongis, Kessler, and Schilling (1989) found that interpersonal stressors are by far the most upsetting of all daily stressors, accounting for more than 80 percent of the explained variance in daily mood. Within the conflict literature, theory and research has traditionally focused on individual and team effectiveness, and productivity, with far less attention being devoted to the outcomes of health and well-being (De Dreu and Beersma, 2005). Nevertheless, there is empirical evidence demonstrating that the occurrence of interpersonal conflict at work results in a decline in physical and psychological functioning (see Spector and Jex, 1998, for a meta-analysis). More specifically, this body of knowledge has reported that interpersonal relationships are associated with employee stress responses (Beehr and Newman, 1978; Jones, Bright, Searle, and Cooper, 1998; Warr, 1994) and psychological disturbance beyond variates of age, health practices, stressful work events, support from work and home, and stressful life events (Gilbreath and Benson, 2004). Associations also have been found between conflict at work and frustration, anxiety, the emotional subset of burnout, physician-diagnosed psychiatric morbidity, and physical complaints (Dijkstra, van Dierendonck, and Evers, 2005; Frone, 2000; Leiter, 1991; Rahim, 1983; Richardsen, Burke, and Leiter, 1992; Romanov et al., 1996; Skogstad et al., 2007; Spector et al., 2000; Van Dierendonck, Schaufeli, and Sixma, 1994). Lastly, the concept of "conflict stress," a stress response from exposure to conflict, was introduced by Giebels and Janssen (2005). These authors argued that conflict stress is positively related to emotional exhaustion, and is stronger when it emanates from relationship conflict compared to task conflict.

It also is important to note that related to relationship conflict at work is harassment and bullying (De Dreu and Beersma, 2005), the effects of which can lead to outcomes of an even more severe nature (Einarsen, 1999). The harassment or bullying literature provides some specific support for the link between this type of conflict and employee ill-health, with research demonstrating that employees who experienced or witnessed bullying reported more symptoms of anxiety, depression, and somatization, as well as having levels of salivary cortisol that have been associated with post-traumatic stress disorder and chronic fatigue (Hansen, Hogh, Persson, Karlson, Garde, and Orbæk, 2006; Vartia, 2001). Further support for the relationship between harassment and employee strain was found in a recent meta-analysis (Bowling and Beehr, 2006). In this research, harassment was positively associated with negative emotions at work, frustration, anxiety, depression, burnout, and physical symptoms (with effect sizes ranging from 0.31 to 0.46), and was negatively associated with job satisfaction with an effect size of 0.35. In addition, there has been research conducted on the effects of bullying on bystanders which concludes that both bullying targets and bystanders suffer when someone is bullied in the workplace, such that bullying becomes a problem for the entire workgroup (Hansen et al., 2006; Vartia, 2001).

Thus, the first proposition centers on replicating and adding to the research findings outlined in this section, particularly adding to the body of knowledge recommending that future research make a clear distinction between task and relationship conflict and their respective effects on employee outcomes.

Proposition 1: Workgroup-level perceptions of the presence of conflict in the workgroup will have a negative main effect on individual-level employee adjustment (specifically psychological well-being and job satisfaction).

Role of Supervisory Behaviors in Employee Adjustment

SUPERVISOR SUPPORT

In response to research outlining the negative consequences of task and relationship conflict stressors for an organization and its employees, researchers have investigated factors that may moderate their negative effects. Such moderation effects occur via a two-way interaction in which the presence of an additional variable attenuates, or buffers, the negative effects of work stress on employee adjustment by allowing the employee some means of coping with the demanding situation. The stress-buffering hypothesis is commonly used to describe the effects of a range of different variables that may protect individuals from adverse life events (Cohen and Edwards, 1989). Indeed, the effects of work stressors on employees have been shown to vary depending on a variety of contextual characteristics related to the climate of the organization (Johlke and Duhan, 2001). As noted by Ganster (1988), the identification of such moderating variables has practical implications. If specific job characteristics can be identified that lessen the negative impact of work stressors, one could create a healthy work environment without necessarily lowering the level of demands. One job characteristic that has attracted extensive research attention as a potential buffer in the stressor–strain relationship is the notion of social support from supervisors (Karasek and Theorell, 1990; for reviews see Van der Doef and Maes, 1998; 1999).

Social support is generally categorized as "instrumental" support or "emotional" support. Instrumental support consists of offering practical help to solve problems or providing tangible assistance or aid in the form of knowledge or advice needed to resolve the issue, whereas emotional support involves offering care or listening sympathetically to another person (Swanson and Power, 2001). Both researchers and laypersons alike have readily accepted social support as a potentially powerful moderator in reducing the impact of stressors on strains. Indeed, there is empirical support for this proposition in the work context (see Wang, 2004, for an example in the prediction of major depression; see also Wang and Patten, 2001), including a meta-analysis by Viswesvaran, Sanchez, and Fisher (1999). However, other studies have failed to find evidence for the stress-buffering role of supervisor support in the prediction of employee adjustment (e.g., Kickul and Posig, 2001; Singh, 1998; Swanson and Power, 2001).

Furthermore, it is not uncommon in this literature for reverse-buffering effects to be detected, with several studies documenting instances in which social support is more harmful than helpful (Elfering, Semmer, Schade, Grund, and Boos, 2002; Glaser, 1999; Kickul and Posig, 2001; see also Deelstra, Peeters, Schaufeli, Stroebe, Zijlstra, and van Doornen, 2003, for a review of such negative associations). Reverse-buffering effects—in which the provision of supervisor support actually increases (i.e., exacerbates) the relationship between the stressor and strain—were first identified by LaRocco, House, and French (1980) and later more directly by Kaufmann and Beehr (1989). More specifically, Kaufman and Beehr found that support involving reaffirming the aversive nature of the work environment will heighten, rather than mitigate, a person's negative stress responses. The content of interactions and behaviors used when giving support may, therefore, be an important factor in determining whether this support will ultimately alleviate or exacerbate strain. We argue that this inconsistent pattern of findings is due to the fact that the specific behavioral intervention strategies used by supervisors when managing stressful conditions at work has not been systematically investigated. Aiming to address these concerns, the following section outlines a broad, systematic, and integrative framework of possible supervisor responses to workgroup conflict.

SUPERVISORS AS A SOURCE OF THIRD PARTY HELP FOR WORKPLACE CONFLICT

Third-party help refers to a specific conflict management strategy or technique of actively involving a third-party in a dispute (Giebels and Janssen, 2005). That third-party intervention has the potential to be useful in conflict resolution is clear. Ting-Toomey and Oetzel (2001) found that accessing third party help could be an additional conflict management style for individual employees that buffers the effect of conflict-related stressors on well-being. Similarly, Giebels and Janssen (2005) found that the effects of distress resulting from task and relationship conflict on exhaustion, absenteeism, and turnover intentions was far more marked for employees who reported using less third-party help. Hyde, Jappinen, Theorell, and Oxenstierna (2006) examined the relationship between conflict management in the workplace and self-report measures of well-being and organizational outcomes, with some focus on management style. Analyses showed that conflict resolved through discussion was least likely to result in a deterioration of well-being. Limitations in some of these studies were the failure to specify the source of this third-party help (i.e., supervisor or colleague) or to specify the nature of assistance provided by the source (for example was it mediation, arbitration, information provision, problem-solving, and so on).

There are, however, relatively few studies that explore supervisors in this capacity. Given that the vast majority of organizations function in a hierarchical manner, it can be argued that supervisors often have the power to set rules and expectations in which to act in certain situations. Thus, they have formal organizational authority and expertise that makes them logical intra-organizational third parties to whom employees can turn when they cannot handle the demanding aspects of the work. Supervisory third-party help differs from formal third parties (Sheppard, Saunders, and Minton, 1988). Formal third parties, such as arbitrators and mediators, have clearly defined and limited roles in handling disputes (see review by Lewicki, Wiess, and Lewin, 1992). In comparison, the conflict handling strategies and techniques available to supervisors are much less constrained, allowing them greater freedom in selecting the style of conflict handling they implement.

Pinkley, Brittain, Neale, and Northcraft (1995) have described the underlying dimensions that characterize the strategies used by supervisors in resolving intra-organizational problems. Based on the earlier work of Karambayya and Brett (1989), Sheppard (1984), and Lewicki and Sheppard (1985), they developed a taxonomy by asking managers to recall behavioral strategies employed when asked to help others within their organization to manage or resolve a problem at work and detected four underlying dimensions that distinguish one set of managerial strategies from another. It has been argued that third party help may provide its buffering effect via promoting accurate information processing, by clarifying the real issues at stake, by setting out procedures to manage conflict, and by helping parties recover control over the process and outcomes of their disputes (Arnold and O'Connor, 1999).

Supporting the need for further research into this area, what most third party research literature does not consider is threefold. First, situations where the supervisor does not identify or accurately assess the conflict are not considered. For supervisors to take informed and effective action they must first, obviously, be aware that the conflict is occurring and accurately assess its severity. Having the emotional competence to both identify and accurately assess conflict is argued to be the first important hurdle for supervisors to clear to enable effective conflict management. Second, the influence of interventions other than helping the individual resolve the conflict (i.e., high systems approaches) has not been systematically evaluated and, third, how employees' group-level perceptions of their supervisors' behaviors influences employee strain has been relatively overlooked.

The model proposed in this chapter is argued to address these gaps in the literature in a number of ways. First, it takes a wider view of supervisors' response to conflict. Rather than the model being isolated to what supervisors do to manage conflict, as is the case with traditional third-party frameworks, the current model starts from a point antecedent to this, that is, whether supervisors are even aware that conflict exists. It also adds a second, new antecedent to previous models by including whether supervisors accurately assess the severity of conflict. Third, it considers interventions taken by supervisors to address conflict and whether these interventions are targeted at the appropriate level of the system. These new ideas offer avenues for research about how and why some supervisor behaviors may be helpful in resolving conflict, while others seem to exacerbate conflict. Last, using Lazarus and Folkman's (1984) Cognitive Appraisal Model as a theoretical base, the proposed model gives central importance to employee perceptions of supervisor behavior, rather than supervisors' self-ratings. Each of the categories of supervisor responses to conflict will now be described in turn.

Proposed Supervisor Responses to Workgroup Conflict

CATEGORY 1: SUPERVISORS' ABILITY TO IDENTIFY CONFLICT

This category of responses examines the extent to which supervisors perceive or *identify the presence* of conflict in their workgroup. It is based on the first step of established workplace health and safety risk management frameworks— *risk identification* (see for example, Queensland Government, 2007). In terms of psychological constructs underpinning this category, it is argued that the emotional intelligence of the supervisor underpins their ability to identify workgroup conflict. Specific constructs of relevance to this proposition are based on some, but not all, of the Mayer and Salovey (1997) model of emotional intelligence. Emotional intelligence is defined as: "the ability to perceive emotions, the ability to access and generate emotions so as to assist thought, to understand emotions and emotional knowledge, and to reflectively regulate emotions so as to promote emotional and intellectual growth" (Mayer and Salovey, 1997: 5). The model of emotional intelligence, as put forward by these authors, has four "branches," each of which has four subsets. Of the 16 subsets of emotional intelligence, there are three constructs that theoretically underpin supervisors' ability to identify conflict in their workgroup: 1) their ability to identify emotions in other people; 2) their ability to use emotions to prioritize thinking by directing attention to important information; and 3) their ability to monitor emotions reflectively in relation to others and recognize how clear, typical, influential, or reasonable they are. That is, where supervisors are able to recognize atypical emotions in their workgroup, they will be more skilled at being able to identify conflict and therefore more able to commence the next stage in third party conflict management as outlined in category 2 below.

CATEGORY 2: SUPERVISORS' ABILITY TO ASSESS THE SEVERITY OF CONFLICT

Once detected, supervisors must accurately *assess the severity* of the workgroup conflict in order to determine whether they need to intervene or take action to manage conflict. This important category of responses is based on the second step of established workplace health and safety risk management frameworks— *risk assessment* (Queensland Government, 2007). It involves decision-making based on the severity and likelihood of negative outcomes from the conflict. Specifically, this category asks the question: Do supervisors ascribe appropriate importance to the conflict? That is, do supervisors under- or over-estimate the severity of outcomes from the conflict and the likelihood of negative outcomes occurring?

We propose that psychological constructs underpinning this category are, again, a number of aspects of emotional intelligence proposed by Mayer and Salovey (1997: 10), including 1) supervisors' "ability to discriminate between accurate and inaccurate, or honest versus dishonest expressions of feeling"; and 2) the extent to which "emotions are sufficiently vivid and available that they can be generated as aids to judgment and memory concerning feelings." Therefore, it is proposed that supervisors who are able to tell the difference between accurate and inaccurate expression of employees' feelings, and supervisors who use emotional content in their judgment and memory, will be better at judging the severity of conflict in their workgroup. For supervisors who do not have this capacity, they may under-estimate the severity and outcomes of the conflict and fail to intervene where action is required. Alternatively, they may over-estimate the severity of the conflict and intervene in situations where no action is required, thereby exacerbating the conflict. In this model, it is argued that workers who perceive their supervisors are able to judge accurately the severity of conflict in their workgroup will have higher levels of adjustment as their supervisors are more like to intervene as appropriate.

CATEGORY 3: LEVEL OF INTERVENTION TAKEN BY SUPERVISORS TO ADDRESS CONFLICT

It is argued that it is appropriate and necessary for supervisors to take action to intervene in some types of conflict and, in fact, this category lines up with *implementing risk controls* in health and safety frameworks (Queensland Government, 2007). The occupational stress research provides a classification method for the types of actions supervisors may take when initiating these interventions. Intervention types for responding to occupational stress have been classified into three groups (Cox and Griffiths, 2000; de Frank and Cooper, 1987) First, those targeted at the individual level for employees who may exhibit negative consequences associated with work stressors (Bunce, 1997). Individual-level interventions are aimed at assisting employees to build resilience and develop a repertoire of coping skills through support, training, education, and behavioral programs. The second intervention type includes those targeted at the individual/organizational interface level or the fit between the two. The third are those interventions targeted at the organizational level, where interventions are aimed at altering parts or components of the organizational system itself (for example initiatives related to job design, managerial training and development and change management practices).

It is important to note that individual-level interventions are limited to the extent that they, at least implicitly, attribute primary responsibility for the management of conflict to employees rather than focusing on systemic ways to reduce conflict in the workplace. Thus, the extent to which employees remain exposed to some types of conflict is not likely to be diminished. A theme evident in the literature is that the majority of stress interventions studied have been individually-focused and remedial (Caulfield, Chang, Dollard, and Elshaug, 2004; Giga, Noblet, Faragher, and Cooper, 2003; Kompier and Cooper, 1999; van der Klink, Blonk, Schene, and van Dijk, 2001). While there is empirical evidence to suggest that some types of individual-level interventions are effective in improving the psychological well-being of employees (Cooper and Cartwright, 1997), overall findings suggest that interventions that utilize a combination of individual *and* organizational-level interventions are the most effective (Caulfield et al., 2004; Cox and Griffiths, 2000; Giga, Cooper, and Faragher, 2003; Giga, Noblet et al., 2003; Semmer, 2003).

The distinction between types of intervention for occupational stress provides an important framework on which the current model is based. That is, the proposed framework suggests that having identified and assessed the conflict accurately, supervisors can take action at the individual level (such as providing individual or joint conflict counseling, coaching, or mediation), the organizational level (such as addressing role demand, role ambiguity, and/or role conflict), or both levels. It is suggested that an error in this category can occur by intervening at the wrong level, for example, focusing on deficits in individual coping skills but not addressing problems in performance management discrepancies. Specifically, it is proposed that, similar to the findings in the general stress research, supervisors who take action to address conflict at both the individual level and organizational level will be most effective.

CATEGORY 4: SUPERVISORS' CONFLICT MANAGEMENT STYLE

To add to our understanding of what is done in terms of supervisor responses, the final category in the framework looks at *how* the supervisors intervene, or their conflict management style. To do this, we draw on the conflict management literature to identify behaviors that might be of use when supervisors are entrusted with the responsibility of managing psychosocial risk factors, such as task or relationship conflict in the workplace.

There are many models of conflict handling style (see Lewicki et al., 1992, for a review); however, for our purposes, we draw on the influential and empirically tested Conflict Management Taxonomy/Grid (Blake and Mouton, 1964) and the related Dual Concern Theory (Pruitt and Rubin, 1986; Thomas, 1992). These models propose four different ways that individuals may respond when they find themselves in a conflict situation. The first way of responding is "contending" (or forcing), in which the individual imposes his or her will on others and may involve threats, bluffs, persuasive arguments, and positional commitments, indicating high concern for self and low concern for others. The second way of responding is "conceding" (or yielding). This involves unilateral concessions and indicates low concern for self and high concern for others. "Avoiding," which involves inaction or withdrawing, is the third way of responding and indicates low concern for self and others. Last, "collaborating" (or problem solving) involves showing insights and making trade-offs between important and unimportant issues indicating a high concern for self and others. Some authors (e.g., Kilmann and Thomas, 1977; Van de Vliert, 1997) have suggested a fifth strategy, "compromising," which indicates intermediate concern for self and others.

It is proposed that the five conflict management strategies that have been researched at the individual level (as outlined above) can apply to a third party or supervisor who may be attempting to resolve a dispute in a workgroup. That is, employees may report that their supervisor managed conflict in their workgroup by 1) looking for a compromise between parties to the conflict, 2) yielding to one of the parties, 3) contending or forcing an outcome, 4) problem-solving or collaborating between parties, or 5) avoiding differences of opinion and confrontation. Further, it is proposed that although there may be times when the conflict management strategies of "avoiding" or "forcing" are better suited to a particular situation (De Dreu and Van Vianen, 2001; Rahim, 1985), it is suggested that, on balance, the more conciliatory styles of "collaborating" or "compromising" are more effective in reducing employee strain (Arnold and O'Connor, 1999; DeChurch, Hamilton, and Haas, 2007; Weider-Hatfield and Hatfield, 1995; 1996). With these four categories in mind, the second proposal relates to the main effects between supervisor responses to conflict and employee outcomes.

Proposition 2: Workgroup-level perceptions that supervisors (i) identify workgroup conflict, (ii) accurately assess the severity of workgroup conflict, (iii) intervene in conflict situations using a combination of individual and organizational methods, and (iv) use a conciliatory conflict handling style (i.e., collaboration or compromise) will have a positive main effect on individual-level employee adjustment.

The Stress-Buffering Effect of Supervisor Responses

The examination of stress-buffering effects have a historical tradition in the occupational stress literature, stemming from such models as the Job Demand-Control-Support Model (Karasek and Theorell, 1990) and the Effort-Reward-Imbalance Model (Siegrist, 1998), and the buffering effect of social support has been outlined in an earlier section of this chapter. Consistent with these theories, which posit that contextual variables in the organization act as psychological resources that serve to mitigate the detrimental effects of stressors, it is argued that the four categories of supervisor responses, as described in the framework, not only have a positive main effect on employee adjustment, but also provide a buffer to employee adjustment when faced with task or relationship conflict in the group (i.e. a moderating relationship).

DeChurch and Marks (2001) found that the way a *group* manages conflict moderates the relationship between task conflict and group performance. In our model, we propose that the way a *supervisor* manages conflict moderates the relationship between task and relationship conflict and employee adjustment. In other words, employees' psychological response occurs via an interaction between the employees' perception of conflict and the competence of their supervisor's response—under conditions of high conflict, and when supervisors are perceived to be competent in the four categories of response, employees will be protected from the negative effects of conflict on their adjustment.

Proposition 3: The negative main effects of workgroup-level conflict on individual-level employee adjustment will be buffered (i.e., reduced) for workgroups who perceive that their supervisor (i) identifies conflict, (ii) accurately assesses the severity of conflict, (iii) intervenes in conflict situations using a combination of individual and organizational methods, and (iv) uses a conciliatory conflict handling style.

Role of Organizational Justice Climate

In an attempt to explain why workgroup conflict may have an influence on employee adjustment, we argue that justice climate (conceptualized at the group level) is likely to mediate the relationship between workgroup conflict and employee adjustment. There are two broad theoretical explanations for why people desire justice (Tyler, 1994). First, the resource-based view argues that people want to maximize outcomes in situations involving social exchange and expect this to be more likely when they are treated in a just manner. Second, the group-value model argues that fair treatment bolsters peoples' sense of self by signaling to them that they are valued members of the group.

Organizational justice, or "attempts to describe and explain the role of fairness as a consideration in the workplace" (Greenberg, 1990), has been conceptualized into a number of subcomponents, namely 1) distributive justice—the fairness of outcomes (Adams, 1965; Leventhal, 1976), 2) procedural justice—the fairness of procedures used to determine the outcomes (Leventhal, 1980), and 3) interactional justice—the quality of interpersonal treatment people receive when procedures are implemented (Bies and Moag, 1986). Greenberg (1993) divided this final subcomponent into a) interactional justice—whether people are treated with respect, dignity, and politeness and b) informational justice—explanations about why certain procedures were used or why outcomes were distributed in a certain way.

The links among stressors, justice, and health have been proposed by a number of authors (Brotheridge, 2003; Elovainio, Kivimäki, Vahtera, Virtanen, and Keltikangas-Järvinen, 2003; Taris, Peelers, Le Blanc, Schreurs, and Schaufeli, 2001; Vermunt and Steensma, 2001; Ylipaavalniemi, Kivimäki, Elovainio, Virtanen, Keltikangas-Järvinen, and Vahtera, 2005), with some concluding that the degree to which people are treated with justice in workplaces is associated with their health, independently of established stressors at work (Kivimäki et al., 2002). Workplace bullying, as a particular workplace stressor of interest, has been found to be negatively associated with justice (-0.35) in a meta-analysis conducted by Bowling and Beehr (2006). Distributive justice, procedural justice, and interactional justice all have been related to positive employee outcomes, such as reduced burnout, and higher levels of satisfaction, commitment, and performance (Cohen-Charash and Spector, 2001), and Brotheridge (2003) noted that organizational justice has emerged as an important psychosocial predictor of health at work.

In addition to the effects at the individual level, organizational justice also has been aggregated to the group level in the form of justice climate (Naumann and Bennett, 2000). Justice climate refers to perception of workgroup members that policies and practices in their unit are fair. It is argued that employees observe how others in their workgroup are treated and make judgments about how that treatment might affect them (Lind, Kray, and Thompson, 1998) and further that procedures being enacted unfairly against one member of a workgroup may be perceived as an injustice against the whole group (Tyler and Lind, 1992). From this, it is suggested that distinct group-level cognitions about how group members are likely to be treated is present. A shared sense of the level of justice is likely due to the following reasons (Naumann and Bennett, 2000; Simons and Roberson, 2003): first, employees in the same work unit are likely to experience similar practices and procedures; second, employees create a mutually-shared perception of the environment by interpersonal interaction and social information processing; and third, attraction/selection/attrition processes create similarity and homogeneity within work units.

Justice climate has been shown to have effects over and above individual-level justice perceptions. For example, procedural justice climate predicted helping behavior after controlling for individual-level perceptions of procedural justice (Naumann and Bennett, 2000). Team-level procedural justice also has been found to significantly affect team performance and absenteeism (Colquitt, Noe, and Jackson, 2002) and department-level procedural and interpersonal justice to increase employee affective commitment, satisfaction with supervision, organizational citizenship behaviors, and intention to remain. In addition, justice climate has recently been linked with psychological strain. For instance, Moliner, Martinez-Tur, Peiró, Ramos, and Cropanzano (2005) found that when members of work units perceived, as a group, that their supervisor treated them appropriately (i.e., interactional justice), levels of exhaustion and cynicism at the work-unit level were reduced. Following on from these research findings, main and mediating relationships among workgroup conflict, injustice climate, and employee adjustment are proposed.

Proposition 4: At the workgroup-level conflict will have a negative main effect on procedural, interactional, and informational justice climate.

Proposition 5: Workgroup-level perceptions of procedural, interactional, and informational justice climate will mediate the relationship between workgroup conflict, and individual-level employee adjustment.

Also, in the context of the proposed theoretical framework, we argue that successful supervisory intervention efforts will be the ones that engender a sense of justice among employees. Although there is limited research on antecedents of justice climate, there is evidence to suggest that managerial and supervisory actions may influence perceptions of justice climate. For instance, Ehrhart (2004) found that leadership style which is comprised of participative, supportive, and nurturing relationships with subordinates helped create a climate of procedural justice. For this reason, the extent to which a shared climate of justice helps workgroups to cope with the demanding aspects of their job will be another avenue of inquiry in this research. With this in mind, Proposition 6 relates to the main effect relationship between supervisory responses to conflict and employees' perceptions of justice climate at the workgroup-level. Specifically, it is argued that supervisors who are perceived to be engaging in appropriate responses to conflict will engender a positive justice climate within the workgroup.

Proposition 6: Workgroups who perceive that their supervisor (i) identifies workgroup conflict, (ii) accurately assesses the severity of workgroup conflict, (iii) intervenes in conflict situations using a combination of individual and organizational methods, and (iv) uses a conciliatory conflict handling style will perceive greater procedural, interactional, and informational justice climate in their workgroup.

Mediated Moderation of Workgroup Conflict and Employee Adjustment

Following on from the main and moderating effects of supervisor responses, it is proposed that the reason successful supervisory intervention buffers against the negative effects of task and relationship conflict on employee adjustment is through a sense of fairness in the way the conflict was handled by the supervisor which is an instance of mediated moderation (Baron and Kenny, 1986). Muller, Judd, and Yzerbyt (2005) noted that mediated moderation is concerned with the mediating process as the explanatory mechanism for the moderating effect on the dependent variable of interest. Therefore, applied to the current model, the explanatory mechanism for why the group-level, two-way interaction predicts individual-level employee adjustment is because of its more proximal effect on justice climate. Given that workgroup conflict can be conceptualized as a work stressor, studies highlighting justice as a mediating variable between work factors and psychological outcomes (Kalimo, Taris, and Schaufeli, 2003) provide an important base for this proposal. Specifically, it is argued in our model that the interactive effect between workgroup conflict and supervisor responses on employee adjustment will be mediated by justice climate and, as such, employees will be protected from the negative consequences of conflict if their supervisor responds appropriately.

Proposition 7: The stress-buffering effect of the four supervisory conflict management behaviors on the negative association between workgroup conflict, and individual-level employee adjustment will be mediated by justice climate.

Conclusion

This chapter proposes a new and integrative framework that gives a much broader perspective on the way supervisors respond to conflict in workgroups, and how this may have incremental effects on employee adjustment. This work is in line with recent calls for more research into precisely what managers can do to both foster feelings of justice and minimize stress reactions among their staff (Greenberg, 2004). Specifically, it is proposed that supervisor responses interact with workgroup conflict, such that it buffers or exacerbates employee strain. Further, the effect of this interaction on employee strain is mediated by workgroup perceptions of procedural, interpersonal, and informational justice.

This framework, especially with its consideration of emotional intelligence-related precursors to supervisor conflict handling, provides additional richness and depth to traditional conflict management models, and notions of supervisor support, by taking a much broader perspective on the issue of third-party responses to conflict. Specifically, it introduces two antecedents to traditional conflict handling models providing empirically testable ideas about whether supervisors have the emotional competence to identify and accurately assess the severity of conflict. It also introduces ideas about whether supervisors intervene in the right level of the system when responding to conflict in their workgroup. Considering the workgroup's perception of the supervisor's conflict management style is another area of theoretical advancement as conflict management frameworks such as these have not been applied to supervisors as a third party before. Similarly, measuring workers' perceptions of their supervisor's behaviors at the workgroup-level is an avenue for research that could be pursued. By investigating these relationships using a multi-level approach, additional knowledge of how group perceptions and processes can effect individual-level adjustment may be gleaned.

If these relationships hold true, these propositions will provide important foundations on which to build appropriate and effective ways for organizations, through their management structures, to intervene in conflict in the workplace. For example, supervisors may develop knowledge of their unique conflict handling responses and/or weaknesses, and subsequently develop skills in one or all of these categories of responses. Further, in covering a wider breadth of responses, this model allows organizations and supervisors to identify areas for improvement that traditional models would not highlight (e.g., in emotional competence to help them identify and accurately assess conflict). Last, by asking at which level supervisors intervene to address conflict, the model shines a light on a number of control methods that organizations may not traditionally consider when attempting to address conflict, such as job design or change management strategies. It is argued that where targeted and empirically driven interventions of these types are utilized in organizations, great benefits for both employee well-being and organizational effectiveness may be achieved.

References

Adams, J.S. (1965). Inequity in social exchange. In L. Berkowitz (ed.), *Advances in Experimental Social Psychology* (pp. 267–99). San Diego, CA: Academic Press.

Anderson, N. and West, M.A. (1998). Measuring climate for work group innovation: development and validation of the team climate inventory. *Journal of Organizational Behavior*, 19, 235–58.

Arnold, J.A. and O'Connor, K.M. (1999). Ombudspersons or peers?: The effect of third-party expertise and recommendations on negotiation. *Journal of Applied Psychology*, 84, 776–85.

Baron, R.A. (1989). Personality and organizational conflict: type A behavior pattern and self monitoring. *Organizational Behavior and Human Decision Processes*, 44, 281–97.

Baron, R. and Kenny, D.A. (1986). The moderator–mediator variable distinction in social psychological research: conceptual, strategic, and statistical considerations. *Journal of Personality and Social Psychology*, 51, 1173–82.

Beehr, T.A. and Newman, J.E. (1978). Job stress, employee health, and organizational effectiveness: a facet analysis, model, and literature review. *Personnel Psychology*, 31, 665–99.

Bies, R.J. and Moag, L.S. (1986). Interactional justice: communication criteria of fairness. In R.J. Lewicki, B.H. Sheppard, and B.H. Bazerman (eds), *Research on Negotiation in Organizations* (pp. 43–55). Greenwich, CT: JAI Press.

Blake, R. and Mouton, J.S. (1964). *The Managerial Grid*. Houston, TX: Gulf.

Bliese, P.D. and Jex, S.M. (1999). Incorporating multiple levels of analysis into occupational stress research. *Work and Stress*, 13, 1–6.

Bolger, N., DeLongis, A., Kessler, R.C., and Schilling, E.A. (1989). Effects of daily stress on negative mood. *Journal of Personality and Social Psychology*, 57, 808–18.

Bowling, N.A. and Beehr, T.A. (2006). Workplace harassment from the victim's perspective: a theoretical model and meta-analysis. *Journal of Applied Psychology*, 91, 998–1012.

Brotheridge, C.M. (2003). The role of fairness in mediating the effects of voice and justification on stress and other outcomes in a climate of organizational change. *International Journal of Stress Management*, 10, 253–68.

Bunce, D. (1997). What factors are associated with the outcome of individual-focused worksite stress management interventions? *Journal of Occupational and Organisational Psychology*, 70, 1–17.

Caulfield, N., Chang, D., Dollard, M.F., and Elshaug, C. (2004). A review of occupational stress interventions in Australia. *International Journal of Stress Management*, 11, 149–66.

Cohen, S. and Edwards, J.R. (1989). Personality characteristics as moderators of the relationship between stress and disorder. In R.W J. Neufeld (ed.), *Advances in the Investigation of Psychological Stress* (pp. 235–83). New York: Wiley.

Cohen-Charash, Y. and Spector, P.E. (2001). The role of justice in organizations: a meta-analysis. *Organizational Behavior and Human Decision Processes*, 86, 278–321.

Colquitt, J.A., Noe, R.A., and Jackson, C.L. (2002). Justice in teams: antecedents and consequences of procedural justice. *Personnel Psychology*, 55, 83–109.

Cooper, C.L. and Cartwright, S. (1997). An intervention strategy for workplace stress. *Journal of Psychosomatic Research*, 43, 7–16.

Cox, T. and Griffiths, A. (2000). *Occupational Stress Interventions*. Sudbury: HSE Books.

DeChurch, L.A., Hamilton, K.L., and Haas, C. (2007). Effects of conflict management strategies on perceptions of intragroup conflict. *Group Dynamics: Theory, Research, and Practice*, 11, 66–78.

DeChurch, L.A. and Marks, M.A. (2001). Maximizing the benefits of task conflict: the role of conflict management. *International Journal of Conflict Management*, 12, 4–22.

De Dreu, C.K.W. and Beersma, B. (2005). Conflict in organizations: beyond effectiveness and performance. *European Journal of Work and Organizational Psychology*, 14, 105–17.

De Dreu, C.K.W. and van de Vliert, E. (1997). *Using Conflict in Organizations*. Thousand Oaks, CA: Sage.

De Dreu, C.K.W., van Dierendonck, D., and De Best-Waldhober, M. (2003). Conflict at work and individual well-being. In M.J. Schabracq, J.A.M. Winnubst, and C.L. Cooper (eds), *The Handbook of Work and Health Psychology* (pp. 495–515). Chichester: Wiley.

De Dreu, C.K.W. and van Vianen, A.E.M. (2001). Managing relationship conflict and the effectiveness of organizational teams. *Journal of Organizational Behavior*, 22, 309–28.

De Dreu, C.K.W. and Weingart, L.R. (2003). Task versus relationship conflict, team performance, and team member satisfaction: a meta-analysis. *Journal of Applied Psychology*, 88, 741–9.

Deelstra, J.T., Peeters, M.C.W., Schaufeli, W.B., Stroebe, W., Zijlstra, F.R.H., and van Doornen, L.P. (2003). Receiving instrumental support at work: when help is not welcome. *Journal of Applied Psychology*, 88, 324–31.

De Frank, R.S. and Cooper, C.L. (1987). Worksite stress management interventions: their effectiveness and conceptualization. *Journal of Managerial Psychology*, 2, 4–10.

Dijkstra, M.T.M., van Dierendonck, D., and Evers, A. (2005). Responding to conflict at work and individual well-being: the mediating role of flight behaviour and feelings of helplessness. *European Journal of Work and Organisational Psychology*, 14, 119–35.

Ehrhart, M.G. (2004). Leadership and procedural justice climate as antecedents of unit-level organizational citizenship behavior. *Personnel Psychology*, 57, 61–94.

Einarsen, S. (1999). The nature and causes of bullying at work. *International Journal of Manpower*, 20, 16–27.

Elfering, A., Semmer, N.K., Schade, V., Grund, S., and Boos, N. (2002). Supportive colleague, unsupportive supervisor: the role of provider-specific constellations of social support at work in the development of low back pain. *Journal of Occupational Health Psychology*, 7, 130–40.

Elovainio, M., Kivimäki, M., Vahtera, J., Virtanen, M., and Keltikangas-Järvinen, L. (2003). Personality as a moderator in the relations between perceptions of organizational justice and sickness absence. *Journal of Vocational Behavior*, 63, 379–95.

Frone, M.R. (2000). Interpersonal conflict at work and psychological outcomes: testing a model among young workers. *Journal of Occupational Health Psychology*, 5, 246–55.

Ganster, D.C. (1988). Improving measures of worker control in occupational stress research. In J.J. Hurrell, L.R. Murphy, S.L. Sauter, and C.L. Cooper (eds), *Occupational Stress: Issues and Developments in Research* (pp. 88–99). New York: Taylor and Francis.

Giebels, E. and Janssen, O. (2005). Conflict stress and reduced well-being at work: the buffering effect of third-party help. *European Journal of Work and Organizational Psychology*, 14, 137–55.

Giga, S.I., Cooper, C.L., and Faragher, B. (2003). The development of a framework for a comprehensive approach to stress management interventions at work. *International Journal of Stress Management*, 10, 280–96.

Giga, S.I., Noblet, A.J. Faragher, B., and Cooper, C.L. (2003). The UK perspective: a review of organizational stress management interventions. *Australian Psychologist*, 38, 158–64.

Gilbreath, B. and Benson, P.G. (2004). The contribution of supervisor behavior to employee psychological well-being. *Work and Stress*, 18, 255–66.

Glaser, D.N. (1999). Workload and social support: effects on performance and stress. *Human Performance*, 12, 155–76.

Greenberg, J. (1990). Organizational justice: yesterday, today, and tomorrow. *Journal of Management*, 16, 399–432.

Greenberg, J. (1993). The social side of fairness: interpersonal and informational classes of organizational justice. In R. Cropanzano (ed.), *Justice in the Workplace: Approaching Fairness in Human Resource Management* (pp. 79–103). Hillsdale, NJ: Erlbaum.

Greenberg, J. (2004). Stress fairness to fare no stress: managing workplace stress by promoting organizational justice. *Organizational Dynamics*, 33, 352–65.

Guetzkow, H. and Gyr, J. (1954). An analysis of conflict in decision-making groups. *Human Relations*, 7, 367–82.

Hansen, Å.M., Hogh, A., Persson, R., Karlson, B., Garde, A.H., and Orbæk, P. (2006). Bullying at work, health outcomes, and physiological stress response. *Journal of Psychosomatic Research*, 60, 63–72.

Hoel, H., Sparks, K., and Cooper, C.L. (2001). *The Cost of Violence/Stress at Work and the Benefits of a Violence/Stress-free Working Environment*. Geneva: International Labor Organization.

Hyde, M., Jappinen, P., Theorell, T., and Oxenstierna, G. (2006). Workplace conflict resolution and the health of employees in the Swedish and Finnish units of an industrial company. *Social Science and Medicine*, 63, 2218–27.

Jehn, K.A. (1995). A multi-method examination of the benefits and detriments of intragroup conflict. *Administrative Science Quarterly*, 40, 256–82.

Jehn, K.A. and Mannix, E. (2001). The dynamic nature of conflict: a longitudinal study of intragroup conflict and group performance. *Academy of Management Journal*, 44, 238–51.

Jex, S.M. (1998). *Stress and Job Performance: Theory, Research, and Implications for Managerial Practice*. Thousand Oaks, CA: Sage.

Jex, S.M. and Beehr, T.A. (1991). Emerging theoretical and methodological issues in the study of work-related stress. *Research in Personnel and Human Resources Management*, 9, 311–65.

Johlke, M.C. and Duhan, D.F. (2001). Supervisor communication practices and boundary spanner role ambiguity. *Journal of Managerial Issues*, 13, 87–101.

Jones, F., Bright, J.E.H., Searle, B., and Cooper, L. (1998). Modelling occupational stress and health: the impact of the demand-control model on academic research and on workplace practice. *Stress Medicine*, 14, 231–6.

Jordan, P.J. and Troth, A.C. (2004). Managing emotions during team problem solving: emotional intelligence and conflict resolution. *Human Performance*, 17, 195–218.

Kalimo, R., Taris, T.W., and Schaufeli, W.B. (2003). The effects of past and anticipated future downsizing on survivor well-being: an equity perspective. *Journal of Occupational Health Psychology*, 8, 91–109.

Karambayya, R. and Brett, J.M. (1989). Managers handling disputes: third-party roles and perceptions of fairness. *Academy of Management Journal*, 32, 687–704.

Karasek, R. and Theorell, T. (1990). *Healthy Work: Stress, Productivity, and the Reconstruction of Working Life*. New York: Basic Books.

Kaufmann, G.M. and Beehr, T.A. (1989). Occupational stressors, individual strains, and social support among police officers. *Human Relations*, 42, 185–97.

Kickul, J. and Posig, M. (2001). Supervisory emotional support and burnout: an explanation of reverse buffering effects. *Journal of Managerial Issues*, 13, 328–44.

Kilmann, R.H. and Thomas, K.W. (1977). Developing a forced-choice measure of conflict-handling behavior: the "MODE" instrument. *Educational and Psychological Measurement*, 37, 309–25.

Kivimäki, M., Leino-Arjas, P., Luukkonen, R., Riihimäki, H., Vahtera, J., and Kirjonen, J. (2002). Work stress and risk of cardiovascular mortality: prospective cohort study of industrial employees. *British Medical Journal*, 325, 857–60.

Kompier, M.A.J. and Cooper, C.L. (1999). *Preventing Stress, Improving Productivity: European Case Studies in the Workplace*. London: Routledge.

Koslowsky, M. (1998). *Modelling the Stress-Strain Relationship in Work Settings*. Florence, KY: Taylor and Frances/Routledge.

Kozlowski, S.W.J. and Klein, K.J. (2000). A multilevel approach to theory and research in organizations: contextual, temporal, and emergent processes. In K.J. Klein and S.W.J. Kozlowski (eds), *Multilevel Theory, Research, and Methods in Organizations: Foundations, Extensions, and New Directions* (pp. 3–90). San Francisco, CA: Jossey-Bass.

LaRocco, J., House, J., and French, J. (1980). Social support, occupational stress and health. *Journal of Health and Social Behavior*, 21, 202–18.

Lazarus, R.S. (1990). Theory based stress management. *Psychological Inquiry*, 1, 3–13.

Lazarus, R.S. and Folkman, S. (1984). *Stress, Appraisal, and Coping*. New York: Springer.

Leiter, M.P. (1991). Coping patterns as predictors of burnout: the function of control and escapist coping patterns. *Journal of Organizational Behavior*, 12, 123–44.

Leventhal, G.S. (1976). The distribution of rewards and resources in groups and organizations. In L. Berkowhz and E. Walster (eds), *Advances in Experimental Social Psychology* (pp. 91–131). San Diego, CA: Academic Press.

Leventhal, G.S. (1980). What should be done with equity theory?: new approaches to the study of fairness in social relationships. In K. Gergen, M. Greenberg, and R. Willis (eds), *Social Exchange: Advances in Theory and Research* (pp. 27–55). New York: Plenum.

Lewicki, R.J. and Sheppard, B.H. (1985). Choosing how to intervene: factors affecting the use of process and outcome control in third party dispute resolution. *Journal of Occupational Behavior*, 6, 49–64.

Lewicki, R.J., Weiss, S.E., and Lewin, D. (1992). Models of conflict, negotiation and third party intervention: a review and synthesis. *Journal of Organizational Behavior*, 13, 209–52.

Lind, E.A., Kray, L., and Thompson, L. (1998). The social construction of injustice: fairness judgments in response to own and others' unfair treatment by authorities. *Organizational Behavior and Human Decision Processes*, 75, 1–22.

Mayer, J.D. and Salovey, P. (1997). What is emotional intelligence? In P. Salovey and David J. Sluyter (eds), *Emotional Development and Emotional Intelligence: Educational Implications* (pp. 3–31). New York: Basic Books.

Moliner, C., Martinez-Tur, V., Peiró, J.M., Ramos, J., and Cropanzano, R. (2005). Relationships between organisational justice and burnout at the work-unit level. *International Journal of Stress Management*, 12, 99–116.

Muller, D., Judd, C.M., and Yzerbyt, V.Y. (2005). When moderation is mediated and mediation is moderated. *Journal of Personality and Social Psychology*, 89, 852–63.

Naumann, S.E. and Bennett, N. (2000). A case for procedural justice climate: development and test of a multilevel model. *Academy of Management Journal*, 43, 881–9.

Pinkley, R.L., Brittain, J., Neale, M.A., and Northcraft, G.B. (1995). Managerial third-party dispute intervention: an inductive analysis of intervenor strategy selection. *Journal of Applied Psychology*, 80, 386–402.

Pruitt, D.G. and Rubin, J. (1986). *Social Conflict: Escalation, Stalemate, and Settlement*. New York: Random House.

Queensland Government (2007). *Risk Management Code of Practice*. Queensland: Go Print.

Quick, J.C., Marik-Frey, M., and Cooper, C.L. (2007). Managerial dimensions of organizational health: the healthy leader at work. *Journal of Management Studies*, 44, 189–205.

Quick, J.C., Quick, J.D., Nelson, D.L., and Hurrell, J.J. (1997). *Preventive Stress Management in Organizations*. Washington, DC: American Psychological Association.

Rahim, M.A. (1983). Measurement of organizational conflict. *Journal of General Psychology*, 109, 189–99.

Rahim, M.A. (1985). A strategy of managing conflict in complex organizations. *Human Relations*, 38, 81–9.

Richardsen, A.M., Burke, R.J., and Leiter, M.P. (1992). Occupational demands, psychological burnout, and anxiety among hospital personnel in Norway. *Anxiety, Stress, and Coping*, 5, 55–68.

Romanov, K., Appelberg, K., Honkasalo, M.L., and Koskenvuo, M. (1996). Recent interpersonal conflict at work and psychiatric morbidity: a prospective study of 15,530 employees aged 24–64. *Journal of Psychosomatic Research*, 40, 169–76.

Salin, D. (2003). Ways of explaining workplace bullying: a review of enabling, motivating, and precipitating structures and processes in the work environment. *Human Relations*, 56, 1213–32.

Semmer, N. (2003). Job stress interventions and organization of work. In J.C. Quick and L.E. Tetrick (eds), *Handbook of Occupational Health Psychology* (pp. 325–53). Washington, DC: American Psychological Association.

Sheppard, B.H. (1984). Third-party conflict intervention: a procedural framework. *Research in Organizational Behavior*, 6, 141–90.

Sheppard, B.H., Saunders, D.M., and Minton, J.W. (1988). Procedural justice from the third-party perspective. *Journal of Personality and Social Psychology*, 54, 629–37.

Siegrist, J. (1998). Adverse health effects of effort-reward imbalance at work. In C. Cooper (ed.), *Theories of Organizational Stress*. Oxford: Oxford University Press.

Simons, T.L. and Roberson, Q. (2003). Why managers should care about fairness: the effects of aggregate justice perceptions on organisational outcomes. *Journal of Applied Psychology*, 88, 432–43.

Singh, J. (1998). Striking a balance in boundary-spanning positions: an investigation of some unconventional influences of role stressors and job characteristics on job outcomes of salespeople. *Journal of Marketing*, 62, 69–86.

Skogstad, A., Einarsen, S., Torsheim, T., Aasland, M.S., and Hetland, H. (2007). The destructiveness of laissez-faire leadership behavior. *Journal of Occupational Health Psychology*, 12, 80–92.

Smith, C.S. and Sulsky, L.M. (1995). An investigation of job-related coping strategies across multiple stressors and samples. In L.R. Murphy, J.J. Hurrell, Jr., S.L. Sauter, and G.P. Keita (eds), *Job Stress Interventions* (pp. 109–23). Washington, DC: American Psychological Association.

Spector, P.E., Chen, P.Y., and O'Connell, B.J. (2000). A longitudinal study of relations between job stressors and job strains while controlling for prior negative affectivity and strains. *Journal of Applied Psychology*, 85, 211–18.

Spector, P.E. and Jex, S.M. (1998). Development of four self-report measures of job stressors and strains: interpersonal conflict at work scale, organizational constraints scale, quantitative workload inventory, and physical symptoms inventory. *Journal of Occupational Health Psychology*, 3, 356–67.

Swanson, V. and Power, K. (2001). Employees' perceptions of organisational restructuring: the role of social support. *Work and Stress*, 15, 161–78.

Taris, T.W., Peelers, M.C.W., Le Blanc, P.M., Schreurs, P.J.G., and Schaufeli, W.B. (2001). From inequity to burnout: the role of job stress. *Journal of Occupational Health Psychology*, 6, 303–23.

Thomas, K.W. (1992). Conflict and negotiation processes in organizations. In M.D. Dunnette and L.M. Hough (eds), *Handbook of Industrial and Organizational Psychology* (pp. 651–717). Palo Alto, CA: Consulting Psychologists Press.

Ting-Toomey, S. and Oetzel, J.G. (2001). *Managing Intercultural Conflict Effectively*. Thousand Oaks, CA: Sage.

Tyler, T.R. (1994). Psychological models of the justice motive: antecedents of distributive and procedural justice. *Journal of Personality and Social Psychology*, 67, 850–63.

Tyler, T.R. and Lind, E.A. (1992). A relational model of authority in groups. In M.P. Zanna (ed.), *Advances in Experimental Social Psychology* (pp. 115–91). San Diego, CA: Academic Press.

van der Doef, M. and Maes, S. (1998). The job demand-control (-support) model and physical health outcomes: a review of the strain and buffer hypothesis. *Psychology and Health*, 13, 909–36.

van der Doef, M. and Maes, S. (1999). The job demand-control (-support) model and psychological well-being: a review of 20 years of empirical research. *Work and Stress*, 13, 87–114.

Van der Klink, J.J.L., Blonk, R.W.B., Schene, A.H., and Van Dijk, F.J.H. (2001). The benefits of interventions for work-related stress. *American Journal of Public Health*, 91, 270–76.

van de Vliert, E. (1997). *Complex Interpersonal Conflict Behavior: Theoretical Frontiers*. Hove: Psychology Press.

van Dierendonck, D., Schaufeli, W.B., and Sixma, H.J. (1994). Burnout among general practitioners: a perspective from equity theory. *Journal of Social and Clinical Psychology*, 13, 86–100.

Vartia, M.A.L. (2001). Consequences of workplace bullying with respect to the well-being of its targets and the observers of bullying. *Scandinavian Journal of Work, Environment, and Health*, 27, 63–9.

Vermunt, R. and Steensma, H. (2001). Stress and justice in organizations: an exploration into justice processes with the aim to find mechanisms to reduce stress. In R. Cropanzano (ed.), *Justice in the Workplace: From Theory to Practice* (pp. 27–48). Mahwah, NJ: Lawrence Erlbaum Associates Publishers.

Viswesvaran, C., Sanchez, J.I., and Fisher, J. (1999). The role of social support in the process of work stress: a meta-analysis. *Journal of Vocational Behavior*, 54, 314–34.

Wall J. and Callister, R. (1995). Conflicts and its management. *Journal of Management*, 21, 515–38.

Wang, J. (2004). Perceived work stress and major depressive episodes in a population of employed Canadians over 18 years old. *Journal of Nervous and Mental Disease*, 192, 160–63.

Wang, J. and Patten, S.B. (2001). Perceived work stress and major depression in the Canadian employed population, 20–49 years old. *Journal of Occupational Health Psychology*, 6, 283–9.

Warr, P.B. (1991). Mental health, well-being, and job satisfaction. In B. Hesketh and A. Adams (eds), *Psychological Perspectives on Occupational Health and Rehabilitation* (pp. 143–65). London: Harcourt Brace.

Warr, P. (1994). A conceptual framework for the study of work and mental health. *Work and Stress*, 8, 84–97.

Weider-Hatfield, D. and Hatfield, J.D. (1995). Relationships among conflict management styles, levels of conflict, and reactions to work. *Journal of Social Psychology*, 135, 687–98.

Weider-Hatfield, D. and Hatfield, J.D. (1996). Superiors conflict management strategies and subordinate outcomes. *Management Communication Quarterly*, 10, 189–208.

Yarker, J., Lewis, R., Donaldson-Feilder, E., and Flaxman, P.E. (2007). *Management Competencies for Preventing and Reducing Stress at Work: Identifying and Developing the Management Behaviors Necessary to Implement the HSE Management Standards*. Sudbury: HSE Books.

Ylipaavalniemi, J., Kivimäki, M., Elovainio, M., Virtanen, M., Keltikangas-Järvinen, L., and Vahtera, J. (2005). Psychosocial work characteristics and incidence of newly diagnosed depression: a prospective cohort study of three different models. *Social Science and Medicine*, 61, 111–22.

12

Determinants of Work Satisfaction, and Physical and Psychological Health in German Managers

Elizabeth Austin, Bruce Kirkcaldy and Terence Martin

Introduction

Although the concept of job stress is widely recognised as an important work- and health-related criterion, determining its contributory antecedents and precise outcomes will present a challenge to those with a low tolerance for ambiguity. The body of literature which has grown around this concept in recent decades can accurately be described as vast. Indeed, any attempt to collect and collate the current extent of published empirical analyses of the phenomenon in diverse occupations would present a monumental logistical problem. This is not surprising in view of the long-standing and largely unresolved debates that have surrounded not only the very definition of the stress concept, but also the issue of establishing the most valid scientific and meaningful techniques by which job stress should be measured (Kasl, 1987; Cox, 1993).

In conventional interactional models, stress is conjectured as a 'lack of fit' between the environment and a person. In these terms stress comes between its antecedent factors and its consequences (effects). Such models define stress as a dynamic system of interaction between the person and the environment. Demand arises externally from the environment and internally from inherent psychological and physiological needs. The central tenet of interactive models concerns one's cognitive appraisal of a putatively stressful situation, and his or her capacity to cope both psychologically and physiologically. The instrument used in this study, 'Pressure Management Indicator' (PMI), provides a global measure as well as differentiated profiles of occupational stress. The outcome measures include work satisfaction, organisational security, organisational satisfaction, and commitment, as well as physical well-being (physical symptoms and exhaustion) and psychological health (anxiety depression, worry and resilience). In addition moderator variables are assessed including type A behaviour, internal locus of control and coping strategies.

Not surprisingly the interactional approach to stress, that incorporates both stimulus-based and response-based approaches has also been referred to as the stimulus-response interaction (Greenberg, 1999) and is sometimes adapted to refer to the transactional approach (Derogatis and Coons, 1993).

Cox extended the common interactional approach to stress, with a focus on the structural characteristics of the person's interaction with their work environment, one step further and proposed that there is another facet to this scenario (Cox, 1990). This theory has been referred to as transactional. The transactional approach takes the stimulus, response, cognitive appraisal of the stressor, coping style of the individual, psychological defences and social milieu into account (Folkman and Lazarus, 1988a; 1988b). A transactional approach suggests that, 'not only does the individual mediate the impact of environmental stimulus upon responses, but, in addition, the perceptual, cognitive, and physiological characteristics of the individual affect and become a significant component of the environment' (Derogatis and Coons, 1993).

Much recent research in this area has focused on the associations between job-related stress, work satisfaction and physical and psychological well-being. Whilst stress is clearly implicated in all these outcomes, it is clear that both work satisfaction and health are multiply caused and that furthermore the causal factors themselves have complex inter-relationships. The literature in this area is too extensive for a full review; here we discuss the main associations that have been found and how they have been modelled. The key variables that have been related to job stress and to the outcomes mentioned above fall into two categories: objectively observable variables, for example age, gender and hours worked, and individual dispositional differences such as personality traits, coping style and locus of control. There is clear evidence that all these contribute to stress, job satisfaction and health.

Dispositional differences which contribute to stress and work-related outcomes include personality and coping style. The personality trait of neuroticism has been particularly associated with these, with people who score high on neuroticism or on a closely related trait of negative affectivity tending to report more stress, less job satisfaction and poorer health (Deary et al., 1996, Watson and Pennebaker, 1989). An emotion-oriented coping style has also been found to be consistently associated with higher stress levels (e.g. Jerusalem, 1993; Deary et al., 1996). Associations between type A personality and stress have also been found (Cooper and Baglioni, 1988; Kirkcaldy, Shephard and Furnham, 2002) and external locus of control has also been found to be associated with stress (Cooper, Kirkcaldy and Brown 1994; Kirkcaldy, Shephard and Furnham, 2002).

Amongst more objective indicators, workload and total hours worked have been found to be associated with higher stress levels (Deary et al., 1996; Kirkcaldy, Trimpop and Levine, 2002) and with lower levels of physical and psychological health (Sparks et al., 1997).

The European Foundation for the Improvement of Living and Working Conditions' (1996) *Working Conditions* report indicated that a high proportion of workers across the EU work long hours (49 percent work more than 40 hours per week, and 23 percent more than 45 hours). The data also revealed that health problems including levels of stress increased with the hours worked. Specifically within research in to long working hours, compressed work weeks, with 12-hour working days, have been associated with feelings of increased fatigue (Rosa et al., 1989). Similarly, studies of occupational groups often associated with long working hours, such as junior health service doctors, have also uncovered increased levels of stress and negative health correlates (Spurgeon, Harrington and Cooper, 1997).

Surprisingly little research attention has been paid to the issue of gender and job stress. In spite of an increase in the numbers of women entering occupations, professions and managerial jobs previously dominated by men, few studies have assessed the differential impact or consequences of job stress on male and female managers. One cross-cultural study examined the sources of occupational stress (stressors), coping and consequences of occupational stress (strains) from male and female managers in four countries – South Africa, the United Kingdom, the United States of America and Taiwan (Miller et al., 2000). Although this study found that there were also virtually no differences in sources of work stress, there were differences in the consequences of work stress for male and female managers. One theme that has appealed to researchers has been that additional challenges for women in the world of work often revolve around balancing work and family roles. Lundberg and Frankenhaeuser (1999) investigated psychological and physiological stress responses related to work and family among female and male managers and professionals. Overall, their results suggested that women experienced greater levels of stress and pressure than males. In particular, women were more stressed by their greater unpaid workload and by a greater responsibility to fulfil duties related to home and family.

In recent years, job stress research has increasingly emphasised the importance of transactional models, highlighting the role of perception, cognitive appraisal and coping mechanisms. Cox and Griffiths (1995) proposed a 'unifying concept of the stress process' which would allow these factors to be understood in their context, both temporally and as they interrelate systemically, 'beginning with ... antecedent factors and ... the cognitive perceptual process which gives rise to the emotional experience of stress' and then considering 'the correlates of that experience'. In a transactional model variables are divided into three categories: antecedent, mediating and outcome. Antecedent variables are characteristics of the individual or their environment which can be regarded as fixed, at least or relatively so. Examples are age, gender, occupation and personality. Mediating variables such as coping style and locus of control intervene between antecedents and outcomes and account for some or all of the associations between them.

Although valuable information can be obtained about the determinants of outcomes such as work satisfaction using regression and correlational approaches, it is necessary to use the structural equation (SEM) method to test transactional models. The SEM method allows a graphical representation of the structure of the correlation matrix and also enables the fit of competing models to be assessed by the use of significance testing.

Using the SEM and closely related path analysis methods a number of studies have explored transactional models of stress, job satisfaction and health. The mediating role of coping has been extensively studied and coping style has been found, for example, to mediate the relationship between personality and stress (Deary et al., 1996) and between stress and health (Cooper and Baglioni, 1988; Jerusalem, 1993), with higher stress and worse health being associated with the emotion-focused coping style. There is also evidence for locus of control acting as a mediator, for example in models of job satisfaction (Noor, 2002) and school satisfaction (Huebner, Ash and Laughlin, 2001). Here the effect direction is that internal locus of control, which corresponds to higher feelings of control over one's situation, is associated with lower stress and better health (Cooper, Kirkcaldy and Brown, 1994).

The Present Study

On the basis of the above literature review, several hypotheses were formulated:

- Stress will be negatively correlated with the use of adaptive coping strategies and with internal locus of control and positively associated with working hours.

- Job satisfaction and psychological well-being will be positively correlated with the use of adaptive coping strategies and with internal locus of control.

- Job satisfaction, physical well-being and psychological well-being will be negatively correlated with stress.

- Gender differences will be expected in terms of occupational stress and psychological and physical health. More specifically, female managers will exhibit higher job stress scores than male managers, and presumably inferior health.

- According to the transactional model prediction, coping and locus of control should mediate the relationship between antecedent variables such as personality and working hours and the outcome of job-related stress.

Methods

PARTICIPANTS

A group of 284 managerial level staff (approx. 70:30 male:female, aged 18–65 years) were recruited from diverse organisations in the public and private sectors throughout Germany, in accordance with a protocol approved by the Institutional Committee on Human Experimentation. The average age was 47 years. The managers were responsible for an average of up to 40 personnel, and were mainly in the administrative and industrial sector. Data were collected over a nine-month period from 1 June 1999 until 30 March 2000, using the pressure management indicator (PMI). Questionnaires were distributed with stamped and addressed envelopes. Generally, they were to be returned to the International Centre for the Study of Occupational and Mental Health (for the Older Federal States). The response rate was very high (over 80 percent) because only those who had expressed an interest in the project were supplied with the questionnaires. Subjects were allowed to complete the inventory in their own time. They were not paid for participation, but they were debriefed wherever possible, and a free individualised case-report narrative regarding their occupational stress profiles was offered if requested.

The Pressure Management Indicator was used, a 120-item self-report questionnaire, shown to be a reliable and comprehensive psychometric tool in assessing diverse facets of working life and health (Williams and Cooper, 1998; Williams, Kirkcaldy and Cooper, 1998). It provides an integrated measure of job satisfaction, organisational satisfaction, organisational security and organisational commitment. The outcome scales are also incorporated to assess physical (physical symptoms and exhaustion) and mental well-being (anxiety depression, resilience and worry). The subjective stress variables include pressure originating from workload, social relationships, recognition, organisational climate, personal responsibility, managerial role, home-work balance and daily hassles. Moreover, an array of moderator variables are also included, such as Type A behaviour (drive and impatience 'need for urgency'), locus of control (decision latitude, personal influence) and coping strategies (problem focus such as 'planning ahead and time management'; social support, and life-work balance). The internal consistencies of the scales vary from +0.64 (daily hassles) to +0.89 (job satisfaction) (Williams, 1996).

Results

Table 12.1 shows the correlation matrix of demographic factors, work factors, work outcomes and aggregate PMI scales. Partial correlations, controlled for age and gender, are also shown. It can be seen from the correlations in the first column that there is evidence of a number of significant between-gender differences; these are discussed in more detail below. Job satisfaction, psychological well-being and physical well-being are all positively intercorrelated. These outcomes are also negatively correlated with stress and positively correlated with internal

Table 12.1 Correlations between demographic, job-related, outcome and personality variables

	Gender	Age	Tenure	Hours	Satis	Psych	Phys	Stress	Type A	Locus
Age	-.29***									
Tenure	-.28***	.62***								
Hours	-.22**	.28***	-.02 (-.19*)							
Satis	-.10	.12	.02 (-.01)	.11 (.07)						
Psych	-.26***	.10	.11 (.04)	.05 (-.12)	.34*** (.24**)					
Phys	-.21***	.10	.13 (.18*)	.05 (-0.16)	.39*** (.36**)	.63*** (.59**)				
Stress	.05	.00	-.08 (-.07)	.13 (0.18*)	-.34*** (-.32**)	-.39** (-.28**)	-.34*** (-.35**)			
Type A	-.02	-.08	.01 (.02)	.11 (.17*)	-.02 (.00)	-.10 (-.05)	-.06 (-.04)	.15* (.14)		
Locus	-.13*	-0.17**	.00 (-.08)	.28*** (.28**)	.49*** (.41***)	.21*** (.13)	.26*** (.22*)	-.19*** (-.13)	.17*** (.20*)	
Coping	0.04	.05	-.03 (.02)	-.06 (-.10)	.20*** (.21*)	.17** (.18*)	.21*** (.27*)	-.04 (.04)	.02 (.08)	.18** (.22*)

Note: Ns range from 194 to 356. Correlations in brackets are controlled for gender and age. * p < 0.05, ** p < 0.01, *** p < 0.001. Gender was coded M = 1, F = 2.

locus of control and coping. Stress is positively correlated with Type A score, negatively correlated with external locus of control and uncorrelated with coping. The sizes of the correlations in Table 12.1 show little change when age and gender are partialled out.

Examination of gender differences using *t*-tests (Table 12.2) showed that males reported longer job tenure and longer working hours than females. Males also scored higher on psychological well-being, physical well-being and locus of control.

Table 12.2 Gender differences for job-related, outcome and personality variables

	Mean (sd) Males	N	Mean (sd) Females	N	t	p
Tenure	13.96 (10.29)	120	8.55 (7.04)	73	3.96	0.00
Hours	46.59 (8.67)	169	42.33 (9.88)	93	3.63	0.00
Satis	87.36 (12.07)	208	84.86 (12.01)	124	1.82	0.07
Psych	45.11 (6.19)	208	41.68 (6.52)	124	4.78	0.00
Phys	31.48 (5.50)	208	28.74 (6.91)	124	3.98	0.00
Stress	120.91 (29.30)	208	123.73 (31.63)	124	-0.83	0.41
Type A	36.08 (5.05)	208	35.85 (4.61)	124	0.42	0.68
Locus	31.96 (4.45)	208	30.69 (4.78)	124	2.43	0.02
Coping	54.00 (7.49)	208	54.65 (7.08)	124	-0.79	0.43

A series of three consecutive linear multiple regression analyses were computed using the three subscales of coping (problem-focused, life-work balance and social support) to identify which specific facets of coping style predicted the various outcome measures (see Table 12.3). In addition, the magnitude of the standardised beta coefficients would provide an estimate of the effect size for each independent variable (coping subscale).

Table 12.3 Linear multiple regression analyses. Subscales of coping as determinants of outcome measures (work satisfaction, psychological and physical health)

Outcome variables	beta	$F(3,352) = 5.99$ t	$P<0.001$
Work satisfaction			
Problem focused	+0.19	+3.42	0.001***
		$F(3,352) = 17.64$	$P<0.001$
Physical health			
Problem-focused	+0.21	+3.95	0.001***
Life-work balance	+0.26	+5.00	0.001***
Social support	-0.20	-3.70	0.001***
		$F(3,352) = 17.50$	$P<0.001$***
Psychological health			
Problem-focused	+0.20	+3.86	0.001***
Life-work balance	+0.24	+4.69	0.001***
Social support	-0.24	-4.58	0.001***

As regards the outcome variable work satisfaction, the regression was statistically significant, but only the first subscale, problem-focused emerged as statistically significant. This scale assesses specific work characteristics, such as effective time management, planning ahead, setting priorities and dealing with problems accordingly, using selective attention, and concentrating on specific problems. In contrast both health outcome measures, physical and psychological health, revealed statistically significant regressions involving all three sub-scales. Furthermore, all three coping subscales displayed significant beta weightings (problem-focused, life-work balance, and 'social support' for physical and psychological health respectively). Social support (talking to sympathetic and understanding friends, seeking as much social support as possible, and sharing my concerns with other people) was significantly related to both health outcome variables, although the direction of the impact was negative. This affords credence to the assertion that social support may serve a double-edged therapeutic function. That is, although social support may be beneficial in alleviating some (job-related) stress, a greater need to seek others' support may be associated with a greater psychological dependency and insecurity, and consequently be coupled with inferior general health. Furthermore, it should also be obvious that 'seeking social support', does not provide any information about whether support is actually obtained, or indeed elaborate with regard to the quality of support.

STRUCTURAL EQUATION MODELLING

Models were constructed using those individuals (N = 284 subjects) with complete data for personality, stress, outcomes and hours worked.

The structural equation modelling technique allows the multivariate associations between measured variables to be explored in more detail than is possible with techniques such as multiple regression and MANOVA. In particular, as discussed in the introduction, the possibility that the relationship between two variables is mediated by a third can be investigated. The method also provides a range of goodness-of-fit indices and tests for the addition and deletion of model paths, allowing competing models to be tested. Structural equation modelling is widely used in the study of the effects of personality, attitudes and other factors (for example stressors) on behaviour (see for example Austin, Deary and Willock, 2001, Deary et al., 1996). For a more detailed account of the use of SEM see Austin et al. (1998).

Models were constructed using the EQS package (Bentler, 1995). Model fit was assessed by examining both the magnitude of the residual covariance matrix elements and the goodness-of-fit indices provided by the EQS package; significance tests related to adding or removing paths from the models were also performed. The final models obtained are shown in Figures 12.1, 12.2 and 12.3; Table 12.3 summarises model fit information. For all three outcomes it was found that the mediating models shown had better fit than regression models in which all predictors contributed directly. In the figures the square of the number beside each model path gives the proportion of variance shared by the corresponding pair of variables. In addition to the paths shown in the figures, each model includes non-zero correlations between locus of control and Type A score and coping. It can be seen from Table 12.4 that all the models are well-fitting and explain a reasonable proportion of variance in their respective outcome variables.

The forms of the best-fitting models are identical for satisfaction and physical well-being. In the model for psychological well-being there is a direct path between age and the outcome (indicating that psychological well-being increases with age) and there is no direct path from locus of control to the outcome.

All the models show that the effect of hours worked, Type A personality and locus of control on the three outcomes are mediated by stress. As would be expected, stress is negatively associated with all three outcomes, so individuals who are more stressed report lower levels of satisfaction and psychological and physical well-being. It can also be seen that number of working hours is positively related to age and that internal locus of control and low Type A scores diminish stress levels, whilst increased working hours increase them. There are also positive relationships between locus of control and both hours worked and age. Locus of control increases (becomes more internal) with age; the positive association between hours worked and locus of control cannot be interpreted unambiguously. It is possible that people with a highly internal locus of control choose to work longer hours, or that they are more likely to undergo a career progression into a job which requires longer hours.

Contrary to predictions, coping style did not act as a mediating variable, but locus of control did mediate the effect of hours worked on stress (although, as discussed above, the interpretation of this path is somewhat ambiguous). Stress acted as a mediator of the effect of hours worked and also of type A personality.

Table 12.4 Fit statistics for the structural equation models

Outcome	Residual	Model χ^2 (df)	NFI	NNFI	CFI	R^2
Satisfaction	0.029	12.63 (10) $p = 0.25$	0.93	0.96	0.98	0.33
Psychological well-being	0.032	13.50 (10) $p = 0.20$	0.91	0.94	0.97	0.21
Physical well-being	0.033	13.95 (10) $p = 0.18$	0.90	0.93	0.97	0.21

Note: $N = 218$. Residual = mean standardised absolute off-diagonal covariance matrix element, values of 0.04 or less indicate a well-fitting model. A non-significant model χ^2 indicates good fit. NFI = normed fit index, NNFI = non-normed fit index, CFI = comparative fit index; these should all be greater than 0.9 for a well-fitting model. For a more detailed discussion of model fitting, see Austin et al. (1998). R^2 is the proportion of variance in the outcome accounted for by the model. Sample size is smaller than for Table 12.3 because only participants with complete data for all variables could be included in the modelling.

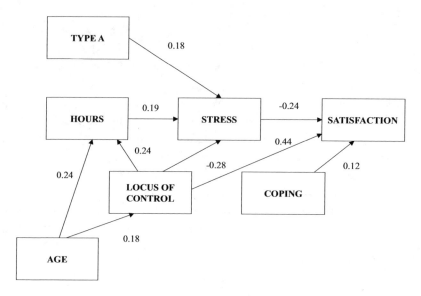

Figure 12.1 Path model, predicting work satisfaction (PMI) from personality (Type A, locus of control), coping style, occupational stress and demographic variables (age and hours of work)

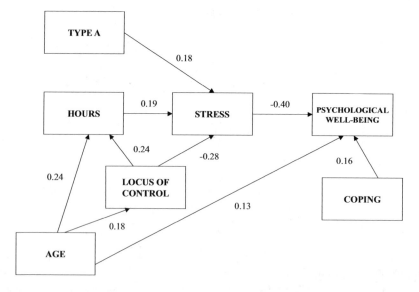

Figure 12.2 Path model, predicting mental health (PMI's psychological well-being) from personality (Type A, locus of control), coping style, occupational stress and demographic variables (age and hours of work)

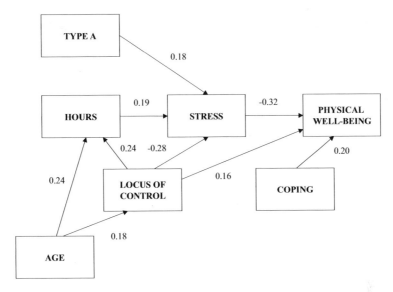

Figure 12.3 Path model, predicting physical health (PMI) from personality (Type A, locus of control), coping style, occupational stress and demographic variables (age and hours of work)

Discussion

In this study of German managers we have confirmed a number of well-known univariate associations in the work/stress/well-being area. It was found that number of hours worked was positively associated with stress levels whilst in turn stress levels were negatively related to physical well-being, psychological well-being and job satisfaction (cf. Kirkcaldy, Levine and Shephard, 2000; Kirkcaldy, Trimpop and Cooper, 1997). It was also found that these three outcome variables were all positively intercorrelated, as was found by Kirkcaldy, Cooper and Brown (1995). Stress levels were found to be negatively related to internal locus of control and positively related to Type A score as found by Goli, Marcoulides, Cooper and Kirkcaldy (1996). Unusually, no association was found between stress and coping style; most studies in this area have found an association (e.g. Deary et al., 1996; Kirkcaldy, Cooper and Brown, 1995).

The inclusion of gender as one of the variables of interest in the current study reflects the fact that the number of women in the workplace has increased steadily in recent years, although women continue to be heavily employed in domains frequently associated with high levels of job stress, such as health, teaching and the voluntary sector. Although the female participants reported working fewer hours than their male counterparts, women displayed higher stress and inferior physical and psychological health. This finding supports previous research that has established work and family roles have different meaning for men than for women, and that these differences can be related to physical and mental health, especially distress (Simon, 1995). Publiesi (1995) examined the differential exposure hypothesis which claims that roles are sources of stressors with respect to gender that impact well-being, and the differential vulnerability hypothesis which claims that gender differences in well-being are sources of social roles in men and women.

One of the principal aims of applying SEM in this study was to attempt to explore the complex interrelationship between multiple antecedents of occupational stress and the ensuing impact on health outcome variables and work satisfaction, in a way that is more informative than the examination of univariate associations or the use of regression models. The magnitudes of the majority of the model coefficients revealed moderate associations, and overall the models displayed highly satisfactory fit. These findings lend credence for the transactional model of psychological and physical health in which stress mediates the relationship between personality and situational factors and outcomes associated with physical or psychological well-being (Deary et al., 1996). Between 21 to 33 percent of the observed variance in the outcome variables could be accurately assigned to the parameters in the model (Type A, locus of control, age, working hours, coping and occupational stress).

One common observation across all three outcome variables was that the two individual difference variables – Type A behaviour and locus of control – both exerted a significant impact of the health variables, albeit mediated through occupational stress. Job-related stress had a negative effect on the outcome variables (increased work dissatisfaction and inferior psychological and physical well-being). Type A behaviour and (external) locus of control were associated with increased occupational stress, as was the number of weekly working hours. The detailed information on the multivariate associations in the data displayed in Figures 12.1, 12.2 and 12.3 illustrates the power of the structural equation method in displaying these associations in a readily understood graphical form. It permits tentative mechanisms explaining the intricate interrelationship between the individual difference variables and occupational stress and the outcome measures of physical and psychological health.

Some methodological shortcomings of the study include: sole reliance on self-report measures; over reliance on a global measure of stress where a multidimensional construct is required (Cooper, Kirkcaldy and Furnham, 1995); failure to distinguish or differentiate managerial groups according to level of management (occupational status); or whether the subjects are employed in the public or private sector. In the current study, the possible interactive effects of internal locus of control and Type A remain unexplored. In addition, parameters of work could be more differentiated and could include, for example, onset of work, duration of lunch break, length of leisure-time and cessation of work. Future studies may take account of these potentially confounding sources.

Implications of the study are manifold. Kirkcaldy, Trimpop and Cooper (1997) reported that not only were individuals who worked in excess of 48 hours more likely to show greater occupational stress, but also that length of working hours had adverse effects on real-life behaviour in areas such as accident rates at work and whilst driving. Evidence has shown that stress can directly and indirectly cause fatigue and a lack of attention and focus which may lead to injury. This finding is of particular relevance to organisations that have a lot of people performing manual labour or working in dangerous areas. Steps should be taken to reduce demands and alleviate time pressures, because when these factors are increased, employees are less likely to take time for safety precautions. This suggests the need for more flexible working hours, and flexplace alternatives, such as working partly at home and partly from central work environments. In addition to the impact on job satisfaction and employee mental and physical health, excessive hours leading to increased stress may encourage or cause talented employees to look for better working environments elsewhere. In such circumstances where extended hours are necessary, employees should see how they and the company benefit, or should receive additional compensation in terms of additional holidays or time-off.

Although legislation may seek to regulate a legal or statutory limit to working hours, additional factors such as commuting between home and work often exert additional pressures on employees. From an organisational perspective, it would seem logical and prudent to consider the role of stress not only in terms of the impact on the organisation or on the employee, but on both. Physical and mental ill health is now commonly associated directly with economic costs, not only in terms of turnover and absenteeism, but ever increasingly in sick days, litigation cases, healthcare and medical expenses. The indirect costs in terms of productivity through reduced morale, commitment, enthusiasm and creativity must also be considered. In direct relation to management, Talbot, Cooper and Barrow (1992) studied 202 managers and found significant negative correlations between stress and the potential for creativity. Clearly the long-term health consequences of job stress among staff will have both a direct and indirect influence on the health and success of the organisation.

References

Austin, E.J., Deary, I.J. and Willock, J. (2001). Personality and intelligence as predictors of economic behaviour in Scottish farmers. *European Journal of Personality*, 15(51) 123–37.

Austin, E.J., Willock, J., Deary, I.J., Gibson, G.J., Dent, J.B., Edwards-Jones, G., Morgan, O., Grieve, R. and Sutherland, A. (1998). Empirical modelling of farmer behaviour using psychological, social and economic variables. Part I: linear models. *Agricultural Systems*, 58, 203–24.

Bentler, P.M. (1995). *EQS Structural Equations Program Manual*. Encino, CA: Multivariate Software Inc.

Cooper, C.L. and Baglioni, A.J. (1988). A structural model approach toward the development of a theory of the link between stress and mental health. *British Journal of Medical Psychology*, 61, 87–102.

Cooper, C.L., Kirkcaldy, B.D. and Brown, J. (1994). A model of job stress and physical health: the role of individual differences. *Personality and Individual Differences*, 16(4), 653–5.

Cooper, C.L., Kirkcaldy, B.D. and Furnham, A.F. (1995). Psychische Belastung von Führungskräften [The impact of organisational stress on managers]. In A. Kieser, G. Reber and R. Wunderer (eds), *Handwörterbuch der Führung (HWFü)* (pp. 1794–807). Stuttgart: Schäffer-Poeschel Verlag.

Cox, T. (1990). The recognition and measurement of stress: conceptual and methodological issues. In: E.N. Corlett and J. Wilson (eds), *Evaluation of Human Work* (pp. 31–9). London: Taylor and Francis.

Cox, T. (1993). *Stress Research and Stress Management: Putting Theory to Work*. Sudbury: Health and Safety Executive.

Cox, T. and Griffiths, A. (1995). The nature and measurement of work stress: theory and practice. In J.R. Wilson and E.N. Corlett (eds), *Evaluation Of Human Work*, 2nd edn. London: Taylor and Francis.

Deary, I.J., Blenkin, H., Agius, R.M., Endler, N.S., Zealley, H. and Wood, R. (1996). Models of job-related stress and personal achievement among consultant doctors. *British Journal of Psychology*, 87, 3–29.

Derogatis, L.R. and Coons, H.L. (1993). Self-report measures of stress. In L. Goldberger and S. Breznitz (eds), *Handbook of Stress: Theoretical and Clinical Aspects*, 2nd edn (pp. 200–233). New York: The Free Press.

European Foundation for the Improvement of Living and Working Conditions (1996). *Second European Survey on Working Conditions in the European Union*. Dublin: European Foundation for the Improvement of Living and Working Conditions.

Folkman, S. and Lazarus, R.S. (1988a). Coping as a mediator of emotion. *Journal of Personality and Social Psychology*, 54(3), 466–75.

Folkman, S. and Lazarus, R.S. (1988b). The relationship between coping and emotion: implications for theory and research. *Social Science Medicine*, 26(3), 309–17.

Goli, A., Marcoulides, G.A., Cooper, C.L. and Kirkcaldy, B.D. (Winter 1996). Testing a model of occupational stress in different countries. *Journal of Business and Management (Special Issue: International Business)*, 3(2), 10–29.

Greenberg, J.S. (1999). *Comprehensive Stress Management*, 6th edn. New York: WCB/McGraw-Hill.

Huebner, E.S., Ash, C. and Laughlin, J.E. (2001). Life experiences, locus of control and school satisfaction in adolescence. *Social Indicators Research*, 55, 167–83.

Jerusalem, M. (1993). Personal resources, environmental constraints and adaptational processes: the predictive power of a theoretical stress model. *Personality and Individual Differences*, 14, 15–24.

Kasl, S.V. (1987). Methodologies in stress and health: past difficulties, present dilemmas, future directions. In S. Kasl (ed.), *Stress and Health: Issues in Research Methodology*. Chichester: John Wiley.

Kirkcaldy, B.D., Cooper, C.L. and Brown, J. (1995). The role of coping in the stress-strain relationship among senior police officers. *International Journal of Stress Management*, 2(2), 69–78.

Kirkcaldy, B.D., Levine, R. and Shephard, R.J. (2000). The impact of working hours on physical and psychological health of German managers. *European Review of Applied Psychology*, 50(4), 443–9.

Kirkcaldy, B.D., Shephard, R.J. and Furnham, A. (2002). The influence of type A behaviour and locus of control upon job satisfaction and occupational health. *Personality and Individual Differences*, 33, 1361–71.

Kirkcaldy, B.D., Trimpop, R. and Cooper, C.L. (1997) . Working hours, job stress, work satisfaction and accident rates among medical practitioners, consultants and allied personnel. *International Journal of Stress Management*, 4(2), 79–87.

Kirkcaldy, B., Trimpop, R. and Levine, R. (2002). The impact of work hours and schedules on physical and psychological well-being in medical practices. *European Psychologist*, 7, 116–24.

Lundberg, U. and Frankenhaeuser, M. (1999). Stress and workload of men and women in high ranking positions. *Journal of Occupational Health Psychology*, 4, 142–51.

Miller, K., Greyling, M., Cooper, C.L., Luo, L., Sparks, K. and Spector, P.E. (2000). Occupational stress and gender: a cross-cultural study. *Stress Medicine*, 16, 271–8.

Noor, N.M. (2002). Work-family conflict, locus of control, and women's well-being: tests of alternative pathways. *Journal of Social Psychology*, 142, 645–62.

Publiesi, K. (1995). Work and well-being: gender differences in the psychological consequences of employment. *Journal of Health and Social Behavior*, 36, 57–71.

Rosa, R.R., Colligan, M.J. and Lewis, P. (1989). Extended workdays: effects of 8-hour and 12-hour rotating shifts schedules on performance, subjective alertness, sleep patterns and psychosocial variables. *Work and Stress*, 3, 2–32.

Simon, R. (1995). Gender, multiple roles, role meaning, and mental health. *Journal of Health and Social Behavior*, 36, 182–94.

Sparks, K., Cooper, C., Fried, Y. and Shirom, A. (1997). The effects of hours of work on health: a meta-analytic review. *Journal of Occupational and Organisational Psychology*, 70, 391–408.

Spurgeon A., Harrington J.M. and Cooper C.L. (1997). Health and safety problems associated with long working hours: a review of the current position. *Occupational And Environmental Medicine*, 54(6), 367–75.

Talbot, R., Cooper, C. and Barrow, S. (1992). Creativity and stress. *Creativity and Innovation Management*, 1(4), 183–93.

Watson, D. and Pennebaker, J.W. (1989). Health complaints, stress, and distress: exploring the central role of negative affectivity. *Psychological Review*, 96, 234–64.

Williams, S. (1996). A critical review and further development of the occupational stress indicator. Doctoral thesis. University of Manchester, Manchester.

Williams, S. and Cooper, C.L. (1998). Measuring occupational stress: development of the pressure management indicator. *Journal of Occupational Health Psychology*, 3(4), 306–21.

Williams, S., Kirkcaldy, B.D. and Cooper, C.L. (1998). *Der Indikator*. (Pressure Management Indicator). Harrogate: Human Resources.

13

Employee Health and Presenteeism: The Challenge for Human Resources Management

Robert A. Roe and Bas van Diepen

Introduction

Employee health is an important issue in organizational contexts. It is commonly assumed that employee sickness results in absenteeism and that organizations suffer from productivity loss and replacement costs, and therefore need to make special efforts to reintegrate employees in order for these to resume their work as early as possible. This story highlights one scenario only, though. As research has shown, many employees continue to work when their health is affected. This so-called "presenteeism" appears to happen with a wide range of illnesses and ailments, and can produce positive as well as negative effects for the employee and the organization. Recent research has shown that presenteeism and absenteeism are related, and emphasized that one should study their joint effects. This chapter reviews the evidence on presenteeism and the factors that seem to determine its prevalence and effects. Special attention is paid to performance effects, impacts on other employees, and long-term health consequences. The role that human resources management (HRM) can and should play with regard to presenteeism and absenteeism is also discussed.

Perspectives and Contexts

There are two main perspectives on health in organizations. The first is that of occupational health and environmental hygiene, which emphasizes the potential impact that exposure to environmental risks and executing certain work tasks can have on employees' health. This perspective highlights the impact of workplace stressors and the damaging effects of prolonged exposure to harmful conditions. It sees absenteeism as a negative and hence to-be-prevented response to a potentially dangerous work situation. The second perspective is a managerial one. It depicts employee sickness as an undesirable phenomenon that limits the organization's dependability, raises costs, and reduces productivity. Both perspectives have an interest in preventing and reducing employee illness, but with a different emphasis. The managerial perspective, which has grown in importance in recent years, focuses on reducing costs and maintaining productivity (Cascio, 2006), limiting the financial burden of absenteeism (e.g., Martocchio, 1992), and securing work flow (e.g., Atkin and Goodman, 1984) as well as employee performance (e.g., Bycio, 1992). Organizational initiatives based on this perspective have mainly aimed at prevention and reduction of absenteeism, and comprised occupational health surveillance, employee screening and monitoring, the prevention of incidents that can lead to injuries and diseases, the design of work tasks, and health education. A certain degree of absenteeism is accepted for the purpose of "removing the injured" for the benefit of the individual and that of colleagues or clients, but it is associated with calls for early return to the work place.

Both the occupational health and the managerial perspective focus on absenteeism and thereby leave certain aspects of the relationship between health and work unaccounted for. First of all, absenteeism is not the only response to sickness. Many employees continue to go to their workplace and keep performing their tasks after falling sick. For some, the consequences of this so-called "presenteeism" may be positive as the work detracts from symptoms and promotes recovery, but for others they may be negative, aggravating the condition and inhibiting recovery. Secondly, absenteeism does not only have negative effects and should not be avoided at all costs. Absenteeism does allow employees to manage their sickness and gives them room for recovery. In some cases it helps them to take a distance and become aware of harmful working conditions that should be changed or avoided. It is important for managers and HRM specialists to take these facets of sickness and work into consideration as dong so provides a better basis for developing effective health policies.

Although it is somewhat underemphasized in the research literature, it is worth noting that the way in which organizations deal with employee health is dependent on the institutional context and particularly on the system of labor relations. Van Diepen, van Iterson, and Roe (2006) have pointed at the contrast between countries with a contract-based system (particularly the United States) and a covenant-based system (most of Europe), which differ in the roles that employers and employees play vis-à-vis each other, and in the expectations stemming from these roles. In contract-based settings the relationship is more short-term and instrumental, whereas in the covenant-based system the relationship is more long-term and built on reciprocal obligations. On the basis of this difference, one would expect that in the United States employers are generally more interested in maintaining productivity and keeping down the health costs they must bear, whereas European employers may be more inclined to find a balance between ensuring productivity and providing an appropriate level of care. Congruous with the differences in labor relations are differences in the wider societal setting, e.g., in the provision of social security and public health care. Differences in legislation on employment and health, both supranational and national, are an expression of this. European employers and employees are subject to European Framework directives (e.g., Directive 89/391) which oblige employers to ensure the safety and health of their workers. European employers must take specific measures (e.g., with respect to the prevention of occupational risks) as well as provide information and training, and establishing the necessary infrastructure for care. They are furthermore required to prevent monotonous work, work at a predetermined rate, and to adapt the work to the individual (e.g., through the design of work places, the choice of work equipment, or the choice of work and production methods) in order to reduce negative impacts on employee health. In addressing these issues employers need to give collective protective measures priority over individual protective measures.

There are also national differences, for instance in legal regulations regarding employer and employee responsibilities and duties in limiting risks, covering costs, and organizing health care at work. For instance, in the United States, the Family and Medical Leave Act provides employees with protection against dismissal in case of sickness while taking accrued paid leave (such as vacation or sick leave). European countries differ in the degree of risk that employees are supposed to bear. In some countries employees are held accountable for health problems due to activities in the private domain (e.g., sports, traffic), while the employer is accountable for problems originating at the work place—in other countries such a distinction is not made.

These institutional differences are important because they may influence both absenteeism and presenteeism. Employees in covenant-based environments are likely to experience less pressure to keep working when ill or to resume the work before full recovery. They may see absenteeism as a "right" or even as a "duty" to restore their health before going back to work. In serious cases, where employees have fallen ill or become disabled due to exposure to work-related hazards, absenteeism may give them the opportunity to reflect on necessary workplace adaptations or possible career changes to avoid future health problems. In such cases employees may call for the support of health or HRM professionals and negotiate changes in working conditions or transfer to another position before the work is resumed. Employees in contract-based environments, on the other hand, may feel pressured to keep working or to resume the work at an earlier moment, possibly before being sufficiently recovered. In cases where a certain amount of sickness days has been agreed, they may take an instrumental attitude and use up the available time even when able to work. In such cases, minor illnesses, ranging from the common cold to "not feeling well," can serve to legitimize the absence.

Presenteeism: Its Nature and Origin

The term "presenteeism" refers to people's tendency to continue working while being sick. Although it seems fair to assume that this phenomenon has always existed, researchers' interest in it has grown conspicuously, especially in the United States. This can be explained by the high costs of health care and the fact that American employers are legally obliged to carry half of the expenses (Goetzel, Hawkins, Ozminkowski, and Wang, 2003). Although the measurement of productivity loss in presenteeism is still in its infancy, there are indications that the costs incurred due to presenteeism are higher than those resulting from absenteeism (Stewart, Ricci, Chee, and Morganstein, 2003). The loss of productive working time due to sickness at work has been estimated to amount to 5 percent to 10 percent (Burton et al., 2005), but there have also been lower (Bunn et al., 2006) and higher estimates (Collins et al., 2005). The estimates vary with the kind of work and the nature of the ailment. Unfortunately the current measurement methods appear to be not very reliable. For instance, a recent study into the effect of headaches (Pransky et al., 2005) found that employees estimated the decrease in their performance to be 20 percent, while an objective measure put the figure at only 8 percent.

At which scale does presenteeism occur and which illnesses are involved? There is not enough research evidence to give a definite answer to these questions. The available evidence suggests that in Western countries at least half of the working population continues working when they could have reported sick. According to a Dutch study among employees in education (Kamphuis and van Poppel, 1998) this applied to 65 percent of non-teaching staff and 75 percent of teaching staff. A British study found a figure of 85 percent or higher for a sample of general practitioners, hospital doctors, accountants, and management consultants (McKevitt, Morgan, Dundas, and Holland, 1997). The aforementioned study by Collins et al. (2005), conducted among employees of Dow Chemical in the United States reported a figure of 65 percent. These presenteeism figures clearly depend on the way in which "going to work when sick" is operationalized. Stewart et al. (2003), who studied a random sample of the American population, found that 38.3 percent of the respondents had been "less productive" as a consequence of a health problem, during at least one day during the past two weeks. Swedish researchers (Aronsson, Gustafsson, and Dallner, 2000) noted that 37 percent of the employees in a national sample had gone to work while preferring to report sick at least twice during the past year. The rates for medical doctors were 49 percent and for teachers 52 percent. This study suggests that presenteeism occurs more frequently in the sectors of care and education.

In interpreting presenteeism figures the institutional context should again be taken into account. The rate of presenteeism may have been higher in the United States where reduction of absenteeism has been a major concern for decades, but in recent years many European countries have undergone liberal reforms producing similar effects. Privatization of health insurance and caps on employee income protection have increased the pressure to curtail absenteeism and to accelerate the return to work. As a consequence the degree of presenteeism may have risen. Evidence from the Netherlands seems to confirm this assumption: in a sample of employees in the care sector 32 percent reported an increase in working while being sick and resuming work more quickly. Thus it seems that employees "substitute" absenteeism by presenteeism, as it was put in a recent Canadian study (Caverley, Cunningham, and MacGregor, 2007).

People can have different *reasons* to go to work while being sick. A primary reason is the negative impact on other people that staying at home has. Among them are both clients (also pupils and patients) and colleagues. The effect is likely to vary with the degree to which one is replaceable. If there is no person to take over the tasks, and the work keeps compiling during one's absence, the tendency to come to work in spite of the illness will be stronger. Relationships with colleagues and the degree of task interdependency also play a role. For instance, a qualitative study by Grinyer and Singleton (2000) found that being a member of a work team increased workers' reluctance to take sick leave. A second reason lies in the negative consequences that absenteeism may have on one's income or employment security. In Europe many people decide to observe the stricter rules regarding absenteeism and return to work, out of fear for loss of income, non-continuation of their contract (especially when sick during a probation period), or negative impacts on their later career (Judiesch and Lyness, 1999). In a recent study by a Dutch temp agency 15 to 20 percent of the respondents said they would continue to work while sick out of fear of dismissal.[1] In the third place, there can be social pressures to come to work, either from co-workers or supervisors, as an expression of social norms on appropriate health behavior. Of course, there may also be positive reasons such as having interesting and stimulating work tasks, and having rewarding relations with colleagues and clients, that make people opt for presenteeism.

From another angle, there is the *nature of the illness* as a factor that may affect the decision to keep working in a number of ways. There are several facets of illness to be considered. First, there is the severity of the condition. In case of a minor illness that does not significantly hinder traveling to work and performing the work tasks, most people will be inclined to go to work. This applies to, for example, headaches, the common cold, and muscle pains, conditions that are normally of short duration and can be effectively treated with medication. Second, there is the legitimacy of absenteeism provided by the illness, that is, the degree to which it is seen as an acceptable excuse for staying home by the social environment (managers, co-workers, people in the same profession, family) of the worker him/herself. Research has shown that people in lower level jobs find it more acceptable to stay home with a common cold, influenza, headache, back pain etc. than do people in higher level jobs (Harvey and Nicholson, 1999), which suggests that social norms are operating, but this may also have to do with the nature of the work tasks. Finally, there are interaction and cumulative effects. People with a good health condition will not immediately report sick when suffering from an occasional illness, while those with a poor health condition may stay home when suffering from a mild affliction. This suggests that presenteeism can be seen as the opposite of absenteeism: factors promoting absenteeism can be seen as hindrances to presenteeism and vice versa.

What are the illnesses that are most associated with presenteeism? According to research these are physical conditions such as headaches, stomach and bowel problems, common cold and influenza, neck and back pain, and mental conditions such as anxiety, depression, and irritation (Bunn et al., 2006;

---

1 Randstad Werkmonitor, February 12, 2004. Available at: http: www.randstad.nl/rnl/download/randstad/onderzoek/Onderzoek%20Ziekteverzuim%20Februari%202004.pdf [Accessed: 17 January 2007].

Stewart et al., 2003). Apart from these minor complaints there are also more serious illnesses. Table 13.1, based on the study by Bunn et al. (2006), lists eleven illnesses from which people suffered during at least one day a year. This list is by no means exhaustive. A study by Collins et al. (2005) into the effects of chronic conditions mentions allergies as well as back/neck disorders and stomach/bowel disorders. An older study (Taylor, 1968) documents that presenteeism happens with a variety of physical ailments. In this study it appeared that 28 percent of employees who were never absent from their work had some organic illness.

Table 13.1 shows that employees are confronted with a broad range of illnesses which can vary widely in their effects. It is important to acknowledge that these illnesses can appear in all sorts of combinations. At one extreme there are employees who are rarely ill and who suffer from a single illness that can be effectively treated with medication. At the other extreme there are employees with chronic health conditions who are repeatedly afflicted by other illnesses that are difficult to cure. Due to a lack of research we know very little about the distribution between these poles, but it is beyond doubt that these varying patterns of illness have diverging impacts on employees' performance.

Table 13.1 Common health conditions in presenteeism

	% Respondents who reported experiencing a condition for at least 1 day per year		
	Men	Women	Total
Allergic rhinitis/hay fever	54.4	59.3	57.3
High stress	36.8	45.8	42.1
Migraine	18.0	33.2	27.0
Arthritis/rheumatism	20.1	22.6	21.6
Respiratory illnesses	12.9	21.8	18.2
Anxiety disorder	14.6	19.1	17.2
Depression	11.4	17.3	14.9
Hypertension	13.4	11.2	12.1
Asthma	9.6	11.8	10.9
Coronary heart disease	5.9	4.5	5.1
Diabetes	4.5	4.8	4.7

Source: Based on Bunn et al. (2006).

Presenteeism: Effects on Performance and Productivity

How does presenteeism affect employees' performance and productivity? The American studies that were quoted above point to various degrees of productivity decline. The study by Stewart et al. (2003), for example, estimated the average loss of productive working time as a direct consequence of illness at 1.32 hours per week. This does not include absenteeism, which resulted in a loss of 0.54 hours per week, on average. It must be noted that these figures are not based on performance measurements but are derived from employee reports about the effects, such as loss of concentration, slower work pace, increased fatigue, less effectiveness, and so on (Collins et al., 2005; Koopman et al., 2002). Therefore they do not provide direct information on how health problems influence people's performance. The literature provides limited evidence on such performance effects. We will review this evidence and rely on notions form the theoretical literature on performance to develop a picture of the illness-performance relationship. In our review we will distinguish between performance as a process and as an outcome (e.g., Roe, 1999).

IMPACTS ON THE PERFORMANCE PROCESS

A number of studies have investigated general impacts of being sick on people's task performance. Matthews, Davies, Westerman, and Stammers (2000: 225–6) describe four ways in which illness can negatively affect the performance process:

- impaired neural functioning as a direct consequence of the illness itself: for example Alzheimer's disease, multiple sclerosis and immunological changes;

- impaired cerebral blood flow due to reduced glucose and oxygen metabolism as a result of cardiovascular disease, hypertension, diabetes and the like;

- symptom effects resulting from negative mental conditions such as anxiety, depression and fatigue;

- health behaviors, that is, effects of using of antihistaminic, sedating and other drugs, and ideas about the patient role such as "taking it easy."

A more detailed image of health impacts on the performance process can be constructed by looking at theoretical models of the various mental and physical regulation mechanisms involved in work performance (Roe, 1999; 2007). For instance, the *action regulation mechanism* that underlies task execution requires an undisturbed functioning of the central nervous system, the perceptual apparatus, and the motor apparatus. Any major disturbance, whether reduced brain metabolism, impaired perception, or muscle lesion will result in performance decline, unless this can be prevented or compensated by a change of work strategy. For instance, an employee might opt for an alternative strategy that allows him/her to perform the task by relying more heavily on routines, extending the activities over time, or using other muscle groups. The *energetic regulation* will be affected when coping with the illness adds to a person's workload, and a greater expenditure of effort becomes necessary. In such a case the capacity to accommodate work load variations by mobilizing additional effort decreases. Spending still extra effort can cause the person to overtax him/herself, who is then forced to give up. *Emotional regulation* at work can be negatively affected when the person suffers from illnesses accompanied by emotional instability or mood changes, as is the case with depression or burnout. This will cause problems in emotionally demanding work.

Apart from these effects, illness will nearly always have an impact on the person's *vital regulation*, the process by which the person's vitality is controlled. The person needs time to recover and must make efforts to reduce or compensate the symptoms and consequences of the illness. He/she may need more sleep and more time and attention for medication and personal care, which implies less time spent on work. There may also be implications for the regulation of a person's *self-image*, but here individual differences are to be expected. Being sick can be a difficult condition for people who have just started a job and who want to avoid making a wrong impression. It can also pose a problem those who foster a reputation of "never being ill" or who want to "give a good example" as a manager. They would rather keep working than admit to the "weakness" of having to stay home. Here, personal norms may interact with social norms held by others at work or in the family. When the social environment disapproves, presenteeism can become a stressor that enhances the effect of illness on performance.

What will be the result of all these impacts on the performance process? Hockey (2000: 220–22) has posited that action regulation naturally implies a certain *resistance to degradation*: people strive to accomplish their work goals in spite of possible hindrances. When faced with hindrances they will expend additional effort, change their work strategy, persist longer—but rather not give up. Hockey mentions three modes of working, which can be differentiated physiologically:

- *engagement*: the stressor is immediately coped with within the limits of the energetic budget, the performance outcome is maintained as far as possible;

- *disengagement*: the subjective task is adjusted, resulting in a downward adjustment of the performance outcome;

- *strain*: extra effort is spent with the aim to maintain the performance outcomes.

It is important to note that the second mode, which implies a decline of performance outcomes, is not readily chosen. Performance decline usually takes the form of a graceful degradation (Navon and Gopher, 1979) rather than of a total disintegration. In connection with presenteeism it is important to note that the person pays a price for this in the form of an extra and perhaps excessive, and therefore potentially harmful, expenditure of effort. Hockey (2000) speaks about a "latent performance decrement": at the surface there are no important performance changes but underneath, at the level of regulation of the activity and the required resources, an undesirable change may take place. The person may neglect certain subordinate tasks, spend less effort than really needed, develop more fatigue, or take more risky decisions.

IMPACTS ON PERFORMANCE OUTCOMES

Empirical research on performance outcomes has hitherto been limited to specific illnesses and test tasks carried out in laboratory settings. A distinction should be made between acute and chronic conditions. Among the acute conditions, respiratory illnesses—especially influenza and the common cold—have attracted most research attention. A British study (Smith, 1992) has shown that these illnesses have very different effects. Influenza causes a deterioration of performance in simple detection and reaction tasks, which hints at impairment of the attention mechanism. The common cold leads to a deterioration of tracking tasks (tasks requiring the pursuit of a moving target though eye-hand coordination), whereas performance in memory tasks does not suffer. The common cold can lead to lower arousal, but the stimulating effect of a cup of coffee suffices to compensate for this.

Research on *chronic conditions* has concentrated on the effects of the Human Immunodeficiency Virus (HIV), the chronic fatigue syndrome (CFS), and diabetes. The effects of HIV become manifest in later stages of the disease. They comprise amnesia, impaired thinking, retarded motor functioning, and so on. CFS is associated with impairment of several cognitive functions. In (insulin dependent) diabetes, evidence of impaired cognitive performance during and after hypoglycemic periods has been found. These examples only serve to illustrate the diversity of the effects that illness can have on work performance. Future research will have to establish which specific effects are produced by which illnesses. It is also important to pay attention to the use of medication during illness, since drugs do not only suppress the symptoms of an illness but can also affect the performance level directly. Effects on the capacity to drive or operate machines are widely known, but other types of performance can be influenced as well.

Drawing a general conclusion about the effects of presenteeism on performance, it seems unlikely that performance effectiveness will suffer greatly, at least in the short run. There are several reasons to support this expectation. First, presenteeism will often be confined to cases of minor illness of which the symptoms can be suppressed by using drugs. Second, one would expect to see the phenomenon of performance protection that was mentioned above—even in those with more serious conditions. However, personal efficiency will decline since the same task requires more time and effort due to the person's lower capacity. Over time, personal costs can accumulate considerably. This can result in delayed recovery and can negatively influence performance in the long run. Other effects should be expected among people who return to work after a period of serious illness. Depending on the condition they suffered from, the performance level can be markedly lower, especially when they were not fully recovered in the moment of resuming the work. This applies, for instance, to the case of people resuming work after a back or limb operation (e.g., Lotters, Meerding, and Burdorff, 2005).

It is important to acknowledge individual differences in the effects of illness on performance. For instance, greater performance deterioration is to be expected among people who are ill more often and/or who suffer from a chronic condition. Interactions with an unhealthy life style should also be considered. Research (e.g., Bunn et al., 2006; Stewart et al., 2003) has shown that smoking, excessive alcohol use, and obesity can enhance the negative effects on performance of illness. Compared to non-smokers, smokers are ill more frequently and they show greater performance decrements. For certain health conditions there are also differences between men and women. For instance, women compared to men report more anxiety, depression, and stress, as well as grater impacts on their work (Bunn et al., 2006). The latter finding might be explained by the fact that presenteeism in women involves other diseases than presenteeism in men.

The effects of illness on performance are not limited to individual performance. Evidence from everyday life shows that employees who come to work in spite of illness are often supported by their colleagues, so that the collective performance is somehow maintained. However, in case of an employee carrying an infectious disease, there is a chance that other employees or customers become infected. This is a clear risk factor in settings that imply a close contact between people. In such cases the individual performance need not be much lower, but the joint performance may decline significantly. In case of insufficient recovery the overall effect may not be sustainable and team performance may yet decline.

IMPACTS ON PERFORMANCE IN VARIOUS OCCUPATIONS

For a valid assessment of the relationship between illness and performance it is not sufficient to study specific illnesses and their general effects on human cognition and action. One will also have to consider the nature of the work to be performed, since the effects of a particular illness may vary with the task demands. For instance, the common cold can pose a serious hindrance in the work of an air pilot, whereas it may not have much impact on the work of a secretary or gardener. On theoretical grounds one would expect that illnesses involving general malaise, migraine, headache, and dizziness will pose a hindrance to activities involving high cognitive demands. Likewise mental conditions such as anxiety, depression, irritation, and burnout are impediments to work involving high emotional demands. Disorders involving the muscular-skeletal system, including RSI, neck and back problems, arthritis, and so on, seem to hinder work implying high physical demands. Altogether it would seem that performance in higher level jobs will suffer more from the first group of illnesses (general malaise and the like) and mental conditions, than from physical ailments. For lower level jobs effects are likely to be different because of a greater variety of work demands.

Following the logic of Functional Job Analysis (Fine and Cronshaw, 1999) which classifies jobs according to the degree of involvement with things, people, and data as work objects, one would predict that employees working with "things" — like factory workers, drivers, and operators — will mostly be hindered by disorders of the muscular-skeletal system. Those working with "people" — for example, flight attendants, teachers, nurses, social workers — will mainly be hindered by mental conditions, like those working with "data," who can also suffer from afflictions of the muscular-skeletal system. Of course, these are merely hypothetical ideas that need to be tested in empirical research.

Effects of Presenteeism and Performance on Employee Health

In the previous section attention focused on the impact of health on performance, but one can also raise the question of how performance influences health, and subsequently how health and performance reciprocally influence each other. These questions are difficult to answer because many factors are involved. Research on work and mental health (e.g., Warr, 1987; 2007) has shown that having a paid job generally contributes to good health while unemployment leads to depression and illness. For people who have been unable to work because of a physical or mental disorder, work can act as a medicine, as is apparent in expressions such as "occupational therapy" and "vocational rehabilitation". The reason for this may be that assuming a work role helps one to become active and to leave the patient role behind. Moreover, performing work tasks structures the activity stream, activates and stimulates several mental and bodily functions, and redirects attention from negative thoughts and towards work content. Successfully performing work tasks may lead to positive feedback and appreciation from others, which can enhance the self image even more and counterbalance the efforts involved in working. These therapeutic effects can provide people with a reason to go to work in spite of ill health.

Although this suggests that presenteeism can have positive health effects, opposite outcomes may also occur. Much will depend on whether the employee is able to reach an adequate level of performance without overtaxing him/herself or otherwise hinder the process of recovery. A key factor seems to lie in the adjustment of work norms and working hours. If this is the case, presenteeism may result in effective reintegration and rehabilitation. In this connection it is interesting to note that a greater deterioration of performance has been observed in jobs with fewer regulation possibilities (little control) (Stewart et al., 2003). When adjustments are impossible it may be difficult to achieve acceptable outcomes, and the drive to perform can turn into a stressor that impedes recovery. This may necessitate the person stopping work, which turns presenteeism into absenteeism, and annihilates the therapeutic effect.

Support by colleagues and the supervisor is also a factor to consider. If support is perceived as facilitating it can enhance the employee's self-image and improve reintegration; if it is perceived as a pressure to perform it can act as a stressor that impedes reintegration (Deelstra et al., 2003). Thus, for performance to have a positive influence on health, a number of conditions will have to be fulfilled. The working environment should be free of harmful influences, the workload should be calibrated, there should be sufficient opportunity to adjust the method of working to optimize recovery, and there should be adequate support from the social environment. An implication is that others in the organization will have to accept a lower productivity for some time, but the relationships between work demands and abilities, work load and capacity, effort and rewards are important as well.

Presenteeism, Absenteeism, and HRM

Growing insights into the nature and effects of presenteeism will necessitate employers reconsidering their position regarding work and illness. It now seems that the focus on curtailing absenteeism, while understandable from an occupational health and managerial perspective, has been shortsighted. Not only do the costs of absenteeism seem to be lower than those of presenteeism (Stewart et al., 2003), the estimates for presenteeism are very high indeed, amounting to US$180 billion a year for the United States as a whole (Hemp, 2004; Samuel and Wilson, 2007). For Europe no such estimates are known, but it can safely be assumed that the costs are substantial as well. Costs should not be the only concern, however. Low absenteeism, and high presenteeism, may also affect the long-term health and well-being of the work force as a whole, and thereby undermine the health and agility of the organization.

Now that presenteeism and absenteeism are known to be related, it is clear that too much emphasis on either side will give suboptimal results. A heavy reliance on reducing absenteeism may seem effective as a way to curtail productivity decline due to employee absence and losses from temporary replacements. However, raising presenteeism evokes alternative and disguised forms of productivity decline due to poorer performance of sick employees, compensatory action by colleagues, consequent sickness of colleagues and the like. Also, it obstructs and prolongs the recovery process, which leads to suboptimal employee health and raises costs in the long term. Too much emphasis on reducing presenteeism has the opposite effects. While better protecting employee health and reducing the costs of productivity loss due to working while sick, it causes greater absenteeism which implies productivity loss due to absence and replacement costs. Knowledge on the relation between health and performance, even though limited, leads to another important conclusion: the optimal balance between presenteeism and absenteeism differs with the nature of the illness, the type of work, and the room for reintegration and rehabilitation given the severity of the illness and the stage of recovery. In some cases employees will benefit most from going back to work early, while in other cases they should rather stay home and wait for complete recovery. Thus, an approach to presenteeism is needed that distinguishes between cases when it should be encouraged or facilitated (because of positive impacts), and cases when it should be discouraged (because of negative consequences).

An important insight from the literature is that employees do not merely respond in a passive way to the organization's health and work policies, but take an active role in making a choice between staying home or going to work while sick. Although acute and serious illness may force them into a patient role, there seems to be a range of health conditions in which they consider their behavioral options and weigh their consequences before making the choice. A recent study has suggested that employees do trade off their responses to sickness (Caverley, Cunningham, and MacGregor, 2007). Several factors may influence this choice between absence and presenteeism. For instance, the relationship with the organization may have an influence, as presenteeism can be seen as a form of organizational citizenship by which the employee reciprocates something the organization has provided, or fulfills a felt obligation (Coyle Shapiro, Kessler, and Purcell, 2004), and absenteeism as a way to express discontent or as a means of retaliation. Other factors, such as perceived interdependence between colleagues, the level of workload, and reduced career opportunities (Judiesch and Lyness, 1999) may also play a role. Of course, absenteeism and presenteeism are not the only options open to employees. If employee health is under jeopardy by harmful conditions at work, the employee can also look for another job with, for example, a lower work load, less exposure to hazards, or less taxing working hours. In the context of a boundaryless career (Arthur, 1994) this represents a meaningful option from the individual's point of view. In some organizations health and safety related career changes may contribute significantly to employee mobility, and thereby be a subject to merit managerial attention.

Although it is customary to take a medical perspective on employee health, one may obtain better insight into organizational issues by broadening the perspective, so as to include psychological, organizational, social, and cultural factors, and by examining its link with the health of the organization

(McIntosh, MacLean, and Burns, 2007). For instance, organizational programs for improving organizational health (aggregate) may harm individual health and how individual employees anticipate and react to influences on their health. Such an analysis shows that individual and organizational health are interdependent but also reveals that the relationship is not necessarily symbiotic. In other words, what is good for the organization (for instance, low absenteeism) may not necessarily be good for individual employees. Adopting a broader perspective helps to make sense of studies which have shown that the relative incidence of presenteeism and absenteeism is associated with factors such as organizational size, unemployment rates, and group norms (Markham and McKee, 1991; 1995), grade, position and age (Harvey and Nicholson, 1999), and various psychosocial factors (MacGregor, Cunningham, and Caverley, 2007). Apparently, the phenomena of presenteeism and absenteeism have organizational and societal dimensions that reach beyond the behavior of the individual employee (McIntosh, MacLean, and Burns, 2007).

Developing a balanced and differentiated approach to health and work that acknowledges the facts and insights that research have brought is a great challenge for organizations. It will not be easy to define a policy that optimally serves organizational and employee interests, and produces the best possible short- and long-term outcomes. Nor will it be simple to combine the necessary differentiation with employees' demands for fairness. Yet, this challenge is one that human resource management will have to deal with in order to avoid unnecessary harm to the organization and its employees. The aim of a balanced and differentiated policy does not have to be an optimum cost level or a statistical health parameter. A more meaningful approach would start with *defining a strategy* that acknowledges the role of health in pursuing the interests of the organization's main stakeholder groups, employees being one of them, and that makes sense from the viewpoint of corporate social responsibility. Developing such a strategy may take a different route in contract and covenant based environments, but in both some degree of consultation with employee representatives will be expedient to achieve the needed legitimacy and acceptance.

Following from this strategy would be *sickness prevention* and *health optimization*, to be implemented with well known means such as deliberate job and work place design, protection against hazards, non-aversive work time scheduling, and realistic planning and task allocation, combined with health monitoring and fitness programs. Employing these means requires not only many resources and facilities, but also methods for surveying critical indicators of 1) potentially harmful and beneficial work place factors, and 2) employee health, sickness, and recovery needs, that can help to set targets and evaluate the effectiveness of various practices. Information about such indicators, derived from occupational medicine, would also be needed as a basis for striking an *acceptable balance between absenteeism and presenteeism*. Here, two types of action seem to be appropriate. Most important is to avoid a one-sided emphasis on minimizing absenteeism as well as on minimizing presenteeism, as either extreme is likely to be detrimental for the organization and for the employees. But in addition, a differentiated position could be taken with regard to (un)desirability of absenteeism and presenteeism in particular jobs, for particular illness, or for particular combinations of both. Obviously, such an approach would not only require information on work and employee health indicators, but also expertise to make the necessary judgments. The challenge for HRM will not be limited to developing methods for this latter purpose but also to develop a new kind of expertise that integrates contributions from medical, psychological, work, and management disciplines. Translating judgments in specific measures that would encourage or restrain employees to opt for absenteeism or presenteeism might be done in different ways. One would think of guidelines on how to act in particular types of jobs and illnesses, and of rules for particular combinations that imply special risks. With such tools, which might vary with the industry and the institutional context, one would be able to achieve the *differentiation* that is needed to ensure that the choice for absenteeism or presenteeism produces the desired therapeutic effects and thereby contributes optimally to reintegration and rehabilitation. Another type of HRM activity is the active *support of reintegration and rehabilitation*. A prerequisite is that employees returning to the work place have recovered to a sufficient degree, and that the work activity allows further recovery. Attention should not be limited to their work capacity, but it must also be secured that they perceive the return to work as meaningful and that they receive adequate social support (Deelstra et al., 2003; Svensson, Mussener, and Alexanderson, 2006).

Although the focus of this chapter is on employee health and presenteeism, and on specific policies to optimize the work-health relationship, it should be acknowledged that there are other domains of HRM activity, such as recruitment, selection, training, and career development that can help to achieve a good person-environment fit and thereby to reduce the incidence of work-related illnesses. Thus, a balanced and differentiated approach to presenteeism and absenteeism should be seen as part of a broader HRM portfolio. It should also be noted that HRM is not the sole party carrying responsibility for promoting and maintaining employee health. This is also a responsibility for line managers and even more for employees themselves (Quick and Quick, 2004). Educating them and providing them with information can also be seen as a role for HRM (Samuel and Wilson, 2007). Raising their awareness of the costs and risks involved in presenteeism should help managers and employees to resist the pressures to minimal absenteeism and earliest possible return to work that emerge from contract based environments and to a growing degree also from covenant based environments. When better educated and informed they will also be able to look for alternatives that can ensure greater health and productivity in the long run.

References

Aronsson, G., Gustafsson, K., and Dallner, M. (2000). Sick but yet at work: an empirical study of sickness presenteeism. *Journal of Epidemiology and Community Health*, 54(7), 502–9.

Arthur, M.B. (1994). The boundaryless career: a new perspective for organizational inquiry. *Journal of Organizational Behavior*, 15(4), 295–306.

Atkin, R.S. and Goodman, P.S. (1984). *Absenteeism: New Approaches to Understanding. Measuring and Managing Employee Absence*. San Francisco, CA: Jossey-Bass Publishers.

Bunn, W.B., Stave, G.M., Downs, K.E., Alvir, J.M., and Dirani, R. (2006). Effect of smoking status on productivity loss. *Journal of Occupational and Environmental Medicine*, 48(10), 1099–108.

Burton, W.N., Chen, C.Y., Conti, D.J., Schultz, A.B., Pransky, G., and Edington, D.W. (2005). The association of health risks with on-the-job productivity. *Journal of Occupational and Environmental Medicine*, 47(8), 769–77.

Bycio, P. (1992). Job performance and absenteeism: a review and meta-analysis. *Human Relations*, 45, 193–220.

Cascio, W.F. (2006). *Managing Human Resources: Productivity, Quality of life, Profits*, 7th edn. New York: McGraw-Hill.

Caverley, N., Cunningham, J.B., and MacGregor, J.N. (2007). Sickness presenteeism, sickness absenteeism, and health following restructuring in a public service organization. *Journal of Management Studies*, 44(2), 304–19.

Collins, J.J., Baase, C.M., Sharda, C.E., Ozminkowski, R.J., Nicholson, S., Billotti, G.M., et al. (2005). The assessment of chronic health conditions on work performance, absence, and total economic impact for employer. *Journal of Occupational and Environmental Medicine*, 47(6), 547–57.

Coyle Shapiro, J.A.M., Kessler, I., and Purcell, J. (2004). Reciprocity or "It's my job": exploring organizationally directed citizenship behavior in a National Health Service setting. *Journal of Management Studies*, 41(1), 85–106.

Deelstra, J.T., Peeters, M.C.W., Schaufeli, W.B., Stroebe, W., Zijlstra, F.R.H., and van Doornen, L.P. (2003). Receiving instrumental support at work: when help is not welcome. *Journal of Applied Psychology*, 88(2), 324–31.

Fine, S.A. and Cronshaw, S.F. (1999). *Functional Job Analysis: A Foundation for Human Resources Management*. Mahwah, NJ and London: Lawrence Erlbaum.

Goetzel, R.Z., Hawkins, K., Ozminkowski, R.J., and Wang, S. (2003). The health and productivity cost burden of the "top 10" physical and mental health conditions affecting six large US employers in 1999. *Journal of Occupational and Environmental Medicine*, 45(1), 5–14.

Grinyer, A. and Singleton, V. (2000). Sickness absence as risk-taking behaviour: a study of organisational and cultural factors in the public sector. *Health, Risk and Society*, 2(1), 7–21.

Harvey, J. and Nicholson, N. (1999). Minor illness as a legitimate reason for absence. *Journal of Organizational Behavior*, 20(6), 979–93.

Hemp, P. (2004). Presenteeism: At work — burn out of it. *Harvard Business Review*, 82(10), 49–58.

Hockey, G.R.J. (2000). Work environments and performance. In N. Chmiel (ed.), *Introduction to Work and Organizational Psychology: A European Perspective* (pp. 206–30). Oxford: Blackwell.

Judiesch, M.K. and Lyness, K.S. (1999). Left behind? The impact of leaves of absence on managers' career success. *Academy of Management Journal*, 42(6), 641–51.

Kamphuis, P. and van Poppel, J. (1998). Van ziek doorwerken wordt niemand beter. *Arbeidsomstandigheden*, 74(1), 24–7.

Koopman, C., Pelletier, K.R., Murray, J.F., Sharda, C.E., Berger, M.L., Turpin, R.S., et al. (2002). Stanford presenteeism scale: health status and employee productivity. *Journal of Occupational and Environmental Medicine*, 44(1), 14–20.

Lotters, F., Meerding, W.J., and Burdorff, A. (2005). Reduced productivity after sickness absence due to musculoskeletal disorders and its relation to health outcomes. *Scandinavian Journal of Environmental Health*, 31(5), 367–74.

MacGregor, J.N., Cunningham, J.B., and Caverley, N. (2007). Psychosocial correlates of absenteeism and presenteeism. Unpublished paper, University of Victoria.

Markham, S.E. and McKee, G.H. (1991). Declining organizational size and increasing unemployment rates: predicting employee absenteeism from within- and between-plant perspectives. *Academy of Management Journal*, 34, 952–65.

Markham, S.E. and McKee, G.H. (1995). Group absence behavior and standards: a multilevel analysis. *Academy of Management Journal*, 38(4), 1174–90.

Martocchio, J.J. (1992). The financial costs of absence decisions. *Journal of Management*, 18(1), 133–52.

Matthews, G., Davies, D.R., Westerman, S.J., and Stammers, R.B. (2000). *Human Performance: Cognition, Stress and Individual Differences*. Hove: Psychology Press.

McIntosh, R.J., MacLean, D., and Burns, H. (2007). Health in organizations: towards a process-based view. *Journal of Management Studies*, 44(2), 206–21.

McKevitt, C., Morgan, M., Dundas, R., and Holland, W.W. (1997). Sickness absence and "working through" illness: a comparison of two professional groups. *Journal of Public Health Medicine*, 19(3), 295–300.

Navon, D. and Gopher, D. (1979). On the economy of human information processing. *Psychological review*, 86, 214–55.

Pransky, G.S., Berndt, E., Finkelstein, S.N., Verma, S., and Agrawal, A. (2005). Performance decrements resulting from illness in the workplace: the effect of headaches. *Journal of Occupational and Environmental Medicine*, 47(1), 34–40.

Quick, J.C. and Quick, J.D. (2004). Healthy, happy, productive work: a leadership challenge. *Employee Benefit Plan Review*, 61(11), 5–7.

Roe, R.A. (1999). Work performance: a multiple regulation perspective. *International Review of Industrial and Organizational Psychology*, 14, 231–335.

Roe, R.A. (2007). Gezondheid en prestaties. In W. Schaufeli and A. Bakker (eds), *De psychologie van arbeid en gezondheid* (pp. 373–88). Houten: Bohn Stafleu Van Loghum.

Samuel, R.J. and Wilson, L.M. (2007). Is presenteeism hurting your workforce? *Employee Benefit Plan Review*, 61(11), 5–7.

Smith, A.P. (1992). Colds, influenza and performance. In A.P. Smith and D.M. Jones (eds), *Handbook of Human Performance*, vol. 2. London: Academic Press.

Stewart, W.F., Ricci, J.A., Chee, E., and Morganstein, D. (2003). Lost productive work time costs from health conditions in the United States: results from the American Productivity Audit. *Journal of Occupational and Environmental Medicine*, 45(12), 1234–46.

Svensson, T., Mussener, U., and Alexanderson, K. (2006). Pride, empowerment, and return to work: on the significance of promoting positive social emotions among sickness absentees. *Work*, 27(1), 57–65.

Taylor, P.J. (1968). Personal factors associated with sickness absence. *British Journal of Industrial Medicine*, 25, 106–18.

van Diepen, B., van Iterson, A., and Roe, R.A. (2006). Human resources management in Europe and North America: similarities and differences. In C. Cooper and R. Burke (eds), *The Human Resources Revolution: Research and Practice*. New York: Elsevier.

Warr, P.B. (1987). *Work, Unemployment and Mental Health*. Oxford: Clarendon Press.

Warr, P.B. (2007). *Work, Happiness and Unhappiness*. Mahwah, NJ: Lawrence Erlbaum.

14

Non-Standard Work Schedules and Retention Management

Robert R. Sinclair and Kristin E. Charles

Non-Standard Work Schedules and Retention Management

Many organizations now operate on 24-hours-a-day, seven-days-a-week schedules. The factors contributing to the need for these schedules include globalization, technological developments, the use of round-the-clock production strategies, and increased customer demand for 24-hour access to services. As a result, people increasingly work on schedules that differ from the traditional notion of a work week composed of five eight-hour days with Saturdays and Sundays off. For example, in the United States, although estimates vary depending on the year, operational definitions, and data sources, at least 30–40 percent of employees now work on non-standard work schedules (Bureau of Labor Statistics, 2006a; 2006b; Presser, 2003). It is unlikely that the forces driving the utilization of non-standard work schedules will abate and such work schedules probably will be increasingly common in the future.

Much of the existing literature refers to shift work and shift workers rather than non-standard work schedules. Totterdell (2005: 36) defines shift work as "a system of working in which one group of workers replaces another group during the workday" and a shift worker "as someone who regularly starts or ends work outside of daytime hours (e.g., 7 a.m. to 7 p.m.)." Traditional conceptions of shift work are still common in manufacturing, public safety, and to a certain extent in health care. However, many work schedules bear little resemblance to traditional shift work. Moreover, schedule-related challenges differ dramatically across occupations, ranging from various forms of extended shifts (e.g., long-haul truckers, deployed military personnel, nurses), to schedules that change from week to week or even day to day (e.g., retail, casual dining, call centers), to schedules that require extended travel (e.g., business consultants, flight attendants). Thus, we use the term non-standard work schedules as a broad term that includes long work hours, shift work, and other work arrangements that share the common feature that they do not entail five eight-hour week day shifts.

Non-standard work schedules have clear costs and benefits, both for employers and employees. The health-related costs of such schedules for employees have been well-documented. For example, a recent review identified over 50 studies on the health effects of work schedules and long work hours published between 1995 and 2002 (Carusso et al., 2004). In contrast, relatively few studies have examined the relationship between work schedules and employee retention. Retention research can contribute to previous schedule literature by identifying possible undesirable outcomes for employees (i.e., desiring to leave one's job) and, given the costs of turnover for employers, can help make the business case for greater attention to how organizations manage their work schedules. Therefore, our main goal in this chapter is to describe a conceptual framework linking schedule design considerations and employees' schedule perceptions to retention outcomes.

COSTS OF NON-STANDARD WORK SCHEDULES FOR EMPLOYEES

Most work schedule research focuses on the negative effects of working non-standard schedules (see Totterdell, 2005 for a recent review of this literature). For example, research has linked working night or rotating shifts to physical health problems including gastrointestinal complaints (Costa, 1996; Parkes, 1999), women's reproductive disorders (Costa, 1996; Nurminen, 1989), breast cancer (Swerdlow, 2003), cardiovascular disease (Costa, 1996), and sleep disorders (Parkes, 1999). Furthermore, the poor sleep quality associated with non-standard schedules can lead to fatigue (Bourdouxhe et al., 1999; Costa, 1996), attention lapses, slowed reaction times, and increased error rates on performance tasks (Khaleque, 1999). When employees experience excessive fatigue as a result of their work schedules they also are more likely to experience injuries and accidents (Circadian Technologies, 2003; Monk, Folkard, and Wedderburn, 1996). Finally, studies have linked non-standard work schedules to psychological problems such as learned helplessness and depression (Healy, Minors, and Waterhouse, 1993), mental and emotional health (Jamal, 1981), loneliness (Bohle and Tilley, 1998), and psychological distress (Shields, 2002). Although not all studies find similar relationships (cf. Goodrich and Weaver, 1998), past research supports the general conclusion that non-standard schedules are associated with negative psychological and physical health outcomes.

Research also generally indicates negative effects of non-standard schedules on family and social life outcomes. Khaleque (1999) found that rotating shift workers reported that their work schedules disturbed their family and social lives, leisure activities, and mealtimes. Non-standard schedules have been linked to difficulty scheduling family activities, less time in family roles, and higher levels of work-family conflict (Staines and Pleck, 1984). Additionally, non-standard schedules have been associated with increased instance of separation and divorce for couples with children (Presser, 2003).

Non-standard schedules also are associated with poorer job attitudes. Jamal (1981) compared nurses working fixed schedules (i.e., the same schedule each week) with nurses working mixed schedules (i.e., when work days and times change from week to week). The nurses working mixed schedules reported lower job satisfaction, less social involvement, and weaker organizational commitment, as well as higher absenteeism and stronger turnover intentions. Similarly, Jamal and Baba (1992) concluded that mixed shift workers reported more job stress, stronger turnover intentions, and poor job satisfaction. Finally, Pattanayak (2002) found that supervisors working a three-shift, non-standard schedule reported lower organizational commitment than those working a standard (nine-to-five) schedule.

BENEFITS OF NON-STANDARD WORK SCHEDULES FOR EMPLOYEES

It is important to acknowledge that people often choose to work non-standard schedules in response to other demands from other roles. For example, many high school and college students work at night or on weekends to pay educational costs and generate discretionary income. Other people work non-standard schedules that complement a spouse's standard schedule, so the family can avoid expensive childcare costs. Still others may be moonlighters, working a second job at night or on the weekends to bring in additional family income. Employees also may receive financial benefits from non-standard schedules in the form of wage premiums for extra hours or for night or weekend work. Some task demands (e.g., customer interaction, workload, or work pace) also may be lighter on off-business hours, such as at night. Thus, while most employees may not prefer non-standard schedules, they may be functional, in that employees experience some benefits from these schedules.

A Model of Work Schedule Effects on Retention

Prior reviews have pointed out that relatively little work schedule literature has focused on theory testing (e.g., Totterdell, 2005; Taylor, Briner, and Folkard, 1997). Past schedule models range from broad conceptual frameworks that do not generate testable hypotheses to complex dynamic models that Totterdell (2005) characterized as producing "increased diversity in shift work research but at the cost of a lack of clarity and falsifiability (p. 40)." As shown in Figure 14.1, we sought to address these concerns by developing a model of the relationship between work schedules and retention that strikes a balance between being overly general and unnecessarily complex. Our model is organized around five broad propositions about the effects of work schedules on retention drivers and retention outcomes. Each proposition implies several testable hypotheses that form the foundation of an agenda for future schedule research in relation to retention outcomes.

Proposition 1: Undesirable schedules (night/evening, longer, rotating, etc.) are associated with more negative perceptions of schedule justice.

Proposition 2: Undesirable schedules (night/evening, longer, rotating, etc.) are associated with a weaker desire to stay with the organization/profession and higher perceived ease of movement to a new position.

Proposition 3: Higher levels of schedule justice are associated with a stronger desire to stay with the organization/profession and lower perceived ease of movement to a new position.

Proposition 4: Schedule justice moderates the effects of undesirable schedules on desirability of staying and ease of movement such that undesirable schedules have stronger effects for employees who perceive low levels of schedule justice.

Proposition 5: Employees' non-work role demands moderate the effects of undesirable schedules and schedule justice on desirability of staying and ease of movement, such that the negative effects of undesirable schedules are stronger for employees with more non-work role demands.

Our model includes a path reflecting the relationship between the retention drivers and the retention outcomes (i.e., turnover intentions and voluntary turnover behavior). This reflects our assumption that schedules affect retention

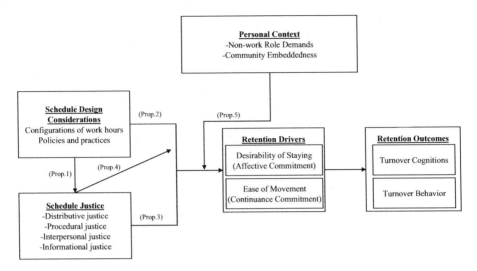

Figure 14.1 A model of work schedule effects on retention outcomes

through their effects on an employee's analysis of the desirability of staying with the organization relative to the ease of obtaining a more desirable job. We will address some other possibilities from the turnover literature as emerging issues below. However, in our opinion, this model reflects core processes from the turnover literature that organizations can influence through changes in schedule-related policies and practices.

We view our model as serving three purposes. First, as discussed above, the model includes specific theoretical propositions intended to facilitate the development of testable hypotheses concerning the effects of work schedules on retention. Second, the model facilitates communication with lay audiences (e.g., managers) by being both reasonably straightforward and empirically plausible. Third, our model facilitates the development of theoretical links to other areas of organizational psychology likely to influence employees' reactions to their schedules such as personality, leadership, and motivation. For example, although they are not a central focus of our model, researchers might consider whether personality traits differentially relate to schedule fairness, retention drivers, or retention outcomes and how these effects might vary for employees with different kinds of schedules or non-work demands.

SCHEDULE DESIGN CONSIDERATIONS

Schedule design considerations refer to the schedule policies and practices employers choose from when creating work schedules. We regard these as features of the work environment that can be distinguished from employees' reactions to their schedules. They include both the configurations of work hours that constitute the schedule and managerial practices related to the implementation of the schedule. Examples of variables related to the configuration of work hours include the extent to which the schedule changes from week to week, involves night work or unusual changeover times, or requires extended hours. Differences in managerial policies and practices include how much input employees have into their schedules, whether employees can change their schedules once they have been posted, whether employees have flexibility in their schedule, and how frequently managers change employees' schedules once they have been posted. These policies and practices include formal elements, such as staffing rules codified in law, company policies, or union contracts, as well as informal elements that reflect differences across business units in terms of how organizations manage schedule issues.

Considering all of these variables highlights the challenges of conducting work schedule research. For example, one full-time employee may work a ten-hour shift that rotates between night and day shifts with limited flexibility to change schedules. That employee may have a co-worker who works part-time on weekends and another who works an eight-hour day shift Monday through Friday that begins and ends at the same time each day. These possibilities highlight the critical need for research that can distinguish the effects of multiple schedule design considerations (cf. Blau and Lunz, 1999; Demerouti et al., 2004). For the purpose of linking these variables to retention, we assume that these schedule design considerations can generally be characterized as more or less desirable (cf. Presser, 2003). Other factors being equal, we assume employees find non-standard schedules less desirable than standard schedules.

Mixed versus fixed shift work

Mixed versus fixed shift work refers to the level of regularity in a person's schedule. In fixed shift schedules, employees work the same hours at the same times from week to week. Mixed shifts change on either a regular or an irregular pattern. Perhaps the most common form of mixed shift is a rotating schedule where the work days and times change at fixed intervals, often every week or every month (Smith, Folkard, and Fuller, 2003). Rotating schedules can be forward rotating (morning to evening to night shifts) or backward rotating (night to evening to morning). Research suggests that longer intervals between schedule changes and forward rotation result in more positive employee outcomes (Knauth, 1996). However, many organizations (e.g., healthcare, retail) use mixed schedules to spread out night work among employees or to respond to irregular staffing demands and shortages. We would expect employees to find these irregular and/or unpredictable schedules to be very undesirable.

Day versus night shift work

Approximately 8 percent of US employees work during the evening or at night (US Census Bureau, 2006). Night work can be a permanent shift, or part of a mixed shift system. For example, some people work only at night (fixed night shift), whereas others may work a mixture of night and day shifts. As we noted above, a large literature has generally shown more negative health, family, and attitudinal outcomes from more frequent night work (Smith, Folkard, and Fuller, 2003; Totterdell, 2005).

Changeover times

Changeover times of shifts, or the start and stop times of shifts, can influence the effects of night work on employees. Tucker et al. (1998) found that for employees working in the early morning, starting work later allows individuals to get more sleep, since most people go to bed at the same time regardless of when they have to get up. However, for individuals who sleep during the day, early changeovers are more favorable. Getting off work later may cut afternoon sleep short because of children, housework, and other daytime distractions. Flexibility over changeover times can help accommodate individual preferences and reduce sleep-related problems.

Extended hours shift work

Many people work shifts that last longer than eight hours. Some organizations have implemented compressed workweeks, where employees work 10 to 12-hour shifts, three to four days a week. This type of schedule allows employees more time to recover from night work and more time for non-work activities. However, there is still some debate about the effects of compressed workweeks. For example, although workers report several benefits of working extended shifts (cf. Johnson and Sharit, 2001; Pierce and Dunham, 1992; Tucker et al., 1998), they also are associated with several poor mental and physical health outcomes (Bourdouxhe et al., 1999; Kundi et al., 1995).

Schedule control and flexibility

Employees often face unexpected events that require them to change their schedules; the ability to adjust their schedule may influence whether some decide to quit. For example, many organizations have policies that allow employees to change their schedules if they can find someone to cover their shift and no overtime results. This type of policy allows employees to address unexpected scheduling constraints and can be beneficial for both employees and organizations. A growing body of research has established several favorable outcomes for employees who have more flexible schedules and/or who work schedules that are congruent with their non-work lives (Burke and Greenglass, 2000; Havlovic, Lau, and Pinfield, 2002; Ng et al., 2005). For example, workers who choose to work at night suffer fewer negative consequences, are better able to adapt to night work, and report more positive job attitudes (Barton, 1994). Similarly, employees who are awarded preferences for scheduling report higher satisfaction and commitment, better job performance, and are less likely to quit (Holtom, Lee, and Tidd, 2002). Schedule control also has been associated with higher levels of commitment, satisfaction, and work-home balance, and lower levels of burnout, distress, and general health (Fenwick and Tausig, 2001; Krausz, Sagie, and Bidermann, 2000).

Schedule stability

In many industries (e.g., retail, casual dining, nursing), employers face constant staffing shortages and high turnover. Often when someone unexpectedly quits and/or an organization cannot fill a position, employees' schedules may be altered to meet staffing demands. While this may be necessary from an operational standpoint, it can create hardships for employees. For example, when employees do not know their schedule in advance it is harder for them to plan for childcare needs, college classes, vacations, or demands of another job. When schedules change frequently, employees may become frustrated and may leave the organization. This can create a vicious cycle of frequent quits and continued schedule instability.

WORK SCHEDULE JUSTICE

Schedule design considerations should have both direct effects on retention processes and effects on employees' reactions to their work schedules. Accordingly, the second component of our model reflects employees' perceptions of the fairness of their work schedules—or work schedule justice.

Nearly three decades of research has established the benefits of organizational justice for employees and their employers, including reduced turnover (cf. Colquitt et al., 2001; Greenberg and Colquitt, 2005). Moreover, justice models provide a conceptual framework for integrating past research on schedule-related attitudes.

Colquitt et al. (2001) described four components of organizational justice. First, *distributive justice* refers to the fairness of outcomes employees receive, in comparison to other people or to their own needs, or relative to their contributions to the organization. These outcomes might include pay, promotions, or work assignments. Second, *procedural justice* refers to the fairness of the procedures used to determine those outcomes. Procedures are viewed as fair when they are applied consistently, are free from bias, and include opportunities for people to provide input. Third, *interpersonal fairness* concerns how people are treated during the implementation of organizational procedures. Finally, employees perceive higher levels of *informational justice* when they receive explanations for decisions that affect them, when organizational changes are communicated in a timely manner, and when communications are tailored to employee needs.

Extending the four-component model to refer to work schedules, *distributive schedule justice* reflects employees' sense of the fairness of their schedules in comparison to those of other people or to their own needs, or relative to their contributions to the organization. For example, if two employees have equal tenure and experience but one never works weekends, the weekend worker should perceive less distributive schedule justice. A more just approach might be to employ a schedule where weekends are rotated, so both employees have some weekends free. Schedule stability also probably influences distributive schedule justice. Schedules may be perceived as unfair if employees are frequently scheduled for extra shifts with little or no advanced notice, or scheduled for shifts they were told they would not have to work when they were hired, such as night shifts.

Schedule satisfaction research suggests the likely benefits of distributive schedule fairness. For example, in a sample of female physicians, the extent to which the schedule met the physicians' needs mediated the relationship between the number of hours worked and burnout (Barnett, Gareis, and Brennan, 1999). Additionally, nurses who work their desired work schedules report fewer rest and sleep-related problems, less interference with their family and social activities, greater satisfaction towards their current work schedules and better quality of service to patients (Havlovic et al., 2002).

Sinclair et al. (2007) found that distributive work schedule justice predicted employed college students' self-reports of pain, gastrointestinal distress, and work-school conflict. Further, Krausz et al. (2000) found that nurses who worked a preferred schedule (a likely contributor to distributive schedule justice) reported higher job satisfaction, stronger organizational commitment, and less burnout. Other research has shown that distributive schedule justice is related to nurses' job satisfaction (Charles and Sinclair, 2007) and intentions to change schedules (Charles, 2007). Although few studies have investigated retention, existing research suggests that lower distributive schedule justice is associated with higher turnover.

Procedural schedule justice captures whether procedures used to determine work schedules are applied consistently, are free from bias, and include opportunities for people to provide input (cf. Posthuma, Maertz, and Dworkin, 2007; Sinclair et al., 2007). The ability to adjust one's schedule for personal needs and perceptions of control over one's schedule contribute to perceptions of procedural schedule justice. Thus, efforts to make schedules compatible with employees' preferences and provide them input into their schedules should be associated with more favorable outcomes.

Sinclair et al. (2007) examined stress-related effects of students' procedural schedule justice but found few effects. The one exception was that students who reported higher levels of procedural schedule justice also reported lower levels of work-school conflict. Other studies have linked procedural schedule justice to likely antecedents of retention, such as perceived organizational support (Charles and Sinclair, 2007). However, only one study has directly studied an objective measure of voluntary employee turnover. Posthuma et al. (2007) examined four forms of procedural justice related to work schedules: advance notice, consistency in schedules, representativeness of employees' views, and opportunities for input. In a sample of 190 nurses, they found that two of the facets: representativeness of views and advance notice were associated with lower voluntary turnover.

Interpersonal schedule justice captures the extent to which authority figures (e.g., supervisors) treat people well during the implementation of work schedule assignment processes. The person responsible for assigning work schedules (who may or may not be an employee's direct supervisor) can be extremely influential on employee perceptions of schedule justice. A schedule coordinator who treats employees with respect, who does her best to help accommodate personal and family needs, and who genuinely cares about employees will generate increased perceptions of interpersonal schedule justice. For example, when employees request shift changes, schedule coordinators can be understanding and try to help the employee find someone to cover the shift, or they can be unhelpful and dismissive. Even if an employee ultimately is not able to change her schedule, a supportive schedule coordinator may lessen her feelings of unfairness because she knows the schedule coordinator made a good-faith effort to help.

Finally, *informational schedule justice* reflects the extent to which schedule makers explain schedule processes, communicate changes in a timely manner, and tailor communications to individual needs. Because of high turnover in some industries and geographic areas, some employers often have more shifts to fill than employees scheduled. These demands often result in employees working double shifts and overtime. Employees who work for a supervisor who is disorganized or for an organization that is severely understaffed may experience unpredictable and continuously changing schedules. This can create problems for employees trying to plan family and social events, arrange childcare, or enroll in school. For employees to have positive perceptions of informational schedule justice, supervisors must communicate schedules in advance and explain any necessary changes.

Three studies have investigated informational and interpersonal schedule justice and have found some benefits. Sinclair et al. (2007) found that interpersonal schedule justice predicted self-reports of gastrointestinal distress (but not other outcomes) and informational schedule justice was not related to any outcomes. Charles (2007) found that both interpersonal and informational schedule justice predicted intentions to leave the nursing industry, and informational schedule justice predicted a measure of engagement. Similarly, Charles and Sinclair (2007) found that informational schedule justice predicted perceived organizational support and interpersonal schedule justice predicted job satisfaction. Although these studies suggest the importance of informational and interpersonal schedule justice, these three studies were cross-sectional studies of a limited set of variables and two of the studies analyzed different outcomes in the same sample (e.g., Charles, 2007; Charles and Sinclair, 2007).

Taken as a whole, the small literature on work schedule justice suggests its promise as a construct to help guide schedule attitude research. The critical assumption guiding this research is that the way organizations manage their work schedules influences employee attitudes and behavior and these effects can be distinguished from the demands of the schedule itself. Thus, employees may be more willing to tolerate undesirable schedules when they are implemented using fair procedures, when they are sufficiently informed about their schedule, and when they receive considerate treatment in the implementation of schedule policies. Moreover, undesirable schedules might be seen as distributively fair if they are assigned based on a reasonable standard, such as tenure.

RETENTION DRIVERS

March and Simon (1958) argued that turnover is a function of an employee's analysis of the desirability of remaining with his or her organization relative to the ease of obtaining another position. We label these two proximate processes as retention drivers. Thus, we contend that work schedules primarily affect retention through their effects on the desirability of staying and the ease of leaving. To our knowledge, no study has investigated schedule justice effects on retention, or other outcomes, through these retention drivers.

Desirability of staying and affective commitment

Desirability of staying is typically captured with job attitude measures such as those reflecting organizational commitment. Dozens of studies have established that higher commitment is associated with lower turnover and weaker turnover intentions (cf. Cooper-Hakim and Viswesvaran, 2005). There are multiple forms of commitment that differ in the target of the relationship and in the underlying nature of the person-organization attachment. The form most relevant to the desirability of staying is affective organizational commitment, which reflects shared values between the person and the organization, willingness to exert extra effort on behalf of the organization, and a strong desire to remain a member of the organization (cf. Meyer and Allen, 1997).

While most commitment research focuses on employees' attachments to the global organization, employees form multiple attachments to different targets or constituencies (cf. Cohen, 2003). Professional commitment may be an important consideration for schedule research. For example, for organizations that employ nurses (hospitals, long-term care providers, etc.), engendering organizational commitment is critical, as labor market shortages often enable nurses to obtain jobs with a more desirable schedule. However, there also is a broader societal concern about nurses leaving the profession altogether. Thus, research on the desirability of staying with one's current employer needs to include an examination of both professional and organizational commitment.

Past literature supports the idea that qualities of and reactions to work schedules should be associated with affective commitment. For example, applications of social exchange theory to work assume that work conditions signal employees about the extent to which they are valued by the organization (cf. Rhoades and Eisenberger, 2002). Social exchange theory suggests that employees who work on undesirable schedules or who feel unfairly treated in the process of schedule administration are likely to respond with weaker professional and organizational commitment. In contrast, employees with desirable schedules and/or who feel fairly treated by the employer should be more likely to develop and maintain strong attachments.

Second, some researchers have begun to consider injustice as a source of stress that would presumably decrease one's desirability of staying with the current employer (cf. Cropanzano, Goldman, and Benson, 2005). The job demands-resources (JD-R) model suggests that burnout mediates the effects of job demands on health outcomes and employee engagement mediates the effects of job resources on retention outcomes (cf. Demerouti, Bakker, Nachreiner, and Schaufeli, 2001; Schaufeli and Bakker, 2004). In the case of work schedules, undesirable work schedules could be conceptualized as demands and work schedule fairness viewed as a resource (i.e., because fairness presumably helps people cope with the negative effects of demanding schedules). However, research has not directly applied the JD-R model to work schedule issues.

Ease of movement and continuance commitment

Ease of movement refers to employees' sense of their ability to obtain another job that is similar to or better than their current position. Researchers typically capture ease of movement with objective labor market measures (e.g., unemployment rates) or employees' perceptions of the quality of available alternatives (cf. Lee et al., 2004). Within the organizational commitment literature, measures of *continuance organizational commitment* provide a useful assessment of ease of movement. Employees who have strong continuance commitment (sometimes labeled calculative commitment) perceive the social and economic costs of leaving the organization to be too high and/or believe that they have few viable employment alternatives (Meyer and Allen, 1997).

The concept of continuance commitment can be extended to professions as well, enabling researchers to distinguish between continuance professional commitment and continuance organizational commitment. This might be a particularly useful distinction in schedule research as some workers on non-standard schedules likely contemplate costs of leaving their current organization and think about leaving their current profession. To summarize, our discussion of retention drivers emphasizes four concepts drawn from the commitment literature: affective and continuance organizational commitment and affective and continuance professional commitment. We encourage interested readers to conduct a more thorough review of that literature for useful theoretical models, well-developed measures, and a large body of supporting empirical research.

RETENTION OUTCOMES

Our model positions voluntary turnover behavior as the primary retention outcome of interest. A long standing assumption in psychology is that people engage in various cognitive processes prior to acting, particularly for life-changing decisions such as leaving one's job or profession. As Worrell (2005) notes, most research assumes the turnover process unfolds through a reasonably well-ordered causal chain of events in which workers first become dissatisfied with their jobs, then evaluate their job relative to alternatives, and eventually form intentions to stay in or leave their current jobs. Thus, turnover researchers view turnover cognitions as an important precursor to turnover behavior. This model has received a good deal of empirical support as turnover cognitions have been shown to be moderately strong predictors of voluntary turnover (cf. Tett and Meyer, 1993; Griffeth, Hom, and Gaertner, 2000). On the other hand, as we note below, recent turnover research suggests other possibilities that warrant further investigation.

PERSONAL CONTEXT

Employees who work undesirable schedules decide to remain with their employer for several reasons that may not be directly related to their working conditions. Thus, the final component of our model refers to the personal context of work schedules and includes demands from other roles and community embeddedness as critical influences on retention. These labels encompass many possible variables and possible relationships with the core processes on our model. However, our basic expectation is that the influence of schedules on turnover depends on the extent to which the job enables employees to meet non-work role demands and the extent to which employees feel embedded in their communities.

Non-work role demands

Non-work demands may be particularly challenging for employees working non-standard schedules. Examples of non-work demands include school schedules or religious and social activities with the majority of research focusing on family role demands. Women may be more vulnerable to the negative effects of non-standard schedules (especially night work) because they also often have household and childcare responsibilities that prevent them from getting enough sleep (Presser, 1995). For example, the number of domestic commitments in a household is related to reduced sleep duration, more sleep difficulties, and reduced on-shift alertness (Spelten et al., 1995). Additionally, married night workers report more complaints than single workers and employees with more children report getting less sleep after afternoon and night shifts than those with fewer children (Akerstedt and Torsvall, 1981). Additionally, non-standard schedules can cause distress among family members in relation to intimacy, support, sharing, and companionship (Smith and Folkard, 1993).

However, some people may prefer night work and other non-standard schedules that enable them to spend more time with their children during the day, avoid childcare costs, or meet other family needs (cf. Presser, 1995; Barnett, Gareis, and Brennan, 1999). These findings suggest that non-standard schedules are associated with fewer negative outcomes when the schedule fits an employee's non-work demands and conversely, that non-work demands may exacerbate the negative effects of non-standard schedules. This may have important implications for developing schedule-related supports and may help researchers understand the conditions under which schedules are likely to have particularly negative effects.

Community embeddedness

Embeddedness research assumes that organizational behavior is affected by the extent to which employees are socially enmeshed (or embedded) in their employing organization and in their community (cf. Lee et al., 2004; Mitchell et al., 2001). Mitchell et al. (2001) describe three dimensions of embeddedness: links, fit, and sacrifice. People with strong *links* have more formal and informal connections to others in their community or organization. People with strong *fit* feel more compatible with and/or comfortable in their community. Finally, *sacrifice* refers to the perceived costs of leaving a community; higher sacrifice means that people would have to give up more to leave the community. Lee et al. (2004) found that after controlling for job satisfaction and organizational commitment, community embeddedness predicted turnover outcomes while organizational embeddedness did not. Based on their findings, we would expect community embeddedness to influence whether workers are likely to leave an organization in response to dissatisfaction with or stress from their non-standard work schedule, particularly for people who would have to relocate to find a new job.

A Brief Agenda for Schedule Research

The sets of proposed relationships described above are fairly well supported in terms of prior research and theory. However, other schedule studies suggest interesting research directions and/or have produced mixed findings to date, implying the need for further investigation. These topics include emerging directions in justice work, personality and circadian type influences on schedule adaptation, and a series of other understudied topics in work schedule and retention research.

DIRECTIONS IN ORGANIZATIONAL JUSTICE

One of the desirable features of justice research is that, in addition to many studies of justice antecedents, processes, and outcomes, there is a large body of theoretical and empirical literature to guide future studies (cf. Colquitt et al., 2001; Cropanzano et al., 2001; Greenberg and Colquitt, 2005). We recommend three additional research directions that would contribute both to justice and work schedule literature. First, some justice researchers have discussed the idea of injustice thresholds—which refer to the cumulative number of justice violations necessary to evoke responses from those who experience the injustice (cf. Gilliland, Benson, and Schepers, 1998). Poorly managed work schedules create a ripe opportunity for experiences of injustice through events such as receiving an undesirable schedule, poor communication about schedule changes, and poor treatment by schedule makers.

The justice threshold idea can be linked to turnover literature in that instances of injustice in work schedules represent an example of what turnover researchers call shocks—events that cause employees to contemplate leaving the organization (cf. Lee and Mitchell, 1994; Lee, et al., 2004; Worrell, 2005). For example, Worrell (2005) found that nurses who left their jobs fit one of three profiles: those who left because of work-related shocks, such as realizing the organization would not honor a commitment to let the nurse change rotations; those who left because of non-work related shocks, such as a nurse whose spouse obtained a desirable job overseas; and those who followed the traditional turnover model (i.e., turnover prompted by dissatisfaction and weighing costs and benefits of leaving). Events that produce perceptions of work schedule injustice probably serve as a work-related shock. However, this has not been directly investigated and several interesting questions remain about the effects of work schedule injustice as compared with other forms of poor treatment.

A second direction for justice research would be further examination of the multidimensional model of schedule justice. Justice scholars have expressed a range of opinions about the appropriate number of dimensions of justice (cf. Cropanzano et al., 2001). Although the procedural-distributive distinction seems generally accepted, there is less consensus about the interpersonal and informational components. Some factor analytic research supports the four-dimensional model of work schedule justice (e.g., Charles, 2007; Sinclair et al., 2007), but additional studies are needed to test competing measurement models. Another possibility would be focusing on justice facets—narrower content domain areas within each broad justice dimension. Posthuma et al.'s (2007) procedural justice study is the only research we know of in this area. Research is needed to replicate their findings and to consider the usefulness of examining facets of other justice dimensions.

Finally, both in work schedule justice research and in the broader justice literature, there is some consideration of interactions among components of justice. For example, Sinclair et al. (2007) found interactions of distributive schedule justice with interpersonal and procedural schedule justice, in the prediction of health and academic outcomes. In each case, distributive schedule justice was more strongly related to favorable outcomes when the other component was also strong. Similarly, Charles (2007) found that both interpersonal and informational schedule justice interacted with distributive schedule justice to influence long-term care nurses' intentions to leave the job and the industry. Additionally, the interaction between informational and distributive schedule justice predicted employee engagement. When distributive schedule justice was low, the influence of informational schedule justice did not affect engagement or intentions to leave the job and interpersonal schedule justice did not affect intentions to leave the job either. In other words, interpersonal and informational justice only increased positive outcomes when distributive justice was high. To date, no single pattern of interactions has emerged from this research and several patterns are conceivable. However, future research on justice × justice interactions stands to make an important contribution to both the schedule and justice literatures.

CIRCADIAN TYPE AND SCHEDULE ADAPTATION

Circadian rhythms refer to the performance of various body functions that occur on a 24-hour cycle. These rhythms include core body temperature, heart rate, metabolic rate, wakefulness, blood pressure, and flexibility. Humans are biologically geared towards daytime activity and sleeping at night. However, the peaks and valleys of individuals' daily cycles vary (Smith, Folkard, and Fuller, 2003) and daily cycles also appear to be affected by experience. Accordingly, several studies have investigated individual differences in workers' ability to tolerate or adapt to non-standard work schedules.

The basic assumption of circadian type (or morningness/eveningness) research is that certain people have preferences for the extremes of the day, and when given the opportunity, will act in accordance with these preferences (Horne and Ostberg, 1976). Morning types prefer early morning activity; evening types prefer activities in the late evening. Thus, morning types should be better suited for early morning work and evening types should be best on late night shifts (Tankova, Adan, and Buela-Casal, 1994). There is a small, but growing literature on morningness/eveningness that offers some support for circadian type as a predictor of adjustment to shift work, sleep quality, and other outcomes, but also some inconsistencies in findings across studies and some construct validity questions about its measurement (Akerstedt and Torsvall, 1981; Charles, 2007; Hildebrandt and Stratmann, 1979; Ognianova, Dalbokova, and Stanchev, 1998; Smith, Folkard, and Fuller, 2003; Steele et al., 2000; Taillard, Philip, and Bioulac, 1999). However, there is enough supporting evidence to recommend continued research in this area.

PERSONALITY AND SCHEDULE ADAPTATION

Neuroticism and extroversion offer some promise for shift work research. Shift workers with higher neuroticism/negative affectivity tend to experience higher levels of chronic fatigue, digestive problems, and cardiovascular disease (Prizmic and Kaliterna, 1995) as well as higher psychosomatic complaints and psychological distress (Parkes, 1999). Similarly, introverts appear to have an earlier circadian phase than extroverts (Vidacek, Kaliterna, and Radosevic-Vidacek, 1988), possibly because extraversion is negatively correlated with morningness (Frost and Jamal, 1979). Thus, introverts may have more difficulty adapting to night work (Colquhoun and Condon, 1980; Costa et al., 1989).

Taken as a whole though, the literature on personality and non-standard work schedules is somewhat underdeveloped. Moreover, it is unclear whether trait variations are a cause or a consequence of shift work. For example, although neuroticism is correlated with current shift work tolerance, it has not been found to predict *future* shift work tolerance (Vidacek, Kaliterna, and Radosevic-Vidacek, 1987). This suggests that neuroticism may be a symptom of current shift work intolerance rather than a signal of future concerns (Kaliterna et al., 1995). Thus, while few conclusions can be confidently drawn from this literature, there are enough compelling findings to encourage future research on personality-related differences in schedule adaptation.

EMERGING ISSUES IN WORK SCHEDULE RESEARCH

Several other topics offer potentially interesting directions for schedule research. For example, the influence of work schedules on retention outcomes may depend on whether people are working full- or part-time. In an unpublished study, Martin et al. (2007) found that full-time employees who worked weekends were more likely to leave the organization than full-time employees who did not, but found no turnover differences for part-time employees related to whether they worked weekends. Thus, the effects of work schedules on employee outcomes also may depend on how often employees work on a particular schedule.

Unionization also may affect how people react to schedule-related demands. For example, in unionized organizations there may be limited variability in schedule policies and practices with the central fairness issue being whether workers perceive assigning desirable schedules based on tenure to be fair. On the other hand, in industries where employees work widely varied schedules developed by their individual supervisors (e.g., retail, small businesses), the interpersonal aspects of schedule justice may be more important.

There have been several new developments in retention research that have not been well integrated into occupational health studies and that may present exciting opportunities for future schedule research. For example, researchers have shown that the turnover process may unfold through a variety of patterns, some of which involve dissatisfaction and turnover intentions and others that involve quitting without extensive deliberations (cf. Harman et al., 2007; Lee and Mitchell, 1994; Maertz and Campion, 2004). Examples of these patterns include leaving without an advance plan, having a pre-determined *definite* plan to quit *when* a particular event occurs (such as a child finishing school), and having an *indefinite* plan to quit *if* a particular event happens (such as having a child). Work schedules likely have different effects on people depending on their plans and may lead people to change their plans if work schedule demands become intolerable.

Finally, non-standard work schedules may have several outcomes that have not received sufficient research attention. Examples include differences in access to mentoring when potential mentors work during the day, opportunities to participate in union meetings which might be held at times that fit some schedules but not others, and opportunities for recognition at work which might be limited for employees who work when fewer supervisors are present (such as nights or weekends). Non-standard work schedules also may exacerbate the effects of other stressors. Resource-based models of job stress (e.g., Hobfoll, 1989) assume employees have a limited pool of resources to cope with stressors. Schedule demands drain that pool of resources, leaving less to cope with other sources of stress (e.g., job demands, family conflict).

WORK SCHEDULE INTERVENTION RESEARCH

As in many areas of occupational health, there is a critical need for intervention research in relation to work schedules. Occupational health psychology emphasizes three influences on occupational health—the individual worker, the work-family interface, and the work environment (e.g., Quick, 1999a; 1999b). Regarding the work-family interface, flexible work schedules are perhaps the standard schedule-related practice designed to facilitate employees' ability to meet work and family demands. There is a large literature on the benefits of this and other family supportive policies and practices (cf. Neal and Hammer, 2007). The individual emphasis concerns addressing characteristics of workers that influence schedule tolerance. Personnel selection procedures aimed at identifying workers with high levels of schedule tolerance or the ability to adapt to changing schedules might be useful. However, there is little scientific consensus about what individual difference factors to focus on and it seems premature to recommend selection interventions for that purpose. Other individually-focused interventions include education and counseling programs to assist individuals with shift work adaptation (Smith, Folkard, and Fuller, 2003) and the use of prescription sleep aids such as melatonin for shift workers (Arendt and Deacon, 1997).

In terms of the organization of work, interventions could focus on changing characteristics of the work environment, such as placing bright lights in the work space to affect employees' circadian rhythms. Our emphasis on work schedule justice also highlights the need for interventions aimed at how schedules are managed. These might include schedule premiums aimed at enhancing distributive justice (e.g., by increasing employees' outcomes), or manager development interventions aimed at increasing procedural, informational, and interpersonal justice in schedule administration. Some employers use other interventions such as using contract agencies to absorb unexpected staffing demands or using automated scheduling tools to help both employers and employees manage schedule demands. However, there is relatively little empirical research on the effectiveness of any of these strategies, particularly in relation to retention outcomes.

Conclusion

We hope that this chapter has highlighted some of the connections between work schedule management and retention related outcomes. We certainly believe that a similar model could be used to link schedules to other outcomes valued by organizations and/or employees with one example being in the general area of performance outcomes such as organizational citizenship behavior and counterproductive behavior. Despite our emphasis on retention, we encourage readers to remember that a sizeable body of research has documented the potentially detrimental effects of work schedules on safety, health, and well-being outcomes. These effects occur for employees who work non-standard schedules either out of choice or by necessity and we conclude by recommending that researchers keep occupational safety and health concerns at the forefront of their research.

References

Akerstedt, T. and Torsvall, L. (1981). Shift work: shift-dependent well-being and individual differences. *Ergonomics*, 24, 265–73.

Arendt, J. and Deacon, S. (1997). Treatment of circadian rhythm disorders-melatonin. *Chronobiology International*, 14, 185–204.

Barnett, R.C., Gareis, K.C., and Brennan, R.T. (1999). Fit as a mediator of the relationship between work hours and burnout. *Journal of Occupational Health Psychology*, 4, 307–17.

Barton, J. (1994). Choosing to work at night: a moderating influence on individual tolerance to shift work. *Journal of Applied Psychology*, 79, 449–54.

Blau, G.J. and Lunz, M. (1999). Testing the impact of shift schedules on organizational variables. *Journal of Organizational Behavior*, 20, 933–42.

Bohle, P. and Tilley, A.J. (1998). Early experiences of shiftwork: influences on attitudes. *Journal of Occupational and Organizational Psychology*, 71, 61–79.

Bourdouxhe, M.A., Queinnec, Y., Granger, D., Baril, R.H., Guertin, S.C., Massicotte, P.R. (1999). Aging and shiftwork: The effects of 20 years of rotating 12-hour shifts among petroleum refinery operators. *Experimental Aging Research*, 25, 323–9.

Bureau of Labor Statistics (2006a). *Career Guide to Industries, 2006–07 Edition, Health Care*. [Online]. Available at: http://www.bls.gov/oco/cg/cgs035.htm [Accessed: September 2, 2006].

Bureau of Labor Statistics (2006b). *Occupational Outlook Handbook, 2006–07 Edition, Nursing, Psychiatric, and Home Health Aid*. [Online]. Available at: http://www.bls.gov/oco/ocos165.htm [Accessed: September 2, 2006].

Burke, R.J. and Greenglass, E.R. (2000). Work status congruence, work outcomes, and psychological well-being. *Stress Medicine*, 16, 91–9.

Carusso, C.C., Hitchcock, E.M., Dick, R.B., Russo, J.M., and Schmit, J.M. (2004). *Overtime and Extended Work Shifts: Recent Findings on Illnesses, Injuries, and Health*. DHHS (NIOSH) Publication No. 2004-143.

Charles, K.E. (2007). Shift work in the long-term care industry: an examination of organizational and individual factors that influence employee outcomes. Doctoral Dissertation, Portland State University, Department of Psychology.

Charles, K.E. and Sinclair, R.R. (April, 2007). Examining work-schedule management for direct-care workers in the long-term care industry. Paper presented at the 22nd annual conference of the Society for Industrial and Organizational Psychology, New York.

Circadian Technologies, Inc. (2003). *Overtime in US Extended Hour Operations Continues to Rise*. [Online]. Available at: http://www.circadian.com/media/2003_press_overtime.htm [Accessed: February 2, 2003].

Cohen, A. (2003). *Multiple Commitments in the Workplace: An Integrative Approach*. Mahwah, NJ: Erlbaum.

Colquhoun, W.P. and Condon, R. (1980). Introversion-extraversion and the adjustment of the body-temperature rhythm to night work. In A. Reinberg, N. Vieux, and P. Andlauer (eds), *Night and Shift Work: Biological and Social Aspects* (pp. 449–55). Oxford: Pentagon Press.

Colquitt, J.A., Conlon, D.E., Wesson, M.J., Porter, C.O.L.H., and Ng, K.Y. (2001). Justice at the millennium: a meta-analytic review of 25 years of organizational justice research. *Journal of Applied Psychology*, 86, 425–45.

Cooper-Hakim, A. and Viswesvaran, C. (2005). The construct of work commitment: testing an integrative framework. *Psychological Bulletin*, 131, 241–59.

Costa, G. (1996). The impact of shift and night work on health. *Applied Ergonomics*, 27, 9–16.

Costa, G., Lievore, F., Casaletti, G., Gaffuri, E., and Folkard, S. (1989). Circadian characteristics influencing interindividual differences in tolerance and adjustment to shiftwork. *Ergonomics*, 32, 373–85.

Cropanzano, R., Goldman, B.M., and Benson, L. III (2005). Organizational justice. In J. Barling, E.K. Kelloway, and M.R. Frone (eds), *Handbook of Work Stress* (pp. 63–87). Thousand Oaks, CA: Sage.

Cropanzano, R., Rupp, D.E., Mohler, C.J., Schminke, M. (2001). Three roads to organizational justice. In G.R. Ferris (ed.), *Research in Personnel and Human Resources Management*, 20, 1–113.

Demerouti, E., Bakker, A.B., Nachreiner, F., and Schaufeli, W.B. (2001). The job demands-resources model of burnout. *Journal of Applied Psychology*, 86, 499–512.

Demerouti, E., Geurts, S.A., Bakker, A.B., and Euwema, M. (2004). The impact of shiftwork on work-home conflict, job attitudes and health. *Ergonomics*, 47, 987–1002.

Fenwick, R. and Tausig, M. (2001). Scheduling stress: family and health outcomes of shift work and schedule control. *American Behavioral Scientist*, 44, 1179–98.

Frost, P.J. and Jamal, M. (1979). Shift work, attitudes, and reported behavior: some associations between individual characteristics and hours of work and leisure. *Journal of Applied Psychology*, 64, 66–70.

Gilliland, S.W., Benson, L. III., and Schepers, D.H. (1998). A rejection threshold in justice evaluations: effects on judgment and decision making. *Organizational Behavior and Human Decision Processes*, 76, 113–31.

Goodrich, S. and Weaver, K.A. (1998). Differences in depressive symptoms between traditional workers and shiftworkers. *Psychological Reports*, 83, 571–6.

Greenberg, J. and Colquitt, J.A. (eds) (2005). *Handbook of Organizational Justice*. Mahwah, NJ: Erlbaum.

Griffeth, R., Hom, P., and Gaertner, S. (2000). A meta-analysis of antecedents and correlates of employee turnover: update, moderator tests, and research implications for the next millennium. *Journal of Management*, 26(3), 463.

Harman, W.W., Lee, T.W., Mitchell, T.R., Felps, W.O., and Owens, B.P. (2007). The psychology of voluntary employee turnover. *Current Directions in Psychological Science*, 16, 51–4.

Havlovic, S.J., Lau, D.C., and Pinfield, L.T. (2002). Repercussions of work schedule congruence among full-time, part-time, and contingent nurses. *Health Care Management Review*, 27, 30–41.

Healy, D., Minors, D.S., and Waterhouse, J.M. (1993). Shiftwork, helplessness, and depression. *Journal of Affective Disorders*, 29, 17–25.

Hildebrandt, G. and Stratmann, I. (1979). Circadian system response to night work in relation to the individual circadian phase position. *International Archives of Occupational and Environmental Health*, 43, 73–83.

Hobfoll, S.E. (1989). Conservation of resources: a new attempt at conceptualizing stress. *American Psychologist*, 44, 513–24.

Holtom, B.C., Lee, T.W., and Tidd, S.T. (2002). The relationship between work status congruence and work-related attitudes and behaviors. *Journal of Applied Psychology*, 87, 903–15.

Horne, J.A. and Ostberg, O. (1976). A self-assessment questionnaire to determining morningness-eveningness in human circadian rhythms. *International Journal of Chronobiology*, 4, 97–110.

Jamal, M. (1981). Shift work related to job attitudes, social participation and withdrawal behavior: a study of nurses and industrial workers. *Personnel Psychology*, 34, 535–47.

Jamal, M. and Baba, V.V. (1992). Shiftwork and department-type related job stress, work attitudes and behavioral intentions: a study of nurses. *Journal of Organizational Behavior*, 13, 449–64.

Johnson, D.R. and Sharit, J. (2001). Impact of change from an 8h to 12h shift schedule on workers and occupational injury rates. *International Journal of Industrial Ergonomics*, 36, 15–28.

Kaliterna, L., Vidacek, S., Prizmic, Z., and Radosevic-Vidacek, B. (1995). Is tolerance to shiftwork predictable from individual difference measures? *Work and Stress*, 9, 140–47.

Khaleque, A. (1999). Sleep deficiency and quality of life on shift workers. *Social Indicators Research*, 46, 181–9.

Knauth, P. (1996). Designing better shift systems. *Applied Ergonomics*, 27, 39–44.

Krausz, M., Sagie, A., and Bidermann, Y. (2000). Actual and preferred work schedules and schedule control as determinants of job-related attitudes. *Journal of Vocational Behavior*, 56, 1–11.

Kundi, M., Koller, M., Stefan, H., Lehner, L., Kaindlsorfer, S., and Rottenbucher, S. (1995). Attitudes of nurses towards 8-h and 12-h shift systems. *Work and Stress*, 9, 134–9.

Lee, T.W. and Mitchell, T.R. (1994). An alternative approach: the unfolding model of voluntary employee turnover. *Academy of Management Review*, 19, 51–89.

Lee, T.W., Mitchell, T.R., Sablynski, C.J., Burton, J.P., and Holtom, B.C. (2004). The effects of job embeddedness on organizational citizenship, job performance, volitional absences, and voluntary turnover. *Academy of Management Journal*, 47, 711–22.

Maertz, C.P. and Campion, M.A. (2004). Profiles in quitting: integrating process and content in turnover theory. *Academy of Management Journal*, 47, 566–82.

March, J.G. and Simon, H.A. (1958). *Organizations*. New York: Wiley.

Martin, J.E., Charles, K.E., Sinclair, R.R., and Senter, J.L. (2007). Work schedules and employee turnover. Unpublished paper.

Meyer, J.P. and Allen, N.J. (1997). *Commitment in the Workplace: Theory, Research, and Application*. Thousand Oaks, CA: Sage.

Mitchell, T.R., Holtom, B.C., Lee, T.W., Sablynski, C.J., and Erez, M. (2001). Why people stay: using job embeddedness to predict voluntary turnover. *Academy of Management Journal*, 44, 1102–21.

Monk, T., Folkard, S., and Wedderburn, A. (1996). Maintaining safety and high performance on shift work. *Applied Ergonomics*, 27, 17–23.

Neal, M.B. and Hammer, L.B. (2007). *Working Couples Caring for Children and Aging Parents: Effects on Work and Well-being*. Mahwah, NJ: Erlbaum.

Ng, T.W.H., Butts, M.M., Vandenberg, R.J., DeJoy, D.M., and Wilson, M.G. (2005). Effects of management communication, opportunity for learning, and work schedule flexibility on organizational commitment. *Journal of Vocational Behavior*, 68, 474–89.

Nurminen, T. (1989). Shift work, fetal development, and course of pregnancy. *Scandinavian Journal of Work, Environment, and Health*, 15, 395–403.

Ognianova, V.M., Dalbokova, D.L., and Stanchev, V. (1998). Stress states, alertness and individual differences under 12-hour shiftwork. *International Journal of Industrial Ergonomics*, 21, 283–91.

Parkes, K.R. (1999). Shiftwork, job type, and the work environment as joint predictors of health-related outcomes. *Journal of Occupational Health Psychology*, 4, 256–68.

Pattanayak, B. (2002). Effects of shiftwork and hierarchical position in the organization on psychological correlates: a study on an integrated steel plant. *Organization Development Journal*, 20, 71–82.

Pierce, J.L. and Dunham, R.D. (1992). The 12-hour work day: a 48-hour, eight-day week. *Academy of Management Journal*, 35, 1086–98.

Posthuma, R.A., Maertz, C.P., Jr., and Dworkin, J.B. (2007). Procedural justice's relationship with turnover: explaining past inconsistent findings. *Journal of Organizational Behavior*, 28, 381–98.

Presser, H.B. (1995). Job, family, and gender: determinants of nonstandard work schedules among employed Americans in 1991. *Demography*, 32, 577–98.

Presser, H.B. (2003). *Working in a 24/7 Economy*. New York: Russell Sage Foundation.

Prizmic, Z. and Kaliterna, L. (1995). Relationship between positive and negative affect and measures of tolerance to shiftwork. *Psychologica Croatica*, 1, 155–64.

Quick, J.C. (1999a). Occupational health psychology: historical roots and future directions. *Health Psychology*, 18, 82–8.

Quick, J.C. (1999b). Occupational health psychology: the convergence of health and clinical psychology with public health and preventative medicine in an organizational context. *Professional Psychology: Research and Practice*, 30, 123–8.

Rhoades, L. and Eisenberger, R. (2002). Perceived organizational support: a review of the literature. *Journal of Applied Psychology*, 87, 698–714.

Schaufeli, W.B. and Bakker, A.B. (2004). Job demands, job resources, and their relationship with burnout and engagement: a multi-sample study. *Journal of Organizational Behavior*, 25, 293–315.

Shields, M. (2002). Shift work and health. *Health Reports*, 13, 11–33.

Sinclair, R.R., Ford, D.K., Hahn, D.I., Buck, M.A., and Truxillo, D.M. (April, 2007). Work schedule justice effects on employee health and well-being outcomes. Paper presented at the 22nd annual conference of the Society for Industrial and Organizational Psychology, New York.

Smith, L. and Folkard, S. (1993). The perceptions and feelings of shiftworkers' partners. *Ergonomics*, 35, 299–305.

Smith, C.S., Folkard, S., and Fuller, J.A. (2003). Shift work and working hours. In J.C. Quick and L.E. Tetrick (eds), *Handbook of Occupational Health Psychology*. Washington DC: APA.

Spelten, E., Totterdell, P., Barton, J., and Folkard, S. (1995). Effects of age and domestic commitment on the sleep and alertness of female shiftworkers. *Work and Stress*, 9, 165–75.

Staines, G.L. and Pleck, J.H. (1984). Nonstandard work schedules and family life. *Journal of Applied Psychology*, 69, 515–23.

Steele, M.T., Ma, O.J., Watson, W.A., and Thomas, H.A. (2000). Emergency medicine residents' shiftwork tolerance and preference. *Academic Emergency Medicine*, 7, 670–73.

Swerdlow, A. (2003). *Shift Work and Breast Cancer: A Critical Review of the Epidemiological Evidence* (No. 132). Colegate, Norwich: Institute of Cancer Research for the Health and Safety Executive.

Taillard, J., Philip, P., and Bioulac, B. (1999). Morningness/eveningness and the need for sleep. *Journal of Sleep Research*, 8, 291–5.

Tankova, I., Adan, A., and Buela-Casal, G. (1994). Circadian typology and individual differences: a review. *Personality and Individual Differences*, 16, 671–84.

Taylor, E., Briner, R.B., and Folkard, S. (1997). Models of shiftwork and health: an examination of the influence of stress on shiftwork theory. *Human Factors*, 39, 67–82.

Tett, R.P. and Meyer, J.P. (1993). Job satisfaction, organizational commitment, turnover intention and turnover: path analyses based on meta-analytic findings. *Personnel Psychology*, 46, 259–93.

Totterdell, P. (2005). Work schedules. In J. Barling, E.K. Kelloway, and M.R. Frone (eds), *Handbook of Work Stress* (pp. 35–62). Thousand Oaks, CA: Sage.

Tucker, P., Smith, L., Macdonald, I., and Folkard, S. (1998). The impact of early and late shift changeovers on sleep, health, and well-being in 8- and 12-hour shift systems. *Journal of Occupational Health Psychology*, 3, 265–75.

US Census Bureau (2006). *Facts for Features: Labor Day 2006: Sept. 4* (No. CB06-FF.12). Washington DC: US Department of Commerce.

Vidacek, S., Kaliterna, L., and Radosevic-Vidacek, B. (1987). Predictive validity of individual difference measures for health problems in shiftworkers: preliminary results. In A. Oginski, J. Pokorski, and J. Ruthenfranz (eds), *Contemporary Advances in Shiftwork Research* (pp. 53–65). Krakow: Medical Academy.

Vidacek, S., Kaliterna, L., and Radosevic-Vidacek, B. (1988). Personality differences in the phase of circadian rhythms: a comparison of morningness and extraversion. *Ergonomics*, 31, 873–88.

Worrell, K. (2005). Toward a typology of nursing turnover: the role of shocks in nurses' decisions to leave. *Nursing and Health Care Management and Policy*, 49, 315–22.

PART IV
Job Insecurity, Unemployment and Mental Health

15

Health Effects of Unemployment and Job Insecurity

Gisela Mohr and Kathleen Otto

Unemployment has become ever-present in Western societies, as well as in developing parts of the world. It is, nevertheless, often difficult to obtain clear statistics on the phenomenon in many countries or to compare statistics across national economies. Although occupational stress research has shown that paid work not only has positive effects on health, but can also be perceived as a threat, the underlying general assumption of unemployment research is that loss of paid work can be a risk to a person's health status.

Unemployment and Mental Health: Results from More Than Seven Decades of Research

One of the very first studies of unemployment was the 'Marienthal' study, named after a little village in which a factory that had provided work to a large part of the working population had shut down (Eisenberg and Lazarsfeld 1938). The book, first published in 1933 (Jahoda, Lazarsfeld and Zeisel 1933), gives an illustrative report about life in the community after the plant had closed down: people stopped using the public library, even though they now had more free time and it was free of charge; aggression increased, as indicated by trivial offences reported to the police. The following years – the years of the great economic recession/depression – saw the publication of several other important studies (Bakke 1933; Komarovsky 1940; Men without work 1938; Shlionsky, Preu and Rose 1937; Woolston 1934). They had one common feature: they were mostly homogenous in respect of the occupations sampled – for the most part focusing on workers of lower qualifications. After the Second World War, unemployment was no longer a concern for most Western countries, either in the actual economy or in research. Indeed it was not until 1975 that unemployment made it into the newspapers in Germany again, when the number of unemployed breached the one million mark, higher than it had ever been. Since then, the unemployment rate has never been below this, averaging around four million, or 10 percent, in Germany. In October 2007, it was, on average, 7.7 percent in Germany, 6.8 percent in the European Union (Eurostat 2007) and about 4.7 percent in the United States (US Bureau of Labor Statistics 2007). The new phase of high unemployment reached in the 1970s once again stimulated research on the possible psychological aspects involved. In the beginning, one of the main questions concerned whether or not unemployment causes mental illness or whether mental illness is a cause for being dismissed (the 'chicken and egg' problem). Later, a shift in research focus took place. As unemployment became costly, the more urgent question concerned which models would help the unemployed return to the job market.

Several meta-analyses dealing with the original 'chicken and egg' problem were reported. Based on numerous longitudinal studies, they appeared to offer a solution: their results showed that both effects – unemployment as a result of mental impairment (selection effect) as well as mental impairment as a result of unemployment (socialisation effect) – are valid. However, the selection effect is lower than the socialisation effect. Effect sizes for the socialization effect – across different meta-analyses – were small to medium (Paul and Moser 2006a). Nevertheless, in times of mass unemployment, this means the health of millions of people is at risk. In practical terms, twice as many mentally impaired subjects were found among unemployed compared to employed individuals (Paul, Hassel and Moser 2006). Interestingly, the meta-analysis revealed that the positive effect of finding a new job on health was bigger than the negative effect of job loss (Paul and Moser 2006a). One explanation for this finding could be that an underestimation of unemployment effects has taken place, as in most studies the majority of participants were not long-term unemployed (one year or more). However, in some cases re-employment does not lead to a health benefit. Baker and North (1999) describe a subsample of single mothers living on welfare. Their movement from welfare to work did not go along with an improvement in their health status. Furthermore, Dooley and Prause (1997; Dooley, Prause and Ham-Rowbottom 2000) reported that school leavers who received employment were no better off than those staying unemployed in cases where job design was poor ('bad jobs') or where work volume and income was not sufficient ('underemployment').

The psychological reaction most often researched is depression, although elevated anxiety and negative effects on self-esteem are also well documented. Results concerning physical health effects and psychosomatic complaints are not without contradiction. Assumedly, the physical demands of the former job may initially result in physical regeneration effects at the beginning of unemployment. Catalano, Dooley, Wilson and Hough (1993) were first to prove, on the basis of their epidemiological longitudinal data, that unemployment can not only intensify alcohol consumption (and foster consumption of other drugs, such as prescription medications [Henkel 1985]) but can also 'cure' alcoholism. Other longitudinal studies demonstrated that unemployment early in adult life has long-lasting effects for later life (Wadsworth, Montgomery and Bartley 1999). Hammarström and Janlert (2005) confirmed that early unemployment is still a predictor for health 14 years later in life.

The meta-analysis gave no hint of a moderating effect of age or ethnicity, but gender, country, duration of unemployment and commitment had an influence: effect size for a health impact of unemployment was stronger for males, stronger in British studies, and stronger for the long-term unemployed. Commitment was related positively to distress in the unemployed, whereas this relationship was negative for the employed (Paul and Moser 2006a). The discovery that effects of unemployment are stronger in British studies should motivate researchers to evaluate the influence of British labour market policy. Furthermore, the role of commitment and length of unemployment should be taken into account when developing programmes to reduce unemployment. We will comment on the role of gender later, when we discuss further unresolved issues.

In addition to considering these results, some further details demand our consideration. In particular, we will discuss important influential issues concerning an individual's financial situation, the role of social support, political attitudes towards the unemployed and the crime rate within the group of unemployed.

Some Additional Empirical Results

In most countries, being unemployed for a longer period of time results in reduced financial resources. Studies have shown that there is a correlation between reduced financial funds and mental impairment (Elovainio, Kivimäki, Kortteinen and Tuomikoski 2001; Leana and Feldman 1992; Mallinckrodt and

Bennet 1992; Viinamäki, Koskela, Niskanen and Arnkill 1993). In some studies, the financial situation even proved to be a mediator for depression (Frese and Mohr 1987; Kokko and Pulkkinen 1998). It is evident that the availability of financial resources allows the unemployed to take part in everyday life, determines their way of life, may be related to identity, and, last but not least, provides mobility by making transport affordable. Some governments are concerned about the degree of financial assistance they should pay to unemployed people, based on the assumption that earning money is an important motivator for job search activities. Kong, Perrucci and Perrucci (1993) showed that people who received financial assistance for longer also stayed unemployed for longer. At first glance, this seems to support the idea that financial assistance could have a de-activating effect. However, two matters need to be taken into consideration. First, in the study conducted by Kong et al. (1993), no long-term unemployed people were included. Second, data from Klein (1990) demonstrated that those who were first to return to the labour market were also the first to leave it again. Thus, a willingness to make concessions and to escape unemployment as soon as possible may turn out to be the beginning of a downward spiral in one's occupational career. With regard to job search behaviour, there is no clear picture about the relation between this and the amount of assistance received. However, the studies of van Hooft, Born, Taris, van der Flier and Blonk (2004) and Vuori and Vesalainen (1999) indicate that it is not the net amount of money that explains job search behaviour, but the subjective feeling of financial decline. Furthermore, the feeling that one's financial situation is worsening goes hand in hand with a decline in health, which in turn threatens job searching behaviour as it makes the process more laborious (e.g. can one 'survive' the job interview?) (see Vinokur and Schul 2002).

Social support also proves to be relevant for coping with unemployment. In particular, emotional support showed positive effects ('reassurance of worth', Mallinckrodt and Bennett 1992), especially when this support came from other unemployed people (Rife and Belcher 1993). But social support may also imply a threat and may go along with 'undermining' (Vinokur and van Ryan 1993). Indeed, some authors describe that one's social network becomes smaller with ongoing unemployment (Jackson 1988; Jones 1991). This is a critical process because Granovetter (1974) was able to demonstrate that those who successfully re-entered the labour market were those with more of those weak social ties (Brown 2000; Zippay 1990).

Two assumptions often voiced in public are: unemployed people may be more prone to adhere to nationalistic views because they consider foreigners to be competitors in the national labour market; and unemployed people may be prone to criminality because of their increased state of poverty.

So far empirical data do not support a general connection between a rise in right-wing aggression and an increasing unemployment rate. McLaren (1999) found that right-wing aggressive behaviour was more common when the unemployment rate and the rate of foreigners were rising at the same time. It is still to be proven whether this correlation is specific to Germany or if it is a general pattern and what the underlying mechanism may be.

Again, concerning crime rate, no relation could be established using a time series analysis. (Kapuscinski, Braithwaite and Chapman 1998). However, although Sampson and Laub (1990) found that school leavers without work are more prone to be involved in crime, conditions during childhood were strong predictors for criminality and unemployment. Based on a German sample of young people, Sturzbecher, Dietrich and Kohlstruck (1994) also concluded that neither unemployment nor even economic hardship *per se* are predictors of violent behaviour, but that emotional deprivation during childhood is.

Overall it can be assumed that the empirical data concerning the negative health effects of unemployment are an underestimation of real changes in health status. One reason has already been mentioned: most studies do not include long-term unemployment, though duration of unemployment proves to be an important moderator. Another reason for this underestimation is that most unemployment research starts when people have already been laid off (as an exception, see Mohr 2000). Taking the mental status after dismissal as the base line ignores, however, that mental health may already have been affected by a forgoing phase of job insecurity.

It Starts before It Really Happens: The Experience of Job-Insecurity

The meta-analysis performed by Sverke, Hellgren and Näswall (2002) demonstrated that job insecurity is related to mental impairment and also to a worsening of physical health, although the latter effects are lower than the former. Furthermore, the effects of job insecurity also occurred in those not being dismissed after a phase of restructuring and downsizing. Keeping in mind that the number of fixed-term contracts is growing dramatically in most Western countries, this effect will become a relevant issue in future research and practice.

What Actually Happens: Theoretical Approaches and Explanations

Although a high level of consistency can be found in the research concerning the above mentioned health effects of unemployment, theoretical reasoning varies. Because theoretical models are rare in unemployment research, no model until now has proven to be superior. Some authors adhere to the idea that loss of (paid) work can be considered a loss of positive psychological functions (manifest functions, such as economical ones, and latent functions, such as time structuring [Jahoda 1983]; or the loss of the 'vitamins' contained in work [Taris 2002; Warr 1987]).

Other authors emphasize that unemployment should not be considered a life event, but a process. Fryer (1995) considered unemployment to be a process of 'psychological corrosive poverty'. Ezzy (1993), adhering to identity theories, also stresses the need to consider unemployment as a process. When considering unemployment, not as a life event but as a process, the aspect of adaption comes into consideration (de Witte 1993). Two lines of action seem to be adaptive in the sense that they reduce ongoing health impairment: a low or medium rather than high work commitment (Pernice 1996; Wanberg and Marchese 1994) and job search behaviour with a greater focus on quality instead of quantity (Vuori and Vesalainen 1999). The latter seems obvious in times of high unemployment rates, when the failure of job searches is common. Lucas, Clark, Georgellis and Diener (2004) demonstrate that the unemployed react strongly to the loss of a job, but that they shift back towards their baseline level of life satisfaction. However, they argue that this is not to be seen as a complete recovery in the unemployed, not even in cases when people become re-employed. Stress theories are also used to explain the process of unemployment. The approach is not only to see dismissal as a single stressor but also to analyse the daily hassles the unemployed have to cope with. In this regard, Ockenfels et al. (1995) were able to demonstrate physiological stress markers in the unemployed.

Often, unemployment is seen as a loss of control over one's life (see, Frese and Mohr 1987; Westaby and Braithwaite 2003). In studying this, occasionally Ajzen's concept of planned behaviour is used as a model (see van Hooft et al. 2004; Westaby and Braithwaite 2003), while recently, some authors have made use of justice-theories (Dalbert 2006; Naumann, Bennett, Bies and Martin 1999).

Paul and Moser (2006b) introduced a new approach when they considered the situation of the unemployed as a status of incongruence between preferred job (measured by the concepts of 'employment commitment', 'work involvement', 'work ethic' and others) and actual job status. Other approaches used within the last years have relied on equity or exchange models, such as the concept of effort-reward-imbalance (Siegrist 2005) or the concept of (breach of) the psychological contract, which is used in studies examining job insecurity (Schalk et al. 2010).

Some Unresolved Issues

Despite the long tradition of unemployment research, little is known about what unemployed people really do all day long, having lost a job that usually took up more than eight hours of their day (including transportation time to and from work). Information about gender differences is extensive but unsatisfactory. Relations to suicide – often assumed – could not be established firmly. Results concerning self-esteem are highly contradictory. Research assessing the role of discrimination is missing. Furthermore, studies looking at the effects of unemployment on family members are rare. In spite of this, some arguments dealing with these topics can be presented.

A qualitative survey of a small sample of blue-collar, unemployed women revealed that, for them, the time schedules of their social surrounding helped to structure their day and week (Mohr and Müller 2000). It can be assumed that the type and amount of activity displayed during unemployment is highly related to activities learned during employment. Feather and Bond (1983) consider those activities that are perceived as purposeful and focused on important personal goals to have a positive effect on health. But this does not seem to apply to young unemployed individuals (O'Brien, Feather and Kabanoff 1994; Rantakeisu, Starrin and Hagquist 1999; Winefield, Tiggemann and Winefield 1992). Little is known about the effects of voluntary work and alternative types of work, such as housework, vocational training or subsidiary work. In 1990, Sjoeberg and Magneberg stated that volunteer work is not very common, either among the unemployed or among the employed. Unemployed people taking part in volunteer programmes or non-profit work seem to benefit from that type of work as long as they are involved, but the positive effect on health does not hold after leaving the programme (Nitsche and Richter 2003; Richter, Nitsche and Rothländer 2003). Ambrosino (2003) showed that unemployed persons engaged in clubs or registered associations are better off than those not involved in such activities, but this could be a selection effect. Although it is often assumed that housework will have a positive effect for unemployed women, no study has really analysed whether or not this type of work actually leads to positive health effects. However, in general, meta-analyses show that housewives do not have better health than employed women (Klumb and Lampert 2004). One of the main problems with this type of research, however, is that it does not distinguish between the group of women that have chosen to be housewives and those who have lost their job and have consequently involuntarily settled on the role and self-ascription of housewife. The few studies on alternative work that have been conducted to date demonstrate that it is not work *per se* that supports mental health, but specific characteristics of work. Thus, alternative work arrangements should also fulfil criteria of good work design (Göttling 2007; Metzer 2006).

It is also worth mentioning that, although social support is a high impact topic in research, no one to date has tried to uncover exactly how the giving of social support to others (for example, helping relatives or neighbours with child care) can lead to productive coping with the abundance of time and with the sense of worthlessness which may occur in the unemployed.

Concerning gender differences, at first glance, the overall picture seems to be clear: a meta-analysis (Paul and Moser 2006a) revealed stronger effect sizes of unemployment on health for men than for women. But what does this really mean? The greater effect size for men should be analysed further if the type of measurement use for the dependent or independent variable makes a difference. Concerning the independent variable: are the unemployed women involved in the study sample really unemployed, or do they include women who did not want to work, that is, voluntary housewives? As to the dependent variable: one of the main dependent variables in unemployment research is depression. It is a well-known fact that females have higher depression levels. Thus, the augmentations may be fewer in the case of unemployment, because the baseline is originally higher. Additionally, results concerning gender differences may depend on the type of comparison made. Comparisons can be made between health *status* of unemployed men and unemployed women, or between the *decreases* in health in the move from employment to unemployment within each group. In the latter case, ceiling effects may again play a role. It could be argued that gender appropriate unemployment research needs to be gender sensible and may need to look at different outcomes for unemployed males and females. For example, earning one's own money goes along with greater decision-making power within the family and the loss of this power may be a special threat for women. Furthermore, one has to take into account that a large portion of women nowadays can no longer rely on spousal support for a lifetime, thus job loss and loss of own income (and reduced retirement pay) may show harsh effects only very late in life. An example of different effects depending on the variables under research can be found in Hammarström and Janlert (2006), who used longitudinal data drawn from young men and women to reveal that unemployment decreases the gender gap in mental ill health, but increases the gap in health behaviour. Last but not least, in many countries, women are at higher risk for long-term unemployment, and it is precisely the long-term unemployed that are under-represented in unemployment studies.

Although a number of studies exist in different countries relating unemployment rate to suicide rate, no causal link has thus far been established (cf. Eliason and Storrie 2004; Lester and Yang 2003). However, higher suicide ideation in the unemployed has been reported by Claussen (2006) based on a longitudinal study. It must be emphasized that this finding does not exclude a link between unemployment and suicide in some individual cases, simply that suicide cannot be considered a typical reaction. It can be assumed that additional circumstances are also necessary before this drastic response is elicited, for example social isolation (see Agerbo 2003). Analysing national statistics, Grobe (2006) assessed nearly three quarters of a million subjects and discovered that the death rate is higher among the unemployed. The risk of death is 3.9 times higher among the long-term unemployed than the continuously employed. This does not apply to those unemployed only for a short time (less than six months). This epidemiological study does not suggest causal links, but demonstrates an impressive rise in odd ratios for the unemployed.

Concerning the effects of unemployment on self-esteem, there are studies showing that, as may be expected, unemployed people have significantly greater negative self-esteem (Wacker and Kolobkova 2000). However, results are in fact inconsistent (Goldsmith, Veum and Darity 1997; Hartley 1980; Kokko and Pulkkinen 1998). There may be several reasons for this unclear picture. First of all, self-esteem is a rather stable construct. Epstein (1979) argues that self-esteem is based on general and higher order postulates that are not related to the experience of specific situations. Thus, self-esteem is not immediately altered by negative events. The well established self-serving bias in healthy individuals can be seen as a confirmation of this model. Thus, we would expect self-esteem to change only after a longer duration of unemployment. Furthermore, the way self-esteem is measured in these cases is important. Warr (1984) discovered that global measurements of the self-esteem of the unemployed did not change, but, when specific postulates were included in the measurements, changes could indeed be observed.

The lamented decline of native populations, a topic in some Western countries like Germany, also appears to be unexpectedly deepened when one takes into account some results from unemployment research. The decline of native populations is mainly caused by a drop in birth-rate. Yet, while this drop occurs across all Western population groups, this effect seems to be particularly strong for the unemployed.

Regarding families, Eckert-Jaffe and Solaz (2001) state that unemployed individuals commit themselves to long-term relationships later than their employed counterparts, get married less often and have fewer children. The divorce rate within the first four years of marriage is three times higher for unemployed men than for employed men. Furthermore, several studies indicate that children of unemployed parents are burdened with some disadvantages: their weight at birth is lower, they display slower growth and are more prone to accidents (Ström 2002; 2003), they exhibit more self-destructive behaviour, they drop out of school more often and are more often unemployed as adults ('intergenerational unemployment', see Ström 2003). Only a few of these studies take into account the influence of additional variables, such as substance abuse in the case of assessing the physical status of babies. In fact, those unemployed mothers of babies with a low birth weight did consume more nicotine than others. But even when controlling for additional variables, a main affect of job status seems to be relevant, indicating that unemployment is a strong predictor for increased risks in the development of children (Ström 2003). Jones (1997) argues that social emotional deprivation is more relevant than economic status. He concludes that skilled educational support by parents and good emotional ties between parents and children may be able to prevent the spill-over of negative effects of parent's employment on children. This is in line with the results of Caspi, Wright, Moffitt and Silva (1998), who followed the lives of children until the age of 21 years, and the longitudinal study by Hammer (2000). Both studies show that future unemployment can be predicted by the conditions that are present before reaching adulthood. Low parental support, family conflicts, low school commitment and antisocial behaviour are predictors of later unemployment. The results of de Goede, Spruijt, Maas and Duindam (2000) indicate that predictors of unemployment are different for boys and girls: for boys, parental unemployment was a predictor of later unemployment, whereas for girls, malfunctioning family life was a more important predictor of later unemployment.

Groups at Risk

With the expansion of the service industry in many countries within the last two decades, more jobs have been taken on by females than by males. Nevertheless, in most European countries, the female unemployment rate (7.7 percent) is still higher than the male rate (6.1 percent, on average, in the EU) (see Eurostat, 2007).

In some countries, school leavers and the 'young elderly' are prone to experience unemployment. In Germany, for example, the group aged 52 to 59 is at special risk. They are considered too old to be employed again, but they are also too young to receive a pension (Bender, Konietzka and Sopp 2000). Laws against discrimination (including age) have become valid only very recently in Europe and it has yet to be observed if this alters the chances of re-employment for the elderly.

The long-term unemployed are prone to face social exclusion (Kieselbach 2003). Statistics show that having been unemployed raises the probability of becoming unemployed again. Other interruptions in a person's career do not have such negative effects (Bender et al. 2000).

The situation of school leavers deserves special attention. Paul and Moser (2001) concluded that, after leaving school, young adults show an amelioration of health, even when they do not enter the labour market. Interestingly, a study conducted by Winefield, Tiggemann and Winefield (1991), involving Australian young people, led to the conclusion that the unemployed do not in fact have a lower health status, but that employed young adults experience a gain in mental health. Thus, unemployment in young people may be considered a hindrance in further development. However, overall, the results concerning the effects of unemployment in young people are not consistent (Breslin and Mustard 2003; Prause and Dooley 2001; Schaufeli and van Yperen 1993). This may be attributed to the fact that control groups of employed youth may be working in 'bad jobs' or in states of 'underemployment' (Dooley and Prause 1997; Dooley et al. 2000) and thus are ultimately no better off than the unemployed. The 14-year follow-up study with school leavers conducted by Hammarström and Janlert (2005) indicated that early unemployment has long-lasting effects for adult health status.

What Helps, What Doesn't: The Responsibility of Psychology and Psychologists

Considering the above mentioned results concerning the negative impacts of unemployment, it is evident that the best remedy for the unemployed would be a job. But the conclusion is not that any job will be better than no job. In order to have a less negative health impact than unemployment, the job has to contain some basic features of human work design. This means it must provide a person with the means to live, give the person a chance to use and develop skills, make it possible for the person to take part in social life, and allow the person to make plans for the future. Providing a job clearly goes beyond psychology, and into the realm of politics and economics, but when we ask the question 'what helps (to cope with unemployment and to re-enter the labour market) and what hinders', we are asking about the role of psychology. First of all, it needs to be clear what the goal of any intervention could be. In cases where the unemployment rate is very high – as it is, for example, in some rural regions in Germany with a rate of about 20 percent (or even considerably higher when those individuals who do not appear in any statistics but nevertheless experienced involuntary job loss are also included) – coping with long-lasting unemployment and trying to secure mental health should include the further development of one's job qualifications for the lower qualified. In those regions, however, where a sufficient number of jobs theoretically exist or where self-employment is an option, re-employment should be the target.

Vuori and Vesalainen (1999) evaluated three quite different interventions with the unemployed: 1) raising the quality of applications for employment and improving skills for the employment interview or tests, including developing knowledge about niches of the labour market and knowledge about personal abilities, 2) acquiring additional occupational skills (like language, software etc.), and 3) job creation schemes. The first intervention type showed the greatest impact in terms of re-employment success. It was also the shortest measure. This measure focuses on the *quality* of job search behaviour, and is in line with the results of the meta-analysis of Kanfer, Wanberg and Kantrowitz (2001), which revealed that job search intensity alone has only a mean correlation of $r = .18$, but effort of $r = .30$ to re-employment. Thus a number of other conditions have to be taken into account in order to explain re-employment. In addition to the regional unemployment rate, the quality, and not only quantity, of job search activities should be the focus of attention.

When designing interventions for the unemployed, psychologists should refrain from several practices. The first is creating the illusion that the amount of activity is a predictor of re-employment. In contrast, psychologists should be aware that the mere amount of activity may be a risk for the mental health of the unemployed, who then have to cope with being declined.

Other misdirected practices which psychologists may be inclined to implement are the supporting of unrealistic optimism and the encouragement of a strong work commitment. In a longitudinal study, Frese and Mohr (1987) found that those individuals who had high hopes of regaining employment and were still unemployed one and a half years later had the highest level of depression. And those unemployed who showed a lower or only medium level of work commitment were better off in regard to mental health (Leana and Feldman 1995; Pernice 1996; Wanberg and Marchese 1994).

Coercing a willingness to make concessions may also be counterproductive. As Klein (1990) found in an analysis of national statistics, three quarters of those unemployed who obtained a job were unemployed again within four years. In a study conducted by Leana and Feldman (1995), the health status of re-employed individuals who perceived their job to be unsatisfactory was close to that of the still unemployed. Readiness to make concessions may be functional when related to formal aspects of the contract, but not in relation to qualitative dimensions of the job.

Another pitfall for psychologists may be to try to change the way in which unemployed individuals attribute blame for their situation. Chambres, Granier and Marescaux (2000) noted that the internal attribution of failure to the labour market grew with the length of unemployment. Psychologists may be inclined to foster external causal attributions in the unemployed, instead of self-blame, in order to prevent feelings of guilt and depressive emotions. But two studies showed that the unemployed who made external attributions had greater difficulty gaining re-employment than those who made internal attributions (Chauvot 1997; Miller and Hoppe 1994). As Miller and Hoppe (1994) point out, internal attributions of failure are no hindrance to re-employment as long as the attribution is tied to changeable aspects of one's self (e.g. being lazy instead of being too small).

The results summarized above point out that social integration, the maintenance of weak ties and the ability to cope with family life have to be taken into account when working with the unemployed. Encouraging the development of cognitive abilities and initiative-taking seems to be a promising approach. In a longitudinal study, Zempel and Frese (2000) were able to show that people with these abilities experienced the shortest duration of unemployment, even under the harsh conditions of the reunification of the former German Democratic Republic with the Federal Republic of Germany. As the necessary cognitive abilities and initiative-taking skills are not developed 'overnight', the best prevention is to design jobs that develop and sustain cognitive abilities and initiative-taking in the first place.

In those cases where jobs are truly dispensable, the best prevention against the negative effects of unemployment would be to offer an outplacement-programme – not only for managers but also for blue-collar workers (Solomon 1983). In this way, people can be helped to find a new job before they have been dismissed. Even if the outplacement-programme does not prevent unemployment, it seems to have a positive effect on mental health (Isaksson, Hellgren and Pettersson 2005). It is likely that this effect results from the appreciation that the people feel they are being shown by their company when such programmes are offered to them.

For the most part, interventions appear to have a positive effect on mental health, but this effect does not last. Nor does the improvement in physical health during the intervention last over time (Westerlund, Bergström and Theorell 2004). One exception is presented by Price, van Ryan and Vinokur (1992), who were able to demonstrate positive effects of the intervention even two and a half years after the end of the programme. It must be added, however, that their participants had been short-term unemployed (four months). Vuori and Silvonen (2005), adapting the programme Price et al. (1992) had developed and evaluated, found a lagged effect on the mental health of participants involved in an intervention programme. Positive effects were found, not in the first, but in the second wave, two years after the programme was finished. Here persons unemployed for a longer duration (a mean duration of 10 months) were also included. The authors argue that the programme was especially effective in helping people cope with long-lasting unemployment, with setbacks, and with further financial and social degradation (see also Kieselbach, Klink, Scharf and Schulz 1998). As Price at al. (1992) were able to show, those unemployed with the worst health status reaped the highest profit from the programme (see also Creed, Machin and Hicks 1996; Machin and Creed 2003).

Thus, psychology and psychologists can do a good job in helping the unemployed. But they should be aware that there are pitfalls to be avoided and that the real remedy would be to create secure jobs. Occupational conditions also play a role in future unemployment (Bildt and Michélsen 2003), thus ensuring the good design of work places is also a strategy for helping people to deal with unemployment before it happens.

References

Agerbo, E. (2003), 'Unemployment and suicide', *Journal of Epidemiology and Community Health*, vol. 57, no. 8, pp. 560–61.

Ambrosino, V. (2003), 'Aider les chômeurs à reconstruire leurs repères temporels: une étude des stratégies mises en place pours mieux vivre le chômage', *Orientation Scolaire et Professionnelle*, vol. 32, no. 1, pp. 123–44.

Baker, D. and North, K. (1999), 'Does employment improve the health of lone mothers?', *Social Science and Medicine*, vol. 49, no. 1, pp. 121–31.

Bakke, E.W. (1933), *The Unemployed Man*, London: Nisbet and Co.

Bender, S., Konietzka, D. and Sopp, P. (2000), 'Diskontinuität im Erwerbsverlauf und betrieblicher Kontext', *Kölner Zeitschrift für Soziologie und Sozialpsychologie*, vol. 52, no. 3, pp. 475–99.

Bildt, C. and Michélsen, H. (2003), 'Occupational conditions exceed the importance of non-occupational conditions and ill health in explaining future unemployment among women and men', *Archives of Women's Mental Health*, vol. 6, pp. 115–26.

Breslin, F.C. and Mustard, C. (2003), 'Factors influencing the impact of unemployment on mental health among young and older adults in a longitudinal, population-based survey', *Scandinavian Journal of Work, Environment and Health*, vol. 29, no. 1, pp. 5–14.

Brown, D.W. (2000), 'Job searching in a labyrinth of opportunity: the strategies, the contacts, the outcomes', *Journal of Social Behavior and Personality*, vol. 15, no. 2, pp. 227–42.

Caspi, A., Wright, B.R.E., Moffitt, T.E. and Silva, P.A. (1998), 'Early failure in the labor market: childhood and adolescent predictors of unemployment in the transition adulthood', *American Sociological Review*, vol. 63, no. 3, pp. 424–51.

Catalano, R., Dooley, D., Wilson, G. and Hough, R. (1993), 'Job loss and alcohol abuse: a test using data from the epidemiologic catchment area project', *Journal of Health and Social Behavior*, vol. 34, no. 3, pp. 215–25.

Chambres, P., Granier, S. and Marescaux, P.-J. (2000), 'Causal attribution, learned helplessness and autonomy in job seeking: a typology', *European Review of Applied Psychology*, vol. 50, no. 4, pp. 383–92.

Chauvot, P. (1997), 'L'attribution de l'echec chez les cadres. Attribution of failure among managers', *Orientation Scolaire et Professionnelle*, vol. 26, no. 4, pp. 527–57.

Claussen, B. (2006), 'Suicidal ideation in the long-term unemployed: a five-year longitudinal study', in T. Kieselbach, A. Winefield, C. Byod and S. Anderson (eds), *Unemployment and Health*, Brisbane: Australian Academic Press, pp. 109–18.

Creed, P.A., Machin, M.A. and Hicks, R. (1996), 'Neuroticism and mental health outcomes for long term unemployed youth attending occupational skills training programs', *Personality and Individual Differences*, vol. 21, no. 4, pp. 537–44.

Dalbert, C. (2006), Justice concerns and mental health during unemployment, in T Kieselbach, A Winefield, C. Byod and S. Anderson (eds), *Unemployment and Health*, Brisbane: Australian Academic Press, pp. 35–50.

de Goede, M., Spruijt, E., Maas, C. and Duindam, V. (2000), 'Family problems and youth unemployment', *Adolescence*, vol. 35, no. 139, pp. 587–601.

de Witte, H. (1993), 'Gevolgen van langdurige werklossheid voor het psychisch welzijn: overzicht van de onderzoeksiteratuur' [Psychological consequences of long-term unemployment: review of the literature], *Psychologica Belgica*, vol. 33, no. 1, pp. 1–35.

Dooley, D. and Prause, J.A. (1997), 'Effects of favourable employment change on alcohol abuse: one- and five-year follow-ups in the National Longitudinal Survey of Youth', *American Journal of Community Psychology*, vol. 25, no. 6, pp. 787–807.

Dooley, D., Pause, J.A. and Ham-Rowbottom, K.A. (2000), 'Underemployment and depression: longitudinal relationships', *Journal of Health and Social Behavior*, vol. 41, no. 4, pp. 421–36.

Eckert-Jaffe, O. and Solaz, A. (2001), 'Unemployment, marriage and cohabitation in France', *Journal of Socio-Economics*, vol. 30, pp. 75–98.

Eisenberg, P. and Lazarsfeld, P.F. (1938), 'The psychological effects of unemployment', *Psychological Bulletin*, vol. 35, pp. 358–90.

Eliason, M. and Storrie, D. (2004), 'Does job loss shorten life?', Paper presented at the 3rd International Expert Conference on Unemployment and Health, University of Bremen, Germany.

Elovainio, M., Kivimäki, M., Kortteinen, M. and Tuomikoski, H. (2001), 'Socioeconomic status, hostility and health', *Personality and Individual Differences*, vol. 31, pp. 303–15.

Epstein, S. (1979), 'Entwurf einer Integrativen Persönlichkeitstheorie', in S.H. Filipp (ed.), *Selbstkonzept-Forschung*, Stuttgart: Klett, pp. 15–46.

Eurostat (2007), Harmonized unemployment rates, -/+ 25 years, monthly data. [Online]. Available at: http://epp.eurostat.ec.europa.eu [Accessed: 6 December 2007].

Ezzy, D. (1993), 'Unemployment and mental health: a critical review', *Social Science and Medicine*, vol. 37, no. 1, pp. 41–52.

Feather, N.T. and Bond, M.J. (1983), 'Time structure and purposeful activity among employed and unemployed university graduates', *Journal of Occupational Psychology*, vol. 56, pp. 241–54.

Frese, M. and Mohr, G. (1987), 'Prolonged unemployment and depression in older workers: a longitudinal study of intervening variables', *Social Science and Medicine*, vol. 25, pp. 173–8.

Fryer, D.M. (1995), 'Benefit agency? Labour market disadvantage, deprivation and mental health', *The Psychologist*, vol. June, pp. 265–72.

Goldsmith, A.H., Veum, J.R. and Darity, W. Jr. (1997), 'Unemployment, "joblessness, psychological well-being and self-esteem: theory and evidence', *Journal of Socio-Economics*, vol. 26, no. 2, pp. 133–58.

Göttling, S. (2007), 'Die Arbeit der "Arbeitslosen" – Tätigkeiten von Menschen mit geringem Einkommen in Ostdeutschland', in P.G. Richter, R. Rau and S. Mühlpford (eds), *Arbeit und Gesundheit: Zum aktuellen Stand in einem Forschungs- und Praxisfeld*, Lengerich: Pabst Science Publishers, pp. 399–412.

Granovetter, M. (1974), *Getting a Job*, Cambridge: Cambridge University Press.

Grobe, T. (2006), 'Sterben Arbeitslose früher?', in A. Hollederer and H. Brand (eds), *Arbeitslosigkeit, Gesundheit und Krankheit*, Bern: Huber, pp. 75–83.

Hammarström, U. and Janlert, U. (2005), 'Early unemployment can contribute to adult health problems: results from a longitudinal study of school leavers', *Journal of Epidemiology and Community Health*, vol. 56, pp. 624–30.

Hammarström, U. and Janlert, U. (2006), 'Do the health consequences of unemployment differ for young men and women?', in T. Kieselbach, A. Winefield, C. Byod and S. Anderson (eds), *Unemployment and Health*, Brisbane: Australian Academic Press, pp. 135–42.

Hammer, T. (2000), 'Mental health and social exclusion among unemployed youth in Scandinavia: a comparative study', *International Journal of Social Welfare*, vol. 9, pp. 53–63.

Hartley, J. (1980), 'Psychological approaches to unemployment', *Bulletin of the British Psychological Society*, vol. 33, pp. 412–14.

Henkel, D. (1985), 'Arbeitslosigkeit als Risikofaktor für Alkoholgefährdung und Hindernis für Rehabilitationsprozesse', in T. Kieselbach and A. Wacker (eds), *Individuelle und gesellschaftliche Kosten der Massenarbeitslosigkeit*, Weinheim: Beltz, pp. 66–90.

Isaksson, K., Hellgren, J. and Pettersson, P. (2005), 'Union involvement during downsizing and its relation to attitudes and distress among workers', in H. de Witte (ed.), *Job Insecurity, Union Involvement and Union Activism*, London: Ashgate, pp. 97–116.

Jackson, P.R. (1988), 'Personal networks, support mobilization and unemployment', *Psychological Medicine*, vol. 18, no. 2, pp. 397–404.

Jahoda, M. (1983), *Wieviel Arbeit braucht der Mensch? Arbeit und Arbeitslosigkeit im 20. Jahrhundert*, Weinheim: Beltz.

Jahoda, M., Lazarsfeld, P.F. and Zeisel, H. (1933), *Die Arbeitslosen von Marienthal*, Frankfurt/Main: Suhrkamp.

Jones, L. (1991), 'Specifying the temporal relationship between job loss and consequences: Implication for service delivery', *Journal of Applied Social Sciences*, vol. 16, no. 1, pp. 37–62.

Jones, L. (1997), 'The psychological correlates of parental employment status in a sample of foster children', *Journal of Applied Social Science*, vol. 21, no. 2, pp. 71–83.

Kanfer, R., Wanberg, C.R. and Kantrowitz, T.M. (2001), 'Job search and employment: a personality-motivational analysis and meta-analytic review', *Journal of Applied Psychology*, vol. 86, pp. 837–55.

Kapuscinski, C.A., Braithwaite, J. and Chapman, B. (1998), 'Unemployment and crime: toward resolving the paradox', *Journal of Quantitative Criminology*, vol. 14, no. 3, pp. 215–43.

Kieselbach, T. (2003), 'Long-term unemployment among young people: the risk of social exclusion', *American Journal of Community Psychology*, vol. 32, nos 1–2, pp. 69–76.

Kieselbach, T., Klink, F., Scharf, G. and Schulz, S. (1998), *Ich wäre sonst ja nie wieder an Arbeit rangekommen! Evaluation einer Reintegrationsmaßnahme für Langzeiterwerbslose: Psychologie sozialer Ungleichheit*, Weinheim: Deutscher Studienverlag.

Klein, T. (1990), 'Arbeitslosigkeit und Wiederbeschäftigung im Erwerbsverlauf. Theorieansätze und theoretische Befunde', *Kölner Zeitschrift für Soziologie und Sozialpsychologie*, vol. 42, pp. 688–705.

Klumb, P.L. and Lampert, T. (2004), 'Women, work, and well-being 1950–2000: a review and methodological critique', *Social Science and Medicine*, vol. 58, pp. 1007–24.

Kokko, K. and Pulkkinen, L. (1998), 'Unemployment and psychological distress: mediator effects', *Journal of Adult Development*, vol. 5, no. 4, pp. 205–17.

Komarovsky, M. (1940), *The Unemployed Man and His Family*, New York: Dryden Press.

Kong, F., Perrucci, C.C. and Perrucci, R. (1993), 'The impact of unemployment and economic stress on social support', *Community Mental Health Journal*, vol. 29, no. 3, pp. 205–21.

Leana, C.R. and Feldman, D.C. (1992), *Coping with Job Loss: How Individuals, Organizations and Communities Respond to Layoffs*, New York: Macmillan/ Lexington Books.

Leana, C.R. and Feldman, D.C. (1995), 'Finding new jobs after a plant closing: antecedents and outcomes of the occurrence and quality of reemployment', *Human Relations*, vol. 48, no. 12, pp. 1381–401.

Lester, D. and Yang, B. (2003), 'Unemployment and suicidal behaviour', *Journal of Epidemiology and Community Health*, vol. 57, no. 8, pp. 558–9.

Lucas, R.E., Clark, A.E., Georgellis, Y. and Diener, E. (2004), 'Unemployment alters the set point for life satisfaction', *Psychological Science*, vol. 15, pp. 8–12.

Machin, M.A. and Creed, P.A. (2003), 'Understanding the differential benefits of training for the unemployed', *Australian Journal of Psychology*, vol. 55, no. 2, pp. 104–13.

Mallinckrodt, B. and Bennett, J. (1992), 'Social support and the impact of job loss in dislocated blue-collar workers', *Journal of Counseling Psychology*, vol. 39, no. 4, pp. 482–9.

McLaren, L.M. (1999), 'Explaining right-wing violence in Germany: a time series analysis', *Social Science Quarterly*, vol. 80, no. 1, pp. 166–80.

Men without work (1938), *A Report Made to the Pilgrims Trust*, New York: Greenwood Press.

Metzer, J. (2006), 'Can volunteering be a moderator of the detrimental effects of engagement in (un) employment?', in T. Kieselbach, A. Winefield, C. Byod and S. Anderson (eds), *Unemployment and Health*, Brisbane: Australian Academic Press, pp. 259–65.

Miller, M.V. and Hoppe, S.K. (1994), 'Attributions for job termination and psychological distress', *Human Relations*, vol. 47, no. 3, pp. 307–27.

Mohr, G. (2000), 'The changing significance of different stressors after the announcement of bankruptcy: a longitudinal investigation with special emphasis on job insecurity', *Journal of Organizational Behavior*, vol. 21, pp. 337–59.

Mohr, G. and Müller, K. (2000), 'Zeitstrukturierung in der Erwerbslosigkeit am Beispiel von Industriearbeiterinnen. Eine qualitative Analyse', *Verhaltenstherapie und Psychosoziale Praxis*, vol. 32, pp. 53–64.

Naumann, S.E., Bennett, N., Bies, R.J. and Martin C.L. (1999), 'Laid off, but still loyal: the influence of perceived justice and organizational support', *International Journal of Conflict Management*, vol. 9, no. 4, pp. 356–68.

Nitsche, I. and Richter, P. (2003), *Tätigkeiten außerhalb der Erwerbsarbeit. Evaluation des TAURIS-Projektes*, Münster: LIT Verlag.

O'Brien, G.E., Feather, N.T. and Kabanoff, B. (1994), 'Quality of activities and the adjustment of unemployed youth', *Australian Journal of Psychology*, vol. 46, no. 1, pp. 29–34.

Ockenfels, M.C., Porter, L., Smyth, J., Kirschbaum, C., Hellhammer, D.H. and Stone, A. (1995), 'Effect of chronic stress associated with unemployment on salivary cortisol: overall cortisol levels, diurnal rhythm, and acute stress reactivity', *Psychosomatic Medicine*, vol. 57, pp. 460–67.

Paul, K., Hassel, A. and Moser, K. (2006), 'Die Auswirkung von Arbeitslosigkeit auf die psychische Gesundheit', in A. Hollederer and H. Brand (eds), *Arbeitslosigkeit, Gesundheit und Krankheit*, Bern: Huber, pp. 35–51.

Paul, K. and Moser, K. (2001), 'Negatives psychisches Befinden als Wirkung und als Ursache von Arbeitslosigkeit: Ergebnisse einer Metaanalyse', in J. Zempel, J. Bacher and K. Moser (eds), *Erwerbslosigkeit. Ursachen, Auswirkungen und Interventionen*, Opladen: Leske and Buderich, pp. 83–110.

Paul, K. and Moser, K. (2006a), 'Quantitative reviews in psychological unemployment research: an overview', in T. Kieselbach, A. Winefield, C. Byod and S. Anderson (eds), *Unemployment and Health*, Brisbane: Australian Academic Press, pp. 51–9.

Paul, K. and Moser, K. (2006b), 'Incongruence as an explanation for the negative mental health effects of unemployment: meta-analytic evidence', *Journal of Occupational and Organizational Psychology*, vol. 79, pp. 595–621.

Pernice, R. (1996), 'Methodological issues in unemployment research: quantitative and/or qualitative approaches?' *Journal of Occupational and Organizational Psychology*, vol. 69, no. 4, pp. 339–49.

Prause, J. and Dooley, D. (2001), 'Favourable employment status change and psychological depression: a two-year follow-up analysis of the national Longitudinal Survey of Youth', *Applied Psychology: An International Review*, vol. 50, no. 29, pp. 282–304.

Price, R., van Ryan, M. and Vinokur, A. (1992), 'Impact of preventive job search intervention on the likelihood of depression among the unemployed', *Journal of Health and Social Behavior*, vol. 33, pp. 158–67.

Rantakeisu, U., Starrin, B. and Hagquist, C. (1999), 'Financial hardship and shame: a tentative model to understand the social and health effects of unemployment', *British Journal of Social Work*, vol. 29, no. 6, pp. 877–901.

Richter, P., Nitsche, I. and Rothländer, K. (2003), 'Long term unemployment and mental health: stabilizing effects of tasks in the volunteering sector', in C. Weikert, E. Torkelson and J. Pryce (eds), *Occupational Health Psychology in Europe: Empowerment, Participation and Health at Work*, Vienna: AUVA, pp. 152–6.

Rife, J.C. and Belcher, J.R. (1993), 'Social support and job search intensity among older unemployed workers: implications for employment counselors', *Journal of Employment Counseling*, vol. 30, no. 3, pp. 98–107.

Sampson, R.J. and Laub, J.H. (1990), 'Crime and deviance over the life course: the salience of adult social bonds', *American Sociological Review*, vol. 55, no. 5, pp. 609–27.

Schalk, R., De Jong, J., Rigotti, T., Mohr, G., Peiró, J.-M. and Caballer, A. (2010), 'The psychological contracts of temporary and permanent workers, in D. Guest, K. Isaksson and H. de Witte (eds), *Employment Contracts, Psychological Contracts and Employee Well-Being*, Oxford: Oxford University Press, pp. 89–119.

Schaufeli, W. and van Yperen, N. (1993), 'Success and failure on the labour market', *Journal of Organizational Behavior*, vol. 14, pp. 559–72.

Shlionsky, H., Preu, P.W. and Rose, M. (1937), 'Clinical observations on the reaction of a group of transients to unemployment', *Journal of Social Psychology*, vol. 8, pp. 73–86.

Siegrist, J. (2005), 'Social reciprocity and health: new scientific evidence and policy implications', *Psychoneuroendocrinology*, vol. 30, pp. 1033–8.

Sjoeberg, L. and Magneberg, R. (1990), 'Action and emotion in everyday life', *Scandinavian Journal of Psychology*, vol. 31, no. 1, pp. 9–27.

Solomon, L.J. (1983), 'Considerations in laying off employees: a program description', *Journal of Organizational Behavior*, vol. 5, no. 1, pp. 53–62.

Ström, S. (2002), 'Keep out of the reach of children: parental unemployment and children's accident risks in Sweden 1991–1993', *International Journal of Social Welfare*, vol. 11, no. 1, pp. 40–52.

Ström, S. (2003), 'Unemployment and families: a review of research', *Social Service Review*, vol. 77, no. 3, pp. 399–430.

Sturzbecher, D., Dietrich, P. and Kohlstruck, M. (1994), *Jugend in Brandenburg 93*, Potsdam: Staatskanzlei Brandenburg, Brandenburgische Landeszentrale für politische Bildung.

Sverke, M., Hellgren, J. and Näswall, K. (2002), 'No security: A meta-analysis and review of job insecurity and its consequences', *Journal of Occupational Health Psychology*, vol. 7, no. 3, pp. 242–64.

Taris, T.W. (2002), 'Unemployment and mental health: a longitudinal perspective', *International Journal of Stress Management*, vol. 9, no. 1, pp. 43–57.

US Bureau of Labor Statistics (2007), 'Selected unemployment indicators, seasonally adjusted', [Online]. Available at: http://www.bls.gov [Accessed: 6 December 2007].

van Hooft, E.A.J., Born, M., Taris, T.W., van der Flier, H. and Blonk, R.W.B. (2004), 'Predictors of job search behavior among employed and unemployed people', *Personnel Psychology*, vol. 57, pp. 25–59.

Viinamäki, H., Koskela, K., Niskanen, L. and Arnkill, R. (1993), 'Unemployment, financial stress and mental well-being: a factory closure study', *European Journal of Psychiatry*, vol. 7, no. 2, pp. 95–102.

Vinokur, A.D. and Schul, Y. (2002), 'The web of coping resources and pathways to reemployment following a job loss', *Journal of Occupational Health Psychology*, vol. 7, no. 1, pp. 68–83.

Vinokur, A.D. and van Ryan, M. (1993), 'Social support and undermining in close relationships: their independent effects on the mental health of unemployed persons', *Journal of Personality and Social Psychology*, vol. 65, no. 2, pp. 350–59.

Vuori, J. and Silvonen, J. (2005), 'The benefits of a preventive job search program on re-employment and mental health at two-year follow up', *Journal of Occupational and Organizational Psychology*, vol. 78, no. 1, pp. 43–52.

Vuori, J. and Vesalainen, J. (1999), 'Labour market interventions as predictors of re-employment, job seeking activity and psychological distress among the unemployed', *Journal of Occupational and Organizational Psychology*, vol. 72, no. 4, pp. 523–38.

Wacker, A. and Kolobkova, A. (2000), 'Arbeitslosigkeit und Selbstkonzept. Ein Beitrag zu einer kontroversen Diskussion', *Zeitschrift für Arbeits- und Organisationspsychologie*, vol. 44, no. 2, pp. 69–82.

Wadsworth, M.E.J., Montgomery, S.M. and Bartley, M.J. (1999), 'The persisting effect of unemployment on health and social well-being in men early in working life', *Social Science and Medicine*, vol. 48, no. 10, pp. 1491–9.

Wanberg, C.R. and Marchese, M.C. (1994), 'Heterogeneity in the unemployment experience: a cluster analytic investigation', *Journal of Applied Social Psychology*, vol. 24, no. 6, pp. 473–88.

Warr, P. (1984), 'Work and unemployment', in P.J.D. Drenth, H. Thierry, P.J. Willems and C.J. de Wolff (eds), *Handbook of Work and Organizational Psychology*, New York: Wiley, pp. 413–43.

Warr, P. (1987), 'Job characteristics and mental health', in P. Warr (ed.), *Psychology at Work*, London: Penguin, pp. 247–69.

Westaby, J.D. and Braithwaite, K.N. (2003), 'Specific factors underlying reemployments self-efficacy: comparing control belief and motivational reason methods for the recently unemployed', *Journal of Applied Behavioral Science*, vol. 39, no. 4, pp. 415–37.

Westerlund, H., Bergström, A. and Theorell, T. (2004), 'Changes in anabolic and catabolic activity among women taking part in an Alternative Labour Market Programme', *Integrative Physiological and Behavioral Science*, vol. 39, no. 1, pp. 3–15.

Winefield, A., Tiggemann, M. and Winefield, H.R. (1991), 'The psychological impact of unemployment and unsatisfactory employment in young men and woman: longitudinal and cross-sectional data', *British Journal of Psychology*, vol. 82, no. 4, pp. 473–86.

Winefield, A.H., Tiggemann, M. and Winefield, H.R. (1992), 'Spare time use and psychological well-being in employed and unemployed young people. Special Issue: Marienthal and beyond: 20th century research on unemployment and mental health', *Journal of Occupational and Organizational Psychology*, vol. 65, no. 4, pp. 307–13.

Woolston, H.B.P. (1934), 'Psychology of unemployment', *Sociology and Social Research*, vol. 19, pp. 337–40.

Zempel, J. and Frese, M. (2000), 'Prädiktoren der Erwerbslosigkeit und Wiederbeschäftigung', *Verhaltenstherapie and Psychosoziale Praxis*, vol. 32, no. 3, pp. 379–90.

Zippay, A. (1990), 'The limits of intimates: social networks and economic status among displaced industrial workers', *Journal of Applied Social Sciences*, vol. 15, no. 1, pp. 75–95.

16

Job Insecurity: Implications for Occupational Health and Safety

Tahira M. Probst

Introduction

Corporations in many countries are experiencing extreme financial pressures due to commercial rivalries around the globe, government deregulation of industry, and the increasing pace of organizational technology change. As a result, massive layoffs, conversion of full-time jobs to part-time positions, and the increase of temporary workers are sober realities facing organizations and workers today. Organizational restructuring in the form of corporate downsizing, mergers and acquisitions, plant closings, and workforce reorganizations affect millions of workers (blue-collar and white-collar alike) each year. The result of these phenomena has been an increasing prevalence of job insecurity in the workplace.

In Europe, an OECD (Organization for Economic Cooperation and Development, 1997) study found a 12 percent decline in the proportion of surveyed European employees who felt their jobs were secure between the years 1985 and 1995; and, a UK study found levels of job insecurity at their highest levels post-World War Two (Burchell et al., 1999). Similar trends have also been observed in Asia (Rust, McKinley, and Zhao, 2003), where market reforms have had a significant impact on employment security, and in the United States, where annual layoffs hover around one million each year as a result of these transitions (Bureau of Labor Statistics, 2006).

Today's pervasive climate of job insecurity has been shown to have multiple negative consequences for affected employees. Early research by Cobb (1974) found that the stress of possible job termination was associated with significant increases in norepinephrine excretion, serum creatinine, serum uric acid, and serum cholesterol. Subsequent research continues to substantiate the finding that employees with job insecurity report a greater incidence of physical health conditions (Cottington et al., 1986; Dooley, Rook, and Catalano, 1987; Kuhnert, Sims, and Lahey, 1989; Probst, 2000; 2002a; 2003; Roskies and Louis-Guerin, 1990) and higher levels of blood pressure and cholesterol levels (Pollard, 2001) when compared to employees with secure jobs. In fact, Burgard et al. (2006) recently reported that the negative health effects of job insecurity were on a par with the health effects of a serious or life-threatening illness.

Job insecurity has also been associated with higher levels of general psychological distress (Dekker and Schaufeli, 1995; Probst, 2000; 2002a; 2003) and with increased medical consultations for psychological distress (Catalano, Rook, and Dooley, 1986). Roskies and Louis-Guerin (1990) reported that job insecurity among managers was related to an increase in anxiety, depression, and general distress. Similarly, Kuhnert, Sims, and Lahey (1989) found that job insecurity was related to overall increases in somatization, depression, anxiety, and hostility.

There are important job-related outcomes as well. Job insecurity is related to lower levels of employee job satisfaction (Ashford, Lee, and Bobko, 1989; Davy, Kinicki, and Scheck, 1991). The more dissatisfied employees are with their perceived job security, the less committed they are to the organization (Ashford et al., 1989; Davy et al., 1991), the more frequently they engage in work withdrawal behaviors such as absenteeism, tardiness, and work task avoidance (Probst, 2002b), and the more likely they are to quit their job (Ashford et al., 1989; Davy et al., 1991).

Aggregating the results of 72 studies published between 1980 and 1999, Sverke, Hellgren, and Näswell (2002) found that job insecurity was negatively correlated with job satisfaction (-.41), job involvement (-.37), organizational commitment (-.36), trust in management (-.50), physical health (-.16), mental health (-.24), and job performance (-.21); and was positively related to turnover intentions (.28).

While there has clearly been much research documenting the negative effects of job insecurity on employee attitudes and health outcomes, it is only within the past several years that research has investigated the potential effects of job insecurity on employee safety outcomes. Therefore, the goal of this chapter is to examine the theoretical and empirical evidence for the proposition that employee job insecurity can have detrimental effects on worker safety attitudes, behaviors, and outcomes. The first part of the chapter will delineate the possible mechanisms by which job insecurity is expected to adversely affect safety outcomes. Following this, the results of several recent empirical tests of these propositions will be presented. These data—collected in the field and in the laboratory—consistently confirm the negative effects of job insecurity on worker safety outcomes. The last section of the chapter is devoted to an exploration of potential organizational strategies for prevention.

Job Insecurity and Safety: Rationales for a Relationship

Theory and research in the areas of job insecurity and worker safety have largely progressed independently of each other. Researchers in the area of job insecurity have traditionally focused primarily on delineating the attitudinal, behavioral, and job-related consequences of such insecurity, but have largely ignored safety as a potential outcome. Similarly, researchers in the area of workplace safety have identified numerous antecedents of worker safety (e.g., ergonomic conditions, personality, and safety climate). Yet, to date, there has been little research considering employee job insecurity as a predictor of worker safety. Despite the relative independence of empirical research into these two areas, there are numerous theoretical mechanisms that would explain why one might expect to find a link between job insecurity and employee safety.

Proposition 1: Job Insecurity → Stress → Poor Safety Outcomes.

One possible rationale for the link between job insecurity and safety may be the effect that job insecurity has on employee attitudes and stress levels. As noted above, decreased perceptions of job security have consistently been found to be related to lower job satisfaction (e.g., Ashford, Lee, and Bobko, 1989; Davy, Kinicki, and Scheck, 1991; Probst, 2000). Further, job insecurity has been found to be one of the major sources of job stress (Ironson, 1992). When an individual perceives that his or her job security is threatened and is dissatisfied by that perception, it is expected that both safety motivation and safety knowledge will be adversely affected. This prediction can be generated from a cognitive resources framework (Kanfer and Ackerman, 1989) and from Eysenck and Calvo's model of anxiety and performance (1992).

According to Kanfer and Ackerman (1989), there is a set amount of available cognitive resources that each individual has when engaged in the completion of any given task. These finite cognitive resources can be allocated to on-task, off-task, or self-regulatory activities. In a work setting, on-task activities include those behaviors related to production, quality assurance, and safety compliance. Off-task activities include behaviors such as chatting with co-workers, thinking about family, or planning for the weekend. Self-regulatory activities include the monitoring of one's environment. During times of organizational change, the monitoring of job security would be aptly classified as a self-regulatory activity. This involves estimating the chances that one might be affected by the impending organizational transition, how one's job might change as a result, keeping up to date with organizational rumors, and the like.

When individuals have high job security, these self-regulatory activities can be disengaged, leaving more resources available for the on-task activities of production, quality, and safety. However, when job security is perceived to be low, some of those cognitive resources may be funneled into self-regulatory activities aimed at monitoring progress towards the goal of job retention. Thus, during times of organizational transition, valuable cognitive resources may be consumed in the monitoring of job security and in the maintenance of production schedules that would otherwise be utilized to maintain (or increase) safety knowledge, motivation, and compliance. On the other hand, during times of organizational stability and job security, these cognitive resources can be solely devoted to the demands of safety and production.

Other theories also suggest that the stress and dissatisfaction resulting from job insecurity will lead to lowered safety knowledge and motivation. Eysenck and Calvo (1992) suggest that anxiety (such as is expected to result from job insecurity) can either a) drain working memory resources leading to a decrease in performance, or b) increase cognitive arousal, thereby serving as a motivational source that results in performance improvement. Where one will see performance decrements versus performance improvements depends on the employee's perception of the organization's prioritization of safety, quality, and production. Wickens (1992) suggests that safety, in particular, represents an additional task that can compete with performance-related tasks when attention or performance capacities are exceeded. In addition, Sanders and Baron (1975) in their distraction-conflict theory suggest that arousal and anxiety can result in employees relegating workplace hazards to the background. In support of this, Dunbar (1993) found that individuals who have high levels of negative affect, anxiety, and depression are less likely to use their personal protective equipment properly.

Based on these theories and empirical evidence, it can be expected that employees dissatisfied with their job security would report a lowered emphasis on safety knowledge and report lower safety motivation than employees relatively unconcerned about their job security due to the stress resulting from the perceived job insecurity and the associated increase in cognitive demands and anxiety.

Proposition 2: Job Insecurity → Increased Emphasis on Production → Poor Safety Outcomes.

A second possible mechanism by which job insecurity results in poor safety outcomes may be the effect that job insecurity has on employee attitudes towards production. As noted above, stress can lead individuals to focus narrowly on a few specific aspects of their environment (Barthol and Ku, 1959; Mandler, 1982). According to Hofmann and Stetzer (1996), one consequence of this may be that employees tend to focus their attention on productivity rather than safety during times of stress—as might be precipitated by perceived job insecurity.

It has been suggested that workers face an inherent conflict between safety and production (Faverge, 1980; Janssens, Brett, and Smith, 1995; Kjellen, 1984; Leplat and Rasmussen, 1984). The more an organization places an emphasis on production, the more employees perceive that safety is subordinated to the demands of production (Janssens, Brett, and Smith, 1995). Hofmann and Stetzer (1996: 309) summarize this tradeoff and its consequences succinctly:

> *Perceptions of performance pressure can lead workers to perceive that engaging in short cut behavior is an expected, or required, part of the job (Wright, 1986). Specifically, workers who perceive a high degree of performance pressure will focus their attention on completing the work and less on the safety of their work procedures. As a result, they may begin to perceive short cut methods as required to meet the performance demands. (e.g., Wright, 1986)*

The degree to which employees choose production over safety in the safety-production tradeoff will be in part determined by their perceptions regarding organizational reward contingencies. Hofmann and Stetzer (1996) predict that employees who are experiencing job stress will focus on performance rather than safety because performance is more likely to result in salient rewards for the employee. In addition, unsafe behavior may actually be perceived to be rewarding if it allows the employee to perform work tasks more quickly (Slappendal, Laird, Kawachi, Marshall, and Cryer, 1993). Thus, during times of job insecurity, employees desiring to retain their jobs may choose to focus more on performance and less on safety. This increased emphasis on production can then lead to worsened safety outcomes.

Proposition 3: Job Insecurity → Decreased Emphasis on Safety → Poor Safety Outcomes.

Related to the above arguments, it can also be reasoned that job insecurity causes employees to not only place greater emphasis on production, but also correspondingly de-emphasize safety, which in turn results in poor safety outcomes. Simard and Marchand (1997) found that organizations paying lower wages and offering little job security tended to have less managerial participation in safety issues, which in turn was related to a reduction in accident prevention and safety compliance. Therefore, macro-organizational variables were shown to impact micro-level outcomes such as employee safety compliance.

Research suggests that safety knowledge and safety motivation are individual factors that are important in predicting safety compliance (Hofmann, Jacobs, and Landy, 1995; Neal, Griffin, and Hart, 2000). Using a contingency approach, Hofmann et al. predict that employees will be less motivated to comply with safety policies to the extent that they are not rewarded for performing in a safe manner. Perceived organizational contingencies suggesting that greater rewards will follow from completing the work as quickly as possible can lead to employees taking unnecessary shortcuts. In addition, a perception that management is not committed to safety can translate to a lack of motivation on the part of employees to comply with safety policies (Hofmann et al., 1995).

Thus, the third proposition explaining the linkage between job insecurity and reduced safety outcomes is that organizations and jobs with traditionally higher levels of job insecurity tend not to foster organizational cultures supportive of safety due to increased pressures for production in order to survive economically (Simard and Marchand, 1997). Decreased emphasis on safety may result in workers who are less concerned about acquiring and maintaining safety knowledge, are less motivated to comply with safety rules, and subsequently experience a greater incidence of accidents and injuries at work.

Tests of the Job Insecurity–Safety Relationship

A growing body of research suggests that the job insecurity is related to poorer safety outcomes and that the propositions developed above to explain the relationship are largely supported. In perhaps the earliest study on the topic, Landsbergis, Cahill, and Schnall (1999) found detrimental effects on employee health and injury rates in a variety of industries that were implementing lean production cultures. Although this study did not address job insecurity *per se*, it is accepted that one of the hallmarks of lean production is the implementation of organizational downsizing (American Management Association, 1997; Landsbergis et al., 1999). A more recent comprehensive review of more than 90 studies conducted in Europe, North and South America, Asia, and Africa (Quinlan, 2005) found evidence of consistent adverse associations between precarious employment, job insecurity, and occupational safety outcomes such as injury rates, safety knowledge, and safety compliance.

Probst and Brubaker (2001) gathered cross-sectional and longitudinal data in one of the earliest studies to test the mediating mechanisms for the relationship between job insecurity and safety. Participants in that study were sampled from two plants of a large food processing company. Both plants had undergone major organizational changes affecting the job security of the organization's employees. In the first plant, an entire shift of workers was laid off and during focus group interviews employees reported a general feeling that the plant was being slowly phased out of existence in favor of a larger plant located elsewhere. In the second location, the swing shift was being eliminated in favor of a night shift. Employees who could not accommodate the new shift schedule were expected to lose their jobs. Notably, production was expected to remain at former levels during these organizational transitions. Thus, even though there would be fewer employees, overall plant production levels were expected to remain constant.

Employees participated in the study at two different time periods: 1) immediately after the shift changes and elimination were announced, and 2) six months following the organizational restructuring. The results of the two cross-sectional structural equation modeling analyses and the longitudinal multiple regression analyses were quite consistent and supported Proposition 1. Job insecurity was consistently shown to have a strong negative relationship with job satisfaction. In addition, safety motivation and safety knowledge were consistently positively predicted by job satisfaction, suggesting that job insecurity can have an important effect on safety motivation and safety knowledge through its impact on such job attitudes as job security satisfaction, co-worker and supervisor satisfaction, and satisfaction with pay, promotions, and the work itself.

Probst and Brubaker (2001) also assessed the behavioral and physical outcomes of job insecurity and decreased safety motivation and knowledge.

Participants consistently reported less compliance with safety policies when their motivation to comply with safety rules was reduced (i.e., when they perceived few external incentives to comply). Surprisingly, safety knowledge did not appear to be an important predictor of safety compliance in any of the three analyses—perhaps suggesting that safety training programs are bounded in their effectiveness by the employee's motivation to comply with safety policies. With respect to physical health outcomes, greater numbers of workplace accidents and injuries were consistently found when safety compliance was reduced. In two more recent studies of the effects of job insecurity on risky job-related behavior, Rundmo and Iversen (2007) and Storseth (2007) both found that job insecurity was related to risky on-the-job behaviors and that this relationship was partially mediated by job satisfaction.

Although the effects of job insecurity on safety behaviors have been found to be mediated by employee job attitudes and stress levels (in support of Proposition 1), it is also theorized that safety may be compromised when employees feel insecure about their jobs because employees may devote more of their time and energy towards meeting production demands (Proposition 2) and correspondingly less on safety (Proposition 3) in the effort to retain their employment.

To evaluate Propositions 2 and 3, Probst (2002a) designed a follow-up laboratory experiment in order to examine the effects of threatened job loss on employee adherence to safety policies, work quality, and productivity levels in a controlled laboratory setting. Thirty-seven upper-level undergraduates participated in the experiment. Participants were told that they were to be employed by an organization that produced paintings for children's rooms. Their task was to produce as many high quality paintings within a number of work periods as possible while adhering to a number of safety rules designed to minimize their exposure to the potentially irritating paint products. Halfway through the work sessions, students in the experimental condition were told that 50 percent of them would be laid off due to declining sales of the paintings. Layoff decisions would be based on their overall performance (i.e., productivity, work quality, and safety adherence) in the following work period. Employees who were laid off would lose any compensation they had accrued to that point as well as future possibilities for compensation. In the control sessions, no mention of layoffs was made and the sessions continued as before.

There were several pertinent findings from this experiment. First, the results appear to indicate that product quality, safety, and production do, as theorized by Probst and Brubaker (2001), compete for employee resources. As employee production numbers (i.e., number of completed paintings) increased, employee adherence to safety policies decreased and independent ratings of the quality of their work products declined. More importantly, while individuals threatened with layoffs displayed higher productivity than individuals who were not threatened with layoffs, these same individuals also violated more safety policies and produced lower quality paintings than their secure counterparts. In other words, under conditions of job insecurity, productivity was higher, but safety compliance and product quality were significantly lower. Of particular interest was the finding that the effect of job insecurity on quality and safety was fully mediated by the employee's focus on production. In other words, when participants perceived that their jobs were insecure, they responded to this insecurity by increasing their productivity at the expense of their work quality and their safety compliance, comporting with earlier theorizing by Hofmann and Stetzer (1996) that suggested employees will focus on performance rather than safety under conditions of job stress, because performance may be perceived to lead to more salient rewards.

Moving beyond earlier correlational studies, the Probst (2002a) findings appear to indicate that job insecurity can have a causal negative impact on employee safety behaviors. The results also suggest that the underlying explanation for the effect may be that employees perceive production demands to be more important than safety adherence when it comes to retaining their jobs during times of job insecurity.

To further investigate this, Probst and Brubaker (2007) conducted an experimental study to assess the extent to which supervisors take safety versus productivity into account when making layoff recommendations under conditions of differing organizational emphasis on safety versus production. Their laboratory experiment with participants acting as supervisors manipulated the organizational climate to emphasize either safety or production and the safety performance and productivity of four subordinates. Although the results indicated that supervisory layoff recommendations were influenced by the stated organizational climate (e.g., safer workers were recommended to be retained more when safety was an organizational priority), participants consistently predicted that final layoff decisions (to be made by upper management) would eventually result in safe workers being laid off to a greater extent than productive workers. Thus, despite manipulating the organizational emphasis on safety versus production, participants consistently predicted that employees excelling in the area of safety would be laid off by upper management in favor of retaining employees who excel in the area of production. This prediction held true even if participants were told that the organization valued safety above other factors. Thus, it appears to be an ingrained belief that organizations value production over safety even in the face of organizational statements to the contrary.

Based on the results of these initial studies, it appears that job insecurity may adversely affect employee safety in three ways. First, job insecurity appears to cause higher levels of employee stress and job dissatisfaction, which may result in attentional tunneling and a decline in available cognitive resources to properly attend to safety (Proposition 1). Second, job insecurity directly causes employees to focus more on production perhaps in an effort to retain their job (Proposition 2). Third, job insecurity results in perceptions of decreased organizational emphasis on safety. This decreased emphasis on safety leads to lower levels of safety compliance and more subsequent injuries, accidents, and near misses (Proposition 3).

Compounding the results from the above studies, recent research suggests that employee job insecurity may also lead to underreporting of accidents (Probst, 2006b). Data from 359 employees located in four organizations indicated that perceptions of job insecurity may serve to inhibit the reporting of accidents to supervisors. Analyses showed that when job insecurity was low, there was little difference between reported and unreported accidents. However, as job insecurity increased, employees under-reported more accidents. Thus, insecurity may not only lead to more accidents and injuries for the reasons noted earlier, but employees may also be more reluctant to report these injuries to their supervisors—and with good reason. Employees who did report accidents to their supervisors described multiple negative consequences as a result ranging from being unfairly disciplined and given poor performance evaluations to being blamed for ending the company's accident-free record and receiving less favorable job duties. Thus, it is perhaps not surprising that individuals who are already worried about losing their job will underreport accidents to an even greater extent.

Implications for Prevention: Countering the Negative Effects of Job Insecurity on Safety

Although the results of the previous studies may appear discouraging in that there is mounting evidence for the adverse effects of job insecurity on safety outcomes, the same research may also offer clues regarding steps organizations can take to circumvent this cycle. In particular, if the effects of job insecurity on safety are mediated by job stress levels, increased emphasis on production, and decreased emphasis on safety, then interventions targeting these variables may be effective at countering the negative effects of job insecurity on safety. Neal and Griffin's (2004) distinction between safety violations and safety errors is of relevance here. Whereas safety errors are due to unintentional noncompliance with safety regulations, safety violations result from intentional noncompliance. Unintentional noncompliance may be due to higher levels of job stress and the resulting attentional tunneling and cognitive overload, whereas intentional noncompliance may be due to employees deliberately sacrificing safety in order to concentrate their efforts on other aspects of performance such as productivity. Although it may be difficult to alter employee stress levels due to job insecurity (and, therefore, safety errors), organizations can take steps to alter employee perceptions regarding the organization's priorities related to safety (and, thereby, reduce deliberate safety violations).

There has been a lot of attention paid recently to the impact that an organization's safety climate (Zohar, 1980) can have on employee safety behaviors. Research (e.g., Griffin and Neal, 2000; Neal, Griffin, and Hart, 2000) consistently shows that an organization's safety climate is a strong predictor of the level of safety knowledge and motivation exhibited by employees, as well as their level of safety compliance and participation. Thus, it seems clear that organizations with strong safety climates can exert a positive influence on employee behaviors.

Taken in conjunction, research on job insecurity and research on organizational safety climate may suggest that there are ways for an organization to attenuate the negative relationship observed between job insecurity and safety outcomes at work. While organizations may not be able to control employee levels of job insecurity or the resultant stress, organizations can control the message they send to employees during times of organizational transition. Further, organizations can provide incentives and rewards for employee safety, so that employees can see that important job-related outcomes (such as salary, promotions, etc.) are contingent on their adherence to safety procedures, and not just on good production numbers. In this fashion, one might see that a strong organizational climate for safety attenuates the relationship between job insecurity and negative safety outcomes, because employees receive the message that safety need not and should not be subordinated to the demands of production in order to retain their jobs.

Empirical research appears to support this notion. In a field study conducted within a small company engaged in light manufacturing (Probst, 2004), organizational safety climate was found to moderate the impact that job insecurity had on employee safety outcomes. Specifically, employees who perceived a poor safety climate exhibited significant relationships between insecurity and safety outcomes. However, among employees who perceived that management placed a strong value on safety, the relationships between job insecurity and safety knowledge, safety compliance, accidents, and injuries were significantly attenuated. Thus, job insecurity was only related to negative safety outcomes when the organizational safety climate was perceived to be poor.

Similarly, Parker, Axtell, and Turner (2001) conducted a longitudinal study of 161 employees in a glass manufacturing setting to investigate the antecedents of safe working. Job insecurity was hypothesized to be a predictor of safe working, such that more insecurity would be related to less safe work behaviors. However, their results suggested, contrary to their hypothesis, that job insecurity was related to *more positive* safety behaviors among these employees. One explanation for this finding is that the organization described in the Parker et al. study placed a strong emphasis on building a positive safety climate for its workers. As described in the study, there were multiple organizational safety campaigns initiated, new safety training programs introduced, and other safety initiatives which would have clearly indicated to employees that their organization takes safety seriously and that safety outcomes may be considered when making downsizing decisions.

Moreover, a recent study suggests that a positive organizational safety climate can further serve to attenuate the underreporting of accidents. Although a large body of research has found that accident underreporting is widespread (Clarke, 1998; Glendon, 1991; Bridges, 2000), Probst (2006a) found in a study of more than a dozen organizations that underreporting was greatest when the safety climate was perceived to be weak and when supervisors did not consistently enforce safety policies. When the perceived safety climate was positive and enforcement was consistent, employees underreported fewer injuries to their supervisors.

Conclusion

Mounting research has found evidence to suggest that fear of layoffs and job insecurity can result in negative safety outcomes for employees. Job insecurity has been linked with poor safety knowledge, motivation, and compliance; increased levels of accidents and injuries; and a greater tendency to underreport injuries and accidents to supervisors. Reasons for these effects may be heightened levels of job stress, an increased emphasis on production, and/or decreased perceptions of the importance of safety. Yet, research also indicates that organizations can play a key role in circumventing the negative relationship between insecurity and safety by placing a strong emphasis on and building a positive organizational safety climate.

References

American Management Association (1997). *Corporate Job Creation, Job Elimination, and Downsizing*. New York: American Management Association.

Ashford, S., Lee, C., and Bobko, P. (1989). Content, causes, and consequences of job insecurity: a theory-based measure and substantive test. *Academy of Management Journal*, 32, 803–29.

Barthol, R.P. and Ku, N.D. (1959). Regression under stress to first learned behavior. *Journal of Abnormal and Social Psychology*, 59, 134–6.

Bridges, W.G. (2000). Get near misses reported. Process industry incidents: investigation protocols, case histories, lessons learned. In *Proceedings of the Center for Chemical Process Safety International Conference and Workshop* (pp. 379–400). New York: American Institute for Chemical Engineers.

Burchell, B.J., Day, D., Hudson, M., Ladipo, D., Mankelow, R., Nolan, J.P., Reed, H., Wichert, I.C., and Wilkinson, F. (1999). *Job Insecurity and Work Intensification: Flexibility and the Changing Boundaries of Work*. [Online]. Available at: http://www.jrf.org.uk/ KNOWLEDGE/findings/socialpolicy/pdf/F849.pdf [Accessed: July 23, 2007].

Bureau of Labor Statistics (2006). Archived news releases for extended mass layoffs. [Online]. Available at: http://www.bls.gov/schedule/archives/mslo_nr.htm [Accessed: January 22, 2007].

Burgard, S.A., Brand, J.E., and House, J.S. (2006, March). Job insecurity and health among US adults. Paper presented at the Los Angeles Meetings of the Population Association of America, Los Angeles.

Catalano, R., Rook, K., and Dooley, D. (1986). Labor markets and help-seeking: a test of the employment security hypothesis. *Journal of Health and Social Behavior*, 27, 277–87.

Clarke, S. (1998). Organizational factors affecting the incident reporting of train drivers. *Work and Stress*, 12, 6–16.

Cobb, S. (1974). Physiologic changes in men whose jobs were abolished. *Journal of Psychosomatic Research*, 18, 245–58.
Cottington, E.M., Mathews, K.A., Talbot, E., and Kuller, L.H. (1986). Occupational stress, suppressed anger, and hypertension. *Psychosomatic Medicine*, 48, 249–60.
Davy, J., Kinicki, A., and Scheck, C. (1991). Developing and testing a model of survivor responses to layoffs. *Journal of Vocational Behavior*, 38, 302–17.
Dekker, S.W. and Schaufeli, W.B. (1995). The effects of job insecurity on psychological health and withdrawal: a longitudinal study. *Australian Psychologist*, 30, 57–63.
Dooley, D., Rook, K., and Catalano, R. (1987). Job and non-job stressors and their moderators. *Journal of Occupational Psychology*, 60, 115–32.
Dunbar, E. (1993). The role of psychological stress and prior experience in the use of personal protective equipment. *Journal of Safety Research*, 24, 181–7.
Eysenck, M.W. and Calvo, M.G. (1992). Anxiety and performance: the processing efficiency theory. *Cognition and Emotion*, 6, 409–34.
Faverge, J.M. (1980). Le travail en tant qu'activité de récupération. *Bulletin de Psychologie*, 33, 203–6.
Glendon, A.I. (1991). Accident data analysis. *Journal of Health and Safety*, 7, 5–24.
Griffin, M.A. and Neal, A. (2000). Perceptions of safety at work: a framework for linking safety climate to safety performance, knowledge, and motivation. *Journal of Occupational Health Psychology*, 5, 347–58.
Hofmann, D.A., Jacobs, R., and Landy, F. (1995). High reliability process industries: Individual, micro, and macro organizational influences on safety performance. *Journal of Safety Research*, 26, 131–49.
Hofmann, D.A. and Stetzer, A. (1996). A cross-level investigation of factors influencing unsafe behaviors and accidents. *Personnel Psychology*, 49, 307–39.
Ironson, G.H. (1992). Job stress and health. In C.J. Cranny, P.C. Smith, and E.F. Stone (eds), *Job Satisfaction: How People Feel About Their Jobs and How It Affects Their Performance*. New York: Lexington Books.
Janssens, M.J., Brett, J.M., and Smith, F.J. (1995). Confirmatory cross-cultural research: testing the viability of a corporation-wide safety policy. *Academy of Management Journal*, 38, 364–82.
Kanfer, R. and Ackerman, P.L. (1989). Motivation and cognitive abilities: an integrative/aptitude-treatment interaction approach to skill acquisition. *Journal of Applied Psychology*, 74, 657–90.
Kjellen, U. (1984). The deviation concept in occupational accident control. *Accident Analysis and Prevention*, 16, 289–323.
Kuhnert, K., Sims, R., and Lahey, M. (1989). The relationship between job security and employees' health. *Group and Organization Studies*, 14, 399–410.

Landsbergis, P.A., Cahill, J., and Schnall, P. (1999). The impact of lean production and related new systems of work organization on worker health. *Journal of Occupational Health Psychology*, 4, 108–30.

Leplat, J. and Rasmussen, J. (1984). Analysis of human errors in industrial incidents and accidents for improvement of work safety. *Accident Analysis and Prevention*, 16, 77–88.

Mandler, G. (1982). Stress and thought process. In L. Goldberger and S. Breznitz (eds), *Handbook of Stress* (pp. 88–104). New York: Free Press.

Neal, A. and Griffin, M.A. (2004). Safety climate and safety at work. In J. Barling and M. Frone (eds) *Psychology of Workplace Safety*, (pp. 15–34). Washington, DC: American Psychological Association.

Neal, A., Griffin, M.A., and Hart, P.M. (2000). The impact of organizational climate on safety climate and individual behavior. *Safety Science*, 34, 99–109.

OECD (1997). Is job insecurity on the increase in OECD countries? In OECD, *1997 Employment Outlook*. Paris: OECD.

Parker, S.K., Axtell, C.M., and Turner, N. (2001). Designing a safer workplace: importance of job autonomy, communication quality, and supportive supervisors. *Journal of Occupational Health Psychology*, 6, 211–28.

Pollard, T.M. (2001). Changes in mental well-being, blood pressure and total cholesterol levels during workplace reorganization: the impact of uncertainty. *Work and Stress*, 15, 14–28.

Probst, T.M. (2000). Wedded to the job: moderating effects of job involvement on the consequences of job insecurity. *Journal of Occupational Health Psychology*, 5, 63–73.

Probst, T.M. (2002a). Layoffs and tradeoffs: production, quality, and safety demands under the threat of job loss. *Journal of Occupational Health Psychology*, 7, 211–20.

Probst, T.M. (2002b). The impact of job insecurity on employee work attitudes, job adaptation, and organizational withdrawal behaviors. In J.M. Brett and F. Drasgow (eds) *The Psychology of Work: Theoretically Based Empirical Research* (pp. 141–68). Mahwah, NJ: Lawrence Erlbaum.

Probst, T.M. (2003). Exploring employee outcomes of organizational restructuring: a Solomon four-group study. *Group and Organization Management*, 28, 416–39.

Probst, T.M. (2004). Safety and insecurity: exploring the moderating effect of organizational safety climate. *Journal of Occupational Health Psychology*, 9, 3–10.

Probst, T.M. (2006a, October). Individual- and organizational- accident under-reporting: the moderating effect of organizational safety climate. Invited presentation to the Portland Industrial/Organizational Psychology Association, Portland, OR.

Probst, T.M. (2006b, May). Job insecurity and accident underreporting. Paper presented to the 2006 Conference of the Society of Industrial and Organizational Psychology, Dallas, TX.

Probst, T.M. and Brubaker, T.L. (2001). The effects of job insecurity on employee safety outcomes: cross-sectional and longitudinal explorations. *Journal of Occupational Health Psychology*, 6, 139–59.

Probst, T.M. and Brubaker, T.L. (2007). Organizational safety climate and supervisory layoff decisions: preferences versus predictions. *Journal of Applied Social Psychology*, 37, 1630–48.

Quinlan, M. (2005). The hidden epidemic of injuries and illness associated with the global expansion of precarious employment. In C.L. Peterson and C. Mayhew (eds), *Occupational Health and Safety: International Influences and the New Epidemics*. Amityville, NY: Baywood.

Roskies, E. and Louis-Guerin, C. (1990). Job insecurity in managers: antecedents and consequences. *Journal of Organizational Behavior*, 11, 345–59.

Rundmo, T. and Iversen, H. (2007). Is job insecurity a risk factor in occupational health and safety? *International Journal of Risk Assessment and Management*, 7, 165–79.

Rust, K.G., McKinley, W., and Zhao, J. (2003). Business ideologies and perceived breach of contract during downsizing: A China perspective. Unpublished manuscript.

Sanders, G.S. and Baron, R.S. (1975). The motivating effects of distraction on task performance. *Journal of Personality and Social Psychology*, 32, 956–63.

Simard, M. and Marchand, A. (1997). Workgroups' propensity to comply with safety rules: the influence of micro-macro organisational factors. *Ergonomics*, 40(2), 172–88.

Slappendal, C., Laird, I., Kawachi, I., Marshall, S., and Cryer, C. (1993). Factors affecting work-related injury among forestry workers: a review. *Journal of Safety Research*, 24, 19–32.

Storseth, F. (2007). Affective job insecurity and risk taking at work. *International Journal of Risk Assessment and Management*, 7, 189–204.

Sverke, M., Hellgren, J., and Näswell, K. (2002). No security: a meta-analysis and review of job insecurity and its consequences. *Journal of Occupational Health Psychology*, 7, 242–64.

Wickens, C.D. (1992). *Engineering Psychology and Human Performance*. New York: HarperCollins.

Wright, C. (1986). Routine deaths: fatal accidents in the oil industry. *Sociological Review*, 4, 265–89.

Zohar, D. (1980). Safety climate in industrial organizations: theoretical and applied implications. *Journal of Applied Psychology*, 65, 96–102.

17

Mental Health and Unemployment: The Coping Perspective

Alexander-Stamatios Antoniou and Marina Dalla

According to the International Labour Organisation (2007) unemployment covers people who: are out of work; want a job; have actively sought work in the previous four weeks and are available to start work within the next fortnight; or are out of work and have accepted a job that they are waiting to start in the next fortnight. In most European countries, the unemployment rate has increased in the past 30 years, affecting mainly young people and women (Organization for Economic Cooperation and Development, 2009). Increasing globalization and world-wide economic competition have been accompanied by high unemployment rates (Ukpere and Slabbert, 2009).

According to deprivation perspectives (Jahoda, 1982), unemployment or job loss results in a significant deterioration in mental health (Catalano, Raymond, and William, 2002; Dooley, Prause, and Ham-Rowbottom, 2000) as a state of social, emotional and spiritual well-being that provides individuals with the vitality necessary for active living, to achieve goals, and to interact with others in ways that are respectful and just (VicHealth, 1999). The main argument of this theory is that unemployment deprives people of the latent functions of work in their lives: time structure, social contact and participation, status and identity, as well as shared experiences outside the family (Jahoda, 1982). Similarly, Halvorsen (2004) argues that unemployment results in cumulative disadvantages, because of income loss and lower living standards, loss of self-esteem, and an increased risk of poorer mental health.

There is evidence from different countries and time periods that unemployed people have poor psychological health. They suffer from psychosomatic symptoms, anxiety, depression, social dysfunction, reduced happiness, and behavioral problems (Layard, 2005; MacDonald and Shields, 2001; Rodríguez, Frongillo, and Chandra, 2001). Furthermore, unemployed people have a low sense of status and less involvement in social activities, both of which have a negative effect on their psychological health (Waters and Moore, 2002).

However, the relationship between unemployment and well-being does not appear to be linear. According to research, women are less affected by unemployment than men (Waters and Moore, 2002) as a consequence of traditional gender roles that provide some time structure, status, and activity that may compensate for some of the negative effects of unemployment (Artazcoz, Benach, Borrell, and Cortes, 2004; Jahoda, 1982). Furthermore, in many countries, women are considered as the second earner in the household (Georgas, 1989). Likewise, young people experience fewer psychological problems than older people, because they can establish functional alternatives to work and, moreover, they place less value on social position than older persons (Zunker, 1998).

In addition to deprivation theory that attempts to explain the effects of unemployment on well-being, more recent approaches offer a contrasting view of unemployment. The incentive perspective emphasizes that unemployment is a deliberate choice of the unemployed because of weak motivation to search for a job (Goul Andersen, 2001). The proponents of this theory suggest that a notable part of unemployment is more or less voluntary, and that the problem among the unemployed is that their well-being may be too high, rather than too low. According to this view, the behavior of the unemployed can and should be motivated by financial and non-financial incentives that help people to develop and use their full productive capacities.

The key concepts of the deprivation paradigm and the incentive approach have recently been combined in the coping theory (Halvorsen, 1994 in Goul Andersen, 2001). According to this perspective, unemployment is a serious psychosocial problem because it deprives people of latent and manifest benefits. However, a notable number of unemployed people have the resources to cope with the situation. From this perspective, psychological recourses are assumed to be an important precondition for well-being among unemployed people. Psychological resources include a person's perception of self, attitudes towards work, ethical orientation and general outlook in life that represent one's core self evaluations, and one's appraisal of people, events, and things in relation to oneself (Erez and Judge, 2001). Emotional stability and conscientiousness seem to be important resources because careful, responsible, organized, achievement-oriented, and hardworking individuals with low neuroticism are expected to have a high probability of entering employment (Barrick and Mount, 1991). Other psychological traits such as extraversion, agreeableness, and openness to experience are more essential for a job requiring greater interaction or cooperation with others.

Emotion regulation is also an important determinant of well-being (Phillips, Henry, Hosie, and Milne, 2006). Therefore, in evaluating psychological well-being it is important to study anger as one of the most frequently experienced negative emotions (Spielberger, Moscoso, and Brunner, 2005). In terms of social outcomes anger is associated with social maladjustment, especially anger expression within social relationships (Lazarus, 1996). Careful assessment of the experience, expression, and control of anger is essential for understanding problems that are rooted in anger as well as for improving mental and physical health by using adaptive strategies in different situations (Spielberger, Reheiser, Ritterband, Sydeman, and Unger, 1995).

Studying personal and work values and interests, we can understand a person's motivation to engage in job searching to facilitate reemployment. Personal values have been conceptualized as cognitive representations of universal needs (Schwartz, 1996), as enduring states of proper social behavior (Rokeach, 1973), as guiding principles in life, or as part of one's personality affecting goal-oriented behavior and decision making (Schwartz, 1996). Value theory specifies four main dimensions of contrasting values: openness to change values (self-direction, stimulation) which encourage independence of thought, feeling, and action conflicts; conservation values (conformity, tradition, security) that call for self restriction, preserving traditional practices, and protecting stability; self-transcendence values (universalism, benevolence) emphasize the acceptance of others as equals and concern for their welfare conflict; and self-enhancement values (power, achievement) encourage pursuing one's own relative success and dominance over others. Hedonism as a value, then, is seen as sharing elements of openness and self-enhancement. Furthermore, while some studies conclude that self-direction, achievement, and stimulation are positively associated with positive affects, security, conformity, and tradition values are negatively associated (Roccas, Sagiv, Schwartz, and Knafo, 2002).

Work-related values as expressions of more general life values have been defined as goals, or characteristics that can be found in a job (International Research Team, 1987). Work values cover different aspects of work such as creativity, intellectual stimulation, independence, group orientation, prestige, and security (Super, 1995), and after validation in different countries they reflect intrinsic (intellectual stimulation, creativity, and independence) and extrinsic (social orientation, prestige, and security) motivation (Elizur, Borg, Hunt, and Beck, 1991). Intrinsic motivation reflects engaging in an activity simply because it is interesting and enjoyable on its own, while the reasons for extrinsic motivation are different opportunities, separate outcomes, or rewards (Deci and Ryan, 2002). Career interests as likes and dislikes regarding specific activities or objects (Greenhaus, Callanan, and Godshalk, 2000) influence all other aspects of life.

Observing personal and work values in the context of economic change helps people to be more realistic and effective in searching for a new job (Zunker, 2002). Furthermore, values and interests are assumed to be linked to the motivation and the affective system. Some unemployed people might perceive employment as an attractive and personal goal; hence, their behavior is regulated by intrinsic motivation. Others engage in job searching behavior as an opportunity to solve their financial problems; hence, their behavior is characterized by an external perceived motivation. Unemployed people with high external motivation tend to experience job loss as stressful and pressuring, thereby reflecting negative psychological well-being (Vansteenkiste, Lens, Dewitte, DeWitte, and Deci, 2004).

Support for the study of the well-being and other psychological resources of unemployed people comes from developmental training programs. Such programs seek to reduce the negative effects of unemployment on the well-being of unemployed and to improve their basic coping skills for managing transition. One set of skills is related to internal psychological resources and personal strengths which in turn affect motivation and reduce emotional and psychological distress, anger and anxiety, hostile and aggressive behavior (Zunker, 2002). Furthermore, people may analyze discrepancies between existing and desired conditions, identify stressful situations related to implementing goals, and adopt additional skills which facilitate their reentry into employment.

The purpose of this study was to examine the well-being of unemployed people participating in programs which support their technical and vocational training. Usually, the impact of unemployment on well-being is measured by psychological distress, mental health, and satisfaction (Whelan and McGinnity, 2000). We examined a number of aspects of well-being including psychosomatic symptoms, anxiety/insomnia, social dysfunction, severe depression and state and trait anxiety. The aims of this study are: 1) to assess the well-being of unemployed participants, 2) to examine whether there are any gender and age differences in aspects of well-being, and 3) to test if psychological factors (personality traits and state and trait anger) and the personal system of interests and values are related to the well-being of the unemployed. The traditional deprivation perspective is concerned with negative effects of unemployment, while the coping perspective can provide a useful framework when dealing with resources that facilitate re-employment.

To summarize, we expected unemployed people to experience a low degree of well-being following the loss of a job, although earlier results regarding the connection between unemployment and mental health are mixed (Nyman, 2002). Furthermore, we expected that unemployed women would have higher well-being than men, due to their traditional lifestyle. Women are more "homemaker" oriented than men and they place as much or more emphasis on the home as a job (Zunker, 2002). We also expected that unemployment would exert relatively less negative effect (higher well-being) on younger persons than upon older persons.

Finally, following this conceptualization of coping perspective, we examined the relation of personality traits, anger experience, and the personal system of values and work interests to the well-being of the unemployed (psychosomatic symptoms, anxiety/insomnia, social dysfunction, severe depression and state and trait anxiety). We expected emotional stability and conscientiousness to predict positive well-being because people with low neuroticism and high achievement orientation are more likely to engage in job searching (Barrick and Mount, 1991). Extrinsic values were expected to be a positive predictor of negative well-being, because unemployed people with high extrinsic motivation are likely to experience their job search as stressful and harmful for their psychological well-being (Vansteenkiste, Lens, Dewitte, DeWitte, and Deci, 2004).

Method

PARTICIPANTS

The sample comprised 259 people, all of whom were unemployed according to the registration criteria, at the time of vocational training programs offered in the wider region of Athens. There were 61 (23.6%) males and 198 (76.4%) females. Over 28.3% (73) of participants were within the age range of 18 to 25 years, 52.5% (135) were within the range 26–45 years, and 19.4% within the range 46–64 years. There was one missing value with regard to age. All participants were recruited from Vocational Training Centers in the area of Athens.

Measures

WELL-BEING

Well-being was measured using two questionnaires: the General Health Questionnaire (GHQ) (Goldberg and Williams, 1988) and the State-Trait Anxiety Inventory for Adults (STAI) (Spielberger et al., 1995).

- The GHQ-28 (Goldberg and Williams, 1988) asks respondents to describe the level of their recent psychological state in relation to somatic symptoms, anxiety/insomnia, social dysfunction, and severe depression respectively. Responses are provided on a four-point scale: 1: not at all, 2: no more than usual, 3: rather more than usual, 4: much more than usual. The coefficient alphas were: for the Total Score 0.93; for Somatic Symptoms 0.80; for Anxiety and Insomnia 0.97; for Social Dysfunction 0.97; and for Severe Depression 0.97. The total scale score ranges from 28 to 112 and the higher the score the poorer the psychological well-being of the respondents. Subjects were classified as high and low on each of the measures respectively, using the Ward method.

- STAI (Spielberger et al., 1995) provides separate measures of state and trait anxiety using 40 questions. The "state anxiety" (questions 1–20) is a measure of the intensity of anxiety experienced at the time of assessment, while "trait anxiety" (questions 21–40) evaluates stable differences between people in their tendency to perceive a wider range of situations as threatening and in their disposition to experience intense elevations of state anxiety in such situations (Spielberger et al., 2005). The coefficient alphas were: for the Total Score 0.90; for Trait Anxiety 0.80; and for State Anxiety 0.91. Total scores range from a minimum of 20 to a maximum of 80 for trait and state anxiety with higher scores indicating more severe anxiety symptoms. Subjects were classified as high and low on state and trait anxiety respectively, using the Ward method.

PERSONALITY VARIABLES

- Personality traits were measured using a short version of the Adjective Check List–Five Factors (ACL-FF) (Williams, Satterwhite, and Saiz, 1998). The instrument measures neuroticism (N) ($\alpha = 0.70$), extraversion (E) ($\alpha = 0.60$), openness to experience (O) ($\alpha = 0.60$), agreeableness (A) ($\alpha = 0.74$), and conscientiousness (C) ($\alpha = 0.77$). Each scale has six items, and responses are scored on a seven-point rating scale, ranging from "not at all" to "very much."

- The State-Trait Anger Expression Inventory (STAXI-2) (Spielberger, 1988) includes seven independent subscales: State Anger (15 items), Trait Anger (10 items), Anger-in (8 items), Anger-out (8 items), and two anger control factors, Anger/Control-in (8 items) and Anger/Control-out (8 items). State anger ($\alpha = 0.95$) evaluates the level of anger experienced at the time of testing, while Trait anger ($\alpha = 0.87$) measures the general tendency of a person to get angry. The internal expression of anger (Anger-in) ($\alpha = 0.65$) indicates that angry feelings are held in or suppressed, while Anger-out ($\alpha = 0.64$) reflects the outward expression of angry feelings, verbally or via physical aggression towards other people or towards objects in the person's environment. The external control of anger (Anger Control-out) ($\alpha = 0.85$) focuses on anger control by relaxation and calming strategies, and, finally, the internal control of anger (Anger Control-in) ($\alpha = 0.84$) refers to an individual's attempts to control the outward expression of angry feelings. Higher scores on all scales (from one to four) indicate a greater experience of anger and propensity to experience it and a greater tendency to control and to express anger.

THE SYSTEM OF PERSONAL VALUES, INTEREST TYPES AND WORK VALUES

Personal values

The Schwartz Values Survey (Schwartz 1996) was used to determine a system of four types of higher-order values: openness-to-change (self-direction, $\alpha = 0.94$, stimulation, $\alpha = 0.94$), conservation (conformity, $\alpha = 0.92$, security, $\alpha = 0.97$, tradition, $\alpha = 0.97$), self-enhancement (achievement, $\alpha = 0.96$, hedonism, $\alpha = 0.95$, power, $\alpha = 0.86$), and self transcendence (benevolence, $\alpha = 0.62$, universalism, $\alpha = 0.68$). Openness-to-change values relate to the importance of personal autonomy and independence, variety, excitement, and challenge. Conservation values relate to the importance of self-control, safety, and stability in societal and personal relationships, and respecting cultural traditions. Self-enhancement values relate to achieving personal success through demonstrated competence, attaining social status and prestige, and control over others. Self-transcendence values relate to protecting and enhancing the well-being of those with whom one has close contact, as well as the welfare of all people and nature.

Vocational interests

The Vocational Interests Inventory for Adults was used (Holland, Reardon, Latshaw, Rarick, Schneider, Shortridge, and James, 2001) to study six dimensions or interest types. Realistic individuals enjoy working with mechanical devices and working outdoors using machines, tools and objects ($\alpha = 0.86$). Investigative individuals enjoy scientific pursuits, working with abstract ideas, researching and analyzing ($\alpha = 0.89$). Artistic individuals value aesthetics, using their imagination and creativity ($\alpha = 0.84$). Social individuals value service to others and enjoy teaching, helping, and working with people ($\alpha = 0.86$). Enterprising individuals value status and enjoy directing, organizing, and leading ($\alpha = 0.89$). Conventional individuals prefers structured tasks, enjoy practical pursuits and working with things, numbers, or machines to meet precise standards ($\alpha = 0.89$). Vocational interests types were measured using 48-items on a five-point Likert scale (1 = "strongly disinterested"; 5 = "strongly interested").

Work values

Based upon the categorization of values proposed by Super (1995), we used a Work Value Inventory, focused on six basic types of work values: 1) intellectual stimulation ($\alpha = 0.76$), which is associated with work that provides opportunity for independent thinking and learning how and why things work; 2) creativity

(α = 0.65), associated with work that permits individuals to invent new things, design new products or develop new ideas; 3) independence (α = 0.63), which permits individuals to work in their own way, doing what they want according to their level of achievement and direction; 4) group orientation (α = 0.72), associated with work that brings people into contact with fellow workers whom they like; 5) prestige (α = 0.75), associated with work that gives people standing in the eyes of others and evokes respect; and 6) security (α = 0.60), associated with work that provides people with the certainty of having a job, even in hard times. The Work Value Inventory consists of 38 items rated on a five-point Likert scale ranging from "not well at all" to "very well."

This study used the Greek versions of all instruments, which were provided by different authors (Antoniou and Dalla, 2008; Besevegis, Dalla, Gari, and Karademas, 2008; Stalikas, Triliva, and Roussi, 2002).

Results

WELL-BEING OF PARTICIPANTS

The first stage was to use Ward's method to evaluate the distances between people with high and low levels of general health and anxiety. The next step was to test the mean differences between the two groups: high versus low scores on the GHQ-28 and STAI, according to gender and age. One-way Anovas showed significant differences in all variables: Somatic Symptoms $F(1, 258)$ = 361.27, $p<0.001$, Anxiety and Insomnia $F(1, 258)$ = 147.43, $p<0.001$, Social Dysfunction $F(1, 258)$ = 190.34, $p<0.001$, Severe Depression $F(1, 258)$ = 463.662, $p<0.001$, Total GHQ-28 $F(1, 258)$ = 239.560, $p<0.001$; State Anxiety $F(1, 258)$ = 503.08, $p<0.001$, and Trait Anxiety $F(1, 258)$ = 487.60, $p<0.001$.

Means and standard deviations of low and high scores of GHQ-28 and STAI according to Ward analysis are presented in Table 17.1.

The following results (see Table 17.2) reflect crosstab analyses for the samples with low and high scores on GHQ-28 and STAI according to gender. The number of people who experienced high level of general health problems was 37 (7 males and 30 females). The group with the highest somatic symptoms consists of 37 people (7 males and 30 females), while 150 people (30 males and 120 females) experienced high level of anxiety and insomnia, 165 (44 males and 121 females) high social dysfunction, and high levels of severe depression were experienced by

Table 17.1 Means and standard deviation of low and high scores of GHQ-28 and STAI according to Ward analysis

	Low M	Low SD	High M	High SD	Total M	Total SD
GHQ-28						
Somatic Symptoms	9.81	2.40	17.97	2.52	10.98	3.74
Anxiety and Insomnia	8.22	1.85	14.29	3.21	11.74	4.05
Social Dysfunction	9.46	2.20	14.24	2.69	12.51	3.41
Severe Depression	7.25	1.21	14.30	4.01	9.10	3.88
Total GHQ-28	41.04	8.77	64.03	13.85	44.32	11.55
STAI						
State Anxiety	29.32	7.46	52.51	7.75	36.03	12.95
Trait Anxiety	29.43	6.30	48.34	7.46	37.68	11.61

Table 17.2 Participants with low and high scores of GHQ-28 and STAI according to Crosstab analysis

	Male Low f	Male Low %	Male High f	Male High %	Female Low f	Female Low %	Female High f	Female High %
GHQ-28								
Somatic Symptoms	54	88.5	7	11.5	168	84.8	30	14.3
Anxiety and Insomnia	31	50.8	30	49.2	78	71.6	120	60.6
Social Dysfunction	17	27.9	44	72.1	77	38.9	121	61.1
Severe Depression	43	70.5	18	29.5	148	74.7	50	25.3
Total GHQ-28	54	88.5	7	11.5	168	84.5	30	15.2
STAI								
State Anxiety	40	65.6	21	34.4	144	72.7	54	27.3
Trait Anxiety	42	68.9	19	31.1	104	52.5	94	47.5

68 people (18 males and 50 females). Regarding STAI, people reporting high state anxiety amounted to 75 (21 males and 54 females) and 113 participants (19 males and 94 females) experienced high trait anxiety. There were significantly more females than males experiencing high trait anxiety $\chi^2(1, n = 239) = 5.04$, p<0.05. There were no differences for scores on the GHQ-28 and STAI related to age.

AGE AND GENDER DIFFERENCES ON PERSONALITY AND ANGER EXPRESSION VARIABLES

Personality traits

Only neuroticism differentiated between men and women $F(1, 254) = 4.90$, p<0.05, $\eta^2 = 1.9\%$. Women seemed to be more nervous and emotional than men. Age was not significant for any of the personality variables (see Table 17.3).

Table 17.3   Means of personality and anger expression variables as a function of age and gender

	Age 18–25 M.	Age 26–45 M.	Age 46–64 M.	F	η^2	Male M.	Female M.	F	η^2
Check List–Five Factors Personality									
Neuroticism	3.02	3.02	2.81	0.68	0.005	2.79	3.12	4.90*	0.019
Extraversion	4.73	4.65	4.62	2.37	0.019	4.62	4.71	0.77	0.003
Openness	4.52	4.49	4.33	0.37	0.003	4.55	4.34	1.79	0.007
Agreeableness	5.49	5.34	5.78	0.13	0.001	5.45	5.61	0.26	0.001
Conscientiousness	5.58	5.38	5.97	3.45	0.027	5.52	5.78	1.96	0.008
State-Trait Anger Expression Inventory									
State Anger	1.26	1.30	1.13	2.40	0.019	1.32	1.21	1.61	0.006
Trait Anger	1.78	1.88	1.73	2.30	0.018	1.80	1.80	0.02	0.000
Anger-in	2.05	2.17	2.10	2.10	0.016	2.03	2.13	1.27	0.005
Anger-out	1.88	1.86	1.82	0.24	0.002	1.83	1.87	0.23	0.001
Control-in	1.93	1.94	1.91	0.78	0.006	1.92	1.93	0.06	0.000
Control-out	2.73	2.73	2.82	0.10	0.001	2.67	2.77	0.69	0.003

Note: * p<0.05.

State-trait anger expression inventory

There were no age or gender differences for State-Trait Inventory variables (see Table 17.3).

AGE AND GENDER DIFFERENCES ON PERSONAL VALUES

Personal values

Age of participants had a significant effect on preferred personal values (see Table 17.4). Young respondents (18–25 years) were more likely to believe in self direction $F(2, 257) = 6.35$, $p<0.01$, $\eta^2 = 4.8\%$, stimulation $F(2, 257) = 11.3$, $p<0.001$, $\eta^2 = 8.2\%$, achievement $F(2, 257) = 7.23$, $p<0.01$, $\eta^2 = 5.4\%$, hedonism $F(2, 257) = 6.82$, $p<0.01$, $\eta^2 = 4.8\%$, conformity $F(2, 257) = 6.68$, $p<0.01$, $\eta^2 = 5\%$, and power $F(2, 257) = 2.98$, $p<0.05$, $\eta^2 = 2.3\%$. Young (18–25) and older people (46–64) rated higher than people within the age range 26–46 years on security $F(2, 257) = 7.44$, $p<0.01$, $\eta^2 = 5.6\%$, tradition $F(2, 257) = 8.31$, $p<0.001$, $\eta^2 = 6.2\%$, benevolence $F(2, 257) = 8.43$, $p<0.01$, $\eta^2 = 6.3\%$, and universalism $F(2, 257) = 4.68$, $p<0.01$, $\eta^2 = 3.6\%$. There were also significant gender differences for stimulation $F(1, 257) = 6.99$,

Table 17.4 Means of personal value variables as a function of age and gender

	Age					Gender			
	18–25	26–45	46–64			Male	Female		
	M.	M.	M.	F	η^2	M.	M.	F	η^2
Self-direction	4.14a	2.95b	3.41b	6.35**	0.048	3.78	3.45	1.46	0.006
Stimulation	3.88a	2.52b	2.58b	11.3***	0.082	3.54	2.85	6.99**	0.027
Conformity	4.34a	3.16b	3.79 ab	6.68**	0.050	3.99	3.71	0.32	0.004
Security	4.48a	3.25b	4.12a	7.44**	0.056	4.06	3.93	0.67	0.001
Tradition	4.21a	3.05b	3.97a	8.31***	0.062	3.76	3.74	0.01	0.000
Achievement	4.08a	2.91b	3.41b	7.23**	0.054	3.67	3.42	0.87	0.003
Hedonism	4.34a	3.13b	3.61b	6.82**	0.048	3.92	3.65	0.09	0.004
Power	2.85a	2.07b	2.20b	2.98*	0.023	2.81	2.26	4.81*	0.019
Benevolence	4.37a	3.18b	4.07a	8.43***	0.063	3.98	3.85	0.22	0.001
Universalism	3.04a	3.84b	3.04a	4.68**	0.036	3.73	3.56	0.36	0.001

Note: * $p<0.05$; ** $p<0.01$; *** $p<0.001$.

p<0.01, $\eta^2 = 2.7\%$, and power $F(1, 257) = 4.81$, p<0.05, $\eta^2 = 1.9\%$, values. Men were more likely than women to believe in stimulation and power (see Table 17.4).

AGE AND GENDER DIFFERENCES ON INTEREST TYPES AND WORK VALUES

Interest types

Young respondents compared to older people are much more focused on activities that relate to realistic $F(2, 257) = 3.79$, p<0.05, $\eta^2 = 2.9\%$, investigative $F(2, 257) = 3.88$, p<0.05, $\eta^2 = 3.0\%$, and enterprising $F(2, 257) = 5.01$, p<0.01, $\eta^2 = 3.8\%$ occupations. Men rated higher than women on realistic occupations $F(1, 257) = 7.92$, p<0.01, $\eta^2 = 3.0\%$, and on investigative $F(1, 257) = 6.02$, p<0.05, $\eta^2 = 2.3\%$ and enterprising occupations $F(1, 257) = 5.13$, p<0.05, $\eta^2 = 2.0\%$ (see Table 17.5).

Table 17.5 Means of personal interest and work variables as a function of age and gender

	Age 18–25 M.	Age 26–45 M.	Age 46–64 M.	F	η^2	Male M.	Female M.	F	η^2
Interest types									
Realistic	2.18a	1.50ab	1.61b	3.79*	0.029	2.28	1.61	7.92**	0.030
Investigative	2.68a	1.87b	1.91b	3.88*	0.030	2.70	1.98	6.02*	0.023
Artistic	2.43	2.02	1.72	2.48	0.019	2.19	2.01	0.44	0.002
Social	2.80	2.11	2.34	2.46	0.019	2.57	2.36	0.49	0.002
Enterprising	2.78a	1.85b	2.04b	5.01**	0.038	2.73	2.07	5.13*	0.020
Conventional	2.80	2.16	2.12	2.25	0.018	2.50	2.30	0.39	0.002
Work values									
Intellectual stimulation	4.16	3.97	4.16	1.46	0.018	4.09	4.10	0.01	0.00
Creativity	3.53	3.28	3.26	1.27	0.015	3.43	3.34	0.37	0.002
Independence	3.77	3.65	3.44	1.89	0.023	3.46	3.68	1.82	0.011
Group orientation	4.37	4.27	4.51	1.42	0.017	4.22	4.45	4.53*	0.028
Prestige	3.84	3.52	3.64	1.28	0.017	3.74	3.64	0.46	0.003
Security	3.42	3.76	3.82	3.63	0.043	3.61	3.69	0.26	0.002

Note: * p<0.05; ** p<0.01.

Work values

There were no age differences for work values. Regarding gender, men rated lower than women on group orientation $F(1, 257) = 4.53$, $p<0.05$, $\eta^2 = 2.8\%$ (see Table 17.5).

REGRESSION ANALYSES PREDICTING WELL-BEING (GENERAL HEALTH, STATE AND TRAIT ANXIETY) OF PARTICIPANTS FROM PERSONALITY AND WORK-RELATED VARIABLES

Somatic symptoms

According to regression analyses, participants with high neuroticism $\beta = 0.18$, $t = 2.36$, $p<0.01$, high agreeableness $\beta = 0.21$, $t = 2.97$, $p<0.01$, low extraversion $\beta = -0.17$, $t = -2.24$, $p<0.05$, and low conscientiousness $\beta = -0.19$, $t = -2.61$, $p<0,01$ had higher levels of somatic symptoms. Furthermore, high state $\beta = 0.19$, $t = 2.70$, $p<0.01$ and trait anger $\beta = 0.21$, $t = 2.56$, $p<0.01$ was positively related to high levels of somatic symptoms. Low levels of personal values of self-direction $\beta = -0.60$, $t = -2.67$, $p<0.01$ and security $\beta = -0,61$, $t = -2.34$, $p<0.05$, and high levels of benevolence $\beta = 0.50$, $t = 2.38$, $p<0.05$ and universality $\beta = 0.35$, $t = 2.32$, $p<0.05$ were also related to high levels of somatic symptoms. A low level of independence was related to high levels of somatic symptoms $\beta = -0,40$, $t = -2.14$, $p<0.01$ (see Table 17.6).

Anxiety-insomnia

High neuroticism $\beta = 0.22$, $t = 3.50$, $p<0.01$, high agreeableness $\beta = 0.26$, $t = 3.42$, $p<0.01$ and high state $\beta = 0.22$, $t = 3.26$, $p<0.01$ and trait anger $\beta = 0.32$, $t = 3.95$, $p<0.001$ predicted anxiety-insomnia (see Table 17.6).

Social dysfunction

High neuroticism $\beta = 0.19$, $t = 2.70$, $p<0.01$, high agreeableness $\beta = 0.17$, $t = 1.96$, $p<0.05$, and high state $\beta = 0.14$, $t = 1.82$, $p<0.05$ and trait anger $\beta = 0.18$, $t = 1,91$, $p<0.05$ predicted social dysfunction. Furthermore, work values of independence are positively $\beta = 0.36$, $t = 1.99$, $p<0.05$ related to social dysfunction (see Table 17.6).

Severe depression

High agreeableness β = 0.30, t = 3.52, p<0.01, low extraversion β = -0.30, t = -3.73, p<0.001, and high state β = 0.23, t = 3.08, p<0.01 and trait anger β = 0.23, t = 2.61, p<0.01 were significant predictors of severe depression (see Table 17.6).

State anxiety

High agreeableness β = 0.17, t = 1.93, p<0.05, low extraversion β = -0.20, t = -2.44, p<0.01, high state anger β = 0.32, t = 4.18, p<0.05, and low external control of anger β = -0.15, t = -2.1, p<0.05 were significantly related to high state anxiety (see Table 17.6).

Trait anxiety

Low extraversion β = -0.24, t = -3.14, p<0.01, high trait anger β = 0.38, t = 4.53, p<0.001, high anger-in β = 0.17, t = 2.19, p<0.05, and low external control of anger β = -0.16, t = -2.35, p<0.05 were related to high trait anxiety. Furthermore, individuals valuing service to others and working with other people tended to experience more state anxiety β = 0.44, t = 2.88, p<0.01 (see Table 17.6).

In general, women reported higher somatic symptoms and trait anxiety than men (see Table 17.6).

Discussion

In this cross-sectional study, we investigated the well-being of unemployed people according to gender and age using the GHQ-28 (Goldberg and Williams, 1988) and State-Trait Anxiety Inventory for Adults (Spielberger et al., 1995). Our main finding is that more than 50 percent of unemployed people experience high levels of anxiety/insomnia and increased social dysfunction. Our results also indicated that for 15 percent of unemployed people the level of somatic symptoms is high, and 26 percent of the sample reported high severe depression. Similarly, most people report high trait and state anger (more than 50 percent). An important finding is that most unemployed individuals have negative subjective well-being. It has been shown in past research that unemployment as a psychological and social concept has a negative effect on the mental health of individuals (Blanchflower and Oswald, 2004). For individuals who lose their jobs, it is not just the loss of income or financial benefits that matter, it is also the loss of latent functions of work (Frey and Stutzer, 2002).

Table 17.6 Hierarchical regression for the prediction of well being (general health and state trait anxiety) from gender, age, personality and work variables

	Somatic symptoms	Anxiety-insomnia	Social dysfunction	Depression	State anxiety	Trait anxiety
	β	β	β	β	β	β
1. Gender	0.14*	0.07	0.02	0.04	0.07	0.15**
2. Age	0.07	0.05	0.07	0.11	0.10	-0.02
3. Check list – five factors personality						
Neuroticism	0.18**	0.22**	0.19**	0.10	0.06	0.07
Extraversion	-0.17*	-0.08	-0.14	-0.30***	-0.20**	-0.24**
Openness	0.11	0.03	0.08	0.08	0.008	0.05
Agreeableness	0.21**	0.26**	0.17*	0.30**	0.17*	0.03
Conscientiousness	-0.19**	-0.14	-0.14	-0.10	0.02	-0.02
4. State-trait anger expression inventory						
State anger	0.19**	0.22**	0.14*	0.23**	0.32*	0.08
Trait anger	0.21**	0.32***	0.18*	0.23**	0.07	0.38***
Anger-in	0.08	0.11	0.12	0.11	-0.03	0.17*
Anger-out	0.13	-0.08	-0.09	-0.01	-0.07	-0.26
Control-in	-0.24	-0.05	-0.02	-0.14	-0.05	0.22
Control-out	0.01	-0.16	-0.03	-0.07	-0.15*	-0.16*
5. Personal values						
Self-direction	-0.60**	0.06	-0.13	0.13	-0.16	-0.36
Stimulation	0.10	-0.06	-0.10	0.07	0.18	0.14
Conformity	-0.08	-0.09	-0.12	-0.02	-0.07	-0.15
Security	-0.61*	-0.14	0.37	-0.02	0.09	-0.11
Tradition	-0.31	-0.07	-0.36	-0.37	-0.34	-0.26
Achievement	0.22	-0.01	0.14	0.19	-0.06	0.28
Hedonism	0.16	-0.09	-0.14	-0.04	0.27	0.19
Power	0.02	0.19	-0.08	-0.07	0.02	-0.17
Benevolence	0.50*	-0.08	0.23	0.04	-0.03	0.27
Universalism	0.35*	0.09	0.05	0.31	-0.22	-0.05

Table 17.6 continued

	Somatic symptoms	Anxiety-insomnia	Social dysfunction	Depression	State anxiety	Trait anxiety
	β	β	β	β	β	β
6. Interest types						
Realistic	0.01	-0.04	-0.06	0.01	0.01	-0.02
Investigative	0.10	0.01	-0.02	0.02	0.04	-0.12
Artistic	-0.15	0.17	0.06	-0.06	0.08	-0.05
Social	0.16	0.10	-0.14	-0.07	0.05	0.44**
Enterprising	0.12	-0.19	0.25	0.15	0.06	-0.04
Conventional	-0.22	-0.07	-0.07	0.03	-0.19	0.09
7. Work values						
Intellectual stimulation	0.16	-0.12	0.25	-0.25	-0.07	0.10
Creativity	-0.08	0.23	-0.07	0.10	-0.26	0.16
Independence	-0.40**	0.01	0.36*	0.28	0.02	-0.16
Group orientation	-0.20	0.07	-0.48	-0.06	0.34	-0.31
Prestige	0.14	-0.02	-0.19	0.21	0.16	0.22
Security	-0.17	-0.02	-0.05	-0.14	0.08	0.12

Note: * p<0.05; ** p<0.01; *** p<0.001.

However, not all unemployed people experience low levels of well-being. In evaluating the effect of unemployment on individual well-being, individual, familiar, and macroeconomic variables should be considered (Blanchflower and Oswald, 2004). For example, employment is a key element of individual and social well-being for those who wish to work (Clark, 2010). Family relations also moderate the stress of unemployment (Berkman and Glass, 2000). Unemployment benefit systems and other determinants of job finding probabilities are important factors behind the consequences of unemployment for individual well-being (Clark, 2010).

The study results demonstrate no differences between men and women in general health. However, a greater number of unemployed women report high trait anxiety and neuroticism. These findings do not provide any support for the hypothesis of differences between unemployed men and women, but they are consistent with the observation that in adulthood, the prevalence of anxiety is much higher in women than in men (WHO, 2005). Current explanations for these gender differences (internalizing versus externalizing) refer to the greater susceptibility of women to conformity pressures (Berry, Poortinga, Segall, and Dasen, 1992/2002).

Furthermore, females are socialized to be more concerned than males when forming connections with others and are therefore more affected by relational stresses (De Coster, 2005). This finding is confirmed by our study which indicates that females are more impulsive than men in personality traits, and more group-oriented in the work place. On the other hand, men scored significantly higher than women on the power and stimulation values and showed an increased preference for realistic, investigative and enterprising types of occupations. Stimulation and power emphasize the affective autonomy and the legitimacy of a hierarchical role, whereas group orientation indicates that interests of the group are not seen as distinct from those of the individual.

The hypothesis that unemployment exerts fewer psychological problems on younger people than upon older persons is not supported. For all age groups, becoming unemployed did not elicit differences on well-being, on trait and state anxiety, and other personality variables such as personality traits and anger experience and expression. There is evidence supporting the argument that the psychological costs of unemployment go beyond those arising from age (Winefield, 2002).

What are the psychological factors related to the low well-being of unemployed people? According to our results, unemployed women experience the largest reduction in psychological and physical health. The main determinants of the negative mental health of unemployed people are neuroticism, agreeableness, state and trait anger, and self-transcendence values (universalism, benevolence) that emphasize equality among people. Furthermore, social individuals valuing service to others, understanding, and empathy experience more anxiety than other unemployed people.

The negative correlation between extraversion and well-being indicates that social interaction and assertive behavior reduce the harmful effect of unemployment on well-being. Unemployed individuals with high extraversion experience fewer somatic symptoms and less severe depression, and less state and trait anxiety. The other determinants of positive well-being (low somatic symptoms and low trait and state anxiety) are; 1) conscientiousness, characterized by achievement motivation and organization, 2) anger control-out, reducing the intensity of anger by relaxing, 3) high self direction and security values. Work independence that allows individuals to work in their own way, doing what they want according to their level of achievement and direction, is associated with low somatic symptoms but high social dysfunction.

In summary, unemployment is widely considered to have negative effects on well-being (Clark, Georgellis, and Sanfey, 2001), but our results do not provide support for this hypothesis. An important proportion of unemployed people reported positive well-being which is associated with low neuroticism, high achievement motivation, low social isolation, high self direction, high safety, and stability in societal and personal relationships. People with positive well-being are less likely to experience frequent intense angry feelings, and more likely to invest in attempts to monitor and prevent negative expressions.

Previous studies have demonstrated that the health-related effects resulting from unemployment are considered highly heterogeneous across countries (Kieselbach, 2000). In Greece, in general, the health problems of long-term unemployed young people are seen as a pre-existing condition and are not considered as a result of unemployment. Furthermore, the high level of family support is viewed as a protective factor for unemployed people (Kieselbach, 2000). From the perspective of coping theory, most unemployed people have resources to cope with the problem and to maintain a normal way of life. On the contrary, an important proportion of unemployed people lose the manifest (income) and latent functions of work, and this has a negative impact on their psychological well-being.

References

Antoniou, S. and Dalla, M. (2008). Immigration, unemployment and career counseling: a multicultural perspective. In A.S. Antoniou, C. Cooper, G. Chrousos, Ch. Spielberger, and M. Eysenck (eds), *Handbook of Managerial Behavior and Occupational Health* (pp. 311–28). Northampton, MA: Edward Elgar.

Artazcoz, L., Benach, J., Borrell, C., and Cortes, I. (2004). Unemployment and mental health: understanding the interactions among gender, family roles, and social class. *American Journal of Public Health*, 94, 82–8.

Barrick, M.B. and Mount, K.M. (1991). The big five personality dimensions and job performance: a meta-analysis. *Personnel Psychology*, 44, 1–26.

Berkman, L.F. and Glass, T. (2000). Social integration, social networks, social support, and health. In L.F. Berkman and I. Kawachi (eds), *Social Epidemiology* (pp. 137–73). Oxford: Oxford University Press.

Berry, J.W., Poortinga, Y.H., Segall, M.H., and Dasen, P.R. (1992/2002). *Cross-cultural Psychology: Research and Applications*. New York: Cambridge University Press.

Besevegis, E., Dalla, M., Gari, A., and Karademas, C.E. (2008). The adaptation of State-State Anger Expression Inventory (STAXI-II) in the Greek language (in Greek). *Psychology*, 15(2), 171–88.

Blanchflower, D. and Oswald, A. (2004). Well-being over time in Britain and the USA. *Journal of Public Economics*, 88, 1359–86.

Catalano, R., Raymond, N., and William, M. (2002). Layoffs and violence revisited. *Aggressive Behavior*, 28, 233–47.

Clark, A.E. (2010). Work, jobs and well-being across the millennium. In E. Diener, J. Helliwell, and D. Kahneman (eds), *International Differences in Well-Being* (pp. 436–68). Oxford: Oxford University Press.

Clark, A., Georgellis, Y., and Sanfey, P. (2001). Scarring: the psychological impact of past unemployment. *Economica*, 68, 221–41.

De Coster, S. (2005). Depression and law violation: gendered responses to gendered stresses. *Sociological Perspectives*, 48, 155–87.

Deci, E.L. and Ryan, R.M. (2002). *Handbook of Self-Determination Research*. Rochester, NY: The University of Rochester Press.

Dooley, D., Prause, J., and Ham-Rowbottom, K. (2000). Underemployment and depression: longitudinal relationships. *Journal of Health and Social Behavior*, 41, 421–36.

Elizur, D., Borg, I., Hunt, R., and Beck, I.M. (1991). The structure of work values: a cross-cultural comparison. *Journal of Organizational Behavior*, 12, 313–22.

Erez, A. and Judge, T.A. (2001). Relationship of core self-evaluations to goal setting, motivation, and performance. *Journal of Applied Psychology*, 86, 1270–79.

Frey, B.S. and Stutzer, A. (2002). *Happiness and Economics*. Princeton, NJ: Princeton University Press.

Georgas, J. (1989). Changing family values in Greece: from collectivist to individualist. *Journal of Cross-Cultural Psychology*, 20, 80–91.

Goldberg, D. and Williams, P. (1988). *A User's Guide to the General Health Questionnaire*. Windsor: NFER Nelson.

Goul Andersen, J. (2001). Coping with long-term unemployment: economic security, labour market integration and well-being. Paper prepared for the ESF/EURESCU conference "Labour Market Change, Unemployment and Citizenship in Europe", Helsinki, April 20–25, 2001.

Greenhaus, J.H., Callanan, G.A., and Godshalk, V.M. (2000). *Career Management*, 3rd edn. Orlando, FL: Harcourt.

Halvorsen, K. (2004). *How to Combat Unemployment?* Centre for Comparative Welfare Studies (CCWS) Department of Economics, Politics and Public Administration, Aalborg University. [Online]. Available at: http://www.epa.aau.dk/fileadmin/user_upload/ime/CCWS/workingpapers/2004-32-Howtocombatunemployment-knut.pdf [Accessed: 20 October 2007].

Holland, J.L., Reardon, R.C., Latshaw, R.J., Rarick, S.R., Schneider, S., Shortridge, M.A., and James, S.A. (2001). *Self-Directed Search Form R Internet Version 2.0*. [Online]. Available: http://www.self-directed-search.com [Accessed: 20 February 2002].

International Labour Organisation (2007). *Global Employment Trends Brief*. Geneva: ILO.

International Research Team (1987). *The Meaning of Working*. London: Academic Press.

Jahoda, M. (1982). *Employment and Unemployment: A Social-Psychological Analysis*. Cambridge: Cambridge University Press.

Kieselbach, T. (2000). *Long-term Unemployment among Young People in Europe: A Qualitative Comparative Study for Psychology of Work, Unemployment and Health (IPG)*. EU-Workshop on Unemployment, Work and Welfare. European Commission (DG Research), Brussels, 9–11 November.

Layard, R. (2005). *Happiness: Lessons from a New Science*. New York: Penguin.

Lazarus, R.S. (1996). The role of coping in the emotions and how coping changes over the life course. In C. Magai and S.H. McFadden (eds), *Handbook of Emotion, Adult Development, and Aging* (pp. 289–306). San Diego, CA: Academic Press.

MacDonald, Z. and Shields, M.A. (2001). The impact of alcohol consumption on occupational attainment in England. *Economica*, 68, 427–53.

Nyman, J. (2002). *Does Unemployment Contribute to Ill-being: Results from a Panel. Study among Adult Finns, 1989/90 and 1997*. National Health Institute, A4/2002.

Organization for Economic Cooperation and Development (2009). *OECD Harmonized Unemployment Rates*. (May 11) Paris: OECD. Available at: http://www.oecd.org/ dataoecd/9/6/42721197.pdf [Accessed: 20 May 2008].

Phillips, H.L., Henry, D.J., Hosie, A.J., and Milne, B.A. (2006). Age, anger regulation and well-being. *Aging and Mental Health*, 10(3), 250–56.

Roccas, S., Sagiv, L., Schwartz, H.S., and Knafo, A. (2002). The big five personality factors and personal values. *Personality and Social Psychology Bulletin*, 28, 789–801.

Rodríguez, E., Frongillo, E.A., and Chandra, P. (2001). Do social programmes contribute to mental well-being? The long-term impact of unemployment on depression in the United States. *International Journal of Epidemiology*, 30, 163–70.

Rokeach, M. (1973). *The Nature of Human Values*. New York: The Free Press.

Schwartz, S.H. (1996). Value priorities and behavior: applying a theory of integrated value systems. In C. Seligman, J.M. Olson, and M.P. Zanna (eds), *The Psychology of Values: The Ontario Symposium*, vol. 8 (pp. 1–24). Hillsdale, NJ: Erlbaum.

Spielberger, C.D. (1988). *Manual for the State-Trait Anger Expression Inventory (STAXI)*. Odessa, FL: Psychological Assessment Resources.

Spielberger, C.D., Moscoso, M.S., and Brunner, Th.M. (2005). Cross-cultural assessment of emotional states and personality traits. In R.K. Hambleton, C.D. Spielberger, and P.F. Merenda (eds), *Adapting Educational and Psychological Tests for Cross-Cultural Assessment* (pp. 343–68). Mahwah, NJ: Erlbaum.

Spielberger, C.D., Reheiser, E.C., Ritterband, L.M., Sydeman, S.J., and Unger, K.K. (1995). Assessment of emotional states and personality traits: measuring psychological vital signs. In J.N. Butcher (ed.), *Clinical Personality Assessment: Practical Approaches* (pp. 42–58). New York: Oxford University Press.

Stalikas, A., Triliva, S., and Roussi, P. (2002). *Psychometric Instruments in Greece* (in Greek). Athens: Ellinika Grammata.

Super, D. (1995). Values: their nature, assessment, and practical use. In D.E. Super and B. Sverko (eds), *Life Roles, Values, and Careers* (pp. 54–61). San Francisco, CA: Jossey Bass.

Ukpere, W.I. and Slabbert, A.D. (2009). A relationship between current globalization, unemployment, inequality and poverty. *International Journal of Social Economics*, 36, 37–46.

Vansteenkiste, M., Lens, W., Dewitte, S., DeWitte, H., and Deci, E.L. (2004). The "why" and "why not" of job search behaviour: their relation to searching, unemployment experience and wellbeing. *European Journal of Social Psychology*, 34, 345–63.

VicHealth (1999). *Mental Health Promotion Plan Foundation Document: 1999–2002*. Melbourne, Victorian Health Promotion Foundation.

Waters, L. and Moore, K. (2002). Reducing latent deprivation during unemployment: the role of meaningful leisure activity. *Journal of Occupational and Organizational Psychology*, 75, 15–32.

Whelan, C.T. and McGinnity, F. (2000). Unemployment and satisfaction: a European analysis. In D. Gallie and S. Paugam (eds), *Welfare Regimes and the Experience of Unemployment in Europe* (pp. 286–306). Oxford: Oxford University Press.

WHO (2005). *Gender in Mental Health Research*. Geneva: WHO.
Williams, J.E., Satterwhite, R.C., and Saiz, J.L. (1998). *The Importance of Psychological Traits: A Cross-cultural Study*. New York: Plenum.
Winefield, A.H. (2002). The psychology of unemployment. In L. Bäckman and C. von Hofsten (eds), *Psychology at the Turn of the Millennium: Social, Developmental and Clinical Perspectives* (vol. 2, pp. 393–408). Hove: Psychology Press.
Zunker, V.G. (1998). *Career STH Counseling: Applied Concepts of Life Planning*. Pacific Grove, CA: Brooks/Cole Publishing.
Zunker, V.G. (2002). *Career Counseling: Applied Concepts of Life Planning*, 6th edn. Pacific Grove, CA: Brooks/Cole Publishing.

PART V
Specific Issues of Occupational Health Psychology

18

Brain versus Nature: How the Internet Affects Physical Activity

Panagiotis Perros and Alexander-Stamatios Antoniou

Introduction

Gutenberg's introduction of moveable type and the printing press revolutionized the way in which scientific and other ideas and research could be shared, creating the potential for humankind to reap massive benefits. But how accessible were sources of knowledge to those on the other side of the world? How much effort would be required to collect this knowledge in order to develop scientific or art and literature research? It is well known that scientists and artists are continuously learning how to discover knowledge and useful data, but when their access to the sources is limited, the potential for development is also restricted.

The Internet has for some time now been considered the ultimate solution for data storage and publishing, providing straightforward and easy access to data, communication with people, and interaction with institutions, organizations, and various commercial activities. Moreover it saves a great deal of time. A researcher only has to care about her work and its rational progress. There's no need to deal with travel plans and costs, transportation inconveniences, and pointless meetings. Furthermore, the Internet provides pure usable data, though it could be questioned how "natural" are the processes involved in attaining it. Mining and using data from the Internet tends to be an introverted mental activity lacking real life, real time interaction with the environment. However, the ease of using the Internet is by itself so attractive that it can result in a constant, tireless desire to acquire and employ new technologies. Consequently software has become an instant problem-solver which tends to replace other traditional ways of solving problems.

The Internet, however, is not only utilized to promote science, art, and rational thought in general. It is often used to promote new forms of entertainment and recreation. Technology has an almost magical ability to engage a person's imagination by producing an ideal virtual environment in which that person can turn almost every aspect of it towards satisfying their own personal pleasures. Moreover, this kind of entertainment appears to be safer and easier than, for instance, playing soccer in a dirty alley with its associated risk of physical pain and injury.

Rational thought, science, and logic tend to create a new kind of reality, one that ignores or suppresses the rules of nature. This highlights a dualistic concept—a "battle" between the truth deriving from our minds and the truth originating from nature—that has a heritage stretching back to pre-Socratic philosophers and especially Thales, who was the first to form a rational band of primary (though actually rather naïve in the perspective of later thought and science) logic rules to explain the origin and development of the world. This thought launched the study of science and furthermore initiated the idea that we are not manipulated by nature, rather the opposite, we could dominate nature, we could put nature under scientific examination, under the microscope of the most thorough scientific investigators. As a result, we have become something else, and it is logic that provides the rules. Are we, however, ready to face the physical consequences of such a radical change in our civilization?

Misapprehending Physical Activity: The Case of Cyber Sexual Behavior

The most common case of misreading physical activity takes place when the semantic borders between the physical world and the Internet seem quite uncertain. Even in the seventeenth century philosophers believed that we are maybe misled by sensory information and that we could actually be prisoners of a virtual world or a plausible dream (Descartes, 1641). Nowadays technology has come to obscure further the limits of real and virtual life as virtual experience tends to become even more concrete and tangible. A representative instance of this kind of misapprehension is the cyber sexual interaction. As widely known

> *Cybersex is a subcategory of online sexual activities (OSA) and is defined as when two or more people are engaging in sexual talk while online for the purposes of sexual pleasure and may or may not include*

masturbation. Cybersex is a growing phenomenon with a significant impact on participants. (Daneback et al., 2005)

This kind of activity usually involves two individuals participating in a fantasy which is not necessarily mutual. Each one enjoys different kinds of feelings without being in direct physical contact with the other. However, cyber sexual activity could even take place with just one individual expressing his or her one-sided sexual activity while accessing websites with adult content. This kind of Internet surfing has become a very common online behavior, leading to the belief that pornography is more vivid and attractive than ever before (Renshaw, 2007). This vividness has led some to consider the virtual world synonymous with the physical world.

With regard to close human-to-human interaction (such as sexual activity) the absence of touch and physical contact can be seen as an obstacle to the simultaneous reciprocation of feelings, a situation which, in its continuous and systematic expression, psychology might describe as "sexual autism." Such behavior could be considered normal during teenage life (as a primary stage of future normal sexual activity) but it usually indicates a pathological behavior among adults (Askitis, 2008). Indeed, an adult who systematically prefers cyber sexual instead of physical activity could easily become sexually distant or even sexually timorous. Furthermore, the anonymity and safety promised by the Internet could in some cases lead to the quick and easy spread of illegal activity such as trafficking and child exploitation (Ferraro et al., 2004). Illegal activity aside, constant cyber sex isolation has proved to be a mainly problematic behavior concerning the field of sexual (and consequently cyber-sexual) compulsivity, a condition defined as "an insistent, repetitive, intrusive, and unwanted urge to perform specific acts often in ritualized or routinized fashions" (Kalichman and Rompa, 1995). Moreover, someone addicted to expressing his or her sexuality through cyber, mostly virtual means tends to confuse their physical and cyber lives without being able to discern the barriers between the brain-made world and the conventional natural world. Such behavior is accompanied by high levels of distress (Cooper et al., 2000) when an individual cannot pro-actively control his or her (cyber) sexual compulsivity levels.

A more prudent approach to cyber life could include more moderate Internet behavior. Despite the fact that online activities like cyber sex may result in some kind of addiction (when pathologically repeated), such activity may also occasion a more social expression. In this regard, cyber sexual activity (as a moderate, non-pathological habit) can result in promoting real-world, natural sexual activity, as recent research has declared (Daneback et al., 2005). Indeed, individuals engaged in cyber sex tend to have more offline sex partners than those not engaging in cyber sex. This may of course increase the risk of contracting and spreading sexually transmitted diseases (McFarlane and Bull, 2007) but it does not in any case promote the virtual world over the real one. When participated in moderately, activity in the virtual world boosts participation in a conventional, natural life.

Promoting Physical Activity

Medical sources assure us that a virtual environment can actually offer the potential for significant gains in cognitive function. This has been proved during rehabilitation procedures among patients suffering from brain injuries (Grealy et al., 1999). Broadening the axiological examination of the Internet and computer applications in regard to human nature, we can nowadays observe that a virtual environment, apart from improving brain functions, can become a tool of physical activity, boosting the ideal of healthy living in a more direct way. Indeed, in the field of preventive medicine the Internet is considered a great opportunity to move beyond the heretofore reliance on strictly face-to-face modes of communication and a chance to begin to use newer technologies more comprehensively (Marcus et al., 2000), promoting physical activity with interactive communications. For instance, during the last few years fitness equipment (e.g. treadmills) directly connected to the Internet for downloading exercise guidelines and programs without the need for a personal trainer have been introduced into the marketplace. In fact, Internet and computer technology can improve the sport experience for all. For instance, through computer technology, sport can be made a safer and more enjoyable experience that should contribute to the emotional and physical well-being of all participants (Katz, 2003). Apart from useful software, web-based video or streaming video on demand, and participating in multimedia platforms can help us exercise more effectively, even utilizing a personalized methodology based on the user's submitted data.

The potential benefits of the Internet are not restricted to just physical activity though. It can also make us more extravert, willing to travel, to take ourselves physically to different parts of the world. We can become familiar with places we've never been before. Furthermore, we can transcend doctrines and prejudices held regarding foreign societies and nations. For example, a young Greek boy living in a remote village in northern Greece sometimes hears his grandmother say that Sicily is the home of the mafia and that it is therefore a very hazardous place to visit, even on a one-off vacation. Such prejudice, passed from generation to generation, and which Internet access could help undermine, ignores the reality of this beautiful region of Italy.

Published in the 1970s, the famous book *Midnight Express* (Hayes, 1977) (which was later made into a successful film) describes the utter and surreal ordeal that a convicted hashish smuggler endured while incarcerated in the Turkish prison system. The book describes a system designed to devalue human existence and destroy human dignity. As a result of this so-called "nightmarish narrative" a wide belief was formed among people in the United States and other countries that Turkey was not a hospitable place to visit. Similarly, in recent years, the popular horror film *Hostel* depicted tourists visiting Bratislava in Slovakia following the temptations of a beautiful woman and later discovering that they had been sold to a sadistic group that intended to torture and kill them. The plot presented the sadistic group as being protected by Slovakian authorities and by some money-grabbing locals (*Hostel*, 2005). What image would average citizens of, for example, the United States form regarding Turkey and Slovakia when weighing up options for a summer holiday if they didn't have access to information that could dispel the impressions established by *Midnight Express* and *Hostel*? Most likely, a negative one. Fortunately, the Internet makes information easily accessible and removes any dependence on bestselling books and films. The Internet enables us to explore Slovakia and Turkey online, to learn about daily life and traditions and even to communicate with Slovak or Turkish people by email, through online communities, and via live chat applications. Prejudices about "bad foreigners" or even "barbarians" can reduce one's physical activities (traveling, walking, coming into real-world contact with other people), resulting in an intense introversion and unsocial xenophobic behavior. But for those who really know how to obtain and make use of genuine information on the Internet, prejudices can soon be swept away.

Considering the above mentioned example, the Internet can be seen to promote extraversion when employed as a tool to extend real-life social behavior: for example, when someone who owns a bicycle joins a club of other cyclists who organize weekly excursions. Considering bicycles are not so popular in some European capitals, such as Athens, the Internet could be highly valuable to an Athenian cyclist seeking friends to help her escape what for her has become the boredom and isolation of cycling alone. Consequently, in direct or indirect ways, the Internet can help us improve our standards of living by promoting extraverted behavior and physical exercise.

Reducing Physical Activity

How can the Internet reduce physical activity in general? As already mentioned, parents might assume that their 11-year old boy would be safer and more secure playing a web-based RPG (role playing game) than risking his physical integrity in a dirty alley playing soccer or basketball with a bunch of other children. But what do parents achieve by maintaining such behavior? Should they care that their son's weight could be increased if he reduced his physical activity? It is commonly known that more than a quarter of US children are considered obese and that this number is increasing dramatically. It is also widely known that physical activity can reduce body fat and blood pressure and improve lipoprotein profile in obese individuals (Bar-or et al., 1998). So by keeping our children from engaging in physical activity out of the fear that they may injure themselves, we actually contribute to their future weak health. Furthermore, the "safe and easy" Internet could become an addiction, especially for children. When, for a child, having fun, meeting (even virtual) new friends, and exploring new worlds merely requires a few clicks of a mouse, Internet surfing can easily become addictive.

In a study conducted in Korea, Internet users were investigated in terms of Internet over-use and related psychological profiles. Among 13,588 users (7,878 males, 5,710 females), 3.5 percent were diagnosed Internet addicts (IA), while 18.4 percent were classified possible Internet addicts (PA).

> *The Internet Addiction Scale showed a strong relationship with dysfunctional social behaviors. More IA tried to escape from reality than PA and Non-addicts (NA). When they got stressed out by work or were just depressed, IA showed a high tendency to access the Internet. The IA group also reported the highest degree of loneliness, depressed mood, and compulsivity compared to the other groups. The IA group seemed to be more vulnerable to interpersonal dangers than others, showing an unusually close feeling for strangers. (Whang et al., 2003)*

Taking these statistics into consideration, for a young boy to incur injury during a neighborhood soccer game should be preferable to him adopting persistent unsociable behavior that could also lead to serious health problems.

However, not only children and youths are susceptible to "Internet addiction." It can occur in all ages: "Why not shop online, rather than go to the mall?" "Why not chat and flirt online, rather than go for a walk with a couple of friends?" "Why not surf instead of walk?" These are not untypical thoughts of an average middle-aged individual. Although such thoughts are often only occasional, when someone tends constantly to avoid being social and/or physically active, they may cross the threshold of "Internet addiction." Moreover, it is commonly recognized that the Internet has many more seductive properties than anyone would have imagined some years ago. Leung found that those considered Internet "dependents" spend most of their time in the synchronous communication environment, seeking pleasure or escape in interactive online games, chat rooms, and ICQ, while "non-dependents" tend to use the information-gathering functions of the Internet (Leung, 2004). This leads us to conclude that non-addictive personalities tend to view the Internet merely as a useful tool (Ito and Okabe, 2003), while addictive personalities view it as a way of life. In this latter view, the Internet is not just a tool, it is not just a way to communicate, it is the communication itself. In this framework the Internet appears to have an independent value: it contains brand new ideas; it may form a completely new ideological system. Consequently, without realizing it, we are endorsing the commonly held belief that the Internet is morally neutral, and in the process avoiding asking ourselves questions about the essential ethical issues pertinent to Internet and technology use in general (Rowe, 1990). Nonetheless, although philosophical and active thinking has to continue, we would prefer to be seen as technology users rather than technology addicts.

Substituting Physical Activity

> *If anybody asks me what the Internet means to me, I will tell him without hesitation: To me (a quadriplegic) the Internet occupies the most important part in my life. It is my feet that can take me to any part of the world; it is my hands which help me to accomplish my work; it is my best friend – it gives my life meaning. (Zhangxu and Aldis, 2001)*

For people with kinetic disabilities the Internet is the main gateway to the physical world. A disabled person has many obstacles to overcome in order to attend university lessons, to solve bureaucracy problems, or even to be among the audience of a music festival or a public political debate. Nevertheless, all of this and much more is accessible online through Internet multimedia technology. A number of studies have examined thoroughly the field of

Internet use in relation to disabled people (Foo and Theng, 2005) generating useful statistics (Pilling et al., 2004). Furthermore, many companies and individuals construct their websites using universal design concepts (Duckett, 2005) and commonly established accessibility guidelines (Hofstader, 2004). Indeed, the global effort to make the Internet a user-friendly world (Paciello, 2000) for both able bodied and disabled people is captured in the motto: "By making an online place accessible for a disabled person, we make it usable for all" (Gillinson at al., 2004). Even technology—such as screen-readers (ADE Glossary, 2008)—designed especially for visually impaired people, often proves to be useful to all.

The Internet can also give people a second-chance physical world. Since the early 1990s the term "netizen" has defined citizens who utilize the Internet from their home, workplace, school, library, or other location, populating the Internet and making it a human resource. Hence these netizens participate in making the Internet both an intellectual and a social resource (Licklider and Taylor, 1994). The Internet is no longer merely a tool, it is a common global means to come together and form a new society, and within this new kind of society, new identities are emerging (Maney, 2007). Some netizens' Internet identities are the same as those they have in the physical world, but others are entirely new and, many times, completely contradictory. An overweight man may be ashamed to wear a skintight t-shirt, a mature woman may not feel comfortable dancing to the rhythms of teenagers' music, a young boy may be afraid to play basketball with older and bigger people: all these restraints disappear in a digital world, where users do not differ according to their physical substance, but are made unique by way of their mental and emotional skills.

People can even start a new life from scratch, in a virtual world where everyone has the opportunity to try to form an ideal environment by somehow correcting the imperfect physical world. Even industries, organizations, and whole nations take part in a second chance world, now online, named Second Life (Secondlife.com). Second Life is an Internet-based virtual world which came to international attention via mainstream news media in late 2006 and early 2007 (Sege, 2006; Harkin, 2006). Virtual residents of the Secondlife software platform can explore, meet other residents, socialize, participate in individual and group activities, and buy items (virtual property) and services from one another. Furthermore, Second Life is only one of several virtual worlds that have been inspired by the cyberpunk literary movement, and particularly by Neal Stephenson's novel *Snow Crash* (Stephenson, 1993). The main aim of these platforms is to create a world like the Metaverse described by Stephenson, a user-defined world of general use in which people can interact, play, do business, and otherwise communicate. Many users of these online applications adopt a completely new identity, as they try to live a new life. Some of them even choose to change their sex. Some of the users participate in this Internet application as a personal experiment ("How would things be if I ...?"), others as a way to entertain themselves and to have fun with others.

To conclude, the Internet is capable of substituting physical activities, but while some people need this substitution, others just want to utilize it in order to give themselves a new chance in their lives.

Effective Use of the Internet

Apparently we are all dependent on nature. Even the most ardent champion of humankind's omnipotent logic would have to admit that she cannot survive without a connection to natural food or water resources. Hence it would be wise to understand how the dualism between civilization and nature works. Living in a civilized world inevitably means you can drive your car on a public road, you can build industries, you can use plastic products, and you can even enjoy your air conditioning and your brand new television set. You would at least use electricity to turn on your artificial lighting. All these acts have a minor or major negative impact on nature. Civilization by itself stands against nature. However, while nature can survive without civilization, civilization cannot exist without nature. So what should an ordinary civilized human being do in order to use the products of civilization to reduce the damage caused to nature and, of course, to his or her own physical existence?

With regards to the Internet, the advice of an ancient Greek philosopher might help. Aristotle (1998) taught that to achieve the good life, one must live a balanced life and avoid excess. This balance, he taught, varies for different persons and in different situations, and exists as a golden mean between two vices—one an excess and one a deficiency. Taking this advice on board, one could use the Internet to acquire knowledge and as a consequence shape one's motives to explore the physical aspect of this knowledge. For instance, one could search for information on "Caretta Caretta Turtles" and learn that these sea turtles live in the Mediterranean and especially in Zakynthos, a Greek island. This knowledge could then create a desire to travel physically to this island where this rare species resides. Even if the traveler never sees one of these turtles, she has already taken a step to learn more about nature and its species.

Many philosophers assert that modern, civilized humankind has destroyed its connection to the original sources of physical sensations, by considering reason more important than the cognitive sources derived from nature itself:

> *We are born capable of sensation and from birth are affected in diverse ways by the objects around us. As soon as we become conscious of our sensations we are inclined to seek or to avoid the objects which produce them: at first, because they are agreeable or disagreeable to us, later because we discover that they suit or do not suit us, and ultimately because of the judgements we pass on them by reference to the idea of happiness of perfection we get from reason. These inclinations extend and strengthen with the growth of sensibility and intelligence, but under the pressure of habit they are changed to some extent with our opinions. The inclinations before this change are what I call our nature. In my view everything ought to be in conformity with these original inclinations. (Rousseau, Émile, Book 1, translation by Boyd 1956: 13; see also, 1911 edition p. 7)*

Rousseau's hope is that we conform to our original inclinations. But we cannot follow his suggestion by completely ignoring how nature ultimately works. Having all grown up in an anthropocentric educational system where humans learn to ignore nature, we have all also been taught that we are allowed to use nature but not to serve the needs of nature. Because of this selfish and so-called civilized way of life we have forgotten that human beings are not the only mammals on earth. Nature has become something quite removed. Nevertheless, the Internet affords easy access to information that can enrich our knowledge regarding aspects of nature we could previously not even have imagined. This information can be accessed at our workplaces, in our homes, in our friends' homes, at libraries. There are no excuses. The Internet gives us access to free and endless data about the environment and ecology, and by learning more about nature, by getting in physical touch with our ecosystem, we learn more about ourselves and about the way a human body must be treated. Indeed, nature always gives us most beautiful and trustworthy guidelines for our wellbeing. That knowledge is only one click away.

References

ADE Glossary (2008) "Screen reader definition," University of Maryland, USA. [Online]. Available at: http://www.umuc.edu/ade/glossary.html [Accessed: July 15, 2008].

Aristotle (1998) *Nicomachean Ethics*. New York: Oxford University Press.

Askitis, Th. (2008) "Sexual problems in man's life", Sexual Health Institute. [Online]. Available at: http://www.askitis.gr/sexproblems_psixologiko.asp [Accessed: November 22, 2008].

Bar-or, O., Foreyt, J., Bouchard, C., Brownell, K., Dietz, W., Ravussin, E., Salbe, A., Schwenger, S., St. Jeor, S., and Torun, B. (1998), "Physical activity, genetic, and nutritional considerations in childhood weight management," *Medicine and Science in Sports and Exercise*, 30(1): 2–10.

Boyd, W. (1956) *Émile for Today: The Émile of Jean Jacques Rousseau*, selected, translated and interpreted by William Boyd. London: Heinemann.

Cooper, A., Delmonico, D.L., and Burg, R. (2000) "Cybersex users, abusers and compulsives: new findings and implications," *Cybersex, the Dark Side of the Force*, a special issue of *Sexual Addiction and Compulsivity*, 7: 5–29.

Daneback, K., Cooper, A., and Månsson, S. (2005) "An Internet Study of Cybersex Participants," *Archives of Sexual Behavior*, 34(3): 321–8.

Descartes R, (1641) *Meditationes de prima philosophia*, transl. by R. Descartes and M. Moriarty (2008) *Meditations on First Philosophy: With Selections from the Objections and Replies*. Oxford: Oxford University Press.

Duckett, J. (2005) *Accessible XHTML and CSS Web Sites: Problem – Design – Solution*. Indianapolis, IN: Wiley.

Ferraro, M., Casey, E., and McGrath, M. (2004) *Investigating Child Exploitation and Pornography: The Internet, Law and Forensic Science*. Amsterdam: Elsevier.

Foo, S. and Theng, Y.-L. (2005) *Design and Usability of Digital Libraries: A Case Study in the Asia Pacific*. Hershey, PA: Idea Group Publishing.

Gillinson, S., Miller, P., and Parker, S. (2004) *Disablism: How to Tackle the Last Prejudice*. London: Demos.

Grealy, M., Johnson, D., and Rushton, S. (1999) "Improving cognitive function after brain injury: the use of exercise and virtual reality," *Archives of Physical Medicine and Rehabilitation*, 80(6): 661–7.

Harkin, J. (2006) "Get a (second) life," *Financial Times*, November 17, 2006. Available at: http://www.ft.com/cms/s/cf9b81c2-753a-11db-aea1-0000779e2340.html [Accessed: February 15, 2007].

Hayes, B. (1977) *Midnight Express*. New York: Warner Books.

Hofstader, Ch. (2004) "Internet accessibility: beyond disability," *Computer*, 37(9): 103–5.

Hostel (2005), dir. E. Roth.

Ito, M. and Okabe, D. (2003) *Technosocial Situations: Emergent Structurings of Mobile Email Use*. Tokyo: Keio University.

Kalichman, S.C. and Rompa, D. (1995) "Sexual sensation seeking and sexual compulsivity scales: validity, and predicting HIV risk behavior," *Journal of Personality Assessment*, 65(3): 586–601.

Katz, L. (2003) "Multimedia and the Internet for sport sciences: applications and innovations," *International Journal of Computer Science in Sport*, 1(1): 4–18.

Leung, L. (2004) "Net-generation attributes and seductive properties of the Internet as predictors of online activities and Internet addiction," *Cyber Psychology and Behavior*, 7(3): 333–48.

Licklider, J.C.R. and Taylor, R.W. (1994) "The netizens and the Internet," *Amateur Computerist*, 6(2–3): 1–3.

Maney, K. (2007) "The king of alter egos is a surprisingly humble guy," *USA Today*, February 5, 2007. Available at: http://www.usatoday.com/printedition/money/20070205/secondlife_cover.art.htm [Accessed: February 20, 2007].

Marcus, B.H., Nigg, C.R., Riebe, D., and Forsyth, L.A.H. (2000) "Interactive communication strategies: implications for population-based physical-activity promotion," *American Journal of Preventive Medicine*, 19(2): 121–6.

McFarlane, M. and Bull, S.S. (2007) "Use of the Internet in STD/HIV prevention." In S.O. Aral and J.M. Douglas (eds), *Behavioral Interventions for Prevention and Control of Sexually Transmitted Diseases* (pp. 214–31). New York: Springer.

Paciello, M, (2000) *Web Accessibility for People with Disabilities*. New York: CMP Books.

Pilling, D., Barrett, P., and Floyd, M. (2004) *Disabled People and the Internet: Experiences, Barriers and Opportunities*. York: Joseph Rowntree Foundation.

Renshaw, D.C. (2007) "Update 2007: delights and dangers of Internet sex," *Comprehensive Therapy*, 33(1): 32–5.

Rowe, S.J. (1990) "Technology and ecology." In S.J. Rowe, *Home Place: Essays in Ecology* (pp. 63–70). Edmonton: NeWest Books.

Sege, I. (2006) "Leading a double life," *The Boston Globe*, October 25, 2006. Available at: http://www.boston.com/news/globe/living/articles/2006/10/25/leading_a_double_life/) [Accessed: February 15, 2007].

Stephenson, L. (1993) *Snow Crash*. New York: Bantam Spectra.

Whang, L.S.-M., Lee, S., and Chang, G. (2003) "Internet over-users' psychological profiles: a behavior sampling analysis on Internet addiction," *Cyber Psychology and Behavior*, 6(2): 143–50.

Zhangxu, J. and Aldis, J. (2001) "No Disability in Digitalized Community," International Center for Disability Resources on the Internet (ICDRI).

19

Health Professionals and Community Stigma toward People who Engage in Substance Abuse

Alexander-Stamatios Antoniou and Marina Dalla

What is Stigma?

The person who is stigmatized is a person whose social identity is devalued, spoiled, or flawed in the eyes of others (Goffman, 1963). The concept dates to ancient Greece and was used to signify the marks that were pricked onto slaves to demonstrate ownership and to reflect their inferior social status. The ancient word for prick was stig, and the resulting mark, a stigma (Falk, 2001). Some authors have described stigma as a social construction associated with categorization and the recognition of a difference, based on a specific characteristic, which is used to devalue and dehumanize the person who possesses it (Dovidio, Major, and Crocker, 2000). Goffman (1963) identified three types of stigma: abominations of the body, deviation in personal traits, and tribal stigmas. Abominations of the body were described as stigmas associated with physical deformations or deviations from a social norm, such as people with physical challenges, missing limbs, or physical deformities, among others. Deviations in personal traits were stigmas associated with a person's character, identity, unnatural passions, or simply their particular way of being. Some of these blemishes can be attributed to drug users, alcoholics, and people with poor mental health, among others. Finally, tribal stigmas referred to the negative evaluation of particular persons due to their association with a group. All of these dimensions could be argued to be part of the stigma that is related to substance use.

Public stigma, what a naive public does to the stigmatized group (Corrigan, and Watson, 2002), occurs when an individual is identified as deviant, linked with negative stereotypes that engender prejudiced attitudes, which are acted upon in discriminatory behavior (Ottati, Bodenhausen, and Newman, 2005). Deviance is related to behavior which is socially abnormal and usually regarded as unacceptable. The mark of deviance initiates an attributional process through which people interpret other aspects of a person in terms of the mark and respond to stigmatized individuals on the basis of their stigma at the expense of their individuality (Kurzban and Leary, 2001). Lemert (1951) distinguished between "primary" and "secondary" deviance. Primary deviance is the initial act or behavior which is the context of behavior which goes against the dominant norms of society. Substance abuse is therefore one example of primary deviance because it brings with it an array of potentially serious consequences. A need for markedly increased amounts of the substance to achieve intoxication or the desired effect, a withdrawal syndrome for the substance, the great deal of time spent in activities necessary to obtain the substance, use the substance, or recover from its effects, the reduction of social, occupational, or recreational activities because of the substance abuse (DSM-IV, 1999), and other kinds of problems related to it (e.g., delinquency) (NIDA, 1976) result in a variety of social and health consequences, both immediate and chronic.

These problems lead to secondary deviation or to stigmatizing responses from others. This involves the assumption of certain "roles" which then become the central way through which the marked or the labeled person is viewed and judged both by him- or herself and by society. The labeling perspective further argues that the stigmatized person becomes, by virtue of the label, isolated from non-stigmatized groups in society (Clinard and Meier, 1992). Public stigma elicits stereotypes that overgeneralize, misattribute, proscribe, and often condemn the behavior and personal characteristics of people that belong to different marked categories (Operario and Fiske, 2001), including drug abusers among other groups. In contrast to stereotypes, prejudicial attitudes, which are a form of antipathy directed at members of devaluated groups (Glick and Fiske, 2001), result in discrimination as an inappropriate treatment meted out to individuals due to their membership in one or more of the groups (Mummendey and Otten, 2001). Discrimination toward people with drug dependence occurs at an interpersonal and at a structural level (Link and Phelan, 2001). At the personal level this reflects a desire for social distance and less contact with people with drug abuse; at the structural level drug users are excluded from public life through a variety of legal, economic, social, and institutional means.

The stigmatization of drug users involves cognitive and behavioral components as culturally induced expectations of rejection are compounded with actual experiences of rejection. Hence, expectations of rejection, that in turn erode confidence, disrupt social interaction, and impair social and occupational functioning, are often reinforced through the experience of rejection (Link, Struening, Rahav, Phelan, and Nuttbrock, 1997). Furthermore, because substance abuse is associated with behaviors that generate negative responses in society, substance users are believed to be criminals whose addiction represents a moral failing that should be punished rather than treated. They are also considered to be unwilling or unable to change their risk behaviors and to be unreliable participants in society. Room (2005) identified two related elements of addiction that influence the degree of social disapproval and moralization associated with behavioral addictions: unpredictability and losing control. The first of these, unpredictability (e.g., abandoning the norm, or sobriety; and losing inhibitions), is associated with intoxication and might cause anxiety for those who come into contact with an intoxicated person. The second, losing personal control to a substance, which Room describes as being characterized by society as a "disease of the will," results in society viewing those who lose control as blameworthy. In addition, stigma due to substance use has become increasingly complex due to its association with HIV infection (Minior, Galea, Stuber, Ahern, Ompad, 2003).

Substance users remain one of the most stigmatized populations in many countries. In a WHO study covering 14 different countries, in which key local informants ranked a list of 18 conditions (chronic mental disorder, intellectual slowness, and others) in terms of degree of social disapproval or stigma, drug dependence ranked near the top. In all 14 countries being a drug addict was reported to be more highly disapproved of or stigmatized than having a criminal record for burglary (Room, Rehm, Trotter, Paglia, and Ÿnsün, 2001). Indeed, stigma towards drug users is so deeply rooted that it continues even in the face of scientific evidence that demonstrates addiction is a treatable disease and even when we know people in our families and communities who live wonderful lives after recovery (Rosenbloom, 2007). Recovery from a drug problem is a process of change through which an individual achieves abstinence, health, wellness, and quality of life after treatment that occurs in a variety of settings, in different forms, and for different periods of time (Scott, Dennis, and Foss, 2005). The ultimate goal of recovery is the substance user's re-entry into society along with them achieving readjustment and gaining independent functioning. This process of rehabilitation relies on the combined and coordinated use of educational, social, and vocational measures for training or retraining the individual to the highest level of functional ability.

But, the recovery and rehabilitation of substance users is often associated with an astonishing variety of terms that attempt to characterize the addict, and the addiction-prone personality, usually with the assumption that they are: "alienated," "passive psychopaths," "aggressive psychopaths," "emotionally unstable," "nomadic," "inebriate," "narcissistic," "dependent," "sociopathic," "hedonistic," "childlike," "paranoid," "rebellious," "hostile," "infantile," "neurotic," "delinquent," etc. (NIDA, 1976).

Belief in a Just World

Most theories view the act of stigmatizing as a means of maintaining and enhancing positive self-esteem or positive social identity through categorization and social comparison (Crocker and Quinn, 2001). But according to Allport (1954), stereotypes, prejudice, and discrimination act as justificatory devices for categorical acceptance or rejection of the target group and as screening or selective devices to maintain simplicity in perception and in thinking. In this way the categorization and justification functions are compatible and mutually reinforcing (Jost and Hamilton, 2005). How people stigmatize a particular group is determined by the intuitive causal attribution theory that those people hold. In many situations, causal attributions implicitly follow a "just world" belief that assumes people get what they deserve and deserve what they get (Lerner, 1998). Belief in a just world is an indicator of justice motives (Schmitt, Maes, and Schmal, 1995) generated to develop long-term reality orientations in order to be able to survive in a complex social world (Lerner, 1980).

According to Lerner's (1980) just world hypothesis, people have the illusory belief that good things happen to good people whereas bad things happen to bad people. To protect their sense of justice and to reaffirm their beliefs, people can use one or more of several possible strategies. For instance, sometimes assistance can be provided to victims that will reduce their suffering. This strategy can resolve injustice directly. Alternatively, the viewpoint can be adopted that the victims deserved to suffer. For instance, their misfortune can be attributed to reckless behavior. Or they can be judged to be bad, unworthy persons whose suffering is not unjust, even if they did not cause the outcome directly. Making such rationalizations allows people to maintain their belief that a similar misfortune will not befall them, as long as they are careful and are of "good" character (Lerner and Miller, 1978). For example, people who hold just world beliefs are more likely than others to adopt the following types of attitudes in regard to substance users: "They chose to use the drug and now they have to live with the consequences"; or "It's their own fault that they are experiencing problems." In such cases, a just-world ideology downplays the role of situational factors and says, in essence, that the problem of social injustice lies not in society but in the victims of prejudice.

More recently, Lipkus, Dalbert, and Siegler (1996) operationalized the distinction between self (or personal) and others (interpersonal), in terms of their belief in a just world (BJW). The authors reported findings that confirmed the value of the differentiation between self and others: BJW-S was found to be more strongly associated to indexes of psychosocial adjustment (Lipkus et al., 1996). On the other hand, BJW-O was significantly correlated to discrimination against the elderly, stigmatization of poverty, and higher penal punishment, while BJW-S was weakly or not related to these variables (Bègue and Bastounis, 2003). Furthermore, Dalbert and Radant (2004) referred to personal experiences of justice within the family, in which everyone gets what they deserve and deserves what they get. If someone has the specific perception that their family is a just one, this may have a positive effect on the belief in a personal just world.

In addition to rational and nonrational coping mechanisms, Lerner (1980) hypothesized two protective strategies, which are characterized by general ways of thinking about the world. First, people preserve a belief in a just world by thinking of the world in terms of ultimate justice, according to which one can be sure that present misfortune will be compensated in the long run. Second, belief in ultimate justice is differentiated from belief in immanent justice according to which present misfortune is seen as a consequence of prior behavior (Maes and Schmitt, 1999). What seems to be unjust in a narrow time perspective (immanent justice) may turn out to be just eventually (ultimate justice). As a consequence, different individuals may judge the same situation as just or unjust, even if they apply the same distribution principle. The studies showed that subjects who believed in immanent justice tended to derogate victims while subjects who believed in ultimate justice did not (Maes, 1994). Another strategy that was discussed in the early literature was termed psychological distancing from the victim. According to this coping mechanism, people tend to reduce the threat to their need to believe in a just world by convincing themselves that similar injustices will not befall them. Injustice appears to occur in the larger world, not in the immediate environment (Hafer and Bègue, 2005).

Just World Beliefs and Stigma towards Substance Users

How might this issue of just world beliefs be relevant to the acceptance or rejection of substance users? Of importance in this regard is the argument that just world beliefs represent a simplistic belief system (e.g., "Bad things happen to bad people") that can be used to formulate rapid judgments about complex social situations (Lerner, 1980) and the manner in which such a system can be understood in terms of attribution. Research and theory has described stigma as a specific application of stereotyping, prejudice, and discrimination (Ottati, Bodenhausen and Newman, 2005) that is closely connected to the way in which social "others" explain the behavior of the stigmatized. These explanations, known in psychology as "causal attributions," are both a symptom and source of prejudice. In addition to just world beliefs, people often have a general tendency to attribute negative behavior to dispositional causes. Even when behaviors are undeniably caused by situational factors, people will sometimes favor dispositional explanations, a misjudgment known as the "fundamental attribution error" (Ross, 1977). Taking the fundamental attribution error one step further, Pettigrew (1979) suggested that an "ultimate attribution error" occurs when people attribute negative behavior to dispositional causes. The belief in a just world has much in common with the fundamental attribution error, and consequently the belief can be interpreted as a bias, which is termed the "just world bias" (Dharmapala and McAdams, 2005).

Leshner (1997) has identified several negative beliefs held about individuals who suffer from addiction. One belief viewed individuals addicted to drugs as victims of their own situation. Another view perceived drug addicts as bad or weak individuals who were unwilling to try to control their gratifications and behaviors in order to lead normal lives. These views support the belief that drug abusers should be handled by the criminal justice system.

To summarize, we expected that belief in a just world (BJW) would affect the way in which people perceive, explain, evaluate, and react to the stigmatization of substance users after recovery. Accordingly, we expected that there would be a positive correlation between belief in a just world and social stigma toward former substance users (H1). A great number of studies have demonstrated empirically that the stronger the BJW, the more people are inclined to engage in several strategies of stigmatization, presumably because of the greater threat to their BJW (Hafer and Bègue, 2005). Following this conceptualization of differences between immanent and ultimate justice beliefs, we expected that ultimate justice would act as a protective belief against the stigmatization of substance users, while immanent justice beliefs would have a negative effect (H2).

Method

PARTICIPANTS

A total of 147 Greek people living in Athens filled in the questionnaire. Among these, 90 (61.2%) were females and 57 (38.8%) males. The participants' mean age was 34.21 and standard deviation 11.76 ranging from 18 to 60 years of age. In terms of their educational background, 87 (59.2%) participants had graduated from higher education ("University"), and 60 (40.8%) from secondary ("Lyceum"), and low-level primary and secondary school ("Elementary and Gymnasium").

MEASURES

Perceived discrimination

Perceptions of group discrimination (Bourguignon, Seron, Yzerbyt, and Herman, 2006) toward substance users were measured with four items: "I think that substance users are undervalued in Greek society," "In Greek society, people often despise substance users," "Substance users meet with more obstacles in their daily life than other people," "Substance users are often confronted with discrimination." These four items were collapsed into an index of perceived group discrimination ($\alpha = 0.80$).

Belief in a just world

Just and unjust world beliefs were measured using six items from Dalbert's (1999) Just World Beliefs Scale that distinguishes the belief in a personal just world from the belief in a general just world. The personal BJW reflects the belief that events in one's life are just ("I believe that, I usually get what I deserve," "I am usually treated fairly," "I believe that most of the things in my life are just") ($\alpha = 70$). And the general BJW reflects the belief that, basically, the world is a just place ("I am convinced that in the long run people will be compensated for injustices," "I firmly believe that injustices in all areas of life are the exceptions rather than the rule," "I believe that, by and large, people get what that deserve") ($\alpha = 66$). The Just Family Climate Scale (Dalbert and Stoeber, 2006) was used to measure the perception of family climate as just ("At home, things are just," "At home, important decisions that are made are usually just," "At home, injustice is the exception rather the rule," "At home, justice finally prevails") ($\alpha = 0.77$). Items were rated on six-point Likert-type scales ranging from 0 ("totally disagree") to 6 ("totally agree"). All items on the scale were worded so as to reflect a positive belief in a just world. The items were collapsed into three indexes: personal BJW, general BJW, and family BJW.

Beliefs in immanent and ultimate justice were measured with Maes' (1998) and Maes and Kals' (2002) scales. Immanent justice presents misfortune as a consequence of prior faults and sins (e.g., "Misfortune is a fair visitation for one's bad character," "Everybody has to attribute his circumstances to himself") ($\alpha = 0.72$) and is differentiated from belief in ultimate justice according to which one can be sure that present misfortune will be compensated in the long run (e.g. "He who must suffer with difficulty, one day will be compensated," "Injustice does exist, but at the end it will be compensated for") ($\alpha = 80$). Participants were asked to report their agreement with the statements on scales ranging from 1 ("do not agree at all") to 5 ("strongly agree"). An index of immanent justice (seven items) and another of ultimate justice (seven items) were created on the basis of these 14 items.

Results

Two separate MANOVAs were performed on measures of responses to a) stigmatization toward substance users, and b) beliefs in a just world (general, personal, and family beliefs) and immanent and ultimate justice beliefs. In all our analyses we controlled for the influence of gender (male vs female) and education (Higher vs Primary and Secondary).

DISCRIMINATION TOWARD DRUG ABUSERS

Table 19.1 presents the means of discrimination against substance users controlling for gender. As can be seen, total perceived group discrimination was the same for men and women. But men believed more than women that substance users are undervalued in Greek society $F(1, 147) = 3.93$, $p<0.05$, $\eta^2 = 2.7\%$ and meet with more obstacles in their daily life than other people $F(1, 147) = 4.25$, $p<0.05$, $\eta^2 = 2.9\%$.

There was a significant main effect of education on the total discrimination $F(1, 147) = 7.66$, $p = 0.01$, $\eta^2 = 5.1\%$ and on the items: "I think that ex-substance users are undervalued in Greek society" $F(1, 147) = 4.17$, $p<0.05$, $\eta^2 = 2.8\%$, "Ex-drug dependent people meet with more obstacles in their daily life than other people" $F(1, 147) = 7.44$, $p<0.01$, $\eta^2 = 4.9\%$, and "Substance users are often

Table 19.1 Means of discrimination as a function of gender

	Gender			
Items	Male	Female	F	η²
	M.	M.		
I think that ex-drug abuser are undervalued in Greek society	0.21	-0.13	3.93*	0.027
In Greek society, people often despise ex-drug abuser	0.18	-0.12	3.14	0.022
Ex-drug dependent people meet with more obstacles in their daily life than other people	0.19	-0.12	4.25*	0.029
Ex-drug dependent people are often confronted with discrimination	-0.03	0.02	0.00	000
Ex-drug dependent people are not accepted in Greek society	0.04	-0.03	0.02	000
Total discrimination	0.17	-0.11	2.25	0.020

Note: * p<0.05.

confronted with discrimination" $F(1, 147) = 4.53$, p<0.05, $\eta^2 = 3.1\%$. According to the results, people with higher education believed more than people with primary and second education that substance users are undervalued and confronted with discrimination in Greek society (Figure 19.1).

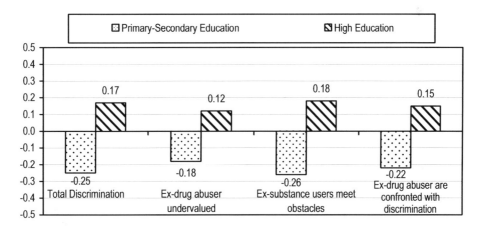

Figure 19.1 Means of discrimination towards substance users as a function of education

BELIEFS IN A JUST WORLD

A 2 (male vs female) × 2 (high vs low education) multivariate analysis of variance (MANOVA) on z-scores of the dependent variables of just world beliefs revealed significant multivariate main effects of gender $F(1, 146) = 6.16$, $p<0.01$, $\eta^2 = 4.1\%$ and education $F(1, 146) = 7.71$, $p<0.01$, $\eta^2 = 5.1\%$ on immanent just world beliefs. Men (M = 0, 29) and participants with primary and secondary education (M = 0, 35) scored higher than women (M = -0, 12) and participants with higher education on immanent justice (M = -0, 15).

Regarding the two-way interaction effect (gender and education), there was significant main effect on general $F(1, 146) = 4.13$, $p<0.05$, $\eta^2 = 2.8\%$ and on ultimate justice $F(1, 99) = 4.2$, $p<0.05$, $\eta^2 = 2.8\%$. Males with primary and secondary education and females with higher education believe more than others (males with higher education and females with primary and second education) that the world is a just place. Females with higher education expected more than males of the same category that every injustice could be resolved and compensated at some point in the future (Table 19.2).

Table 19.2   Means of just world beliefs as a function of interaction of gender and education

Just world beliefs	Higher education Male M	Higher education Female M	Primary and secondary Male M	Primary and secondary Female M	F	η^2
Personal JWB	0.16	-0.04	0.20	-0.23	0.44	0.003
Family JWB	0.09	0.12	-0.04	-0.24	0.43	0.003
General JWB	-0.11	0.09	0.27	-0.23	4.13*	0.028
Immanent JWB	-0.27	0.22	0.06	-0.14	0.18	0.001 0.22 0.06 -0.14 0.18
Ultimate JWB	0.03	-0.31	0.56	0.07	4.20*	0.028

Note: * $p<0.05$.

THE PREDICTION OF STIGMATIZATION FROM JUST WORLD BELIEFS

Regression analysis was used in order to test the prediction of stigmatization of substance users from just world beliefs after controlling for affect of gender and education. Step one of the model included gender; step two, personal, family and general-interpersonal just world beliefs; step three, dimensions of justice beliefs, immanent and ultimate justice; and step four, interaction of education with ultimate justice (because there is interaction of ultimate justice with education).

According to the results, men $\beta = -.21$, $t = -2.43$, $p<0.05$, $R^2 = 1.9\%$ believe more than women that substance users are rejected and undervalued in Greek society (Table 19.3).

Beliefs in immanent justice predicted the stigmatization of substance users in Greek society $\beta = -.21$, $t = -2.21$, $p<0.05$, $R^2 = 4.0\%$. High stigma of substance users is predicted from low immanent justice beliefs. In other words, the lower the belief in immanent justice according to which present misfortune is seen

Table 19.3 Hierarchical regression for the prediction of stigmatization from just world beliefs

	Prediction variables	Stigmatization β	t	R^2
1.	Gender	-0.210*	-2.43	0.020
2.	Just world beliefs			0.010
2a.	Personal JWB	-0.050	-0.47	
2b.	Family JWB	0.030	0.32	
2c.	General JWB	-0.230	-1.01	
3.	Justice beliefs			0.040
3a.	Immanent JB	-0.210*	-2.21	
3b.	Ultimate JB	0.120	0.49	
4.	Interaction general JWBXEduc	0.180	0.76	0.005
5.	Interaction ultimate JWBXEduc	-0.006	-0.02	0.000
	Total R2			0.270

Note: * $p<0.05$.

as a consequence of prior behavior, the higher the belief that substance users are undervalued in Greek society. It can also be noted that no prediction of stigmatization from general, family, and personal beliefs in a just world was found. (See Table 19.3.)

Discussion

The present study aimed, firstly, at examining the relation between social stigma toward substance users and just world beliefs. In line with the just world belief model, we expected a positive relation between perceived stigma and general world belief. For example, people with a high orientation toward multiple justice (personal, familiar, general) would have a greater tendency to accept the stigmatization of substance users. According to this model, individuals tend to believe the world is more just than is actually the case, because of either indoctrination during childhood or self-deception that productively offsets imperfect willpower. As a result, people have excessively strong prior beliefs that outcomes are deserved (Lerner, 1980).

The data obtained in our study provide no support for the first hypothesis. They indicate that just world beliefs are not related to the stigmatization and devaluation of substance users. This lack of a significant correlation may be the consequence of having two measures that are rooted in different psychological processes (Gawronski, Deutsch, and Seidel, 2005). Furthermore, the BJW theory states that justice concerns only apply to our world. People will be concerned primarily with their own world, that is, the environment in which they must live and function. To witness and admit to injustices in other environments does not threaten people very much because these events have little relevance for their own fates. As the events take place far from their world, their concern with injustices decreases greatly (Lerner and Miller, 1978).

It seems that people see substance users as belonging to a world other than their own; thus they separate their own just world from the stigmatization of the outgroup. This could be considered a form of psychological distancing, in which substance users are seen as so unlike oneself as to inhabit a different world governed by different rules (Hafer and Bègue, 2005). This psychological distancing from the "fate" of substance users ("They are not like us; therefore, we do not have to be concerned with their fate") does not require the psychological effort involved in, for example, providing help/compensation, denial/withdrawal, or cognitive reinterpretations of the event. Different findings provide evidence that when people are threatened by undesirable features in others, they respond to the threat by psychologically distancing themselves from such individuals and disassociating from them (Schimel, Pyszczynski, Greenberg, O'Mahen, and Arndt, 2000). This coping mechanism allows observers to reduce the threat to their need to believe in a just world by convincing themselves that they will not fall victim to a similar threat. Distancing from people or groups when they display undesirable attributes can serve to deny vulnerability to a feared fate ("I would never do that," "I am not that kind of a person"). Similarly, people have a tendency to project their negative sides (Markus and Nurius, 1987), about which they have fears, or their "shadow" (Jung, 1959) onto others, reducing any perceived similarity with the others, and enhancing the difference, which contributes to stereotyping and prejudice.

Although the present findings do not provide evidence for all our hypotheses, we believe that these results provide broad support for a number of potentially important ideas. First, people seem to separate their just world from the world of stigmatized substance users. They see targets of stigma as belonging to a world other than their own. This could be considered an extreme form of psychological distancing, in which the targets of stigmatization are seen as belonging to another world that is governed by different rules. Different studies suggest that psychological distancing may be a common defensive response, to the fear of specific negative characteristics, that allows people both to dissociate themselves from unsuccessful groups or groups that display undesirable attributes, and to increase their connection to successful groups (Schimel, Pyszczynski, Greenberg, O'Mahen, and Arndt, 2000). Indeed, theory and research suggest that we distance ourselves from and disparage those who have qualities we fear (Schimel et al., 2000). In respect of this, surveys which examine public attitudes and beliefs about substance abuse show that people commonly hold negative and exaggerated views regarding unpredictability and the dangerousness of drug addiction (Gelder, 2001) and indeed, the main problems ascribed to substance use are illness, violence, casualty, and failure in major social roles, particularly at work and in the family (Room, 2005).

Another finding indicated a negative relation between immanent justice and stigma toward ex-substance users. People who have little belief in the idea that justice is inherent in a given outcome are more likely to indicate that substance users are rejected and undervalued in Greek society. These are people who do not define events as being inherently just. They consequently exhibit a lower level of hope over the future of former substance users. Moreover, since they believe people are not personally responsible for what occurs in their world, they are therefore less threatened by substance users who they see as maybe just less similar to themselves (Maes, 1998).

In many societies there is a high degree of marginalization and stigmatization of those who end up in treatment for alcohol or drug problems (Room, 2005). Our study confirmed that former substance users; 1) are undervalued and despised in Greek society, 2) meet more obstacles in their daily life than other people, and 3) are rejected and confronted with discrimination. Stigmatization has adverse consequences at the individual level, such as lowered self-esteem and learned helplessness, negative psychological and social functioning, and increased depression (Shepard and Reif, 2004). Such consequences may create a treatment barrier for individuals seeking help. In addition, stigmatization involves negative consequences at the societal level, particularly discriminatory behavior toward labeled individuals, both from the public and from members of the medical community. Moreover, discrimination as the behavioral consequence of prejudice may be covert or systemic, intentional or unintentional, a consequence of which is employers and society avoid and reject substance users—a situation that persists despite treatment and recovery (Minior, Galea, Stuber, Ahern, Ompad, 2003). Nonetheless, people recovering from substance use can experience better outcomes if their basic needs are met, a consequence of which is the achievement of progressive independence and rehabilitation.

Stable recovery is a reality for many people with substance abuse (Scott, Dennis, and Foss, 2005). Improving the social reintegration of such treated populations will require a better understanding of how and under what conditions marginalization and stigmatization occurs. Quantitative and qualitative studies are needed to understand both the extent and the mechanics of the marginalization and social stigmatization of substance users and those with substance use problems (Room, 2005). In the context of these general studies, priority should be given to the fear that people have of addicts that leads to distancing from them, and to the stigmatization and discrimination of recovering persons.

In this regard, substance professionals should counterbalance the stigma attached to active addiction through interventions responding to false statements made about individuals with substance abuse (NMHA, 2000). Counselors, clinicians, and researchers should educate the public, and attempt to change negative attitudes and perceptions to try to de-stigmatize addiction and ensure its place in the public health realm (Corrigan, Larson, and Kuwabara, 2007). Education programs can help people to identify the inaccurate stereotypes surrounding substance abuse and replace these stereotypes with factual information. This can be accomplished by furnishing an audience with the basic facts about substance abuse and treatment, or by contrasting the myths with the facts. The goal is not to make the audience experts on substance abuse, but rather to provide simple facts so that many of the myths about addiction crumble. Education programs should therefore also focus on the consequences of addiction and the effectiveness and positive outcomes of treatment, and the many cases of recovery.

References

Allport, G.W. (1954). *The Nature of Prejudice*. Reading, MA: Addison-Wesley.

Bègue, L. and Bastounis, M. (2003). Two spheres of belief in justice: extensive support for the bidimensional model of belief in just world. *Journal of Personality*, 71(3), 435–63.

Bourguignon, D., Seron, E., Yzerbyt, V., and Herman, G. (2006). Perceived group and personal discrimination: differential effects on personal self-esteem. *European Journal of Social Psychology*, 36, 773–89.

Clinard, M.B. and Meier, R.F. (1992). *Sociology of Deviant Behaviour*, 8th edn. Fort Worth, TX: Harcourt Brace Jovanovich.

Corrigan, P.W., Larson, J.E., and Kuwabara, S. (2007). Mental illness stigma and the fundamental components of supported employment. *Rehabilitation Psychology*, 52, 451–7.

Corrigan, P.W. and Watson, A.C. (2002). The paradox of self-stigma and mental illness. *Clinical Psychology — Science and Practice*, 9, 35–53.

Crocker, J. and Quinn, D.M. (2001). Psychological consequences of devalued identities. In R. Brown and S. Gaertner (eds), *Blackwell Handbook in Social Psychology, Vol. 4: Intergroup Processes* (pp. 238–57). Malden, MA: Blackwell.

Dalbert, C. (1999). The world is more just for me than generally: about the personal belief in a just world scale's validity. *Social Justice Research*, 12, 79–98.

Dalbert, C. and Radant, M. (2004). Parenting and young adolescents' belief in a just world. In C. Dalbert and H. Sallay (eds), *The Justice Motive in Adolescence and Young Adulthood: Origins and Consequences* (pp. 11–25). London: Routledge.

Dalbert, C. and Stoeber, J. (2006). The belief in a just world and domain-specific beliefs about justice at school and in the family: a longitudinal study with adolescents. *International Journal of Behavioral Development*, 30, 200–207.

Dharmapala, D. and McAdams, R. (2005). Words that kill? An economic model of the influence of speech on behavior (with particular reference to hate speech). *Journal of Legal Studies*, 34, 93–136.

Dovidio, J., Major, B., and Crocker, J. (2000). Stigma: introduction and overview. In T. Heatherton, R. Kleck, M. Hebl, and J. Hull, *The Social Psychology of Stigma* (pp. 1–28). New York: Guilford Press.

Diagnostic and Statistical Manual of Mental Disorders (DSM-IV) (1999). Washington, DC: American Psychiatric Association.

Falk, G. (2001). *Stigma: How We Treat Outsiders*. New York: Prometheus.

Gawronski, B., Deutsch, R., and Seidel, O. (2005). Contextual influences on implicit evaluation: a test of additive versus contrastive effects of evaluative context stimuli in affective priming. *Personality and Social Psychology Bulletin*, 31, 1226–36.

Gelder, M. (2001). The nature of such stigmatization: The Royal College of Psychiatrists' survey of public opinions about mentally ill people. In A.H. Crisp (ed.), *Every Family in the Land: Understanding Prejudice and Discrimination against People with Mental Illness*. London: The Editor and the Sir Robert Mond Memorial Trust.

Glick, P. and Fiske, S.T. (2001). An ambivalent alliance: hostile and benevolent sexism as complementary justifications of gender inequality. *American Psychologist*, 56(2), 109–18.

Goffman, E. (1963). *Stigma: Notes on the Management of Spoiled Identity*. New York: Prentice-Hall.

Hafer, C.L. and Bègue, L. (2005). Experimental research on just-world theory: problems, developments, and future challenges. *Psychological Bulletin*, 131(1), 128–67.

Jost, J.T. and Hamilton, D.L. (2005). Stereotypes in our culture. In J. Dovidio, P. Glick, and L. Rudman (eds), *On the Nature of Prejudice* (pp. 208–224). Oxford: Blackwell.

Jung, C.G. (1959). Aion: researches into the phenomenology of the self (translated by R.F.C. Hull). In H. Reed, M. Fordham, and G. Adler (eds), *The Collected Works of C.G. Jung* (vol. 9, part 2). Princeton, NJ: Princeton University Press. (Original work published 1951.)

Kurzban, R. and Leary, M.R. (2001). Evolutionary origins of stigmatization: the functions of social exclusion. *Psychological Bulletin*, 127(2), 187–208.

Lemert, E.M. (1951). *Social Pathology: A Systematic Approach to the Theory of Sociopathic Behaviour*. New York: McGraw-Hill.

Lerner, M.J. (1980). *The Belief in a Just World: A Fundamental Delusion*. New York: Plenum.

Lerner, M.J. (1998). The two forms of belief in a just world. In L. Montada and M.J. Lerner (eds), *Responses to Victimizations and Belief in a Just World* (pp. 247–69). New York: Plenum.

Lerner, M.J. and Miller, D.T. (1978). Just world research and the attribution process: looking back and ahead. *Psychological Bulletin*, 85, 1030–51.

Leshner, A.I. (1997). Addiction is a brain disease—and it matters. *Science*, 278, 45–7.

Link, B.G. and Phelan, J.C. (2001). On the nature and consequences of stigma. *Annual Review of Sociology*, 27(1), 363–85.

Link, B.G., Struening, E.L., Rahav, M., Phelan, J.C., and Nuttbrock, L. (1997). On stigma and its consequences: evidence from a longitudinal study of men with dual diagnosis of mental illness and substance abuse. *Journal of Health and Social Behavior*, 38, 177–90.

Lipkus, I.M., Dalbert, C., and Siegler, I.C. (1996). The importance of distinguishing the belief in a just world for self versus for others: implications for psychological well-being. *Personality and Social Psychology Bulletin*, 22, 666–77.

Maes, J. (1994). Blaming the victim: belief in control or belief in justice? *Social Justice Research*, 7(1), 69–90.

Maes, J. (1998). Immanent justice and ultimate justice: two ways of believing in justice. In L. Montada and M. Lerner (eds), *Responses to Victimizations and Belief in the Just World* (pp. 247–69). New York: Plenum.

Maes, J. and Kals, E. (2002). Justice beliefs in school: distinguishing ultimate and immanent justice. *Social Justice Research*, 15, 227–44.

Maes, J. and Schmitt, M. (1999). More on ultimate and immanent justice: results from the research project "Justice as a problem within reunified Germany". *Social Justice Research*, 12, 65–78.

Markus, H. and Nurius, P. (1987). Possible selves: the interface between motivation and the self-concept. In K. Yardley and T. Honess (eds), *Self and Identity: Psychosocial Perspectives* (pp. 157–72). Chichester: Wiley.

Minior, Th., Galea, S., Stuber, J., Ahern, J., and Ompad, D. (2003). Racial differences in discrimination experiences and responses among minority substance users. *Ethnicity and Disease*, 13, 521–7.

Mummendey, A. and Otten, S. (2001). Aversive discrimination. In R. Brown and S. Gaertner (eds), *Blackwell Handbook in Social Psychology* (vol. 4: *Intergroup Processes*, pp. 112–32). Cambridge, MA: Blackwell.

National Mental Health Association (NMHA) (2000). *Stigma: Building Awareness of Understanding about Mental Illness*. Alexandria, VA: NMHA. Available at: http://nhma.org/infoctr/factsheets/14.cfm [Accessed: November 23, 2008].

NIDA (1976). *Effects of Labeling the Drug Abuser: An Inquiry*. Rockville, MD: NIDA. Available at: http://www.nida.nih.gov/pdf/monographs/06.pdf [Accessed: November 23, 2008].

Operario, D. and Fiske, S.T. (2001). Stereotypes: processes, structures, content, and context. In R. Brown and S. Gaertner (eds), *Blackwell Handbook in Social Psychology* (vol. 4: *Intergroup Processes*, pp. 22–44). Cambridge, MA: Blackwell.

Ottati, V., Bodenhausen, G.V., and Newman, L.S. (2005). Social psychological models of mental illness stigma. In P.W. Corrigan (ed.), *On the Stigma of Mental Illness: Practical Strategies for Research and Social Change* (pp. 99–128). Washington, DC: APA.

Pettigrew, T.F. (1979). The ultimate attribution error: extending Allport's cognitive analysis of prejudice. *Personality and Social Psychology Bulletin*, 5, 461–76.

Room, R. (2005). Stigma, social inequality and alcohol and drug use. *Drug and Alcohol Review*, 24, 143–55.

Room, R., Rehm, J., Trotter, R.T., Paglia, A., and Ÿnsün, T.B. (2001). Cross-cultural views on stigma, valuation, parity and societal values towards disability. In T.B. Ÿnsün, S. Chatterji, and J.E. Bickenbach et al. (eds), *Disability and Culture: Universalism and Diversity* (pp. 247–91). Seattle, WA: Hogrefe and Huber.

Rosenbloom, D.L. (2007). Coping with the stigma of addiction. *Addiction*. HBO. [Online]. Available at: http://www.hbo.com/addiction/stigma/52_coping_with_stigma.html [Accessed: 17 February 2010].

Ross, L. (1977). The intuitive psychologist and his shortcomings: distortions in the attribution process. In L. Berkowitz (ed.), *Advances in Experimental Social Psychology* (vol. 10, pp. 173–220). New York: Academic Press.

Schmitt, M., Maes, J., and Schmal, A. (1995). *Gerechtigkeit als innerdeutsches Problem: Einstellungen zu Verteilungsprinzipien, Ungerechtigkeitssensibilität und Glaube an eine gerechte Welt als Kovariate* (Berichte aus der Arbeitsgruppe "Verantwortung, Gerechtigkeit, Moral" Nr. 82). Trier: Universität Trier, Fachbereich I - Psychologie.

Schimel, J., Pyszczynski, T., Greenberg, J., O'Mahen, H., and Arndt, J. (2000). Running from the shadow: psychological distancing from others to deny characteristics people fear in themselves. *Journal of Personality and Social Psychology*, 78(3), 446–62.

Scott, C.K., Dennis, M.L., and Foss, M.A. (2005). Recovery management checkups to shorten the cycle of relapse, treatment re-entry, and recovery. *Drug and Alcohol Dependence*, 78, 325–38.

Shepard, D.S. and Reif, S. (2004). The value of vocational rehabilitation in substance user treatment: a cost effectiveness framework. *Substance Use and Misuse*, 39(13–14), 2581–609.

20

Immigration, Acculturation and Responses to Perceived Employment Discrimination: A Study of Albanian and Bulgarian Immigrants in Greece

Marina Dalla and Alexander-Stamatios Antoniou

Introduction

The process of immigration involves acculturation to changes resulting from the contact of immigrants with the host population and intergroup relations that arise from the reciprocal presentation of views held by the contact groups (Berry, 2003). In general, acculturation is based on two dimensions of change: one refers to the extent to which the culture of origin is being maintained or preferred, and the other refers to the extent to which the new host culture is adopted. On the basis of the interaction between these two dimensions, four different acculturation strategies can be employed: assimilation, integration, separation, and marginalization.

Assimilation is the strategy that relinquishes the ethnic heritage and substitutes it with the new, acquired cultural identity. Integration refers to the preservation of the heritage together with the acquisition of some characteristics of the host culture, while separation involves maintaining the culture of origin and rejecting the culture of settlement. Marginalization refers to a rejection of both the culture of settlement and the culture of origin (Berry, 2003). In all cases, integration is the most preferred acculturation strategy and demonstrates the strongest relationship with positive adaptation. Marginalization is the least beneficial strategy for adaptation, while assimilation and separation are intermediate (Liebkind, 2001).

Intergroup relations encompass intergroup attitudes and behavior, including phenomena such as social discrimination directed by the dominant group or society toward the immigrant groups (Liebkind, 2001). The concept of social discrimination is described as inappropriate treatment towards individuals, owing to their group membership (Dovidio, Brigham, Johnson, and Gaertner, 1996) and correspondingly is connected to notions of justice and equality (Mummendey and Otten, 2001). Perceived discrimination is an individual's perception that he/she is treated differently or unfairly because of his/her group membership (Sanchez and Brock, 1996).

Dion (2002) presents an important psychological reality for immigrants regardless of their status as a social indicator of actual discrimination or intolerance. It elicits cognitive appraisals of threat that are exacerbated by the fact that discrimination is arbitrary and often unpredictable. One important response to the stress associated with discrimination is the strengthening of ingroup identification (Dion, 2002). For immigrants, this may take the form of separation from, or of heightened identification with, the heritage culture. Living in close proximity to members of one's own group, offers a form of social support in response to stress created by the rejection associated with discrimination.

Empirical studies (e.g., Hayfron, 2006) have shown that immigrants are likely to experience periods of unemployment, especially in times of economic hardship which may give rise to hiring discrimination or nepotism. Native-born employment seekers may be given priority even though immigrant job seekers might have similar human capital (Hayfron, 2006). According to Intergroup Emotions Theory (Mackie, Devos, and Smith, 2000), in situations such as these, when events or decisions affecting ingroup members are appraised as unfair, or violating principles of equity or justice, or obstructing goals, the dominant emotional responses triggered are anger and disgust. Research addressing responses to such perceived discrimination has also found preferences for different strategies that may be categorized as individualistic versus collectivistic and as behavioral versus cognitive (Mummendey and Otten, 2001). According to Moghaddam (1998), individuals first attempt to achieve mobility on an individual basis, and only resort to collective action when they perceive the system to be closed and the path to the advantaged group to be blocked.

Despite the fact that perceptions of discrimination have direct, negative effects on psychological and behavioral reactions of individuals or groups, this relationship is often complicated by acculturation strategies. Sanchez and Brock (1996) found that employees with higher levels of acculturation perceived less race-based discrimination than their counterparts who scored lower. A high level of acculturation is related to collective strategies such as the readiness to participate in social protest when an immigrant attempts to achieve social mobility within mainstream society but does not achieve the goals that are acceptable to the majority group (Moghaddam, 1998). The perception of such discrimination against one's group is likely to result in negative reactions among group members. However, this effect seems to be dependent on the specific ethnic group. The external attribution of a personal drawback may be easier for culturally more distant groups than for culturally proximal groups (Liebkind, 2001).

The two immigrant groups studied in this research are Albanian and Bulgarian. In the past 20 years Greece has become host to a number of immigrants (IMEPO, 2004), the majority of them coming from Eastern Europe. More than half of all immigrants in Greece are from Albania (Migration Information Programme, 1995), while the second largest immigrant population is from Bulgaria (which is very different from the first group). Other economic migrants and asylum seekers have been arriving from other countries in Eastern Europe, the former Soviet Union, the Middle East, and several Asian and African countries (IMEPO, 2004).

Economic and employment constraints in their own countries have prompted a number of Albanian and Bulgarian groups to emigrate to Greece (Kasimati, 2000). Like all migrants in a new country, they are prone to experience many barriers, often in the form of exclusion from the labor market, or from key social and legal institutions. Employment discrimination poses a most serious problem.

In Greece, Albanians are predominantly engaged in construction, while Eastern Europeans (e.g., Bulgarians) are mostly concentrated in the domestic services (Glystos, 2005). However, a number of negative attributes towards immigrants have been identified, especially towards Albanians. Albanians are often viewed as a low status and inferior group, who deprive native people of material resources, jobs, wages, social benefits, and services (Constantinidou, 2001). Hence, Albanian immigrants in Greece often change their names and religion, and baptize their children in order to be more rapidly integrated and to strengthen the opportunities for future generations. In the case of Bulgarians, cultural distances are much narrower and easier to overcome because of their Orthodox faith which they have in common with the Greeks (Nikova, 2002).

The Present Study

STUDY AIMS

1. To understand acculturation processes among two immigrant groups, and to test the hypothesis that integration is the most preferred acculturation option for Albanian and Bulgarian immigrants in Greece.

2. To identify emotional and behavioral responses following the perception that an ingroup member has been treated unfairly. It is hypothesized that an increased sense of injustice and more intense negative emotional and behavioral reactions will be experienced among immigrants as a consequence of often being viewed as a distant, low status group (Constantinidou, 2001).

3. To identify which strategies of acculturation are associated with emotional and behavioral responses to perceived discrimination. It was expected that assimilation would be related to more negative emotional reactions and active responses to a situation of perceived injustice (Moghaddam, 1998).

METHOD

Participants

A total of 130 immigrant adults in the wider region of Athens, aged between 18 and 62 years participated in the study. The sample included 66 (50.8%) males and 64 (49.2%) females with a total mean age of 36.45. The ethnic composition of the sample consisted of 50.8% (66) Albanian immigrants and 49.2% (64) Bulgarian immigrants. Over 27.8% (36) of immigrants have a higher educational degree, 72.1% (80) have completed secondary education, and 10.1% (13) have completed primary education.

PROCEDURE

Acculturation

To measure general acculturation attitudes of both the host majority and immigrant groups, four questions, based on the Berry acculturation model and adapted from Bourhis, Moise, Perreault, and Senecal (1997) were asked. These items were "immigrants should try to live according to their customs," "immigrants should try to live according to the customs of the host country," "immigrants should try to maintain their heritage and to adopt important features of the majority culture," and "immigrants should be deported to their country of origin." Participants had to indicate, using a five-point scale, the degree of their *agreement* (5) or *disagreement* (1). The scenario and the questionnaire were administered in Greek, Albanian, and Bulgarian. They were translated using a forward translation from Greek into both Albanian and Bulgarian, followed by back translations into Greek, and reconciliation procedures.

Scenario of discrimination

A modified version of a procedure introduced by Devos, Silver, Mackie, and Smith (2002) was applied. Participants read a scenario in which they were asked to imagine that an acquaintance had called them relaying that, despite her excellent academic credentials, the ministry to which she had applied for a job had turned down her application (see Appendix). In her mind, the ministry had given priority to less qualified applicants. Two variables were manipulated in the scenarios. A *situation of discrimination* manipulation involved an interview for a job for which the applicant has the necessary qualifications (*employment*). The second manipulation was the *level of discrimination because of their group membership*—*immigrant* or *native* (see the Scenario in the Appendix). After reading this account, participants completed measures assessing their cognitive, emotional, and behavioral reactions to the situation.

Emotional reactions

Participants indicated to what extent emotional terms such as "angry," "disgusted," "upset," "indifferent," "repulsed," or "unmoved" captured how the situation made them feel. Responses were provided on a five-point Likert-type scale ranging from 1 ("not at all") to 5 ("very much") (items = 12, Cronbach $\alpha = 0.83$).

Behavioral intentions

Participants reported to what extent they would engage in specific actions on the basis of this person's experiences. Items were inspired by previous work on behavioral responses to discrimination (Lalonde, Stronk, and Aleem, 2002). Some items reflected an active or confrontational way of dealing with the situation, such as writing a letter of support, consulting a lawyer, taking legal action (items = 3, α = 0.82). Other items (reversed for coding) expressed a lack of action or resignation, such as to do nothing, to be indifferent about or accept the decision (items = 3, α = 0.72). Responses were provided on a five-point scale ranging from 1 ("not at all") to 5 ("very much").

Perceived injustice

The focus here is on the extent to which the decision was construed as an act of discrimination, injustice, or an intransparent decision (items = 3, α = 0.73). Responses were provided on a five-point scale ranging from 1 ("strongly disagree") to 5 ("strongly agree").

RESULTS

Separate two-way MANOVAS were performed on measures of acculturation, perceived injustice, and responses to perceived injustice using ethnicity (Albanian vs Bulgarian) and gender (male vs female) as the independent variables.

Results from the acculturation measures indicated that Albanian immigrants preferred the integration orientation $F(1, 117) = 30.39$, p<0.001, $\eta^2 = 19.4\%$. Furthermore, they scored lower than Bulgarians with regard to the exclusionist orientation concerning conflictual relations with the native culture $F(1, 117) = 10.79$, p<0.001, $\eta^2 = 7.9\%$. Regarding appraisals of discrimination, Albanian immigrants perceived the manipulated situation as an act of injustice $F(1, 117) = 25.59$, p<0.001, $\eta^2 = 17.1\%$ and discrimination $F(1, 117) = 33.15$, p<0.001, $\eta^2 = 21.1\%$, more than the Bulgarian immigrants. In terms of responses concerning perceived injustice, Albanian immigrants indicated higher scores of negative emotions $F(1, 117) = 49.69$, p<0.001, $\eta^2 = 30.4\%$ and lower scores of unassertive behavior $F(1, 117) = 42.97$, p<0.001, $\eta^2 = 27.4\%$ than Bulgarians. (See Table 20.1.)

Regression analysis was used, in order to test the predicted pattern of behavior responses to discrimination (active reaction, no reaction). Step 1 of the

Table 20.1 Acculturation, perceived injustice and responses to perceived injustice as a function of ethnicity and gender

	Ethnicity				Gender			
	Albanian	Bulgarian			Male	Female		
	M	M	F	η^2	M	M	F	η^2
Acculturation								
Integration	3.83	2.67	30.39***	0.194	3.23	3.27	0.300	0.009
Assimilation	3.78	3.60	0.81	0.005	2.60	2.80	0.817	0.000
Separation	3.28	3.05	1.04	0.008	3.19	3.14	0.795	0.001
Marginalization/exclusion	2.04	2.75	10.79***	0.079	1.94	2.24	0.152	0.016
Perceived injustice								
Act of injustice	4.14	2.90	25.59***	0.171	3.37	3.67	1.576	0.013
Act of discrimination	4.07	2.78	33.15***	0.211	3.34	3.51	0.557	0.004
No transparent decision	3.92	3.55	2.81	0.022	3.75	3.73	0.008	0.000
Responses to perceived injustice								
Negative emotions	3.93	3.04	49.69***	0.304	3.41	3.57	1.575	0.014
Active reaction	2.98	2.93	0.04	0.000	3.03	2.88	0.461	0.004
Lack of action	1.78	2.90	42.97***	0.274	2.29	2.40	0.453	0.004

Note: * p<0.05. ** p<0.01. *** p<0.001.

model included Ethnicity, with Gender entered at Step 2, Perceived Injustice at Step 3, Negative Emotions at Step 4, Acculturation variables at Step 5 and Interaction of Ethnicity with Acculturation at Step 6.

Appraisal of the situation as an act of discrimination predicted the intention to engage in active or confrontational behaviors β = .373, t = 2.804, p< .01, Total R^2 = 19.5%. Separation was generally related to less active behavior toward discrimination β = -1.05, t = -2.169, p< .05, Total R^2 = 3%. Low negative emotions were significantly related to high levels of passive reaction towards discrimination β = -.281, t = -2.429, p< .05, R^2 = 5%.

Under high separation, both groups showed low levels of active reaction. But under low levels of separation, Albanian immigrants were more active than Bulgarian immigrants β = 1.21, t = 2.33, p< .05, Total R^2 = 3.8%.

Table 20.2 Hierarchical regression for the prediction of behavior reaction to discrimination from perceived injustice and acculturation

Prediction variables	ACT β	ACT t	ACT R2	NOA β	NOA t	NOA R2
1. Ethnic group	-0.182	-0.433	0.001	0.430	1.149	0.269
2. Gender	-0.073	-0.804	0.001	0.081	1.057	0.004
3. Perceived injustice			0.195			0.094
3a. Act of injustice	0.114	0.958		-0.141	-1.351	
3b. Act of discrimination	0.373**	2.804		0.044	0.394	
3c. No transparent decision	0.000	0.004		-0.008	-0.090	
4. Negative emotions	0.076	0.560	0.015	-0.281*	-2.429	0.050
5. Acculturation			0.030			0.051
5a. Assimilation	-0.163	-0.341		0.073	0.178	
5b. Integration	0.528	0.974		0.597	1.302	
5c. Separation	-1.051*	-2.169		-0.214	-0.523	
5d. Exclusion	0.130	0.271		-0.147	-0.360	
6. Ethnicity Acculturation			0.038			0.018
6a. Ethnicity × Assimilation	0.331	0.652		-0.217	-0.502	
6b. Ethnicity × Integration	-0.388	-0.791		-0.515	-1.234	
6a. Ethnicity × Separation	1.214*	2.332		0.145	0.327	
6b. Ethnicity × Exclusion	-0.085	-0.155		0.387	0.819	
Total R2			0.282			0.487

Note: * $p<0.05$. ** $p<0.01$.

Conclusions

It is observed that Albanian immigrants strongly favor integration which is based on two identifications, one with their heritage culture and one with the host country. Accordingly, Albanians are more likely than Bulgarians to reject exclusion from the host society. By using integration as an adaptation strategy, and rejecting exclusion from the host country, it appears that Albanian immigrants are able to adapt to a new society, both culturally and socially. Because the majority of Albanians face harsher conditions in their home country

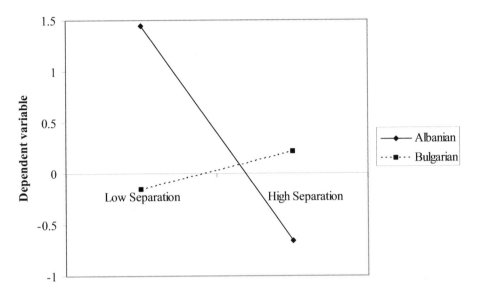

Figure 20.1 Interaction of separation by ethnicity in predicting active reaction toward discrimination

in comparison to Bulgarians, they are perhaps more willing to remain in the host country regardless of the immigration difficulties (Dragoti, Dalla, and Pavlopoulos, 2006). The integration and adaptation of immigrants in general, and Albanian immigrants in particular, is an issue of great importance for the future of Greek society.

As predicted, Albanian immigrants viewed the hypothetical situation of a friend's job application being turned down as a case of ethnic discrimination and as a violation of principles of equality, more so than Bulgarians. They expressed greater feelings of anger and disgust, and a greater desire to engage in confrontational or active ways of dealing with the situation. However, it appears that the perceived appropriateness of responses to discrimination may differ depending on the social standing of the perceiver, at least from a majority/minority perspective as defined by group size.

Several authors have suggested that ethnic prejudice and discrimination against specific outgroups increase with relative group size (Kosic, and Phalet, 2006). They argue that sizeable immigrant groups are more visible, and are therefore perceived as a potential threat to the native population in terms of economic and political power. It seems that high levels of perceived discrimination exacerbates feelings of group threat that reinforces emotional reaction and collective behavior when discrimination takes place. Furthermore, the relative density of ingroup members provides immigrants with the necessary social support to cope with disadvantages (Liebkind, 2001).

Previous research suggests that social identification is often a prerequisite to negative emotions and confrontational methods of dealing with injustice, and indicates the relationship between acculturation and reaction to perceived discrimination (Dovidio, Brigham, Johnson, and Gaertner, 1996; Mummendey and Otten, 2001). According to the results, separation is linked to lower subjective perceptions of collective behavior as a reaction to injustice. Previous studies have found support for the theory that individuals who possess a strong sense of ethnic identity are at greater risk for negative outcomes as the result of perceived discrimination. Other studies have found that strong ethnic identity can serve as a buffer between perceived discrimination and psychological distress. It is possible that currently unidentified moderating and mediating factors are present which impact the effects of acculturation on individual responses to perceived discrimination (Verkuyten, and Nekuee, 1999).

To conclude, our study aims and hypotheses were confirmed to a large extent. It appears that preference of integration as an acculturation option is more prevalent in the Albanian immigrants. As expected, an increased sense of injustice, and more intense negative emotions were identified in the Albanian group. Finally, behavioral intentions following a hypothetical situation were predicted by appraisal of the act of discrimination, separation, and negative emotions, in terms of whether or not to take action. The findings may provide useful to Greece, and to other countries experiencing influxes of immigration, in terms of methods of acculturation and predictors of behavioral intentions in different migrant groups.

Appendix 1: Hypothetical Scenario Given to Participants

Remember I told you that I was applying to the Ministry of Education? Well, guess what? I just found out I was not accepted! I was shocked when I received a letter of rejection! I was certain I was going to be accepted. As you know, I was a pretty good student. My grade point average was excellent. I had other qualifications as well. Can you believe they rejected me in spite of all my qualifications?

I contacted the Ministry to find out what happened. The only explanation I received was that the positions were already filled. I did some research and found out that the requirements for admittance to the Ministry are considerably less than I can fulfill. I truly feel I have been treated unfairly. The Ministry responded that the procedure was meritocratic and moreover that they are proud to hire people coming from immigrant groups. Nonetheless, I feel I am one who has been treated unfairly.

Anyway, I just wanted to keep you informed. Take care.

S.

References

Berry, J.W. (2003). Conceptual approaches to acculturation. In K. Chun, P. Balls-Organista, and G. Marin (eds), *Acculturation: Advances in Theory, Measurement, and Applied Research* (pp. 17–37). Washington, DC: American Psychological Association.

Bourhis, R., Moise, L., Perreault, S., and Senecal, S. (1997). Towards an interactive acculturation model: a social psychological approach. *International Journal of Psychology*, 32(6), 369–86.

Constantinidou, C. (2001). *Social Representations of Crime: Images of Albanian Immigrants' Criminality in the Athenian Press* [in Greek]. Athens: Sakkoulas.

Devos, T., Silver, L.A., Mackie, D.M., and Smith, E.R. (2002). Experiencing intergroup emotions. In D.M. Mackie, and E.R. Smith (eds), *From Prejudice to Intergroup Emotions: Differentiated Reactions to Social Groups* (pp. 111–34). Philadelphia, PA: Psychology Press.

Dion, K.L. (2002). The social psychology of perceived prejudice and discrimination. *Canadian Psychology*, 43, 1–10.

Dovidio, J.F., Brigham, J.C., Johnson, B.T., and Gaertner, S.L. (1996). Stereotyping, prejudice, and discrimination: another look. In N. Macrae, C. Stangor, and M. Hewstone (eds), *Stereotypes and Stereotyping* (pp. 276–319). New York: Guilford.

Dragoti, E., Dalla, M., and Pavlopoulos, V. (2006). Personality and mental health among Albanian immigrants in Greece in comparison to their coethnics in Albania and native Greeks. Paper presented at the 13th European Conference of Personality, July, 22–26, Athens, Greece.

Glytsos, N. (2005). Stepping from illegality to legality and advancing towards integration: the case of immigrants in Greece. *International Migration Review*, 39, 819–40.

Hayfron, J.E. (2006). Immigrants in the labor market. In D.L. Sam, and J.W. Berry (eds), *The Cambridge Handbook of Acculturation Psychology* (pp. 439–51). Cambridge: Cambridge University Press.

Immigration Policy Institute (IMEPO) (2004). *Statistical Data on Immigrants in Greece: An Analytical Study of Available Data and Recommendations for Conformity with European Union Standard.* Athens: Mediterranean Migration Observatory UEHR and Panteion University.

Kasimati, K. (2000). Integration problems of ethnic groups and foreigners in the Greek society. In K. Kasimati (ed.), *Phenomena of Social Pathology in Social Exclusion Groups.* Athens: KEKMOKOP.

Kosic, A. and Phalet, K. (2006). Ethnic categorization of immigrants: the role of prejudice, perceived acculturation strategies and group size. *International Journal of Intercultural Relations: Special Issue,* 30, 769–82.

Lalonde, R.N., Stronk, L.M., and Aleem, R.A. (2002). Representations and preferences of responses of housing and employment discrimination. *Group Processes and Intergroup Relations,* 5(1), 83–102.

Liebkind, K. (2001). Acculturation. In R. Brown and G. Gaertner (eds), *Blackwell Handbook of Social Psychology. Vol. 4: Intergroup Processes* (pp. 386–406). Oxford: Blackwell.

Mackie, D.M., Devos, T., and Smith, E.R. (2000). Intergroup emotions: explaining offensive action tendencies in an intergroup context. *Journal of Personality and Social Psychology,* 79, 602–16.

Migration Information Programme (1995). *Profiles and Motives of Potential Migrants from Albania.* Budapest: IOM.

Moghaddam, F.M. (1998). *Social Psychology: Exploring Universals across Cultures.* New York: W.H. Freeman and Company.

Mummendey, A. and Otten, S. (2001). Aversive discrimination. In R. Brown and S. Gaertner (eds), *Blackwell Handbook of Social Psychology. Vol. 4: Intergroup Processes* (pp. 112–32). Oxford: Blackwell.

Nikova, E. (2002). Economic migration to Greece and the personal and national prospects of Albanians. Unpublished paper.

Sanchez, J.I. and Brock, P. (1996). Outcomes of perceived discrimination among Hispanic employees: is diversity management a luxury or a necessity? *Academy of Management Journal,* 39(3), 704–19.

Verkuyten, M. and Nekuee, S. (1999). Subjective well-being, discrimination and cultural conflict: Iranians living in the Netherlands. *Social Indicators Research,* 47(3), 281–306.

Index

AA *see* Alcoholics Anonymous
ability EI 142
absenteeism
    occupational health 240
    presenteeism balance 255
    United States 243
acculturation and Albanian/Bulgarian immigrants in Greece 385, 389
ACL-FF *see* Adjective Check List-Five Factors
action regulation mechanism 247
addiction-prone personality 370
Adjective Check List-Five Factors (ACL-FF) instrument 335, 339
age/gender differences
    interest types 341
    personal values 340–1
    personality and unemployment 339–40
    work values 341–2
Albanian immigrants in Greece
    integration 387–8, 392–3
    occupations 387
Albanian/Bulgarian immigrants in Greece
    acculturation 385
    assimilation 385
    behavioral intentions 390
    conclusions 392–4
    discrimination 389
    emotional reactions 389
    hypothetical scenario 394–5
    introduction 385–6
    marginalization 385–6
    perceived injustice 390
    research 388–92
alcohol abuse in American adolescents
    consequences 132
    management 133–4
    medications 133
Alcoholics Anonymous (AA) 134
American adolescents and stress
    depression 128–9
    substance abuse
        alcohol 132–4
        tobacco 129–31
American adolescents in the workplace
    defining work 123–4
    employment
        benefits 124–5
        risks 125–6
        types 124
    introduction 123
    prevalence 124
    stress, management 128–34
American Institute of Stress 28
American Psychological Association (APA) 18–20, 26, 30

AMOS modification index 180
ANS *see* autonomic nervous system
APA *see* American Psychological
    Association
Aristotle 363
autonomic nervous system (ANS) 67

Bandura, A. 156
Barling, Julian 20
behavioral intentions and Albanian/
    Bulgarian immigrants in
    Greece 385
belief in just world (BJW)
    community stigma 370–1
    discrimination toward drug
        abusers 374–5
    gender/education 376
    research 373–4
    stigmatization 377–8
    substance abusers 372
Beutell, Nicholas 11–12
biological explanations and gender
    differences in burnout 108,
    116
biomechanical risk factors 45
BJW *see* belief in just world
Black, Carol 35–8
BM *see* Burnout Measure
BMA *see* British Medical Association
book summary 2–3
brain versus nature: Internet and
    physical activity 355–66
Brett, J.M. and Schoh, L.K. 81
British Medical Association (BMA)
    36
Bulgarian immigrants in Greece
    integration 393
    occupations 387
burnout
    description 109–10

human service professionals 110–11
    women 113
Burnout Measure (BM) 113–14

call centers 48
cardiovascular disease 49
CFS *see* chronic fatigue syndrome
*Character Strengths and Virtues :A
    Handbook of Classification* 149
chronic fatigue syndrome (CFS) 249
Chrousos, George 72
circadian type and adaptation
    research 276
Clark, A.E. 345
co-variance of psychological/
    physiological stress response 64
Cobb, S. 313–14
cognitive function and virtual
    environment 358
commuting and work 53
conditions Report 223
Conflict Management Taxonomy/
    Grid 194
construct of self-efficacy 153–4
Cooper, Cary L. 19–20
coping theory
    psychological resources 330–1
    unemployment 330
Cox, T. 222
Cox, T. and Griffiths, A. 224
Cox, Tom 19–20
crime and unemployment 293
"cultural feminists" 109
cyber sex 356–7
cyber sexual behavior and Internet
    activities 356–8

De Dreu, C.K.W. and Beersma, B. 194,
    197
De Frank, R.S. and Cooper, C.L. 194

INDEX

DeChurch, L.A. and Marks, M.A. 206
demand-control-support model 14–16
depression
   American adolescents and stress 128–9
   disorders 129
   psychological therapies 129
deprivation theory and unemployment 330
Descartes, R. 366
Diagnostic and Statistical Manual of Mood Disorders 128
Dion, K.L. 386
discrimination and Albanian immigrants in Greece 389
discrimination towards drug abusers and gender 374–5
Disenchanted Workers (DWs) 91
distributive schedule justice 267
Dow Chemical, US and presenteeism 243
'Drop that Weight or Your Fired!' 37
Dual Concern Theory 194
DWs *see* Disenchanted Workers

EA-OHP *see* European Academy of Occupational Health Psychology
EAs *see* Enthusiastic Addicts (EAs)
emotional intelligence (EI) as personality trait
   ability EI 142
   conclusions 144–5
   introduction 139–40
   trait EI
      ability EI 140–2
      measurement 142–4
'emotional intelligence' (EI) term 139–40

emotional reactions and Albanian/Bulgarian immigrants in Greece 389–90
emotional regulation,
   well-being 331
   work 247
emotional regulation and well being 331
employee health and presenteeism
   employee health 251–2
   illnesses 244–5
   introduction 239
   "nature of illness" 244
   occupations and performance 250–1
   performance 246–8, 248–51
   perspective 239–42
   presenteeism, absenteeism and HRM 252–6
   presenteeism: nature and origin 242–5
employees and supervisors/workgroup conflict 196–8, 198–201, 209
employment contracts 45–9
employment discrimination in Greece and Albanian/Bulgarian immigrants 385–6
energetic regulation 247
Enthusiastic Addicts (EAs) 91, 95
EU *see* European Union
Europe and unemployment 329
European Academy of Occupational Health Psychology (EA-OHP) 19
European Agency for Safety and Health in Work 43
European Foundation for the Improvement of Living and Working Conditions 48, 223
European Framework directives 241

399

European Union (EU)
  unemployment 290
  work hours 223
European Working Conditions
    Survey 52
"everyone drinks alcohol and it is
    OK!" 133
evolutionary theory and gender
    differences in burnout 108
"extreme jobs" 81–3
extrinsic values and unemployment
    333
Eysenck, M.W. and Calvo, M.G. 316

families and unemployment 298
Family and Medical Leave Act, US 241
fibromyalgia (FMS) 74
flexibility and work patterns 49–53
FMS *see* fibromyalgia
Functional Job Analysis 250–1
"fundamental attribution error" 372

gender
  discrimination towards drug
      abusers 374–5
  job stress 223–4
  unemployment 296–7, 330
gender differences in burnout
  biological explanations 108, 116
  conclusions 17
  cross-cultural differences 116–17
  culture 115
  employment status 115–16
  literature review 107–17
  social theories 108
  see also women and burnout
General Health Questionnaire (GHQ)
    48, 334, 337–9, 343
Germany and unemployment 290,
    299, 302

GHQ *see* General Health
    Questionnaire
Grealy, M. et al 358
Greece
  Albanian/Bulgarian immigrants
      385–96
  unemployment 347
Greenhaus, Jeffrey 11–12
Grinyer, A. and Singleton, V. 241–2
groups at risk in unemployment 299

harassment and bullying in
    workplace 197
'health economists' 38
health effects and unemployment/job
    insecurity
  empirical results 291–3
  families 298, 301
  gender 296–7
  groups at risk 299–300
  introduction 289
  job-insecurity 293
  mental health 289–91
  psychology/psychologists 300–3
  self-esteem 297
  suicide 29
  theory 294–5
  unresolved issues 295–8
health optimization 254
health professionals and community
    stigma
  belief in just world 370–2, 382
  discussion 378–81
  education programs 381
  research 373–8
  stigma and substance abuse
      367–70, 372
Health and Safety Executive (HSE) 28
health and safety risk management
    193

hedonism and unemployment 331
Hewlett, S.A. Luce, C.B. 81–2
HIV *see* Human Immunodeficiency Virus
home working 80
Hostel 359
HPAA *see* hypothalamus-pituitary-adrenalin axis
HRM *see* human resource management
Human Immunodeficiency Virus (HIV) 249
human resource management (HRM) and employee health/presenteeism 239–58
human service professionals 110–11
hypertension 49
hypocortisolism 73–4
'hypocortisolism triad' 73
hypothalamus-pituitary-adrenalin axis (HPAA) 67, 69, 74

IAs *see* Internet addicts
illnesses and performance 246–8
ILO *see* International Labor Organization; International Labour Organization
immanent justice 376, 379–80
immigrants
    Albanian/Bulgarian to Greece 385–96
    unemployment 386
incentive perspective and unemployment 330
informational schedule 269
Institute for Social Research, Michigan, US 10–11
Institute of Work Psychology 16–17
interest types and age/gender differences 341

Intergroup Emotions Theory 386
International Labor Organization (ILO) 19, 329
Internet
    physical activity
        balanced life 363
        cyber sexual behavior 356–8
        effective uses of Internet 363–4
        introduction 355–6
        nature 364
        preventive medicine 358
        promotion 358–60
        reduction 360–1
        substitution 361–3
Internet addicts (IAs) 360
interpersonal schedule justice 268–9

Jackson, Susan 13–14, 20
Jahoda, Marie 8–9, 329
Jamal, M. 261
Japan and "karoshi" 83, 87
job insecurity
    mental health 49
    occupational health and safety
        conclusions 324–5
        insecurity-safety relationship tests 318–22
        introduction 313–15
        negative effects (prevention) 322–4
        psychological distress 314
        safety 315–18, 322–4
        safety relationship tests 318–22
    organizational restructuring 48–9
jobs
    burnout 13–14, 20
    insecurity 45–9
    stress research 224
JOHP *see Journal of Occupational Psychology*

Journal of Occupational Behavior 19
Journal of Occupational Psychology (JOHP) 18–20
Journal of Organizational Behavior 19–20
Just Family Climate Scale 373

Kahn, Robert 10–11
Kanfer, R. and Ackerman, P.L. 315–16
Karasek, Robert 14–16
"karoshi" (Japan) 83, 87
Keita, Gwendolyn 19
Klein, T. 301
Kornhauser, Arthur 9–10

Labe, L. 9
labor relations and work 240–1
Leiter, M.P. 110
Lerner, M.J. 370–1, 378
Leshner, A.I. 372
Luthans, F. 157

'Marienthal' study (mental health) 289–90
Marmot, Michael 12–13
Maslach Burnout Inventory (MBI) 113
Maslach, Christina 13–14, 20
Maslow, Abraham 25, 27
Mayo, Elton 25
mental health
   'Marienthal' study 289–90
   unemployment
      discussion 343–7
      introduction 329–33
      job insecurity 49, 289–91, 302
      research 334–43
Midnight Express 359
mood disorders 129

MSDs *see* musculoskeletal disorders
musculoskeletal disorders (MSDs) 44, 52

NAs *see* non-addicts
National Institute for Occupational Safety and Health (NIOSH) 1, 18–19, 50, 124
National Institutes of Health (NIH) 72
National Longitudinal Survey of Youth (NLSY) 126
nationalistic views and unemployment 292–3
"nature of illness" and employee health/presenteeism 244
nature and Internet 364
negative emphasis and preventative interventions 27–30
"netizen" term 362
neurobehavioral medicine 63–6
Neuropattern Circle 70
Neuropattern Test Set (NTS) 68–71, 73
nicotine addiction
   American adolescents 130–1
   medications 131–2
   nasal spray 131
nicotine replacement (NT) therapy 130
NIOSH *see* National Institute for Occupational Safety and Health
NLSY *see* National Longitudinal Survey of Youth
non-addicts (NAs) 360
non-standard work schedules
   overtime 53
   rehabilitation 53
   retention management benefits 262–3

INDEX

conclusions 279
costs and employees 261–2
drivers/outcomes 270–2
introduction 259–60
justice 266–70
model 262–6
personal context 272–4
research 274–9
NT *see* nicotine replacement
NTS *see* Neuropattern Test Set
nursing in SARS crisis in Canada/China 169–88

OCCSEFF *see* Occupational Self-efficacy Scale
occupational health psychology (OHP)
  biography
    Beutell, Nicholas 11–12
    Greenhaus, Jeffrey 11–12
    Jackson, Susan 13–14
    Jahoda, Marie 8–9
    Kahn, Robert 10–11
    Karasek, Robert 14–16
    Kornhauser, Arthur 9–10
    Marmot, Michael 12–13
    Maslasch, Christina 13–14
    Theorell, Töres 14–16
    Wall, Toby 16–17
    Warr, Peter 16–17
    Zohar, Dov 17–18
  editors 19–21
  "health" term 1
  introduction 1, 7–8
  organizations 18–19
occupational health and safety, job insecurity 313–28
occupational health services 29–30
occupational safety and health (OSH) 43

Occupational Safety and Health Administration (OSHA) 125–6, 128
occupational safety (Zohar, Dov) 17–18
occupational self-efficacy 155
Occupational Self-efficacy Scale (OCCSEFF) 155, 160–3
OECD *see* Organization for Economic Co-operation and Development
online sexual activities (OSA) 356–7
Organization for Economic Co-operation and Development (OECD) 47, 313
organization wellness programmes (OWP) 32
organizational justice
  research 274–5
  supervisors/workgroup conflict 206–9
organizational practices 45–9
OSA *see* online sexual activities
OSH *see* occupational safety and health
OSHA *see* Occupational Safety and Health Administration
outplacement-programmes and unemployment 302
OWP *see* organization wellness programmes

part-time employees 48
PAs *see* possible Internet addicts
Paul, K. and Moser, K. 290, 294–5
People Management 36
perceived discrimination and community stigma 373
perceived injustice and Albanian/Bulgarian immigrants in Greece 390

personal values
   age/gender differences 340–1
   community embeddedness 273–4
   economic change 332
   non-work role 273
   research results 336
   unemployment 331, 336–7
   work-related 332–3
personality type and adaptation
   research 276–7
personality and unemployment
   addiction-prone 370
   age/gender differences 339–40
   anger expression 339–40
   measurement 335–7
Peterson, C. and Seligman, M.E.P. 149
PNI *see* pressure management indicator
positive organizational behavior (POB) 149–51
positive organizational scholarship (POS) 149
positive psychology 30, 35, 147–9
possible Internet addicts (PAs) 360
poverty and unemployment 293
presenteeism
   absenteeism balance 255
   absenteeism and HRM 253–6
   nature and origin 242–5
   see also employee heath and presenteeism
"presenteeism" term 242
pressure management indicator (PMI) 226, 232
Probst, T.M. and Brubaker, T.L. 319, 321
procedural schedule justice 268
professional efficacy and social support in nurses during SARS crisis in Canada/China

control coping 169–70
coping, social support and burnout 170–3
discussion 182–5
introduction 169–70
research 173–82
PsyCap (psychological capacity) concept 151
psychoanalytic theory and gender differences in burnout 108
'psychological corrosive poverty' and unemployment 294
psychological resources and coping theory 330–1
psychology/psychologists and unemployment 300–3

Quick, James 20

Raymond, Jonathan 9
regression analyses in unemployment research 342–3, 344–5
reintegration and rehabilitation 255
Relaxed Workers (RW) 91
resistance to degradation 247–8
restrictive 'medical' model 34–5
Rogers, Carl 25, 27
role-playing game (RPG) 360
Rousseau, Émile 364
Royal Mail, UK 32
RPG *see* role-playing game
RW *see* relaxed workers (RW)

safety
   climate in organizations 323–4
   see also occupational health and safety
Sanchez, J.I. and Block P. 387
SARS *see* severe acute respiratory syndrome

school leavers and unemployment 299
Schwartz Value Survey 336
Second Life (secondlife.com) 362
self-efficacy
   construct 153–4
   human actions 156–7
   initiative taking 158
   occupational 155
   POB skill 157
   work engagement 159–63
   work and organizations 157–9
self-efficacy and positive organizational behavior
   capacity 152–3
   conclusions 163–4
   growth 147–51
   motivational/behavioral outcomes 155–63
   "state-like" capacity 152–5
self-employed workforce 47–8
self-esteem and unemployment 297, 329
self-image 247
Seligman, Martin 26, 30, 35
SEM *see* structural equation modelling
severe acute respiratory syndrome (SARS) 169–86
sexually transmitted diseases and Internet activities 358
sickness prevention 254
Simard, M. and Marchand, A. 318
Sinclair, R.R. et al 268
Smith, A.P. 248–9
social construction theory and gender differences in burnout 108–9
social role theory and gender differences in burnout 108
social theories and gender differences in burnout 108
STAI *see* State-Trait Anxiety Inventory for Adults
State-Trait Anxiety Inventory for Adults (STAI) 334–5, 337–40, 343
Stewart W.F. at al 246
stigma and substance abuse 367–70, 371
stress medicine
   clinical endophenotypes
      biological assessment 73–4
      psychological assessment 72–3
   conclusions 74–5
   diagnostic assessment
      brain and body 67
      clinical applicability 68–70
      exchange/update of data 71–2
      individual interventions 71
      neuropatterns 66–8
   introduction 63
   neurobehavioral medicine
      aetiological mechanisms 64–5
      co-variance of psychological/physiological stress response 64
      qualified treatment 65–6
      therapeutic efficacy/cost efficacy 66
      translational requirements 65
stress-buffering and supervisors/workgroup conflict 205–6
stressor-adjustment and supervisors/workgroup conflict 195–6
structural equation modelling (SEM) 182–3, 230–3, 234
substance abuse and community stigma 367–84
suicide and unemployment 297
supervisors and workgroup conflict conclusions 209–11

employees 196–8, 198–201, 209
　identification 201–2
　intervention 203–4
　introduction 191–2
　management 204–5
　model 192–5
　moderation 209
　organizational justice 206–9
　responses 201–5
　severity 202–3
　stress 195–8
　stress-buffering 205–6
　stressor-adjustment 195–6
　third-party help 199–200

TEIQue *see* Trait Emotional
　　Intelligence Questionnaire
Tetrick, Lois 20
Thales (philosopher) 356
The Wall Street Journal 32
Theorell, Töres 14–16
Time and Work: Duration of Work 50–1
trait EI
　ability EI 140–2
　measurement 142–4
Trait Emotional Intelligence
　　Questionnaire (TEIQue) 143–4

Ukpere, W.I. and Slabbert A.D. 329
"ultimate attribution error" 372
unemployment
　control of life 294
　crime and poverty 293
　European Union 290
　families 298
　Germany 290, 299, 302
　groups at risk 299
　immigrants 386
　mental health
　　coping theory 330

　　deprivation theory 330
　　discussion 343–7
　　European rate 329
　　extrinsic values 333
　　gender 330
　　Greece 347
　　incentive perspective 330
　　Jahoda, Marie 8–9
　　Kornhauser, Arthur 9–10
　　latent functions of work 329
　　motivation for re-employment
　　　331
　　personal values 331, 336–7
　　personality 335
　　psychological issues 330
　　research 334–43
　　suicide 297
　　well-being 330–5, 345–7
　　work values 336–7
　nationalistic views 292–3
　outplacement-programmes 302
　'psychological corrosive poverty'
　　294
　psychology/psychologists 300–3
　self-esteem 297, 329
　school leavers 299
　United States 290
Unengaged Workers (UWs) 91
United States (US)
　absenteeism 243
　Family and Medical Leave Act 241
　job insecurity 313
　presenteeism 242
　unemployment 290
US *see* United States
UWs *see* Unengaged Workers

vital regulation 247
Vocational Interests Inventory for
　　Adults 336

vocational interests research results 336
Vuori, J. and Veselainen, J. 294, 300

Wall, Toby 16–17
Warr, Peter 16–17
WAs *see* Work Addicts
well-being
    unemployment
        deprivation theory 330
        development training 332
        emotional regulation 331
        research 334–5, 337–8, 345–7
well-being at work
    current status 30–3
    definition 26
    external pressure and influences 33–8
    future 33–8
    health issues 31–3
    introduction 25–7
    negative emphasis and preventative interventions 27–30
    occupational health services 29–30
    restrictive "medical" model 34–5
WEs *see* Work Enthusiasts
Whitehall studies 12–13
women and burnout
    levels compared to men 113
    occupations 111–13
    professions 112
    sex role stereotypes 111
work
    absenteeism 240
    addiction and workaholism 80, 90–1
    change
        computerization 44–5
        employment contracts 45–9
        flexibility and work patterns 49–53
        introduction 43–4
        job insecurity 45–9
        new technology 44
        organizational practices 45–9
    commuting 53
    disengagement 248
    emotional regulation 247
    engagement 248
    engagement and self-efficacy 159–63
    "extreme jobs" 81–3
    home 80
    hours
        commuting 53
        concerns 87–9
        effects 83–7
        European Union 223
        importance 80
        long 50–3
        non-standard 53
        overtime 50, 53
        patterns 80–1
    intensity 89–90
    labor relations 240–1
    mental health 9–10
    motivation 79
    patterns and flexibility 49–53
    personal values 332–3
    research
        extra-work and family 96
        job behaviors 92
        organizational values 94–5
        outcomes 95
        personal demographics 92
        psychological well-being 96
    schedules 277–9
    Type A behavior 94
    workaholism 93–8

retention drivers 270–1, 272–3
risks and rewards 98
satisfaction and health in German managers
   discussion 233–6
   introduction 221–5
   methods 225–6
   research 225
   results 226–30
   structural equation modelling 224, 230–3
schedules
   changeover times 265
   control and flexibility 266
   day versus night shift 265
   design 263–4
   emerging issues research 277–8
   extended hours shift work 265
   intervention research 278–9
   justice 266–70
   mixed versus fixed shift 264–5
   model 262–3
   stability 266
   see also non-standard
self-employed 47–8

strain 248
see also well-being at work; workaholism
Work Addicts (WAs) 91, 93, 95
Work Enthusiasts (WEs) 91, 93, 95
Work and Stress 20
work values
   age/gender differences 341–2
   economic change 332
   research results 336–7
   unemployment 336–7
workaholism
   addiction 80, 90–1
   antecedents 93–4
   definition 91
   flow at work 95–6
   outcomes 95
   workaholics 91–2
workgroup conflict *see* supervisors and workgroup conflict
Working Conditions report
Working for a Healthier Tomorrow 35
World Health Organization (WHO) 369

Zempel, J. and Frese, M. 302
Zohar, D. 17–18, 323